"A JUSTIFIABLE OBSESSION"

Conservative Ontario's Relations with Ottawa, 1943–1985

"*A Justifiable Obsession*" traces the evolution of Ontario's relationship with the federal government in the years following the Second World War. Through extensive archival research in both national and provincial sources, P.E. Bryden demonstrates that the province's successive Conservative governments played a crucial role in framing the national agenda – although this central relationship has received little attention compared with those that have been more volatile. As such, Bryden's study sheds light on an important but largely ignored chapter in Canadian political history.

Bryden focuses on the politicians and strategists who guided the province through the negotiation of intergovernmental economic, social, and constitutional issues, including tax policies, the design of the new social welfare net, and efforts to patriate the constitution. Written in a lucid, engaging style that captures the spirit of the politics of postwar Canada, "*A Justifiable Obsession*" is a significant contribution to our understanding of Ontario's politics and political culture.

P.E. BRYDEN is an associate professor in the Department of History at the University of Victoria.

P.E. BRYDEN

"A Justifiable Obsession"

Conservative Ontario's Relations with Ottawa, 1943–1985

Ontario's willingness and ability to face the challenges posed by the political structure, and the changing circumstances of the country, go without saying. Confederation has always been a justifiable obsession for Ontarians. For we have, traditionally, always looked upon ourselves as Canadians first and, I would like to believe, we have never hesitated when it was required, to put national interests ahead of those of a more parochial nature.

The Honourable William G. Davis, Premier of Ontario,
at the Empire Club, 5 March 1981

UNIVERSITY OF TORONTO PRESS
Toronto Buffalo London

© University of Toronto Press 2013
Toronto Buffalo London
www.utppublishing.com
Printed in Canada

ISBN 978-1-4426-4586-8 (cloth)
ISBN 978-1-4426-1406-2 (paper)

Printed on acid-free, 100% post-consumer recycled paper with
vegetable-based inks

Library and Archives Canada Cataloguing in Publication

Bryden, Penny
    "A justifiable obsession" : Conservative Ontario's relations with Ottawa,
    1943–1985 / P.E. Bryden.

    Includes bibliographical references and index.
    ISBN 978-1-4426-4586-8 (bound)   ISBN 978-1-4426-1406-2 (pbk.)

    1. Ontario – Politics and government – 1943–1985.   2. Federal-provincial
    relations – Ontario.   I. Title.

    FC3076.2.B79 2013   971.3′04   C2013-901325-3

University of Toronto Press acknowledges the financial assistance to its
publishing program of the Canada Council for the Arts and the Ontario
Arts Council.

Canada Council   Conseil des Arts
for the Arts   du Canada

ONTARIO ARTS COUNCIL
CONSEIL DES ARTS DE L'ONTARIO
50 YEARS OF ONTARIO GOVERNMENT SUPPORT OF THE ARTS
50 ANS DE SOUTIEN DU GOUVERNEMENT DE L'ONTARIO AUX ARTS

University of Toronto Press acknowledges the financial support of the
Government of Canada through the Canada Book Fund for its publishing
activities.

This book has been published with the help of a grant from the Canadian
Federation for the Humanities and Social Sciences, through the Awards to
Scholarly Publications Program, using funds provided by the Social Sciences
and Humanities Research Council of Canada.

For my mother, Patricia Rowe
An Ontario federalist

Contents

Epilogue   226

Illustrations follow page 86

Acknowledgments

Where to begin? With a book as long in the making as this one, there are multiple beginnings, and just as many people to thank for the help along the way. My most heartfelt thanks to –

- My mother, whose fascination with both Ontario and politics – not necessarily together – perhaps laid the groundwork for my own interests
- Three extraordinary professors: Bruce Hodgins for introducing me to federalism, Chris Armstrong for feeding that fascination, and John Saywell for pushing it even further
- A small army of research assistants for hunting down sources, copying endless documents, rechecking material and getting excited about intergovernmental relations: Gordon Barrett, Jennifer Bottos, Andrew Clark, Christine Clayton, April Clyburne-Sherin, Rachael Conway, Karine Duhamel, Anthony Hampton, Caitlin Hayward, David Larlee, and Patrick Webber
- The staff of the Ontario Archives for tracking down information, cataloguing material so that I could examine it, and photocopying what seemed like a million pieces of paper for me in a pre–digital camera era
- The institutions that provided financial support for this project: Mount Allison University, the University of Victoria, and the Social Sciences and Humanities Research Council of Canada
- The Ontario politicians and bureaucrats who talked to me openly and enthusiastically about their own experiences with the federal government, happily reliving both victories and defeats
- Colleagues and friends who read parts of this book in manuscript,

discussed ideas, pushed for completion, and didn't seem to care how long that took: Dimitry Anastakis, Raymond Blake, Kelly Buehler, Simon Devereaux, Bill Godfrey, Jack Granatstein, Norman Knowles, Chris Manfredi, Andrea McKenzie, Elaine Naylor, Sara Stratton, and David Torrance

- Kevin Oliver, for letting me use his dad's archive after Peter Oliver's death – and for serendipitously providing me with a title – and to Jim Phillips for suggesting that I might benefit from the material
- The two anonymous reviewers whose critiques made this a better and more readable book, and the staff at the University of Toronto Press – and in particular Len Husband – for spearheading the process of publication
- And special thanks – and love – to two people who came to this project just in time: Rob Alexander agreed, without complaint, to share a life that included intergovernmental relations, and Lizzie's arrival introduced us both to a different sort of "justifiable obsession."

"A JUSTIFIABLE OBSESSION"

Conservative Ontario's Relations with Ottawa, 1943–1985

Introduction

In the nineteenth century, Ontario's relationship with Ottawa was virtually a spectator sport. In one corner was Oliver Mowat, the long-serving Liberal premier of Ontario, who questioned the extent of federal jurisdiction over natural resources, the powers of the lieutenant governor, and the determination of the territorial boundaries of the province. In the other was Conservative Prime Minister John A. Macdonald, disallowing legislation, referring questions to the courts, and generally poking the provincial premier into a fight. The two were political adversaries in as many ways as possible – their party, legislature, and approach to governance were all widely divergent – and they were certainly not friends, but nevertheless they agreed that they should "try to work the new machine ... with as little friction as possible."[1] Their personal antipathy, borne out of both their public and private differences, combined with a need to clarify the meaning of the British North America Act in those first few decades of its existence, led to some extraordinary battles. With the Liberal *Globe* lining up behind its premier, and the Conservative *Mail* trumpeting the cause of the federal government, the act was a hard one to ignore.

In the end, Mowat probably came out on top of the intergovernmental skirmishes, more than earning the moniker of "father of provincial rights," and securing judicial interpretations of provincial powers that seemed to move the country away from the centralism of the original agreement. In Ontario, at least, Mowat cast a long shadow. Subsequent premiers were quick to emulate his vigorous defence of provincial rights in the hopes of also repeating his success at the polls. Sometimes, the barbs were clearly partisan: James Pliny Whitney, a Conservative premier during Wilfrid Laurier's prime ministership, called the Liberal justice

minister "the most infantile specimen of politician" he had ever met, and
Mackenzie King called another Conservative premier, Howard Ferguson,
a "skunk."[2] On other occasions, however, the participants in the battle
were of the same political stripe. Some of the most heated exchanges
occurred between Mitch Hepburn and King, both Liberals but with very
different ideas about government and jurisdiction. At an intergovernmental meeting described as "the god damnedest exhibition circus you
can imagine," Hepburn attacked the Rowell-Sirois Report recommendations for transferring tax power from the provinces to the federal government. "We are not behind you, we are ahead of you," he told King and
his ministers. "Don't smash this confederation and stir up [a] possible
racial feud in your efforts."[3]

The intergovernmental battles in the period leading up to the Second
World War were important in the determination of the shape of Canadian federalism. Judicial decisions tended to find in favour of a generous
reading of provincial jurisdiction, and a more circumscribed definition
of what Ottawa could do than successive prime ministers might have preferred. By the 1930s, the balance had tilted so far in favour of the provinces that there was little the federal government could do – even had
Prime Ministers R.B. Bennett or King been willing to try – to alleviate the
effects of the Depression. Through much of the period, it was Ontario
politicians who led the charge for provincial rights. But after the war,
that job increasingly seemed to fall on Quebec premiers or, in the 1970s
and 1980s, on politicians from Alberta. Colourful characters like Maurice Duplessis and René Lévesque, or wealthy provincial pseudo-CEOs
like Peter Lougheed, overtook the Ontario politicians of an earlier generation in the public imagination. Moreover, they also seemed to play a
bigger role in determining the direction of Canadian federalism than
their Ontario counterparts.

The story, as it has been told by scholars and, to some extent, participants, has been clear: Ontario was an important player in the intergovernmental battles of the first half of Canada's history, but it has not
played a pivotal role in the second. By focusing attention on the more
apparently colourful characters of federal-provincial relations, however,
we have been blind to the intriguing tale of Ontario's shifting strategies, failed gambits, and unlikely alliances, and to its shocking role re-
versals and occasional mistaken identities along the way. While perhaps
not quite Shakespearean in its unfolding, the intergovernmental relationship that was forged between the politicians and the bureaucrats in
Ontario's Big Blue Machine and a largely Liberal Ottawa in the years

between 1943 and 1985 certainly deserves more scrutiny than it has received. The enormous centralization of power that was a side effect of the Second World War meant that there was simply no way that Ontario could continue to deal with Ottawa in the manner that had been the case under premiers like Oliver Mowat, when recourse to the courts was so often the road to securing broader provincial rights. On the one hand, war had given the federal politicians and bureaucrats the excuse to monopolize taxing powers, and postwar reconstruction suggested a justification for controlling social policies as well. On the other hand, the tenure of the province-friendly Judicial Committee of the Privy Council was about to end, with Canadian appeals eliminated in 1949. These two realities had an overwhelming effect on how the provinces would be able manage their relationship with the federal government after the Second World War. When George Drew was elected the premier of Ontario in the summer of 1943 – the first Conservative in almost a decade – it marked the beginning of a realization that the intergovernmental playing field had shifted profoundly. This book is about successive Ontario governments' search for a new intergovernmental strategy. While the goal of carving out a larger and more autonomous role for Ontario remained the same as had been the case since the early days of Confederation, the means were different – more sophisticated, more integrative – and, ultimately, less successful.

By looking carefully at a relationship that has avoided much attention because it has seemed so benign, this study seeks to add to our understanding not only of Canadian federalism and intergovernmental relations, but also of postwar Ontario politics and political culture. It traces the evolution of a strategy in the federal-provincial arena that was slowly perfected over the course of more than forty years of Conservative government in Ontario. Under George Drew, the provincial politicians and bureaucrats began designing policies that would serve as alternatives to those that were being put forward by the Mackenzie King Liberals in Ottawa. Although the policies were unquestionably designed with an eye to Ontario's own interests, Drew and his colleagues still sought out provincial allies in their campaign against the further centralization of power in Ottawa. When Leslie Frost took over as premier, he continued the strategy, but paid increasing attention to couching the Ontario alternatives in the language of national interest, and to ensuring that Quebec remained included in the federal family. The national interest was of paramount importance to the government of John Robarts during the tumultuous 1960s, when the province offered not so much alternatives to federal schemes but initiated action in areas that many thought more appropriately the realm of federal activity. Removed somewhat from the bilateral relationship that characterizes intergovernmental relations, the Ontario strategy began to shift towards ensuring that federalism remained a functional system in the Canadian environment. By the time Bill Davis took the helm, Ontario's evolving strategy had come to emphasize core elements of the federal system – a form of mega-intergovernmentalism – that put the constitution ahead of the economic and social policy that had dominated earlier intergovernmental debates. The political environment in postwar Ontario, and in the country as a whole, was profoundly shaped by the relationship that each of these four premiers developed with their counterparts in Ottawa.

Scholars have taken their cues from the public, favouring analyses of the more flamboyant or bellicose participants in the intergovernmental battlefields of post–Second World War Canada, and leaving the consideration of Ontario's role in federal-provincial relations mouldering on the grave of Mitch Hepburn. Conflicts, or at least the more obvious ones, have been more attractive sources of inspiration for historians than the apparent calm of Ontario's relations with Ottawa.[4] This focus on the rising tide of separatism in Quebec, or on the powerful role of energy in the new west, has had an effect on our understanding of Canadian federalism. Not only does it exaggerate the role of societal rather than institutional factors in an assessment of Canadian federalism, but also it suggests that the balance of power has been determined by those provinces with either the will or the wealth to leave.[5] Like the majority of Canadian scholarship, this study acknowledges the key role that institutions play in shaping Canadian federalism, emphasizing in particular the role of the constitution in both shaping and being shaped by economic and social policy; in privileging the role of one particular province, however, this work also accepts that societal factors such as history, culture, geography, and economy have an impact on the pressures that are brought to bear on the institutions of federalism. But in examining the ways in which a province increasingly began to articulate a national vision – however much it may have been in the provincial interest to do so – this study weaves together both institutional and societal frameworks in an analysis that underscores the intrastate possibilities of provincial politics.

Although scholars have tended to understand the intrastate features of Canadian federalism – cabinet, Senate, and Supreme Court, most obviously – as being institutions within which regional viewpoints could be heard at the national level, this study offers a model of inverted intrastate federalism. In gradually articulating not just a national *vision*, but also, ultimately, an *approach* to fundamental institutional issues within the Canadian federal structure, Ontario governments gave voice to national concerns at the provincial level. While conspicuously *not* providing national representation at the provincial level, the Ontario approach nevertheless provided a provincial platform (in many cases, an unwelcome one) for the expression of national objectives. In illuminating this quirk of Canadian federalism, this study recasts our understanding of the division of powers, the role of both institutional and societal factors, and the relationship between all three. Federalism in Canada takes on a different appearance when viewed through the lens of the Ontario state.

One of the other peculiarities of the study of federalism in Canada is the dominant role that is accorded to elites. Whether the summit federalism of intergovernmental first ministers' conferences, or the executive federalism of the almost daily contact between ministers and officials at the two levels of government, government-to-government contact is the norm in the Canadian example.[6] Moreover, our understanding of the federal-provincial dynamic in the years after 1945 is shaped almost exclusively through an examination of the elite players – the premiers and prime ministers – who have given faces, voices, and invective to the relationship. What we know about Ontario politics has come to us largely though the lives of the premiers who dominated the postwar landscape.[7] A generation of able biographers focused on the individuals of Queen's Park, examining federalism and the intergovernmental relationship through the eyes of the premier. These studies have been useful, but by viewing the people through the lens of federalism, rather than the reverse, this book offers a different interpretation of Ontario politics and political culture. In the intergovernmental arena, the Ontario politicians – and the plethora of advisers who designed the policies that shaped their administrations – can be seen more clearly to have feet of clay. Viewed from this perspective, Ontario is neither as supportive of the federal government as it might otherwise have appeared to be, nor as confident in its role within the federation. This book seeks, then, to showcase the struggles and conflicts of successive Ontario governments in addressing the federal fact in Canada.

This approach allows us a clearer picture of the party system in Ontario. Political parties themselves have been common topics for scholarly analyses; the long-lasting dominance of the Conservative party in postwar Ontario, however, has largely eluded study. The Big Blue Machine is frequently referenced, but rarely understood. In this area, too, it seems that scholars have been more interested in the oddities of party development elsewhere.[8] Although this book is not an evaluation of a party, the period being considered mirrors the tenure of the Conservatives in Ontario, and therefore inevitably comments on the issues of policy and personnel that shaped both the party and postwar Ontario. Relations with Ottawa were a big part of the work of the Ontario government, and in making decisions about leaders and about election platforms, the managers of the Conservative party itself devised their strategies carefully. Nevertheless, the full study of one of the most successful political dynasties in Canadian history remains to be written.[9]

One of the topics that has *not* been ignored in postwar Ontario is the question of political culture. Although it was once possible to ask "does Ontario exist?"[10] defining the province's political culture has been something of a holy grail for scholars in Ontario, where the task of explaining what seems normative has had long-lasting appeal. Discussions of Ontario's political culture inevitably comment on the province's dominance within the federation, both in terms of size and wealth, the complacency of its population, and the tendency to equate "Ontario" with "Canada."[11] This is perhaps one of the reasons that postwar intergovernmental relations have received so little attention: when John Robarts provocatively and only half-teasingly stated "what's good for Ontario is good for the country," he was expressing a sentiment that few Canadians will doubt was said, thought, and acted upon most of the time. This is one of the reasons, I contend, that few scholars have really examined the Ontario-Ottawa relationship in the years following the Second World War: this simple narrative says it all, offering a convincing explanation for Ontario's position on everything from tax rental agreements to health insurance. Our certainty, then, that Ontario political culture is predicated on a conflation of province and nation, skews our interest in actually examining the real nature of the relationship. This book offers a corrective, suggesting an Ontario culture that does not simply conflate province and nation, but takes responsibility for the idea of nation.

The praxis of federalism in Canada has made it possible for a large, multicultural nation to function and, indeed, to thrive.[12] As such, it has been much studied both at home and abroad. But we know vastly more about the moments when the federal system was threatened than when it held fast, and we know more about the people and provinces and policies that questioned or undermined or rejected federalism than we do about the glue that has held it together. This is a book about the efforts in one province to work with the federal system while at the same time

strengthening the federation, and about an obsession with intergovernmental affairs that at times verged on the unseemly. It is a story that digs
into the very core of what it meant to be Ontarian in the four decades following the Second World War and illuminates a moment that provided
the foundation for the "new Ontario" of today.[13]

Chapter One

"The 'Keystone' Province": George Drew's Ontario, 1943–1946

George Drew, leader of the Conservative party in Ontario from 1938 until he assumed the same position with the national party a decade later, and premier of Ontario from 1943 until 1948, was responsible for initiating what would be a fundamental reorientation of the relationship between Ontario and Ottawa. The shift was determined as much by circumstance as by inclination: Drew inherited a province that faced a much more muscular federal government than had any of his predecessors. The exigencies of wartime gave Ottawa the excuse for centralization, and the courts were increasingly reluctant to expand provincial powers in the way characteristic of the late nineteenth and early twentieth centuries. So while Drew might have preferred to have followed the tactics of the previous generations of Ontario premiers, those avenues were no longer open to him. Instead, he set out in a new direction. Rather than confront the federal government directly, or challenge legislation in the courts, he began a strategy that would be used – and refined – by successive Conservative premiers after him. In response to Prime Minister Mackenzie King's reconstruction plans, Drew offered provincially designed alternatives that had been crafted to address Ontario's specific concerns but also to begin to tackle the problems that other provinces were facing at the end of war. His strategy depended on alliances, so he forged them. George Drew's Ontario did not shift so far from its roots to become a foot soldier for the federal government, but it did begin to articulate an alternative national position on the important policy issues of the day. It was an important beginning for a new intergovernmental relationship.

Drew in Office and on the Warpath

Ontario's relationship with the federal government was on extremely shaky footing in the early years of the Second World War. With the hard-drinking, "deep-dimpled, dynamic" Mitch Hepburn in the premier's office, and Mackenzie King – the "poetry-loving bachelor"[1] – in Ottawa, it made little difference that both were members of the Liberal party; their approaches to party, politics, and government were so divergent that it was difficult to find many, if any, points of agreement between the two. During the Depression, they had crossed swords over the appropriate role that each level of government should play. Hepburn advocated an interventionist approach, at least insofar as the federal government was concerned. King's failure to come up with more money for provincial purposes, "consult with provinces on relief, and accept responsibility for the unemployed" were among the issues that led Hepburn to announce emphatically in 1937 that "I am a Reformer – but I am not a Mackenzie King Liberal any more."[2] By the time war was declared in 1939, the two governments were clearly on different tracks. King treated the early months of the "phony war" period as a time to limit Canada's liabilities; Hepburn advocated a more aggressive approach to war, and condemned the federal government from the Ontario legislature in January 1940. His actions precipitated a federal election, which King won handily. Hepburn may have had continued support from the Ontario electorate, but the same group was just as content with King's more managerial style at the federal level.[3] It was a classic Ontario election in many ways, showcasing the Janus-faced nature of Ontario voters, who seemed to like their premiers feisty and their prime ministers sober. That the two were often incompatible didn't seem to bother the province's voters.

The leader of the opposition at the time of Hepburn's motion of censure against the King government's handling of the war was hardly the same sort of street-fighter as the premier. Conservative George Drew was tall and patrician, had studied at the best schools in Ontario, and was a lawyer by training. Although he had been mayor of Guelph, and was initially the MPP for a riding outside Toronto, he could never quite shake the appearance and reputation of being part of Toronto's monied elite.[4] But if Drew was refined where Hepburn was brash, it made little difference to their views of the prime minister. Drew had been an active participant in the debate in the Ontario legislature regarding King's war effort, delivering a speech that was a stinging indictment of the war of limited liability.[5] Three years later, after Hepburn had resigned as premier, and the Liberal party floundered trying to find an acceptable successor, Drew had his own chance to wage war against the federal government.

George Drew's victory in 1943 can in part be understood as a result of the internal bickering among the Liberals, both within the provinces, where it was unexpected and unseemly, and between the provincial and federal wings of the party, where it was expected but verged on fratricidal. Moreover, there was a vacuum at the top, with Harry Nixon finally being persuaded to occupy the premier's office. Early on, Drew advised his party that "it may be wise for us to take advantage of their difficulties,"[6] but there was more to the Conservative victory than simply the Liberal demise. The membership of the party had undertaken some important restructuring and rethinking at both the national and provincial levels, and by 1943 clearly held some appeal to Ontario voters. The Port Hope thinkers conference in 1942 had resulted in a turn to the left with a manifesto that contained a renewed commitment to the principles of free enterprise, combined with the recognition of a more active role for government in the provision of a wide array of social security measures. Progressive Premier John Bracken of Manitoba soon took the helm of the new national Progressive Conservative Party.

In Ontario, under Drew's leadership, the Conservatives sketched out their own platform, influenced by the turn to the left but not wedded to the details of the Port Hope conference. The Conservative member from Lindsay, Leslie Frost, urged "that a national point of view should be cultivated and instilled." He failed to see "how Canada can exist in this world if her people are not determined to regard the country's interest from every standpoint as being paramount."[7] This point undoubtedly resonated with Drew, who never wavered in propounding what was, in his opinion at least, a position that held the nation's interest to be the chief concern. When he finally unveiled a platform, devised through private, not public, consultation, there was considerable evidence of this national perspective. When he subsequently named Alex McKenzie, an early opponent of the Port Hope conference and Drew loyalist, into the inner circle as chairman of the organizing committee for the provincial ridings, Drew's control over the party machinery in Ontario was clear.[8] Even with the party firmly under his thumb, however, Drew was only just able to oversee the drafting of a coherent policy platform in time for the election called for 4 August 1943.

The provincial Conservative party executives, meeting on 3 July in Toronto shortly after Premier Nixon called the election, agreed to follow their national brethren in adopting the name "Progressive" Conservatives and, more importantly, approved what was to become known as the "Twenty-two Point Programme."[9] The proposal contained evidence of the influence of the Port Hope declaration in its commitment to protect labour, cut school taxes, depoliticize the Hydro-Electric Power Commission, and provide sweeping social security protection for the citizens of Ontario. The first two points in this Progressive Conservative manifesto, however, were pure Drew, unblemished by any hint of the work of the interested laymen the summer before. First, Drew pledged that a government under his leadership would "maintain British institutions and strengthen the British partnership by every means within the constitutional power of the Government of Ontario." As far as that constitutional power was concerned, however, in his second point Drew pledged not only to "work in effective cooperation with the Dominion Government" but to "insist that the constitutional rights of the people of Ontario be preserved and that the Government of Ontario exercise full control of its own provincial affairs."[10] In short, Drew pledged to cooperate and work with the Empire and with the nation, but as a partner, not a pawn, ever mindful of possible encroachments on the clear jurisdiction of the province.

When Liberal Premier Harry Nixon opted to campaign on a platform of putting an end to the federal-provincial feud of the Hepburn era, George Drew quickly countered by combining the policy proposals of the twenty-two–point program with attacks on both King and his perceived stronghold of Quebec. Seeking to take advantage of anti-French sentiment in Ontario, based in part on the continuing question mark over the implementation of conscription, Drew argued that if the Ontario government remained a mere puppet of the federal government, then national policy would continue to be determined by Quebec. Re-elect the Liberals, he claimed, and "the voice may be the voice of Nixon but the words will be the words of Mackenzie King."[11] As far as Frost was concerned, Ontario voters had already had enough of the "timidity, log-rolling and compromise of a government dominated by Quebec," and he came to the conclusion that "there has been enough appeasement in that direction that it has reached the stage where so-called national unity will be harmed if there are any further concessions."[12] When the votes had all been counted late on the evening of 4 August, the Tories sat with a slim minority of thirty-eight seats, the CCF had been turned away from government and would have to be content with thirty-four members and Official Opposition status, and the Liberals were sent into the political wilderness with a rump of fifteen seats. Although the governing Liberals had been ousted, Drew could hardly claim total victory; the strong showing of the CCF under the popular leadership of Ted Jolliffe served to keep the Conservatives firmly tied to their promises of social betterment and a commitment to active postwar planning.

However modest Drew's initial victory in 1943 was, he achieved it on a platform that extended well beyond the borders of Ontario. The twenty-two points were really part of a plan for reconstruction, a proposal for re-building Canada, not just Ontario, in the aftermath of war. Drew's attacks on the federal government, a mainstay of provincial election campaigns since the Confederation era, had strayed into more unfamiliar territory. He did not simply criticize the federal government's relationship with Ontario, but attacked its relationship with *other* provinces. The CCF, with their own plans for reconstruction, had pushed the Conservatives into thinking beyond the provincial borders, but now that he had stepped into that abyss, Drew began to embrace the possibility of a more pan-Canadian role. Changing the entire country from his office in Queen's Park was a tall order, but one that Drew and his army of advisers, or-ganizers, and MPPs nevertheless attempted. While he failed to convince Bracken to move the federal party headquarters to Toronto, he was more persuasive outside his own party. His main concern, as illustrated in the 1943 campaign, was planning for the end of the war, and in this he could find much common ground with other premiers.

Despite his anti-French rhetoric on the campaign trail, his first official visit was to Quebec early in his term in office, with very satisfying results. He was "greatly taken with Mr. Godbout, and in fact with most of his cabinet" and in general was "most cordially received" and felt "confident that there will be generous co-operation in the future."[13] Drew confined his enthusiasm, however, to Adelard Godbout's Liberal administration, which represented the only alternative to what the Ontario premier as-sumed would be "an Anti-British Government headed by either [Mau-rice] Duplessis [of the Union Nationale] or [Maxime] Raymond" of the new anti-conscription Bloc Populaire party.[14] Although an agreeable Quebec would be Ontario's most important ally in any negotiations with the federal government, Drew was also interested in establishing closer ties with the western provinces. By spearheading a discussion of common intergovernmental problems, particularly those facing postwar Canada, Drew hoped "to consolidate the people of the various sections into one great Canadian unit." His motives were hardly pure, however. The point of initiating a national discussion was at least in part "that [it] would add to our prestige and our influence in the international world, as well as create a sense of pride and inspiration amongst ourselves. We can do this if we will all join in that single purpose."[15] Nevertheless, Drew had good reason to think that Ontario might be able to find common ground with some of the western provinces. Earlier in the year, Treasury Department official Chester Walters had discussed the possibility of holding an inter-provincial conference with Manitoba's Liberal Premier Stuart Garson. At the time, Garson declared that the issues were "of such transcendent importance ... that you will find us most co-operative in dealing with the other provinces."[16]

Drew's initial concern was that there was a policy vacuum in Ottawa in regards to postwar planning, and his early friendly visits to other provincial capitals combined with his fact-finding entreaties were designed to mobilize the premiers into filling that hole. News over the Christmas recess, however, that federal Liberals were designing reconstruction strategies unilaterally, forced Drew to take the next step. Early in January 1944, he wrote to King, urging "that a Dominion-Provincial Conference be called at the earliest possible date" to discuss postwar planning and financing.[17] Potential legislation dealing with education, health, and social security clearly affected provincial jurisdiction, and Drew was adamantly opposed to any decisions being made in these areas "until we have reached some understanding in regard to the present and future constitutional relationship of the various governments."[18] Perhaps even more important, the Wartime Tax Rental Agreements, reluctantly entered into by the provinces in 1941, gave the federal government control over all areas of taxation – both direct and indirect – for the duration of hostilities as a way to finance the war effort.[19] The normal, pre-war, arrangement whereby the provinces were free to levy personal, corporate, and succession taxes, would have to be reinstated before any serious reconstruction planning could be undertaken.

The federal Liberals were suspicious of Drew's motives: in the PMO, Jack Pickersgill assumed that Drew "hoped to derive some political advantage for himself."[20] King was probably just as suspicious of Drew's motives as was Pickersgill but opted to move slowly on Drew's suggestion. He first wrote to all of the provincial premiers to survey their opinion on holding a conference, and asked for a list of suitable dates to be submitted.[21] Two weeks later, during the Speech from the Throne, the government noted its intention to establish a Department of Veterans Affairs, a Department of Reconstruction, and a Department of Social Welfare. The speech also indicated that a nationwide health insurance scheme, and a national system of contributory old age pensions, would be topics for future discussions with the provinces in preparation for the postwar period. More ominously, without commenting on provincial consultation, the governor general stated that "to aid in ensuring a minimum of well-being to the children of the nation and to help gain for them a closer approach to equality of opportunity in the battle of life you will be asked to approve a measure making provision for family allowances."[22] By the middle of February, King had appointed a cabinet committee to organize the "preparatory work" involved in holding a dominion-provincial conference on reconstruction.[23] The fact that he named Manitoban Thomas Crerar as chair of the committee, a cabinet minister who was opposed to state interference in the provision of social security measures and someone who was particularly opposed to family allowances, points to King's ambivalent attitude towards extensive reconstruction plans.[24]

Three months into the new year and the situation had not changed much from the Ontario perspective, despite the calls to convene an intergovernmental conference at the earliest possible date. The federal government had indicated at least some interest in the problems that Canada would face at the end of the war, but the concrete solutions proposed were still unilateral in nature and had been reached without concern for the provincial jurisdiction that would be affected. Drew became increasingly irritated with what he regarded as stalling on the timing of the conference. What was needed, he argued, was a preliminary conference on "the practical measures" that might be taken to facilitate intergovernmental cooperation.[25] The federal cabinet committee concluded that such a meeting "could produce only sound and fury," largely because it had already established the scope of the federal-provincial conference, should it ever be called. From the federal perspective, the conference would have to address the continuation of the Wartime Tax Rental Agreements, the addition of succession duties as an exclusive dominion field, control over relief for the able-bodied unemployed, control over contributory pensions, control over most of health insurance, and full federal power to implement international treaties dealing with areas of exclusive provincial jurisdiction.[26] Drew had no way of knowing that the federal government had already established the agenda for the reconstruction conference; he might have noticed the worrisome movement in the direction of family allowances, however.

Federal politicians had weighed the political and economic costs and benefits of implementing a universal system of family allowances in the summer of 1943 and concluded that it was unlikely anyone "could openly oppose the principle of establishing children's allowances at a reasonable figure."[27] By early autumn of that year, the proposal was "very much at the fore in Canada," and senior Liberals were giving it "pretty serious consideration ... as a means of easing the pressure on the wage ceiling without blowing the price ceiling wide open."[28] Designed to be available to all children without a means test, family allowances could legitimately be kept within federal jurisdiction, and so the question of the constitutional division of powers did not really enter into federal thinking. It certainly occurred to provincial politicians, however. Adelard Godbout heard rumours of the proposed policy, and promptly wrote to the prime minister supporting the principle of family allowances, nevertheless noting that "we cannot agree that it could properly be implemented as a war measure under federal authority." Moreover, as a piece of social security legislation, he warned that family allowances were clearly in provincial jurisdiction and would threaten "the preservation of provincial autonomy" if they were to be continued after the war.[29]

Unconvinced by Godbout's complaints, and buttressed by the support of social welfare groups across the country, the King government pushed ahead with its plan for a universal system of family allowances.[30] Early reports indicated "very favourable comments on the social legislation proposed," and what suspicion there was about family allowances was dismissed as being "colored by prejudice against Quebec" where fecund mothers would receive larger cheques than those with smaller families in other parts of the country.[31] The federal Opposition objected to the measure, enlisting the assistance of Charlotte Whitton, founding director of the Canadian Council on Child Welfare and a prominent Conservative, in the preparation of statements in the House of Commons. In Ontario, however, Drew remained silent. Whitton's arguments "that all social legislation comes within the jurisdiction of the provinces and the Dominion should only act by way of legislation 'in aid'" of the provinces were generally embraced by the Bracken Progressive Conservatives, thus alleviating Drew of the need to make the provincial autonomy argument.[32] Moreover, it appeared that public opinion was turning against the family allowance proposal, which, while popular in Quebec, had "had a cool reception elsewhere" where it was regarded as a "pre-election maneuver."[33] Even after the family allowance bill was introduced in Parliament and the federal Conservatives began to wobble in their opposition, Drew elected to remain silent.[34] Although both Drew and his Minister of Welfare Percy Vivian were convinced that the whole matter was unconstitutional and that the provinces could offer "a better deal and a more economical one if given the power to work with the Dominion," Drew was firm in insisting on not going "on record re baby bonuses."[35] The issue, he was certain, would go away when family allowances were found "ultra vires and of no effect."[36]

˙ Ultimately, the Ontario premier could no longer ignore the potential trampling of provincial jurisdiction posed by family allowances. Provincial Treasurer Leslie Frost informed Drew that the $100 million the program would cost Ontario taxpayers could not only provide more generous allowances but also satisfy several other social services deficits if administered internally.[37] Legal experts Leslie Blackwell and C.R. Magone indicated that, in their opinion, the family allowance bill was unconstitutional.[38] Drew could contain his anger no longer. First, at a Progressive Conservative rally in Richmond Hill, Drew attacked the program as the result of an evil conspiracy with Quebec. "If anyone has any doubt" that family allowances were an intentional bribe to Quebec, Drew raged, "it must have been removed by two speeches made last night. We now have it from Mr. Godbout's own lips that this Baby Bonus is the result of his collaboration with Mr. King. And in the same evening, Mr. King went out of his way in the House of Commons to point out the very special advantages which this Bill offered to the people of Quebec." Drew's outrage at the rally was largely focused on his exclusion from the process of collaboration. "I am the premier of a province with a much larger population than Quebec. I am the premier of the province whose people pay 50% of every Canadian tax dollar. I am the premier of a province whose people contribute just about twice as much in taxes for the fulfillment of any Dominion government undertaking as do the people of the province of which Mr. Godbout is premier. Mr. King collaborates with Mr. Godbout according to Mr. Godbout's own statement. As Premier of Ontario, I have heard nothing from Mr. King at any time about this or any similar Bill."[39] The sense of injustice was palpable.

The Richmond Hill speech was just the first salvo in Drew's war over family allowances. In an emergency meeting of key provincial Conservatives, all discussion of plans for reconstruction was coloured by a perception of "the special privileges which have been extended to Quebec in almost every field."[40] The next day, Drew took to the airwaves with a message for the voters of Ontario. Rather than report on the progress the Conservative government had made in areas such as agriculture, labour laws, education, and mining and forest resources, as had been his original intention, "recent events have raised an issue which it is my duty to discuss with you immediately."[41] The issue was family allowances. After lecturing on the division of powers contained in the British North America Act, detailing his constant calls for the convening of an intergovernmental meeting on reconstruction, explaining the cost to the Ontario taxpayers of family allowances, and once again reporting the collaboration with Quebec but the total absence of communication with Ontario, Drew spelled out what lay at the heart of his opposition. "Are we going to permit one isolationist province to dominate the destiny of a divided Canada? I hope that each on of you will answer with a resounding 'no,' which will be heard in every part of the Province of Quebec."[42]

Drew did not restrict his fire to the odious family allowances. His provincewide broadcast was clearly an attack on Quebec's wartime enlistment record, criticizing the fact that the failure to bear the responsibilities of citizenship was nevertheless rewarded with a federal handout that would be more generously received by the larger Quebec families. The speech was a call "upon the rest of Canada to align itself against Quebec in national affairs."[43] Federal officials regarded Drew's actions as posturing preparatory to calling a provincial election that could be fought on an appeal to racial prejudice, a strategy that had worked well for Maurice Duplessis in his victory over Godbout in the Quebec election of the previous day.[44] The damage that was done by Drew's intemperate remarks, however, would have far-reaching effects on his ability to present himself as a national leader.[45]

Although the Conservative press in Canada predictably came to Drew's defence, calling his a brave stand for national unity and urging an end to the appeasement of Quebec, it was the Liberals who were firmly in control.[46] Drew was immediately accused of fanning the flames of racial prejudice. During the "spirited debate" over the family allowance bill in the Senate, A.K. Hugessen, a Quebec Liberal Senator, charged that "to serve his political ends," George Drew was "willing to do two things – to raise the race cry and to sacrifice the children of Canada."[47] The rhetoric was unnecessary: the Liberal-dominated Senate easily passed the family allowance bill over the protests of the few Conservatives. King was also drawn into the debate. In the House of Commons, he accused anyone who "singled out" one part of the country as "doing the greatest disservice that can be done to Canada's unity and to the Commonwealth."[48] Foreshadowing one of the major issues of the federal election in the following year, King promised to do battle with anyone who attempted to divide the country against itself. Although he did not mention Drew's name, it was clear who King saw his opponent as being.[49]

Drew also faced criticism from other parts of the country, where the focus was not on the anti-French sentiments expressed but on the contention that Ontario was footing much of the bill for social services across the country. Manitoba Liberal Premier Stuart Garson "disagreed sharply" with Drew's calculation that 50 per cent of the cost of family allowances would come from Ontario taxpayers. Much of that money, Garson explained, came in fact from customs duties, excise taxes, and sales tax, which were paid by importers and manufacturers in Ontario. Those taxes were then "written into the cost of the goods and services which these Ontario ... concerns sell in western Canada and the Maritimes." A substantial proportion of the $100 million that Ontario would contribute to a family allowance program, then, would "ultimately come to rest upon taxpayers in western Canada and the Maritimes."[50] Carrying on where Garson left off, the *Winnipeg Free Press* noted that much of the money would also come from corporate taxes, which were paid in Ontario on profits made in poorer regions of the country. Drew's criticism of Quebec, the paper claimed, was designed merely to obscure the real source of his anger: "Mr. Drew's attack is concentrated on the West."[51]

Facing criticism from all sides, Drew tried to clarify his position. Reiterating portions of his 9 August radio broadcast, Drew underlined that he was in favour of measures being taken to provide assistance for families, but that he objected to the timing.[52] His concerns, he maintained, were based on the fact that Ottawa was pledging provincial tax money, over which it had temporary control during wartime, for a program that was clearly within provincial jurisdiction and would be in effect long after the war was over.[53] Wisely, after making his clarifications in the provincial legislature, Drew made a "very sudden decision" to leave the country and deal with "very serious problems" of hospitalization and rehabilitation in England.[54] A further clarification after Drew returned at the end of September did little to change minds that were already made up.[55] The hierarchy of the Conservative party was finally forced to admit that "the criticism of the Dominion legislation has done immeasurable harm" and "cooled" much of Drew's support, even within Ontario.[56]

The contemporary view of Drew's strategy held that in taking a pro-Ontario stance and lashing out at Quebec, the poorer provinces in the west and in the Maritimes, and the federal government, Drew was following the same well-worn track of other Ontario premiers, most particularly Mitch Hepburn.[57] Although the imperialist premier was undoubtedly outraged with what he regarded as the negligible participation of French Canadians in the war effort, and as premier he could not help but shudder at the sums of tax dollars that would be collected in Ontario and spent elsewhere through the family allowance program, his real anger was reserved for the federal government and what the program indicated about the future of intergovernmental relations. It was entirely constitutional for the federal government to collect taxes through any means whatsoever, and it was equally constitutional for that money to be spent in any way the federal government might choose. Having embraced Keynesian economics, the Ottawa civil service opted to introduce a system that would put money into the hands of those people most likely to spend it – namely, those people with young families. The increased levels of consumption would prime the economic pump and, it was hoped, would stave off a postwar recession.[58] But from Drew's perspective, family allowances were a costly program that announced that the federal government had no intention of vacating the taxation fields it had occupied since the Wartime Tax Rental Agreements had come into effect in 1942. After months of demanding the immediate convening of an intergovernmental meeting on reconstruction, a meeting that Drew imagined would result in a cooperative postwar effort rather than merely the proclamation of a unilateral reconstruction plan, the Ontario premier was left with the uneasy feeling that cooperation was unlikely. That sense of impotence in the face of the completed federal family allowance scheme left Drew railing against enemies large and small, real and imagined. It also convinced Drew to design new strategies for his dealings with the federal government.

Mending Fences and Making Friends

In simply reacting to a federal fait accompli over family allowances, George Drew had little success and was generally regarded as having weakened the Conservative position in Canada. Over the course of the next year, while not ignoring the baby bonus issue entirely, Drew and the Conservative government of Ontario shifted tactics towards a more proactive defence of provincial rights. Although Mackenzie King steadfastly refused to convene a federal-provincial conference until the summer of 1945, the initial work of preparing a provincial position on reconstruction began in earnest in Ontario in the autumn of 1944. In addition to evaluating the various ways that tax revenues and social responsibilities could be divided between the federal and provincial governments, the Ontario officials began to develop working relationships with the governments of the other provinces. The connections would prove useful once the real work of hammering out a plan for reconstruction began.[59]

Having voiced his opposition to family allowances so loudly, Drew was not in a position to drop the subject entirely, but he expanded his criticisms to include the whole area of federal involvement in social services.

Charlotte Whitton, for example, encouraged the Ontario premier to use his position to stress that shifting postwar revenue towards Ottawa would "seriously impair the ability of every province of Canada, not only to operate its health, welfare and education services but actually [its] basic services, its agriculture, its road systems, etc."[60] Moreover, she pressed Drew to "take the initiative" and call an interprovincial meeting "to discuss the position of the Provinces relating to social security measures generally."[61] Failing that, she urged him to conduct a provincial inquiry into a system of family services that would have "regard to all the factors in the economy, geographical features, stage of development of related services ... in this Province."[62] Drew ultimately commissioned Whitton to prepare a report on family services for the province, in which she raised her voice as one of the few in the community of social welfare workers who was opposed to the existing system of family allowances.[63]

Drew did not take Whitton's advice in calling a meeting of the other premiers to discuss reconstruction plans in the absence of the federal government, although with the continued inaction on the part of Ottawa, there were many times when he considered it.[64] Instead, Drew and Provincial Treasurer Leslie Frost made moves to assess the sentiment in other provinces and make what headway was possible in the direction of interprovincial agreements on issues of taxation. Drew's comments on family allowances had isolated Ontario in the summer of 1944; a few months later, Frost was sent around the country to heal the rifts. His western tour included stops in Vancouver, where Liberal Premier John Hart's meeting with Frost was considered a "reasonable success," and Edmonton, where there was every reason to believe that Social Credit Premier Ernest Manning would approve of the Ontario stance on provincial autonomy.[65] Manitoba, however, did not figure in Frost's travel plans. Drew was "convinced Garson acted in collaboration with Ottawa following my August speech" and advised Frost not to bother with any entreaties.[66] Nor did he stop in Regina, although CCF Premier Tommy Douglas clearly considered Drew the leader in the effort to convene an intergovernmental conference when he urged him, a few months later, to protest the arbitrary manner in which the federal government seized the subsidy owing to Saskatchewan. When Douglas argued that any intergovernmental agreement would be impossible if the subsidy was "subject to [the] caprice of [the] federal government," Drew responded that "this merely emphasizes the need for an immediate Dominion-Provincial conference."[67]

Ontario politicians failed to force a full intergovernmental conference; they did, however, experience some success in negotiating agreements with other provinces instead. For example, with little difficulty, Frost was able to negotiate an agreement with Quebec that would eliminate double succession taxation. Although Drew had not yet met the Quebec premier, and perhaps hesitated to do so after the position he had taken the previous August, Frost considered it "a great privilege" to have met Duplessis early in 1945, and he looked forward to further associations "in solving matters of common interest."[68] Nova Scotia entered into a similar agreement with Ontario, and the two completed deals elicited much praise from the business community.[69] But other provinces were less easily convinced of the merits of Ontario's proposals. Notably, Garson suggested that a more appropriate solution to the problem of double taxation was for the provinces to "withdraw entirely from the inheritance tax field in favour of the Dominion, upon condition that the Dominion provides the provinces with other compensatory revenues."[70] Raising the possibility of provincial initiatives in correcting some of the imbalances in the direct tax fields proved to be a useful way for the Ontario government to gauge the likely attitudes of other provinces at a full dominion-provincial conference. Quebec and Nova Scotia had identified themselves as potential allies with Ontario by signing on to the reciprocal tax agreements; Manitoba, however, was clearly more interested in supporting Ottawa's claim over the direct tax fields. Still, Frost was able to report in May 1945 that over the previous "twenty months Provincial relationships have been immeasurably bettered."[71]

By the summer of 1945, the federal government was finally ready to call an intergovernmental conference to begin on 6 August in Ottawa.[72] King had handily won a third straight majority government in the election of 11 June 1945, and the preparatory work of the cabinet committee on the dominion-provincial conference was finally completed and ready for general consumption.[73] The topics open for discussion had been established more than a year earlier and included the maintenance of full employment and high income through the encouragement of private industry and through public improvements, as well as various issues of public welfare and social security.[74] It was unlikely, however, that many provincial politicians knew the extent of the planning that had already gone on in Ottawa. By early February 1945, Alex Skelton had transformed the deliberations of the cabinet committee on the dominion-provincial conference into a concise memo that would become the basis for the federal position outlined in the Green Book proposals. It documented the federal government's intention to remain in the direct tax fields, in return for providing an extensive array of subsidies and social policies. Skelton considered the proposal "so favourable to the provinces that none could refuse it."[75] Nevertheless, the provinces were free to suggest alternatives if they so wished.[76] Although Ontario had made considerable headway in the direction of identifying solutions to the problems of reconstruction, the alternative was not yet ready for unveiling. The Ontario government therefore prepared for the upcoming conference by holding one last, vitally important, meeting.

Still somewhat uncertain of the reception that Drew would receive in Quebec, Frost met with Maurice Duplessis as an emissary of the Ontario government. In addition to dealing with issues of particular concern to the two provinces, such as security laws and hydro-electricity developments, Frost and Duplessis spoke in considerable detail about dominion-provincial relations. On this topic, there was a great deal of agreement. The two politicians concurred that the forthcoming conference would be but a starting point, and a "continuing conference would permit a thorough understanding of the point of view of various governments." They agreed that neither would make formal submissions at the August meeting. "Ontario would insist," said Frost, "on having all the issues placed before the Conference" and would not be forced into dealing with specifics in a piecemeal fashion. Duplessis seemed to agree. Although he kept silent, Frost assumed that Duplessis was not as willing as Ontario was to accept the federal government collecting corporate and personal income taxes as a way to eliminate double taxation. This last point of presumed disagreement was the sort of evidence that Frost used to conclude "that the Quebec people are extreme provincial rightists. They would go much farther along this line than we would. Our attitude towards the Dominion and other provinces has been and is much more generous."[77] All in all, however, the meeting went very well, and nicely broke the ice for Drew's eventual meeting with Duplessis.

At Queen's Park, the Ontario position was solidifying. The Ontario Bureau of Statistics and Research had done a great deal of preparatory work before the dominion-provincial conference, and while they had not prepared a formal submission, their background report for internal use made several points clear. Maintaining the integrity of provincial jurisdiction was key, and the provincial government should be able to exercise power in any way it saw fit in areas that were clearly its constitutional responsibility. So, too, was maintaining a vibrant economy at all costs. Within the limits imposed by these two criteria, then, measures that would address the concerns of other provinces could be considered. Ontario's main goals as it prepared for the conference on reconstruction were thus fairly clear: regain tax room, build up provincial treasuries, and rebuild the economy. All was dependent, however, on the termination of the irksome Wartime Tax Rental Agreements, the system by which the federal government had "temporarily" moved into taxation areas traditionally under provincial jurisdiction as a necessary part of the war effort.

There was no question that this position was particularly attractive for those provinces that were rich in both resources and corporate tax bases. Nevertheless, Drew was attempting to do more than merely outline an alternative to the anticipated federal position. Instead, it was clear from the Ontario brief that it was designed to appeal to a much broader spectrum of the country. For example, the document proposed a system of subsidies for have-not provinces and minimized the usual Ontario rhetoric about the costs of Confederation that were borne by the central province.[78] It ended on a positive note: "We consider that Ontario now has a splendid opportunity as the 'keystone' province to give leadership in establishing subsidies on a sound basis and to improve Dominion-Provincial and interprovincial relations generally."[79]

Despite having given prolonged consideration to the problems facing postwar Canada, neither Ontario nor dominion government participants were entirely certain on the strategy they would pursue at the conference. A week before the opening, King was convinced that although his officials had prepared "a splendid document," it nevertheless set "forth far too much." He recommended further refinement.[80] Drew, on the other hand, received advice on how to proceed from John Bracken, who had gone over the entire problem with Robert Clark. In an effort to ensure that the Conservative party could continue to "appeal for national unity," Clark suggested that Drew endorse a system of subsidies for poorer regions, a commission to regulate such grants-in-aid, and that he "let the Dominion government be the sole agency for collecting the income tax and succession duties." In return, Drew could offer to "take the lead" in abolishing double taxation rather than wait for the other provinces to declare their intentions to do likewise, which would establish "a solid block in the foundation of the alliance which we must build with the Prairie Provinces and the Maritimes if we are to win the next Federal election."[81]

The Ontario Treasury Department had somewhat different advice. Convinced that "every other province, except perhaps Quebec, will be looking to Ontario to walk into the Conference and empty its horn of plenty," Drew and the other Ontario delegates were urged to remember in "negotiating a redistribution of the taxing powers" that "to have a prosperous Canada we must have a prosperous Ontario."[82] Still, without knowing what the federal government intended to unveil at the conference, Drew did not commit himself to one particular course of action but rather waited to see what the meetings held. When the Dominion-Provincial Conference on Reconstruction finally convened on 6 August 1945 it was with a certain display of fireworks. Drew, Duplessis, and New Brunswick's Liberal Premier John McNair all objected to the intended procedure of the conference, with the former arguing that the conference needed to agree on the subjects to be debated before the federal government could be allowed to table its proposals.[83] The Green Book was finally produced, leaving King privately "disgusted with that sort of thing on the part of leaders of two important provinces of Canada."[84]

At least one federal representative, Minister of Health Brooke Claxton, later believed that tabling the Green Book so early was probably a mistake for the proposals it contained were "so much greater than [the provinces] expected that some of the premiers were thrown for a loop ... and resented it."[85] The federal scheme was, not surprisingly to the Ontario delegation, predicated on the continuation of the wartime policy by which the Ottawa collected all direct and indirect taxes and returned to the provinces a premium to compensate for this loss of provincial income. With this added revenue, the federal government pledged to offer a social security package that included unemployment insurance, disability allowances, and pensions and might conceivably be extended to include health insurance. If adopted, the policies would be "the instrument of completely changing the emphasis of administration and legislation on social problems from the provinces to the dominion."[86] The Green Book also promised a system of equalization grants to assist provinces in which the standard of living was considered to be below the national average. Although the first session of the conference, which lasted five days, was devoted primarily to an airing of the federal proposals and very brief preliminary responses from the provincial premiers, the opposition of the Ontario delegation could not be doubted. When the conference adjourned on 10 August 1945, Drew and his colleagues returned to Toronto to begin the task of preparing a response.

A Treasury Department committee immediately began identifying alternatives to the Green Book as well as the "road to an agreement that might be acceptable to the central Government and to the other provinces – and particularly to the people of Ontario."[87] By the middle of October, an Ontario plan was in place. Beginning with an articulation of the detrimental effects that the Green Book proposals would have on "Ontario's budgetary position," and the "undesirability" of the use of population as a means of determining the value of federal subsidies, the Ontario report moved on to tangible alternatives. It called for the centralization of the collection of all direct taxes, the continuation of the British North America Act subsidies, and a clear division of tax sources with Ottawa vacating amusement, gasoline, electricity, security transfer, and succession duty taxes. Welfare costs would be assumed entirely by the dominion, except "minor services" for which the provinces would cover 25 per cent of the costs, and health insurance was to remain in provincial jurisdiction. The complicated question of how the two levels of government would share the direct tax revenue was dealt with in five alternative formulae. The most attractive to the committee was a plan that would see the centralized collection of such taxes, but the preservation of the provincial right to levy the taxes under their own acts. An undetermined formula for equalization was also included, but it was not based purely on population as was the case in the federal proposal.[88] Ontario had objected to this method of determining fiscal-need subsidies as unfair, but even centralist commentators such as Grant Dexter of the *Winnipeg Free Press* considered the federal proposal "old stuff" and unable to "solve the problem."[89]

In countering the Green Book with a proposal of their own, the Ontario drafters were always very wary of the need to earn the support of other provincial leaders. There was some suggestion of holding an interprovincial conference to discuss the merits of the Ontario plan, and Drew tried to win over supporters in an informal way.[90] The Treasury committee found a "compromise" solution to the problem of shared tax fields with "a plan which would be more favourable to Ontario [than the federal plan] and at the same time not unattractive to the 'have not' provinces."[91] Similarly, Drew's public statements, ostensibly addressed to Ontario voters but designed for broader consumption, made clear that the provincial government was preparing its counterproposals with the best interests of the nation in mind. "I believe that a high measure of uniformity of [federal and provincial] legislation and simplification of tax collection is a vital necessity," he informed a Canadian Club audience. "Neither should anything I have said be interpreted as an objection to the pooling of our resources for the welfare of Canada as a whole. I believe that Ontario should take her full share in building the strength and security of every part of Canada." Make no mistake about it, Drew warned, Ontario's position was "not only in the interests of the people of Ontario but it is also in the best interests of the whole of Canada."[92] Although his speech "might be regarded as a discourse on the advantages of decentralized administration," it was less obviously critical of the federal proposals than comments Drew made during the August conference.[93]

Drew could afford to be more conciliatory once a clear Ontario alternative was established. The dominion-provincial conference, which had broken into subcommittees to study the federal proposals following the initial meeting in the summer of 1945, met sporadically during the fall and winter of 1946. An early meeting of first ministers in November made it "evident that all parties believe a way must and will be found to effect a Dominion-Provincial agreement" and despite raising some "tough questions," hopes for a positive outcome "brightened."[94] Only the federal Green Book proposals, however, were on the agenda. For the time being, the Ontario delegation was cautious: the alternative plan remained a closely guarded secret and, until they were ready to make it public, Frost warned the provincial statistician to ensure that "nothing which we suggest by way of agenda would disclose what we have in mind."[95] Until Ontario's scheme was unveiled at the January meetings of the coordinating committee of the conference, study in both Ottawa and the other provincial capitals focused on the details of the plan contained in the Green Book.[96] Public discussion, on the other hand, was generally curtailed: "the provincial authorities seem to regard the Dominion proposals as if they were wartime secrets – to be kept from public sight."[97]

Ontario's Proposals Take Centre Stage

Official Ottawa, where secrets were few and far between, was taken by surprise by the disclosure of Ontario's alternative proposals for postwar federal-provincial relations. Drew had not only done a good job of convincing his cabinet colleagues and officials in the Treasury Department of the need for secrecy, but also he had lulled the federal government into believing that he would support the Green Book proposals virtually unchanged. The Ontario bombshell marked the beginning of four months of intense negotiations, during which sides were drawn, alliances forged, and tactics altered. Despite the frenetic activity, a final agreement on the division of taxing power and jurisdiction was just as elusive in May as it had been in December.

In advance of the reconvening of the Economic Committee of the Dominion-Provincial Conference on Reconstruction on 8 January 1946, Drew released the Ontario counterproposals to the prime minister and the eight other provincial premiers. It was his hope that his "plans for a more effective working combination" of the two levels of government would put an end to "a growing tendency to settle our differences of opinion ... by extended litigation" instead of by discussion.[98] The result was "a flood of comment across the Dominion, largely favourable."[99] Liberal stalwarts, such as *Winnipeg Free Press* correspondent and Ottawa insider Grant Dexter, reacted with "surprise and keen disappointment" at the position that was "so fundamentally opposed to the dominion proposals that compromise is impossible."[100] By the Ontario government's own count, however, eleven newspapers were in favour of the Ontario position, eight were opposed, and thirty-eight contained editorials that were neutral but, according to Conservative organizer Harry Robbins, tended to praise Drew for "producing a highly constructive brief" and demonstrating "statesmanlike" behaviour.[101]

What was clear was that the focus of intergovernmental negotiations had changed dramatically with the receipt of Ontario's alternative, and none of the players were entirely certain of how to respond. Positions changed as rumours of alliances reached provincial capitals and various backrooms in Ottawa. The provincial treasurer of New Brunswick, for example, was certain that the "general opinion" in the other provinces was that Ontario's proposals were not a "satisfactory alternative" to the Green Book offer, and proceeded to outline the net gains that would be available through the dominion plan. Nevertheless, the Ontario proposals had "at first glance" appeared "to be advantageous to N.B."[102] British Columbia had seemed positively disposed as far as Ontario officials had been concerned, yet on the east coast and to Mackenzie King, Premier Hart was regarded as solidly behind the federal offer.[103] In Nova Scotia, meanwhile, former King cabinet member and newly elected Premier Angus L. Macdonald seemed delighted that "Drew's reply to the Dominion proposals," which he believed contained "the germs of some good things," had been met in Ottawa with "considerable consternation."[104]

Ontario's proposals were not formally discussed until the entire conference coordinating committee reconvened at the end of January, although they were certainly frequently referred to in meetings of the various subcommittees.[105] Before debate began in earnest, the provincial delegations had to content themselves with second-guessing their colleagues' responses, and positioning themselves to be able to take advantage of whatever proposal ultimately won the day. Within the inner circle in Ottawa, however, there was little doubt that the Ontario position would be summarily rejected. Claxton, for one, was reportedly "vitriolic" over Drew's proposals, which he considered to be "uneconomic, impossible of implementation, unacceptable to other provinces, and drafted solely with a view to the selfish interests of Ontario."[106] While other members of the government were more measured in their responses, the cabinet coordinating committee expended a great deal of time and effort preparing the refutation of the Ontario proposals. Outwardly "non-committal,"[107] the federal government nevertheless began taking the alternative proposal apart. The suggestion to establish a permanent body of dominion-provincial consultation was lauded; virtually everything else was dismissed.[108]

The federal critique focused on Ontario's alleged misreading of the Green Book proposals and subsequent inconsistencies in its case, and on Ontario's alternative recommendations themselves. The former problems seemed to raise the ire of the federal delegation much more than the alternatives that Drew had offered. Line by line, the Ontario case was rejected. Canada would not become a unitary state if the Green Book proposals were adopted; no constitutional change was necessary to implement the new measures; the provincial governments were not more effective because they were "closer to the people"; and, perhaps most importantly, "Ontario relies upon the outmoded 'Contract' theory as being a substantial reason for turning down the present Dominion Proposals."[109] The document contained ten pages of information correcting the misinterpretation of the federal proposals contained in the Ontario submission, and only one dealing explicitly with the recommendations themselves. On this issue, the federal officials could only complain that Ontario demanded onerous duties of Ottawa, including responsibility for solving unemployment, stimulating international trade, and providing generous old age assistance, while simultaneously "emasculating the Dominion government" by reducing its taxing ability.[110] Both levels of government objected to the other's insistence on retaining taxing authority; Ontario's objections to the Green Book, and Ottawa's objections to Ontario's proposals, were thus remarkably similar.

The federal government flinched first by recognizing that it would have to sweeten its offer somewhat to attract provinces that might waver after they examined the Ontario proposals. Before the first ministers reconvened on 28 January 1946, officials in the federal Finance Department determined that it would be wise to increase the per capita subsidy offered to each province from $12 to $15.[111] But when the prime minister announced the $50 million increase in the federal offer to the gathered premiers, it was not nearly enough to satisfy the critics.[112] Drew had demanded that discussion revolve around the federal proposals, not those submitted by Ontario, as a way of ensuring that he would not be blamed for any breakdown of negotiations, and it was soon clear that there were still serious questions about the federal intentions.[113] Most particularly, the provinces wanted a clear statement of which direct tax fields Ottawa was proposing to occupy.[114] No doubt the reason for the ambiguity with the federal proposal was that the politicians and officials in Ottawa were not of one mind about which fields they ought to occupy, and for how long. Most importantly, King believed that Drew was quite "right in seeking to get an undertaking which would not invade the direct tax field one way or another beyond what we have already gone." He later admitted that he was "very strongly of the position ... that provinces should be left with certain definite fields of taxation."[115] With the prime minister becoming increasingly swayed by premiers Drew, Duplessis, and Macdonald, and the federal advisers equally determined to wrest control over direct tax fields from the provinces, it was not surprising that there was some confusion over exactly what was being proposed.[116]

Despite the uncertainty, there was still an atmosphere of optimism that the conference, when it resumed in full on 25 April, would result in agreement. Those generally supportive of the federal scheme could point to Ottawa's "generous" modifications, while Drew could exclaim that no one had "indicated a greater desire to cooperate ... than did the representatives from this province."[117] With compromises evident on, or at least being claimed by, both sides, the prospects of concluding the conference on a positive note seemed high. Yet the federal government was still divided over how far it was willing to go into new direct tax fields: during the in camera sessions of the coordinating committee at the end of April, Finance Minister Ilsley indicated that Ottawa would need to move into the succession duty field, but King remained pessimistic about a proposal that rested so heavily on "the subsidy business."[118] Under pressure from Drew that the closed meetings of the coordinating committee be replaced by open sessions to eliminate the possibility of views being misrepresented in the press, the full conference reconvened on 29 April 1946.[119] Under the full glare of the press, any spirit of compromise quickly disappeared.

At first, it seemed that "the differences between the Dominion and Ontario are so small that a final settlement may be regarded as assured."[120] The prime minister thought Drew's statement to the various governmental delegations gathered in the Senate Chamber was "very good."[121] The premier's statement stressed the need to reach agreement; the provincial requirement of control over the smaller, direct tax fields such as amusement and gasoline taxes; and the responsibility of providing fiscal aid to poorer provinces in the form of his proposed National Adjustment Grant. He emphasized that the difference between Ontario's position and that contained in the Green Book was not a difference over the goal of using "principal taxes to maintain a high level of income and employment," but rather over the means adopted to achieve that goal. The question was whether the "objective can be better accomplished by the mere process of giving monopoly tax rights to the Dominion than by achieving a bond of close co-operation between the Dominion and the provinces as self-reliant government authorities."[122] Drew's statement was calm and judicious, and demonstrated an acceptance of some of the Keynesian ideas that had by this time permeated the thinking of the Ottawa civil service.[123]

The next days of the open sessions, however, were not so tranquil. Grant Dexter claimed that the conference was on the verge of breaking up on at least six occasions during the 1 May meetings; by the next day, Conservative leader John Bracken had prepared a press statement blaming the failure of the conference, "partial or complete, as the case may be" squarely on the federal government's shoulders.[124] It was clear to everyone that an impasse existed by 2 May, although King remained hopeful that "some kind of an agreement will be reached."[125] But overnight, the positions of both the federal and the provincial governments hardened. When it became clear that the federal government intended to continue its wartime practice of levying a flat gasoline tax, Drew used the example of double taxation in the minor fields as evidence of bad faith on Ottawa's part after Ontario had agreed to vacate the major fields of income and corporate taxes.[126] With the dramatic departure of Maurice Duplessis following lunch on 3 May, the conference adjourned with vitriol but without agreement.[127]

George Drew began his term as premier of Ontario imagining that he would be able to chart a new course in the province's relationship with the federal government. Not only had a decade of acrimony stalled the possibility of any fruitful collaboration between the two governments, but the dream of an autonomous province required a surprising amount of cooperation from the federal government: tax room had to be allocated equitably between the two levels of government, and responsibility for the burgeoning field of social welfare needed to be sorted out. It quickly became clear that a new relationship – based on a federal recognition of provincial autonomy, as Drew hoped – would be impossible, given both Drew's temperament and the centralization that was underway in wartime Ottawa; the premier was nevertheless able to take the intergovernmental relationship in a different direction than that which had characterized much of the pre-war period. It was not a strategy conceived whole cloth, but one stitched one piece at a time in response to the reaction both in Ottawa and in provincial capitals. Seeking first to establish provincial allies, Drew's government sought to offer alternatives to the national vision of those in the nation's capital. The Ontario proposals for reconstruction naturally emphasized the need to return to the pre-war tax system, whereby the provinces had primary access to the direct tax fields; from there, it proposed a system of sharing some responsibility for social services, and an inducement for the poorer provinces. While there were certainly criticisms of Ontario's motives in proposing its scheme for reconstruction, with most opponents pointing to a certain self-serving quality to the proposals, Drew's strategy at the dominion-provincial conference nevertheless represented a departure from that which had been employed in the past. Both in attempting to build provincial networks, and in presenting alternative solutions for national problems, Drew was taking Ontario into new territory that would come to characterize a new provincial approach to its dealings with Ottawa.

Chapter Two

"As Long as We Define the Terms": George Drew's Canada, 1946–1948

In the weeks following the adjournment of the Dominion-Provincial Conference on Reconstruction, Prime Minister King remained convinced that the premiers had been right in accusing Ilsley and others of rigidity. He reprimanded his cabinet ministers for "taking the wrong course in handing the provinces an excuse for an attack on us on the score of centralization."[1] But while privately blame might be placed on the finance minister and his advisers Clifford Clark and Graham Towers, in public it was Drew who was depicted as the "Big Bad Wolf of the Dominion-Provincial Conference" and, along with Duplessis, was accused by one of the participants of having a "calamitous" effect on the country by prohibiting the seven willing provinces from continuing to work towards a compromise.[2] Being painted as the enemy of postwar reconstruction would surely have a deleterious effect on any national leadership ambitions Drew might be harbouring; his next moves would be crucial both for his own future and for that of the province. Dodging blame for the conference collapse by attempting to craft a provincial alliance around an alternative set of reconstruction proposals, Drew was able to polish his national reputation to some extent, but he also set Ontario firmly on the course that it would follow for much of the next several decades.

In his first term in office, Drew had learned just how difficult it was for an Ontario premier to agree with Mackenzie King's approach to tax sharing, the division of powers, and centralization in general. He also learned that there were real, systemic reasons for disagreement transcending the warring personalities that had dominated the intergovernmental playing field for the previous decade. But with a postwar majority government in Ontario, and real popularity at home, Drew was in a position to devise a clear strategy in dealing with the federal government.

He was no longer surprised by the antics of Liberal Ottawa, nor was he forced to play carefully with provincial sentiment, keeping one eye on the next election even in the design of intergovernmental strategies. After 1945, Drew was free to voice his position much more emphatically. Thus, what we see him doing is building provincial allies, articulating alternatives to the policy proposals coming out of Ottawa, and paying attention to what was the real prize in Drew's world – the leadership of the national party and ultimately the prime minister's office. Ontario was his pulpit, and national policy was his message. Where exactly the congregation was, however, is less clear. Drew's allies came and went, his "national" policies oddly and unacceptably Ontario-centric to many observers, and the Ontario-Ottawa relationship suffered as a result of Drew's focus on replacing Bracken. But there was an important bright spot in Drew's somewhat naïve and awkward approach to dealing with the federal government: just off stage, Ontario Treasurer Leslie Frost learned – and learned well – the art of intergovernmental negotiation.

Ontario and the Tax Rental Proposals

In the immediate aftermath of the reconstruction conference, the next step was clearer to the federal government than it was to the provinces. Regardless of who was responsible for the conference ending sine die, the adjournment succeeded in making clear to an exhausted Ilsley the direction he would have to take.[3] On 27 June 1946, Ilsley's budget speech contained both a criticism of the Ontario reconstruction proposals and "an offer ... to each province to enter into a new tax agreement on the expiration of the present wartime tax agreement."[4] The proposal was exactly the same as that which the federal government had offered in May, with the exception that the agreement would extend for three rather than five years, social security measures would not be extended, and if any province decided not to sign the agreement, the other provinces would be required to levy a 5 per cent corporate income tax. The core of the offer, however, was that in return for vacating the income, corporate, and succession tax fields, individual provinces would receive a lump sum "rental" payment, much like the agreements that had been entered into during the war. Essentially, this action undermined the implied "all-or-nothing" nature of the Green Book proposals, and sent Canadian public policy in the direction of "ad-hocracy" or the achievement of change through "informal accommodations."[5] Despite Ilsley's repeated denial that "there is any coercion in this offer at all, [or] ... that there is any big stick in it,"[6] Ontario politicians regarded the federal budget as little more than a way for Ottawa to achieve through force what it could not achieve through negotiation.

Drew's response was both straightforward and strangely convoluted. There was little doubt that Ontario would reject the offer, but in doing so he both courted a wide assortment of provincial allies and exchanged increasingly vituperative barbs with the prime minister. For the more dispassionate Frost, the response was relatively clear. He believed that had the federal government not been "so blind and so petty they would recognize that a big deal is immediately possible."[7] He agreed with Bracken that the only real sticking point was Ottawa's refusal to vacate the minor tax fields, and that it was "folly for the Dominion Government to allow the negotiations to bog down" over this. The new federal offer, however, eliminated any degree of provincial financial flexibility and threatened to "destroy the Federal system."[8] After outlining the economic implications to the province of not accepting the federal offer, which amounted to a loss of slightly more than one million dollars of guaranteed tax revenue in a more that $60 million budget, Frost came to the conclusion that Ontario should reject the tax rental proposal. Convinced that Ilsley was on his way out, the provincial treasurer urged a strategy of patience: "we shall have to sit the matter out and wait for a more enlightened view at Ottawa, which in my opinion can only come from a change in government personnel."[9]

Frost also suggested that a more overtly Ontario-centric stance might now be appropriate. The people of the province needed to understand that the federal position had made it impossible to proceed with some of the postwar programs that had been anticipated. By explaining the complexities of the intergovernmental relationship in dollars and cents terms, Frost felt that "old Man Ontario will bestir himself and will be just as emphatic [in his opposition to Ottawa] as the people of Quebec." In short, Ontario had to stop fretting about pursuing a strategy "calculated to assist our relations with other provinces" and start putting the interests of its own people first. "If necessary we can discuss the matter with some of the provinces whose views are similar to our own," Frost suggested, but the core reaction should be a reasoned rejection of the dominion offer.[10] Drew was incapable of following such a straightforward course. To follow an independent strategy would only serve to isolate Ontario, further proof that the central province had, indeed, been responsible for the failure of the dominion-provincial conference in the first place. Moreover, Drew himself might end up isolated, and for a premier with national ambitions, that was untenable. Although Drew saw merit in his treasurer's suggestions, he simply could not exercise the sort of patience that Frost advised. The next several months saw the Ontario premier racing madly, and frequently angrily, off in all directions in an ultimately futile effort to find allies.

He first struggled to establish provincial partnerships in a formal setting: the conference on reconstruction had not, after all, concluded, so there was nothing to stop it from being reconvened; nothing, of course, except the intransigence of the prime minister. Drew initiated his correspondence with King somewhat disingenuously. He was "still awaiting word from you as Chairman," he began, "as to the date of the next meeting of that Conference." Not surprisingly, King responded that "unless the views of the Government of Ontario as to what would constitute an acceptable agreement have since altered," there would be no point in resuming the formal intergovernmental discussions. The exchange of letters only deteriorated further from there.

Drew's next strategy was to remind King of the "dual role" he occupied as both chair of the conference and prime minister – two roles that King had promised he would "draw a clear distinction between" and at all times recognize "the right of the Conference as a whole to determine its own fate."[11] King replied that there was nothing binding about the conference proceedings. In fact, he went on, only Parliament and legislatures make binding decisions, and having done so in the shape of the Ilsley budget, there was nothing more that the conference as a whole could do.[12] Drew was apoplectic. His line-by-line critique of King's position, which began with the statement that "you have achieved a truly remarkable feat of disingenuous casuistry," was so intemperate that it was never sent.[13] He did, however, post a response that outlined the history of the original Wartime Tax Rental Agreements and the reasons the provinces had agreed to temporarily vacate certain tax fields, followed by Ontario's position that what was now needed was a "definite allocation of taxing powers" between the two levels of government. Ottawa, he reminded the prime minister, "has refused at all times to even consider this proposal."[14] After one more fruitless exchange of letters, Mackenzie King had finally had too much.[15] He put an end to the correspondence by agreeing with the premier "that no further exchange of letters will serve any useful purpose."[16] Although he privately accused Drew and Duplessis of making "the resumption of the Dominion-Provincial conference … a game of the most demagogic type of politics," he also feared that "our Finance Dep[artmen]t has been far too rigid in matters of negotiation."[17] King intimated that his options had been reduced by the actions of his government, but there is little likelihood that acting alone he would have behaved any differently. The Dominion-Provincial Conference on Reconstruction would not be resumed.

Drew's options were still open, however, as he demonstrated by continuing to work other angles. At home, his ministers and their staffs busied themselves picking apart the original federal proposals. The health proposals came under considerable scrutiny as they were not part of the Ilsley budget but might suddenly reappear on the table at an unexpected point in the future.[18] The information pointed Ontario in the direction of serious research in the field of health insurance, but also illustrated the burdensome expense to any province that might accept an agreement with Ottawa to provide health coverage for its population.[19] These were statistics that could serve to deter other provinces flirting with the dominion offer. Furthermore, Charles Magone of the attorney general's office struggled to find a way that the budget itself could be found unconstitutional. Although he concluded that a dominion agreement with a province as proposed in the budget "would be ultra vires the Parliament of Canada," he did not hold out much hope that the courts would see it that way. "Of recent years the trend of the Privy Council decisions has been to expand rather than restrict the powers of the Dominion Parliament," he complained, "because of the so-called accession to international status of Canada."[20]

But if the courts did not provide a likely avenue for redress of Ontario's concerns, the other provincial capitals housed some people who had already indicated sympathy with Ontario's position. The lengthy Drew-King correspondence on the question of reconvening the aborted reconstruction conference had been circulated to all the premiers, and their responses indicated that Drew was far from alone in his opposition to the current tactics of the federal government. Both Ernest Manning of Alberta and Angus Macdonald of Nova Scotia agreed with Drew that the larger issue of the relationship between the two levels of government needed to be settled before any bilateral agreements were signed or smaller issues were dealt with in the context of problem-specific intergovernmental conferences.[21] There was clearly some room for provincial collusion.

Drew and Macdonald, who had been such close allies during the conference itself, were quick to begin plotting. One possibility was to hold a separate conference of the premiers, they thought, but as soon as the terms of the dominion offer were accepted by some provinces, that became a relatively remote possibility. There was always the chance of failure, as Drew noted, but after Manitoba, Saskatchewan, and New Brunswick lined up to sign the agreement with Ottawa, it would be difficult to include them but equally difficult to have a conference without them.[22] However, there were still certain premiers, they agreed, who would not accept the terms of the dominion offer contained in Ilsley's budget. Duplessis would unquestionably reject the offer. British Columbia's Premier John Hart, who "plays his cards close to his chest," nevertheless told an Ontario minister that he strongly disapproved of the federal proposals "and left the impression that they would not accept them."[23] In Alberta, Ernest Manning also agreed with Drew that "no matter what comes out of individual discussions, the major problem in the field of Dominion-Provincial relations ... remains unsolved."[24] While it seemed that Duplessis, Hart, and Manning were sure to stay outside the tax rental agreements, Stuart Garson and John McNair, on the other hand, were suspected of wanting something from the federal government and therefore likely to accept the deal.[25] Further intelligence on Macdonald's part suggested that Manitoba's Garson was pushing for part of the dominion gasoline tax collections, and that New Brunswick's McNair was still negotiating.[26] The time had come, as Drew had proposed earlier to Manning, for a face-to-face meeting between those premiers predisposed to reject the federal proposal.[27]

The Ontario officials were getting used to these secret meetings: in October, representatives of Ontario and Quebec had met to discuss their respective positions on income and corporate taxes. There was some divergence on the former; however, both parties agreed on the level of provincial income tax and the method for calculating it. On the question of corporate tax, the officials from the two provinces were agreed that a tax should be imposed on both capital and income at a rate that was tentatively set at 5 per cent.[28] The relative harmony of the meeting, despite certain disagreements on technical aspects of how best to proceed, boded well for the future of the Ontario-Quebec friendship. It also, no doubt, put the Ontario officials in a good mood to begin serious discussions with other provinces that had also voiced opposition to the federal government's strong-arm approach to fiscal relations. With federal ministers privately boasting that they had done such a good job of managing the economy during wartime, they might as well continue in peacetime, it was as propitious a time as any for discussions with Nova Scotia's Angus Macdonald.[29]

Moreover, Frost and his colleagues in the Ontario Treasury Department had devised another alternative proposal that "could be accepted by provinces which have not yet agreed to Mr. Ilsley's proposals, without disturbing agreements already made with other provinces." The Ontario recommendation was to reduce the amount of the federal subsidy by the amount of the BNA Act subsidy and the average of federal succession duty collections for the years 1943, 1944, and 1945. In exchange, each province would calculate and impose, using a 1942 base, the income and corporate tax rates necessary to equal the balance of the subsidy after those deductions, a process that would result in differing provincial tax rates. Succession duties would be imposed at either "the current provincial rates or at half the Dominion rates." The federal government would both act as the collection agency and vacate entirely the fields of gasoline, amusement, race track pari-mutuel, security transfer, and electricity taxes. According to Frost's advisers, "this proposal costs the Dominion Government no more than it has undertaken to pay in Mr. Ilsley's budget."[30] Armed with a relatively simple fiscal plan, and a barely contained loathing of Mackenzie King, Drew was thus well prepared for his meeting with Macdonald.

The two embittered premiers met in Montreal on Sunday, 17 November. Their discussion centred around whether a correspondence should continue with the prime minister, or whether it was best simply to organize a conference of the six provinces that were not currently negotiating with Ottawa over the terms of the Ilsley budget. In the evening, Maurice Duplessis joined the pair, and the conversation shifted to the relative position of the two large provinces. Duplessis indicated that he would willingly relinquish income and most of the corporate taxes to Ottawa, as long as Quebec could continue to occupy the succession tax field. Drew would give up all three direct tax fields but emphasized, as the Ontario reconstruction submission had originally proposed, that the provinces should be free to levy minor taxes, including gasoline and amusement taxes. After some clearly enjoyable gossip about "why so many people hated King," the threesome parted to consult with their various provincial advisers.[31]

Having Nova Scotia onside clarified some points of strategy for the Ontario government. As one of the poorer provinces, with one of smallest tax bases, the Maritime province was not likely to be moved by any suggestion that the federal offer unfairly cut into provincial tax revenue. The arguments, therefore, had to shift almost entirely onto the theoretical level. Attempting to establish common ground with Nova Scotia, then, Drew explained to Macdonald that "our position ... is that, financially, it will be extremely difficult, if not impossible, for us to carry on without some form of agreement with Ottawa to bolster our revenues." The financial implications of rejecting Ilsley's proposals had to concern all the provinces, but none more so than the poorest. In overstating Ontario's financial insecurity, Drew sought to convince Macdonald that he was not alone in worrying about the effects of rejection on his provincial coffers. The real problem with Ottawa's "present terms is not, therefore, the amount of money we would receive annually," claimed Drew," but the centralized control which they would give Ottawa over our Provincial economy."[32] This, surely, was an objection on which all of the discontented provinces could agree.

Alberta quickly jumped on the provincialist bandwagon, with Premier Manning issuing a press statement that underlined the province's belief that a "voluntary and ... mutually acceptable" intergovernmental fiscal agreement needed to be reached. The objections shared by "most of the other Provinces," apart from the three that had already signed on, indicated that the central provinces were far from marginalized in their clear repudiation of the budget proposals.[33] This was an important public statement of alliance with the Ontario position; privately, Manning went even further. In possession of Frost's proposals for a workable intergovernmental agreement that did not put severe constraints on provincial autonomy, the Alberta premier and his colleagues were "agreed that it represents a generally satisfactory alternative formula, and one which, with perhaps a few modifications, should be acceptable to all of the non-agreeing Provinces."[34] Manning proposed changing the base year for income and corporate tax calculations to 1944, and inserting some guarantees that provincial revenues would not fall below the minimum obtained under the federal proposals.[35]

Frost did not agree that the changes to his original proposal were for the better, and the fragile coalition of discontented provinces began to show signs of breaking. There was an increasing divergence of opinion on whether the point in proposing an alternative fiscal arrangement was to secure better individual terms or to achieve a more equitable agreement across the country that simultaneously respected provincial taxing jurisdiction. Although Manning's changes would, for provinces such as Ontario and Alberta, provide revenue "greatly in excess of the minimum," Frost was not swayed by the westerner's logic. In Ontario, he explained, "we are loathe to asking the Dominion for anything excepting our rights. We want to be in a position to do our job without being a supplicant. We feel that the other provinces should be in a like position."[36] Within the confines of Queen's Park, Frost noted more explicitly that Alberta's proposal "would have small chance of acceptance by the Dominion" and moreover "would place every province accepting it under the jurisdiction of the Dominion to almost, if not entirely, the same extent as if such province accepted the Dominion budget proposals."[37] Ontario would clearly benefit by adopting the Alberta scheme, and yet it was still unacceptable. The province had gone too far along the path of championing a national solution, with the national interest at stake, to forego the course now. Despite sentiment that Drew was motivated by "ambition and the desire for greater power,"[38] Ontario was not prepared to accept a solution to the intergovernmental impasse that addressed the best interests of some at the cost of the others.

Ottawa, apparently, had no such reservations. Reports began circulating that British Columbia's John Hart was returning from a trip to the capital with a particularly sweet deal in his pocket. Drew, anxious for news from the premier about what was being negotiated, waited in his office for a phone call through the night of 11 December, but Hart was clearly making his own deal with the federal government.[39] Having already secured modifications to the federal proposal that benefited his province and his province only, this new agreement promised to introduce a variable in the calculation of the provincial subsidy that would increase British Columbia's amount "in relation to increases in other provinces."[40] The alliances began to shift with the news from British Columbia. New Brunswick's McNair "suspended taxation negotiations with Ottawa" and charged "gross discrimination on the part of the federal government";[41] the federal officials scurried to come up with new options for both New Brunswick and Manitoba, where Premier Garson was also expressing dismay over the news from further west.[42] Ottawa was clearly prepared to negotiate "better terms" for individual provinces, threatening the very viability of the budget proposition.

The news from Ottawa led to increasing optimism that the strategy of negotiating with provinces individually would prove a failure. According to the "Capital Report," "the greatest satisfaction seems to be felt by those who rejected the Dominion's offer last May ... [and] don't seem to want other provinces to take it up, and they seem to be delighted now that Ottawa is making slow progress."[43] Certainly, Drew felt that the deal offered to British Columbia made Ontario's acceptance of a federal offer virtually impossible. As he explained to Angus Macdonald, "he would have to get $90–$100 million to be on par with B.C.," a figure not likely to be forthcoming.[44] Ottawa's approach to bilateral negotiations had unexpectedly handed Ontario the public excuse it needed to not join with the other provinces in signing an agreement. It also destabilized earlier agreements, and threatened to derail the whole ad hoc process.

But if the Ontario politicians recognized the problems inherent in dealing with the provinces on an individual basis, so too did people in Ottawa. With very real complaints emanating from Manitoba and New Brunswick that they deserved "equality of treatment with British Columbia," federal operatives realized that the only two courses open to them were to withdraw the B.C. deal and the offer to Prince Edward Island that depended on it, or revise the offers to the other seven provinces. Ottawa insider Jack Pickersgill proposed a plan that would see the per capita offer increase from $15 to $19, a scheme that was admittedly weak in "that it cost the Dominion too much" but that would address virtually all of the objections raised by the provinces.[45] Instead, the revised federal offer attempted to save a little money, and meet some of the objections; Finance Minister Abbott might be more flexible than his predecessor Ilsley, but he was not about to give away the store. The new proposal contained two alternate methods of calculating the rental payment the federal government would make in return for the occupation of the major tax fields.[46]

The new proposals seemed to come as a surprise to Ontario officials and politicians alike, and Drew again commenced his correspondence with the prime minister, suggesting that the new rental calculation formulae were "an indication that you are now prepared to reconvene the Dominion-Provincial Conference which adjourned last May."[47] Clearly, King had not meant this "act of courtesy" on the part of the finance minister to indicate anything like the resumption of the reconstruction conference.[48] Apart from wanting to reconvene the conference in order to agree on tax sharing between the two levels of government on a more permanent basis, Drew was also concerned about the status of the social services that had been part of the original discussions in 1945 and 1946. For the Ontario government, the offer extended by Abbott was meaningless without some indication of "what responsibility your [federal] Government will take in the matter of Pensions, Unemployment, Health, etc."[49] Finally, according to calculations made in the provincial treasurer's office, the "Drew proposal" of April 1946 was still more beneficial not only to Ontario but also to Alberta, Quebec, New Brunswick, and Nova Scotia than the new Abbott offer.[50] Therefore, Ontario found ways to criticize the new federal proposal on a variety of different levels; the question, remained, however, whether other provinces would continue to share Ontario's sense of outrage.

The revised federal offer proved enormously attractive. Provinces that had been expected to accept Ottawa's rental proposals from the outset, like Saskatchewan, Manitoba, and New Brunswick, finally did so. British Columbia and Prince Edward Island had their better terms, and Ottawa had their agreement. In February, Ernest Manning of Alberta "finally agreed to the Dominion terms but ... with very considerable reluctance."[51] Drew could be virtually positive that Duplessis would reject the federal terms, but without the continued refusal to sign on the part of Nova Scotia, the two wealthy central provinces would be marginalized, and Drew himself would lose credibility as a national spokesman. He therefore stressed to a representative of the Nova Scotia government that that province's "adhesion to present stand is of prime importance. It shows opposition not confined to wealthy provinces but extends to 'have not' provinces and is rooted in principle."[52] But Macdonald was already very close to following the reluctant Manning into an agreement with the federal government.[53]

Drew got wind of Macdonald's change of position during a visit to the capital. He could hardly believe the rumours spread by "tongues [that] wag rather freely in the Chateau Laurier late in the evening" but in case they were true, the Ontario premier wrote to his counterpart in Nova Scotia to urge that he not be lured into the federal clutches. He used a variety of tactics to press his case. He suggested that acceptance of a deal so late in the day would tarnish Macdonald's reputation as "the spokesman of a clear ideal and of a set of principles which were acceptable to all provinces even though some of them later felt that they were compelled to accept the financial terms." He pointed to rumours that Macdonald had only agreed to the federal offer in order to win an upcoming Halifax by-election. And finally, he begged Macdonald to "reconsider your situation if the door is not yet closed," suggesting that a well-timed call for the resumption of the full dominion-provincial conference would surely result in an agreement being reached in "48 hours."[54] No amount of cajoling would work, however, and Nova Scotia became the seventh province to sign a tax rental agreement with the federal government.[55]

Drew and the Redirection of Attention

Angus L. Macdonald's decision left the two central provinces isolated in their refusal to rent the income, corporate, and succession tax fields to the federal government. It also forced Drew to finally stop his efforts to form a provincial alliance against Mackenzie King's Ottawa and to instead direct his efforts elsewhere. The premier found ample other opportunities to press his case for an alternative approach to the postwar intergovernmental arrangements. Social security, both in the form of more substantial pensions and allowances and through new programs such as health insurance, had been raised at the reconstruction conference and then apparently forgotten; Quebec, far more importantly than Ontario, had been isolated by its refusal to sign the tax rental agreements, and that was a situation that needed to be rectified; have-not provinces had received generous financial compensation for vacating tax fields, but the twin questions of how to balance geographical inequities and protect provincial jurisdiction remained far from solved. There was a great deal of work to be done by a Conservative premier who fancied he had a national role to play; with the problem of reconvening the reconstruction conference essentially solved, Drew was free to attack the problems of intergovernmental relations more generally.

Health insurance was one of the first issues to attract provincial attention. In 1946, Ottawa mandarins and social policy planners were considering funding provincial health care planning to the amount of $5,000 plus 5 cents per capita. The next stage was to include partial federal funding for general practitioner and diagnostic or laboratory services, as well as for hospital care. Nursing, dental, and pharmaceutical services were contemplated as a final stage.[56] The Ontario bureaucracy quickly jumped on the federal scheme, complaining about the inequity of the redistributive features of using federal tax money to fund such an endeavour.[57] Instead of the federal scheme, Ontario officials toyed with alternate proposals. The first "counter-proposal," which would see higher estimates being used for the cost of general practitioner, hospital, and diagnostic services and the elimination of nursing, dental, and pharmaceutical services, was not only "more suitable for the needs of Ontario" but also perhaps "acceptable to the other provinces."[58] The key element in the Ontario scheme was that it would begin with full health insurance coverage for those under the age of fourteen. Once again, this was reminiscent of the strategy employed by Ontario at the conference on reconstruction and its aftermath: having defined the federal position as unacceptable, the goal was to produce an alternative that was regarded as more acceptable than the federal offer in other provincial capitals. In this way, the Ontario approach was to design what would essentially be national policy in their own offices, rather than leaving the responsibility with the federal government. Although health insurance was slow to move to the forefront of either the federal or the provincial political agenda, Drew wanted to make sure the Ontario idea was "well implanted in the public mind before [Minister of National Health and Welfare Paul] Martin can actually commit himself to this [federal] proposition."[59]

The dominion's first move into the health insurance field, a tentative one to be sure, took Drew somewhat by surprise. Ottawa announced its intention to provide several "health survey grants" that would assist in things like hospital construction, cancer research, and public health research, provided that the province both match the federal contribution and maintain its present level of funding in these areas.[60] This was hardly health insurance, but was anticipated as a necessary first step before action could be taken to provide more tangible patient services. Nevertheless, Ontario bureaucrats played important and generally helpful roles in determining how to calculate the extent of the federal grant.[61] Previous experience in financing the health needs of a large and relatively wealthy province proved to be extremely useful in identifying the sorts of problems that might face the federal government as it moved into the field. At this stage, however, Ottawa seemed to be interested merely in paying a portion of the bill; Ontario's grant of over $9.5 million was accepted with no complaints and little suspicion that this initial contribution might lead to less acceptable interference on the part of the federal government at some point in the future.[62]

In fact, Ontario politicians and their advisers seemed more than willing to accept money from the federal coffers. Premier Drew's position on social services, expressed at the reconstruction conference and long after, was that Ottawa should leave them to be "carried out by the provinces" but should "provide the money" to do so.[63] The health survey grants seemed to follow this formula: Ottawa offered only limited guidelines on how the money it was providing should be spent and, in many cases, deferred to Ontario's suggestions in defining those guidelines.[64] Similarly, when the federal government amended its Old Age Pension Act to provide both for more generous pensions and for coverage of 75 per cent of the cost of those pensions, Ontario officials did nothing to impede the hasty proclamation of the new legislation.[65] Indeed, Frost claimed that by staying out of the tax rental agreements, and "reliev[ing] Mr. Abbott of raising for us this year no less than $73,969,000," Ottawa would not only be able "to make sweeping reductions in income tax and other forms of taxation, but also to implement the Dominion's social security schemes."[66] In "not permit[ing] ourselves to be lured into a Dominion-Provincial Agreement," Ontario itself was "free from any financial straight-jacket"[67] and was simultaneously ensuring that the federal government could carry out its promises. Although other provincial premiers attacked Ontario and Quebec for "getting all the money,"[68] Ontario politicians and officials had ample opportunity to perfect their particular spin on the intergovernmental situation.

They were also able to smooth over the relationship with the federal wing of the Progressive Conservative party. There had been a great deal of jockeying for control of the party in the years since George Drew took over the premiership of Ontario, as the federal party struggled with questions of leadership and the provincial party demonstrated managerial successes that would have been welcome in Ottawa.[69] But while Bracken tried to curry favour with Drew, and the national party as a whole sought to design a platform that would carry it to victory in at least the provinces that had rejected the ad hoc tax rental arrangements, the Ontario premier had plans of his own. His isolation could, in fact, be used to his advantage. While federal Liberals fretted that "the Drew-Duplessis axis is ... setting up a state within a state,"[70] and commentators warned that economic security could not be ensured "so long as Ontario and Quebec remain aloof,"[71] Drew celebrated his closeness to his Quebec counterpart. "I have dealt with no man in public life," exclaimed Drew, "who has extended a greater measure of co-operation to this government and to the people of this province than has Mr. Duplessis." The good relations between the two premiers and their respective governments had resulted in the development of the Ottawa River, uniformity in taxation, and not least importantly, a united front against the federal government.[72] As Quebec Finance Minister Onesime Gagnon noted to Frost following the 1948 re-election of the Union Nationale, the victory was a "vindication of the policy which we have followed in constructive collaboration with our Ontario friends ... for the greater good of the country and the people of our provinces."[73] The positive nature of the relationship could also be used to showcase George Drew's appeal across linguistic lines and elevate his stature as a potential successor to the hapless John Bracken. Already popular in Ontario, by securing the support of French Canada, Drew stood poised to take advantage of the province that held, according to some, "the keys to the success or failure of our Party."[74]

Drew's national ambitions, however, were being kept in check by Bracken's political timetable; as long as the latter remained at the helm of the national party, Drew was stuck at Queen's Park. But by the spring of 1948, it was generally assumed that Bracken would announce his resignation as leader of the Progressive Conservatives, opening the way for Drew;[75] indeed, it was widely believed that Drew's surprise decision to call an Ontario election just three years into his mandate was precipitated by the Bracken rumours. Another provincial majority would put Drew in an ideal position to claim the national leadership.[76] Instead, however, the early election call had near disastrous results: the Tories reduced their majority by thirteen seats, the CCF increased their numbers by the same thirteen and became Ontario's Official Opposition, and George Drew himself lost his seat in High Park.[77] Attempting to make the best of a bad situation, Drew claimed that the Progressive Conservative party was "in a very strong position as a result of the broad and representative support we have received from every part of the Province."[78] Although it was certainly an inauspicious start to a national leadership campaign, Drew nevertheless entered the race to replace Bracken in the fall of 1948. He was a late entry in the contest, but he was "no doubt the candidate who can set up the best organization" at the last minute.[79] He was also, significantly, the favourite in the three-man field that included Saskatchewan MP John Diefenbaker and Ontario MP Donald Fleming.

Drew had built his reputation on sound management of Canada's largest province as it shifted from a wartime to a peacetime economy, combined with a fierce defence of provincial rights. He consistently argued that had Conservatives rather than Liberals formed the national government during the time of the reconstruction conference, the sort of battles that he himself had played a large role in instigating would not have erupted. At the leadership convention in Ottawa at the beginning of October, hundreds of delegates from across the country were treated to further explanation of Drew's thoughts on the proper intergovernmental relationship. The handsome and wealthy Ontario premier, "looking rather like a swan in a duck pond,"[80] made federal-provincial relations the cornerstone of his campaign. In his nomination address, he declared:

> The federal system under which this country became a united nation calls for the pooling of our resources in a real and effective partnership. That partnership can be built as long as we define the terms and as long as it is clearly understood that every province and every municipality will have its own full and proper share in carrying forward the development of the particular activities that are entrusted to them ... If you do me the very great honour of choosing me as the leader of this party, I will do everything I can to maintain our constitutional federal democracy.[81]

Drew's approach to intergovernmental relations certainly did not appeal to everyone. A disappointed Fleming supporter, who thought that the "fumbling of [Drew's] unparalleled opportunities" was a "national tragedy" found much wanting in Drew's dealings with both Ottawa and other provinces.[82] With a "fatal facility for arousing antagonisms," Drew "indulged in personalities, called names and imputed motives … feuded with Ottawa and teamed up with reactionary forces in Quebec" and thereby "endangered national unity and inter-provincial goodwill."[83] The opinion was clearly not widely shared, however. Of the 1,242 votes cast, 827 were for George Drew, with John Diefenbaker receiving 311 and Donald Fleming garnering 104. As the *Globe and Mail* declared, "he was not only the proper choice, but the popular choice."[84] Canadian Conservatives were ready to embrace Drew's vision that emphasized the "determination to maintain our traditional federal constitution with its decentralization of authority which brings administration closer to the people."[85] Whether the rest of the country was equally ready for George Drew remained to be seen.

Drew's election to the leadership of the national party left him "no choice but to resign as premier of Ontario."[86] Although this had been the anticipated turn of events since Bracken announced his resignation in the spring of 1948, it nevertheless left the Ontario organization in turmoil. The provincial party constitution allowed the leader to appoint a successor, and had Drew followed the constitution he would surely have named his Provincial Treasurer Leslie Frost to the premier's office. However, long-standing rivalries between the urban and rural wings of the party flared in the vacuum created by Drew's impending departure, and as a result a more open convention process was required. Party president Alex McKenzie, a Frost supporter, announced that a leadership convention of 650 delegates would be held in Toronto in April 1949.[87] Tom Kennedy, a loyal member of the Drew machine, was appointed interim premier.[88] First elected in 1919, the seventy-year-old farmer from Peel and mainstay of the party had been agriculture minister during the Drew administrations. Attorney General Leslie Blackwell, one of the most vocal critics of Drew's efforts to name his own successor and the leader of the urban-based reform-oriented wing of the party, objected to Kennedy's appointment, but for most he was regarded as an innocuous seat-warmer until a real leader could be selected.[89] The intervening six months proved to be advantageous to the Frost candidacy.

When Kennedy took over the premiership, he did little to change the environment that Drew had created, which meant, among other things, that Frost continued in the high-profile provincial treasurer portfolio. Behind the scenes, Frost's as-yet-undeclared candidacy for the leadership of the Ontario Conservatives was widely regarded as benefiting from the assistance of Alex McKenzie and the rest of the members of the party machinery who all "worked diligently to turn Mr. Frost into a high profile candidate."[90] Two weeks before the opening of the Tory convention, Frost announced his intention to let his name stand for the leadership. The race was, by later standards, a low-key affair with little of the campaign excess that has come to characterize modern leadership conventions. Nevertheless, the seventeen hundred delegates and twelve hundred alternates that swarmed the Royal York Hotel ensured a political spectacle larger than any before experienced in the Ontario capital. The other candidates for the position, Attorney General Leslie Blackwell, Provincial Secretary Dana Porter, and former Tory backbencher Kelso Roberts, were all regarded as something of long shots for the position, but there was still the appearance of a leadership race.

Although the votes were not made public, Frost was elected in a landslide, garnering, unofficially, 834 votes to Blackwell's 442, with Roberts and Porter far behind at 121 and 65 votes respectively.[91] Frost won partly on the basis of his sound management of the Ontario economy over the previous half-dozen years. As his nominator underlined, "his even temper and sure judgment have done much to preserve the financial independence of the province of Ontario" and ensured that the budget could still be balanced without the imposition of a provincial income tax.[92] But perhaps more importantly, Frost secured the leadership of the party and the premiership of the province because he exuded a genial, small-town, hard-working quality with which the majority of the party members identified. Yet it was the steely determination that was so clear to those who worked closely with Frost that made him a formidable presence on both the provincial and the national stages.

The Drew chapter in Ontario politics formally closed with the selection of Frost as his permanent replacement in the premier's office, but his legacy would continue. Drew had taken the province into some new territory in terms of intergovernmental relations. Although the increasing centralization that was apparent in the years after the Second World War clearly defined the contours of the federal-provincial playing field, it was Drew's own national ambitions that dictated the strategies he would follow on the provincial stage. Drew knew, even if he was incapable of capitalizing on it, that a popular Ontario premier would need more than the support of his home province to make it to 24 Sussex Drive, and so his government consistently played to the larger national audience. Counter-proposals to those offered by the federal government were designed to appeal across the country, and personal friendships and alliances were built to make the Ontario proposals even more acceptable. In the first step – winning the leadership of the national Progressive Conservative party – Drew demonstrated that he had built a national reputation. But that reputation was not enough to catapult him into the prime minister's office or, more importantly for Ontario, to best the federal government in the game of tax plans or social policy formation. When Frost took over as premier, however, he had all the experience in building alliances and offering alternative policy models, without any of the ulterior motivation.

Drew's interest in forging alliances with his provincial counterparts was twofold: he certainly wanted support in his opposition to the federal government, regardless of whether his administration had established alternative proposals or not. He also, however, was keen to secure a national support base for what would ultimately be a successful bid for leadership of the national party. Drew's Ontario fought against the unilateral intergovernmental decisions of the federal government and tried to secure tax policy and social policy decisions that were friendlier to provincial autonomy, but without much success. Most of the other provinces were lured by the rental agreements or the social policy expenditures of the federal government, leaving isolationist Quebec and provincial rights–oriented Ontario little room for anything but complaint. Or, at least, that was how Drew ended up playing his hand, ultimately opting for a higher perch from which to sling his barbs with the leadership of the national party.

Provincial Treasurer Leslie Frost had long been a participant in intergovernmental relations. He had earned his position as Drew's right-hand man through the interminable meetings of the Dominion-Provincial Conference on Reconstruction, and he had been indispensible as Ontario curried favour with other provinces and designed alternatives to the proposals coming out of Ottawa. He was a man who seemed much calmer, less prone to fits of pique, more capable of compromise than George Drew. It was nevertheless clear that intergovernmental relations were of prime importance to Frost, and he was not about to let the federal government trample all over provincial jurisdiction.[93] In accepting the leaderships of the provincial party, Frost stated that "the national income arising in Ontario today is just about that of the whole of Canada ten years ago. From this," he continued, "it is apparent why we should retain our fiscal freedom. The great future of development of Ontario cannot be reduced to a formula. Our problems are many sided and varied. Our sources of revenue must be flexible. Our ability to do the job is in direct relation to the fiscal means with which we have to do it. Rationalized Dominion-Provincial relationships are a must."[94] They would not be easy to achieve, but it was Frost who set Ontario on course towards that elusive goal.

Chapter Three

"Know and Understand the Problems": Leslie Frost Makes His Mark, 1949–1952

While George Drew was settling into his new position as the leader of the federal Progressive Conservatives in the fall of 1948, the Liberals prepared to welcome Louis St. Laurent as the new prime minister. Elected at a convention in mid-summer, there had never been much doubt that St. Laurent was Mackenzie King's chosen successor. Only the justice minister himself had worried about his suitability, with less than a decade of service in elected politics and a francophone background that might split both the Liberal party and the country itself. But after winning a surprisingly large mandate on the first ballot, with more support from English Ontario than from Quebec, St. Laurent began the slow move into the prime minister's office. King was reluctant to leave, wanting to represent Canada at European conferences in the fall, so 15 November 1948 was identified as the day of transition. For Drew, it meant a change from one old nemesis to another: while King had been a constant foil for Drew on intergovernmental issues, St. Laurent had initiated charges against Drew during the war over his criticism of Canadian leadership in Hong Kong. Although they were ultimately dropped, Drew was not so quick to forget the affront to both his integrity and his patriotism.[1] Drew's battles, then, remained much the same. He continued to rail against federal Liberals, but rather than scoring the occasional victory, Drew began racking up defeats. His first electoral loss at the helm of the Progressive Conservatives was in June 1949; another would follow in 1953. Drew's leadership of the national party was a sad end to his ambitions: his Bay Street image did not translate at all well on the national stage, and he was never able to convince voters outside Ontario to support him in Ottawa. Even in his home province, Drew was unable to compete with the popular Liberals, and he did not come close to achieving the support that John Bracken had in the 1945 election.[2]

But if Drew was unable to change the face of Ottawa, there is little doubt that the intergovernmental playing field continued to evolve. Drew had developed a particular approach to dealing with Ottawa: establish alternatives in the shared policy areas, such as taxation or social policy, then lobby other provincial premiers to support the Ontario position rather than the federal position. Drew had been only modestly successful in pursuing the strategy, as the alternatives that came out of Queen's Park seemed to be in Ontario's interest alone, and the strategy itself failed to deliver on its implicit promise of more amicable intergovernmental relations. However, Frost and St. Laurent were different creatures from their predecessors; neither was quite as quick to anger or as likely to hold grudges, and both were committed to establishing a productive relationship. Moreover, the issues that animated the intergovernmental conversation in the late 1940s and early 1950s were different from those of the reconstruction period. Unfinished social policies littered the agenda, and an established approach to sharing tax revenue had to be worked around. Frost continued to offer alternatives to federal policy, but he increasingly portrayed them as in the national interest. The greater Frost's role on the national political canvas, the more he seemed to be asked to do. Moreover, to complicate matters further, the constitutional appeared as a new issue for discussion.

Opening a New Intergovernmental Front

A conference called to discuss the constitution should have appealed to St. Laurent's training and past career as a constitutional lawyer, and it was certainly a move in the direction of goals that had been publicized during the federal election campaign. In a national broadcast in early May, the prime minister had argued that "the record of Canadians in two world wars" was inconsistent with the fact "our adult nationhood is not yet fully recognized in our constitution and our laws." In an effort to correct that imbalance, St. Laurent declared, "it is our intention, after the election, to consult the Provincial governments with a view to working out a method ... of amending the constitution in Canada."[3] Gordon Robertson was "the only one in either the Privy Council Office or the Prime Minister's Office with a background in constitutional law," so to him fell the job of laying out the options for an amending formula and devising a strategy for 1949.[4] Robertson stressed that agreement had very nearly been reached in 1936 on an amending formula that would have seen each level of government independently responsible for changes that affected only their jurisdiction, agreement of the federal government and two-thirds of the provinces representing at least 55 per cent of the population necessary in those cases that had ramifications for both levels of government, and unanimous consent required for change to particular "entrenched classes." Robertson thought any new formula should start from this point.[5] He hoped it might be possible for a final amending formula to be submitted to Britain for approval sometime in 1950.[6]

Prime Minister St. Laurent certainly thought it was important to "recover the initiative"; he was less certain that the way to do that was to follow Robertson's suggestion of a constitutional conference. After giving "quite a lot of thought to the matter," St. Laurent concluded that the best strategy might instead be to "take the right" to amend the strictly federal sections of the constitution "without consulting the provinces" and then immediately to transfer the jurisdiction to amend the BNA Act to Canada from Britain.[7] This particular approach had the advantage of securing an amending formula without invading provincial jurisdiction, and leaving to the courts, rather than to the intergovernmental conference table, the question of "whether or not anything we attempted to do would impinge on a right or privilege of any Province."[8] There was no doubt that this was a strategy that would seize the initiative, but in the process it would also almost certainly raise the hackles of provincial premiers already wary of federal ambitions on constitutional matters. Still, the federal Liberals forged ahead, announcing to the premiers their intention to acquire the right to amend the constitution in relation to matters not coming within provincial jurisdiction, and to hold a later conference to deal with matters affecting both levels of government.[9]

In 1949, the provinces were still reeling from the threat to their jurisdiction posed by the impending abolition of appeals to the Judicial Committee of the Privy Council. The JCPC had been an important tool for the provinces, and particularly for Ontario, in their struggle for greater autonomy, but from the perspective of the federal government its decisions were not only an impediment to legislating for the whole dominion, but also a constant reminder of Canada's continuing colonial status. In 1940, the Supreme Court of Canada accepted the argument that the federal government could abolish appeals to the JCPC.[10] On the appeal of that decision in 1947, Ontario intervened, arguing that the abolition of appeals was an infringement of provincial jurisdiction over the administration of justice within the provinces and a violation of their traditional right to bring civil appeals to the Privy Council. The intervention had no effect on the outcome of the case, and the JCPC upheld the previous Supreme Court ruling.[11] With the federal intention to add a limited amending power to the government's jurisdiction, it was becoming apparent that the Supreme Court – itself "the creature of the Dominion Government" – would now also potentially have the authority to decide the "scope of the federal power of amendment."[12] It was a worrisome turn of events for the provinces.

But the federal proposition that it should acquire the power to amend those parts of the constitution that affected "federal rights" raised provincial concerns about more than merely the omnipotence of the Supreme Court in determining jurisdiction. As Quebec Premier Maurice Duplessis pointed out to St. Laurent, "it would be arbitrary on the part of the Federal Government to decide *ex parte* and of its own authority which are federal rights and which are the rights of the provinces." Surely, he went on, "it does not belong to one of the parties to a multilateral contract to declare itself the supreme arbiter."[13] Frost was, characteristically, more cautious and diplomatic than Duplessis, but he too was horrified by the sudden action being contemplated in Ottawa. He pointed out "that the abolition of appeals to the Privy Council may affect" the situation "more than is generally realized."[14] Frost also expressed concern, this time to federal Minister of Justice Stuart Garson, that the Supreme Court would cease to be bound by Judicial Committee precedent, which had offered such a generous reading of provincial jurisdiction over the years and which, it was hoped, would not be discarded in the race for constitutional maturity.[15] In private, secret, meetings with Duplessis, Frost was undoubtedly not as guarded in expressing his concerns.[16]

From the provincial perspective, however, the conference was not merely about the amending procedure, but also it offered an opportunity to fix some of the damage that had already been done to the intergovernmental relationship. The tax rental agreements and even the federal health grants had proven to be sly ways of moving into provincial jurisdiction, and had made the Ontarians justifiably wary. The provincial politicians and advisers were ready to take advantage of the last minute changes of strategy that occurred in Ottawa. On 16 December 1949, the Cabinet Committee on the Dominion-Provincial Conference agreed that opening positions should be provided by both federal and provincial government representatives.[17] By 20 December, St. Laurent questioned the desirability of the federal government making specific proposals at all;[18] at the opening of the conference, his assistant Jack Pickersgill had finally convinced him that a federal proposal "would simply serve as a target for attack by one or more of the premiers," and St. Laurent allowed the provinces to present the opening salvoes.[19] Leslie Frost came to Ottawa armed with a solid proposal for the full patriation of the constitution, forcing a poorly prepared federal government into the back seat.

The federal cabinet committee had tossed around formulae for the degree of provincial consent necessary for amendment, from six provinces with 75 per cent of the population to seven provinces with 80 per cent, and investigated the effect that each of the six possible combinations would have on Quebec.[20] When it came to actually preparing a strategy for the conference, however, the federal government seemed more concerned that "unemployment insurance would almost inevitably become an early topic for discussion" than it was with preparing for the constitutional debate.[21] According to one report, the federal view was "that the ten Provincial Premiers and their colleagues now have the ball and should have a free field to complete the play."[22] This hardly seemed a fitting follow-up to St. Laurent's bold opening gambit, but it did demonstrate a willingness to discuss intergovernmental issues that was in marked contrast to the Mackenzie King approach.

Frost seemed prepared to "do everything possible to bring about agreement."[23] Noting that he did not think "Ontario's historical links with the British Parliament" would in any way be undermined by an agreement on an amending formula, Frost reassured the collected premiers at the opening of the conference of Ontario's sincerity.[24] While other provincial premiers debated the heads under which types of constitutional amendments should be grouped and the impact of the federal government's partial amending power,[25] the Ontario premier eventually offered up a concrete, if simple, proposal for a full amending procedure. He suggested that unanimous agreement should be required for amendments affecting language, education, schools, and the "legislative jurisdiction of the provinces"; that Parliament and the few affected provincial legislatures could agree to amend the act on matters that did not affect all provinces; that Parliament could unilaterally "amend the Act in respect of all matters concerning the Executive Government of Canada and the Constitution and privileges of the House of Commons and the Senate except with respect to the representation of the provinces in the House of Commons and the Senate"; and that two-thirds of the provincial legislatures needed to agree to an amendment on any other provision of the act.[26] Although this "would be a satisfactory arrangement from Ontario's point of view," Frost made clear that this was merely a starting point for discussion.[27]

The constitutional conference itself had not been conceived with the goal of reaching decisions in the course of the three-day meeting; nevertheless, everyone had certainly hoped that disagreement could be avoided until the matter was shunted off to a committee of constitutional experts. Thanks to the prime minister's clarification that the federal government's partial amending formula should not be considered "an obstacle" to establishing a complete amending procedure, the atmosphere seemed to indicate a "new spirit of unity."[28] The conference participants had agreed that the issue of constitutional amendment really needed to be discussed by attorneys general and their officials, so they established a standing committee to undertake the technical considerations. This committee was charged with identifying appropriate amending procedures for matters "which concern parliament and all of the provincial legislatures," and with addressing the subject of transferring powers from one level of government to the other.[29] The initial stage of discussion was, according to some observers, "untroubled by any controversial issues" although others noted that it had done little besides "agreeing on a series of pigeon holes into which the various sections of the BNA Act are to be placed. The real task will be which sections ... go into one pigeon hole and which will go into another."[30]

In its decision to move decisively into the field of intergovernmental relations, the federal government had succeeded in shifting the focus of negotiations almost exclusively onto the question of the amending formula. Neither a made-in-Canada procedure for making changes to the British North America Act nor the end of the appeals to the Judicial Committee of the Privy Council – the decision that had immediately preceded the current round of constitutional negotiations – had figured particularly prominently in Ontario's list of intergovernmental concerns. Thus, the federal government had succeeded in demonstrating initiative by making a move into a relatively little-studied area. The provinces were not prepared with counter-proposals because none had given much consideration to either constitutional question before Ottawa placed them on the agenda. With the end of the first constitutional conference, however, the time had come to move the discussion back to areas that had been debated innumerable times before and in which the provinces already had clearly established objectives. Certainly Ontario was prepared to return to the terrain of the reconstruction conference, revisiting questions of tax sharing and jurisdiction over social policy. Planning had been conducted in these fields almost unabated since the end of the last full and general first ministers' meeting in 1946, and now under the leadership of Leslie Frost, Ontario was prepared to defend its jurisdiction.

When the Dominion-Provincial Conference on Reconstruction ended *sine die* in May 1946, the entire field of intergovernmental affairs was left in a state of suspended reality. Clearly, the federal government was most interested in reaching some kind of conclusion in regards to the financial proposals that had been on the table, and thus announced with the 1946 budget its intention to continue to rent the lucrative direct tax fields from the provinces. The other issues that had been under discussion, however, remained more like orphans, with neither level of government exactly leaping at the opportunity to wrest exclusive control from the other. Health insurance, old age pensions, and unemployment insurance benefits had all been raised at the reconstruction conference; five years after the conference opened, none had yet found a happy, or a permanent, home. On the other hand, the direct taxes were on the verge of losing their home: the rental agreements of 1947 had a five year life-span and, recognizing that renegotiation might be a time-consuming process, 1950 marked the beginning of the next round of discussions.

The changes to pensions, which Frost acknowledged were necessary, were of a housekeeping sort, unlikely to cause too many disagreements, and ones that he informed the prime minister could "readily be solved by direct approach and consideration. As far as the Government of Ontario is concerned," Frost went on, "we are prepared to start now if you so desire."[31] The problems raised by unemployment assistance were equally easily solved: Ottawa need only fulfil the promise it had made in 1945 and "set up a system of unemployment assistance under which it will pay benefits equal to 85 percent of unemployment benefits to unemployed persons able and willing to work who are not entitled, or who have ceased to be entitled, to unemployment insurance benefits."[32] The only hurdle was the fact that Ottawa maintained that the Green Book promises of the immediate postwar period were impossible without provincial agreement on tax sharing. From the federal perspective, responsibility for the employable unemployed rested squarely with the provinces; from Ontario's vantage point, the onus was on Ottawa. Ontario and the federal government remained at loggerheads for years over which level of government would have to shoulder the expensive task of providing for this group. Since Ottawa was on record as claiming responsibility, there was little if any political damage incurred in Ontario for denying responsibility. As the debate waged on, the toll on both individuals and local charities became undeniable.[33]

Despite the unfinished business of the reconstruction conference, under the new administrations there seemed to be a higher probability that agreements might ultimately be reached. The atmosphere of intergovernmental relations was far from chilly. In his budget speech, Frost, who combined his old position of provincial treasurer with his new office of premier, emphasized the ease with which solutions to intergovernmental problems could be found. The January constitutional conference, he thought, was "the forerunner of many successful meetings."[34] Federal Finance Minister Douglas Abbott was pleased with "the general spirit of goodwill and co-operation in which [Frost approached] the problem of our mutual relations," but he was still uneasy with some of Ontario's proposals. Particularly unsettling was the suggestion that the solution to Ontario's non-participation in the tax rental agreements of 1947 would be for Ottawa to collect income tax for the province, remitting the equivalent amount back to the provincial government on a quarterly basis.[35] Abbott argued that this would amount to "changing the terms of the offer which was made to the provinces in 1946." He also added that he personally believed that "the only sound practice" was for governments to collect their own taxes.[36] Nevertheless, in his budget speech to the province, and subsequently through more private correspondence with the federal finance minister, the Ontario premier made clear that he might contemplate entering into a form of tax rental agreement with Ottawa.[37] He might even be able to persuade other provinces to come onside. British Columbia, for one, "realizes its mistake" and was now prepared to "insist on sharing in the production of its own industry in the form of taxes collected."[38]

It was the new field of constitutional change, however, that remained most intoxicating, offering a clean slate for Ontario to offer alternatives and seek allies. In early March, less than two months after the question of amendment had been formally opened up by the federal government, Ontario officials submitted a draft to the Committee of Attorneys General that had been struck to prepare for the September first ministers' conference. Ontario proposed an amending formula that recognized Ottawa's right to "alter or repeal" any constitutional provision relating "to the Executive Government of Canada and the procedure, constitution and privileges of the House of Commons and the Senate" except on matters of representation and democratic rights. In conjunction with the agreement of the affected province or provinces, the Parliament of Canada could also amend the constitution on matters "which relate to one or more but not all of the Provinces."[39] Agreement on these two categories of amendment seemed likely, as the first was already in place and there had been no prior suggestion that the second would raise any hackles. It was the remaining categories of the amending formula that were somewhat more problematic, as they rested on prior agreement about federal and provincial jurisdiction.

The Ontario proposal included a list of subjects that could not be altered without the unanimous consent of "the Legislatures of all the Provinces." The list included four items:

a) the use of the English and French language;
b) the rights and privileges granted or secured to any class of persons with respect to schools;
c) the procedure for future amendments to the Constitution of Canada;
d) the legislative jurisdiction of the Provincial Legislatures except in relation to matters coming within the following classes of subjects:
   i) the establishment, maintenance and management of public and reformatory prisons in and for the Province;
   ii) the establishment, maintenance and management of hospitals, asylums, charities and eleemosynary institutions in and for the Provinces;
   iii) local works and undertakings;
   iv) the incorporation of companies with Provincial objects;
   v) generally, all matters of a merely local and private nature in the Province.[40]

According to the Ontario plan, all other amendments would require the consent of at least two-thirds of the provinces, representing at least 55 per cent of the population.[41]

This proposal indicated that, once the question of constitutional reform was opened, Ontario was prepared to utilize constitutional means to address the problems that it perceived had been afflicting intergovernmental relations since wartime. In identifying those areas that were fundamental and therefore required unanimous consent, Ontario pinpointed language, education, the amending formula itself, and all of section 92 except for those areas that had been recently hotly debated. These latter fields, including prisons, hospitals, and local businesses, were certainly of interest to both levels of government in much the same way as use of the French and English languages, but they were much more obviously under current consideration. Unanimous consent for change would have been too rigorous for Ontario, hoping as its politicians were for substantial changes to such things as the way businesses were regulated by taxation, and these areas thus fell under the two-thirds rule that Ontario had proposed. The objectives of the Frost government were relatively transparent; nevertheless, the draft constitutional amendment proposals provided an important starting point for discussion, both at Queen's Park and within the committee of attorneys general.

In Ottawa, meanwhile, preparations for the constitutional conference were proceeding with uncharacteristic attention to the position of the provinces. Jack Pickersgill urged the federal cabinet members to retain "a more flexible position" in dealing with their provincial counterparts. The members of the Cabinet Committee on the Constitutional Conference were "against having the federal government indicate that flexibility" and instead argued that "there was a lot to be said for maintaining conditions of uniformity in the framework of government." If, however, the provinces proved dogmatic, "they thought the federal government should be prepared to accept changes in the handling of sections but that we should not take the initiative."[42] Gordon Robertson, from his position in the Privy Council Office, continued to push for a less rigid stance on intergovernmental relations. An examination of the proceedings of the conference on reconstruction gave Robertson some indication of how *not* to manage the constitutional conference. The manner in which the 1945 conference was introduced, the way the agenda was set, and the publication of the federal proposals all "smacked of autocracy and clearly was a psychological error."[43] The mistake would not be repeated this time around.

The second session of the constitutional conference was held in Quebec City. While the location permitted a certain showcasing of Quebec and of Quebec's constitutional designs, it was Frost's political acumen that carried the conference. Ontario's strategy, if not its proposal, had become simpler since its first incarnation in the spring of 1950. Although legal adviser Charles Magone had fleshed the points into appropriately constitutional language, that language had no place at the conference itself; together with Attorney General Dana Porter, Frost boiled the Ontario position down to its very essence.[44] After first reminding the collected politicians and advisers of the traditional role of the courts in deciding jurisdictional issues on which there was some debate, Frost submitted that "no attempt should be made by this conference to allot any particular sections or subject matters to any particular classification." Instead, the Ontario premier proposed "that this conference should adopt a formula or method of amendment and leave it to subsequent agreement among the governments concerned as occasions arise, or upon any failure of agreement, to the courts to determine under what heading any particular section or subject matter should be placed."[45]

Ontario's opening statement was something of a surprise considering that the province had already submitted a fairly extensive categorization of various methods of amendment. Moreover, Ontario had recently expressed concern over the unilateral abolition of appeals to the Judicial Committee of the Privy Council, and many grave doubts over the hearing that provinces would receive at a federally appointed Supreme Court of Canada. But Leslie Frost was a wily politician, unlikely to hand over such sweeping powers to the courts; his opening remarks, "advanced only as a basis for discussion," and not proposed in "a dogmatic way,"[46] reflected Frost's apparently reasonable belief that agreement among the premiers would be difficult. The open sessions of the four-day conference appeared to observers to indicate that the first ministers' "views conflicted widely on method and other detail."[47] Frost's was thus a note of lowered expectations, reminding the participants that in the hotly contested field of constitutional reform, agreement on the categories for amendment would still be a major accomplishment. As the discussion continued, it became increasingly clear to all present that agreement on specifics would be difficult, if not impossible, to reach.

On the second day, Frost proposed that the conference needed first to agree on an amending procedure, second on how the constitution might be patriated, and lastly on what was "meant by a majority of the provinces."[48] By the last day, Frost had agreed that his classifications, which were "by classes of subject rather than by individual sections," should be "referred to the Committee of Attorneys General." The conference as a whole had agreed to reconvene at the end of the next meeting, which was primarily concerned with the equally contentious issue of fiscal arrangements.[49] Frost's genial opening, establishing that the courts had always played an important role in the determination of difficult constitutional issues and suggesting that such could continue to be the case if only the first ministers agreed on a principle, still proved to be too much for the delegates to agree on. For Ontario bureaucrats and politicians, however, the allure of the constitution was already apparent in the 1950s. Amendment offered Ontario bureaucrats and politicians alike the elusive possibility of a universal solution to the debates over both social and economic policy, and their interest in these matters – despite ongoing battles in other intergovernmental arenas – suggests the origins of an obsession. But for the time being, constitutional issues were put off for another day, and more mundane, but equally contentious, issues moved to the top of the agenda.

Intergovernmental Harmony, Frost-Style

The general federal-provincial conference called for early December 1950 quickly began to show signs that it was going to be "round two" of the reconstruction conference. Although originally called to discuss fiscal arrangements between the two levels of governments, and explicitly to consider the continuation of the tax rental agreements, the agenda became increasingly weighted down with the addition of other unfinished items of intergovernmental business.[50] The two levels of government had produced a shopping list of topics to address at the conference, including fiscal issues, social security, investment, income and employment policies, resources development, labour issues, housing, and a variety of topics that were of interest to individual provinces. The list was a daunting one from the federal perspective, especially given that the outbreak of war in Korea "imposed ... financial obligations" and left all Canadians with a sense of "uncertainty as to the future."[51] Without being entirely clear on what would be included under the rubric, St. Laurent proposed and the premiers agreed to limit their discussion to "fiscal and social security matters" and leave other matters to a more general discussion "without any expectation of carrying through to final or definite conclusions at that time."[52] It was still a tall order.

Fiscal arrangements topped the agenda.[53] The need to renegotiate the tax rental agreements meant that there was an opportunity for the federal government to bring Ontario and Quebec, the two non-agreeing provinces, onside, but it also opened up the possibility of losing some of those provinces that had signed on the first time around. According to reconnaissance earlier in the fall, New Brunswick was expected to make "a case for more money" and an Alberta official "passed some comment ... that the next agreement would cost the Federal Government real money." As for Ontario, British Columbia, and Quebec, the three provinces most likely to reject an extension of the current rental agreements, their officials were either too "taciturn, enigmatic or preoccupied with other matters" to indicate their intentions before the meeting itself.[54]

Ontario, however, had provided ample evidence that it "might be interested in a tax agreement if a suitable tax-sharing option was available."[55] Frost had given every indication since assuming office that he was amenable to smoothing over the intergovernmental relationship, although not at the cost of provincial autonomy. His demeanour was friendly and open, he had kept the federal officials carefully informed of his government's intentions, and his appearances at federal-provincial conferences had not been characterized by either dogmatic or vitriolic presentations. Confronted with an Ontario premier who seemed reasonable, federal officials put a considerable amount of effort into identifying tax-sharing possibilities, most of which revolved around the issue of compensation.[56] As the date of the conference neared, Finance Minister Abbott suggested to the Cabinet Committee on Federal-Provincial Relations that the most appropriate strategy might be to "offer all provinces a renewal of tax rental agreements on a basis similar to that now in existence" on the understanding that there would be some amendment "to take into consideration the high tax potentials of the provinces of Ontario and British Columbia."[57] St. Laurent seemed to agree: he thought that "Ontario might well agree to rent its taxes provided the higher tax potential of that province were recognized." He therefore suggested that it was "preferable to offer at the outset some plan which would in fact take into consideration the special positions of the Provinces of Ontario and British Columbia."[58]

For the Ontario delegation, the 1950 meeting was more than just about tax rental agreements; it was an opportunity to essentially complete the reconstruction conference and reshape Canadian federalism. Frost wanted to address his opposition to the means test for old age pensions, as well as open up the issue of unemployment assistance for "unemployables."[59] The suspicion was that providing any kind of benefits for this group of people "would involve a very widespread programme"; the implication was that this was not very high on Ontario's list of priorities.[60] Although responsibility for this category of unemployed persons was far from clear, at least as far as people in the Department of National Health and Welfare were concerned, it was certainly clear that the extension of coverage would be a costly proposition. Neither level of government demonstrated any particular enthusiasm for taking it on.

In combination with discussions about social policy responsibilities, the December conference was also charged with picking up the dangling threads of the issue of constitutional amendment. The provinces had finally agreed, after some initial concern from New Brunswick and Quebec, that "it would be desirable to establish the constitution in Canada."[61] There were technical difficulties inherent in achieving this, as the existing British document would have to be repealed simultaneous to the "substitution of constitutional instruments passed in Canada by a means other than action of the Parliament of Canada *alone*."[62] Gordon Robertson proposed several ways in which the new provisions could be established in Canada. A referendum could be held, although "the constitutional provisions would inevitably be so complicated as not to be readily comprehensible to the ordinary voter." Quebec and New Brunswick officials had suggested patriating the constitution through a treaty with all ten provinces and the federal government as parties, but Robertson dismissed this as giving too much credence to the compact theory of Confederation. Instead, he advocated passing concurrent resolutions at the federal and provincial levels.[63] The forthcoming meeting of attorneys general was supposed to discuss the various options.

Federal Justice Minister Stuart Garson presided over the late November meeting of his provincial counterparts in an effort to establish some agreement on the outstanding constitutional issues before the meeting of first ministers the following week. Ontario alone had submitted a formula for constitutional amendment, and it then became the basis for discussion. Agreement had already been reached on several issues; what remained to be decided were what sections would require unanimous consent for amendment, the degree of provincial consent necessary for the other shared issues, and precisely where the contents of section 92(13), property and civil rights in the province, fell. In addition, debate ensued around the question of "whether or not a referendum should be used in connection with the amendment of the Constitution."[64] Although little was agreed on, according to Saskatchewan adviser Frank Scott, the proceedings provided an interesting glimpse into provincial strategies. He reported back to Premier Tommy Douglas:

> The three chief topics before us were the referendum, the population factor, and the division of Property and Civil Rights into two or more parts. The first two may be discussed together. Ontario insisted on a population factor, and strongly opposed a referendum; at the same time expressing a willingness to throw all 92(13) into Category 4 [requiring unanimous consent] if these ideas prevailed. This pseudo-generous concession seemed to make a lot of other provinces accept Ontario's position in the interests of harmony. Even Alberta and Manitoba were willing to come around, although New Brunswick stood firm along with ourselves. [New Brunswick Premier] McNair explained very clearly that a requirement that the 2/3 provinces approving an amendment should represent even 51% of the population meant that, if there were no referendum, the two central provinces can veto

all amendments. Thus we can assume that federal social security measures, which necessarily involve a transfer from wealthy to poor provinces, will be extremely difficult to secure. Since Quebec can almost always be counted on to oppose, Ontario can veto when she likes ... I think that if we stand firm on this, pointing out that the population factor without a referendum puts eight provinces under the control of two, we shall have wide support in the country and more than we may think in the conference itself.[65]

There was little evidence of the federal justice minister in Scott's account of the meeting; Ontario seemed to be dictating the direction of discussion, with Quebec's Duplessis occasionally meriting recognition because of his refusal to contribute substantively to a debate that often revolved around the perception of Quebec's constitutional needs.[66] Yet despite Scott's apparent displeasure with the position that Ontario was taking on several issues, his comments suggest that the central province operated under a certain sense of obligation. Any deference to the will of the population, as a referendum would entail, was absolutely out of the question for Ontario's conservative patriarchy. Constitutional matters of any kind were far too weighty to be entrusted to a free vote, a sentiment undoubtedly shared by all provinces other than the cooperative bastion of Saskatchewan. But in digging in their heels on this matter, Ontario officials were willing to trade a little on other issues. In other federal-provincial meetings at other times, Ontario presumably also began with certain immutable points, and other areas where flexibility might be possible. In the 1950 meeting of attorneys general, it is especially interesting to note the reaction of the other provincial representatives to Ontario's willingness to compromise. As Frank Scott said, Ontario's "concessions seemed to make a lot of other provinces accept [its] position in the interests of harmony."[67] By acting first in self-interest, then in the national interest, Ontario seemed to be able to convince at least some of the others to follow its lead. The federal government was all but lost in the manoeuvring.

Under Frost's leadership, Ontario continued to publically advance a strategy of federal-provincial harmony. At the opening of the first ministers' conference in early December, the Ontario premier made clear that he was willing to consider a variety of changes to the existing social security and financial arrangements currently under debate. His comments on the fiscal arrangements were particularly illuminating. "What is needed," Frost argued, "is the frank recognition that there must be joint occupation of these [major tax] fields ... The federal system of government is a partnership and if it is to operate efficiently it must be a working partnership."[68] However, while he might have indicated a willingness on the part of Ontario to enter into a renewal of the tax rental agreements, he was quick to point out that the high costs of industrial expansion would mean that Ontario would find it difficult to heed the federal finance minister's admonition to curb inflation. The postwar economic boom in the central province had, according to Frost, "led to all manner of problems, from the requirement for more roads, more schools, more municipal assistance to those of conservation and stream pollution. This growth in industry and population has added tremendously heavy costs to the provincial and municipal governments of Ontario."[69] The premier of Canada's newest province, Newfoundland's Joey Smallwood, recalls responding sarcastically, "Stop, you're breaking my heart," but Frost was not immune to the plight of the have-not provinces, calling explicitly for a subsidy formula to assist the Atlantic and Prairie provinces.[70]

All signs pointed to this being a far different conference than the previous one. The participants seemed amenable to reaching an agreement on virtually all of the items on the agenda. In fact, Frost even closed his comments on the first day by saying that "the Province of Ontario is here today to consider on its merits any proposal which may be made by any government. We are anxious to know and understand the problems of the other provinces. We are anxious to know and understand the problems of the federal government, which are formidable indeed. We are anxious that the other governments should know and understand our problems. We are hopeful that arrangements can be made here which will safeguard the fundamentals of our federal system, which will be realistic in the light of the days in which we are living and which will be beneficial to all of the people of this nation."[71] The conference was well positioned to make some serious headway on resolving the outstanding issues of joint federal-provincial concern that confronted them.

On the question of old age pensions, while Frost seemed equally willing to reach an agreement across the different levels of government, his motives drew criticism from social welfare advocates. He made it absolutely clear that "in the subject matter of welfare, Ontario would like to see the means test in basic old age pensions abolished."[72] Not because it was humiliating, not because the aged deserved better treatment from the nation they had served so well, not even merely because it was "difficult to administer," although Frost did admit the latter point; no, the means test should be abolished because it "discourages thrift." In the meeting of the Committee on Old Age Security, established on Frost's recommendation on the first day of the full first ministers' conference, Ontario's Welfare Minister W.A. Goodfellow reiterated the sentiment. He voiced his own approval of the existing system that, if increased a bit, should be "adequate to meet actual requirements."[73] Rather than offering wholehearted support for the aged in Ontario, both Frost and Goodfellow used the occasion of an intergovernmental forum to remind the federal government of the pressing problem of unemployment, suggesting "a disability pension for all unemployables between the ages of 21 and 69 as an alternative to the proposed 65–69 means test pension."[74] In the final debate over whether to try to introduce a contributory pension or not, it was the simpler, non-contributory scheme, financed through designated taxes, that carried the day.[75]

For four days, discussion focused on Ottawa's fiscal proposals and old age security. No one stormed out of the conference, which was apparently enough to establish it as "the most amicable and one of the most successful federal-provincial conferences in our history."[76] True, in the end, agreement was reached, but it seemed to be on so little. St. Laurent was given the authority to issue a press statement declaring that "the Conference had discussed: (i) the offer of the federal government for new tax agreements; (ii) the offer of the federal government respecting old age security; (iii) a provincial proposal for an amendment to permit provincial indirect sales taxes at the retail level." A further continuing committee would assess the case of pensions for people under age seventy.[77] Frost essentially answered the question of Ontario's position on the social security issues by releasing his own press statement simultaneously, indicating a willingness to introduce joint federal-provincial pensions for those aged sixty-five to sixty-nine contingent only on Ottawa assuming responsibility for those over seventy.[78] The entire question of constitutional amendment "might be resumed following further study of the tax agreements and related matters,"[79] declared the closing press statement released by the delegates to the conference. Small victories, and little progress, seemed to be the order of the day if a federal-provincial conference had any hope of being considered a success.

The National Interest in the Provincial Narrative

At intergovernmental meetings with sweeping agendas it was difficult to determine the accomplishments. The increasing need for expert advice to navigate through the complex array of financial and population statistics in an effort to establish priorities meant that first ministers were loath to agree to anything that had not been thoroughly assessed by their own government departments. The December 1950 conference, with its agenda of fiscal and social security issues and its hopes to address the unfinished business of constitutional amendment, ended with more high hopes, but little to show for the four days of meetings. The plan had been to deal with the inter-related subjects of economic, social, and constitutional policy in an effort to complete the overhaul of Confederation that daunted the participants at the 1945 conference, but that had proven too complex. Although the conference was regarded by many as "the most harmonious and successful"[80] intergovernmental meeting in recent memory, it was not remarkable in its progress. Frost would later comment that multi-item conferences were impossible, but for the time being Canada's mid-century leaders were faced with the challenge of finishing as much as possible from the intergovernmental agenda.

Some of the loose ends were relatively simple to tie off, although rarely in a completely satisfactory fashion. Constitutional amendment, for example, simply disappeared from the agenda entirely, not to reappear in any consequential manner for another decade.[81] Unemployment assistance seemed destined to be similarly ignored. Justice Minister Garson's much earlier decree that "the constitutional position [on unemployment assistance] was clear" left the problem squarely in the laps of provinces eager for Ottawa to make good on its promise to assume full responsibility.[82] They would have to wait several more years before that promise was fulfilled. Other social policy decisions, however, seemed on the brink of agreement at the conclusion of the conference.

Early in the new year, Garson had sent out a draft proposal of an amendment that would, in his department's opinion, serve to establish the constitutional right of the federal government to legislate in the area of old age pensions. After some input from Ontario, and further clarification, the amendment received unanimous provincial approval by May 1951, and old age pensions successfully lost their means test for people over seventy years of age.[83] There were still debates over the other aspects of the old age pension scheme – in particular, what to do with the group between the ages of sixty-five and sixty-nine. Frost was adamant that the means test should be eliminated for all age categories as he thought that it "encourage[d] people who can do useful work to get out of production." He was even more concerned about the possibility, expressed to him in private by the federal deputy minister of welfare, "that the matter of means test should be left to each individual province." A scheme that depended on a 50 per cent contribution from the federal government, Frost maintained, should be a plan common to all provinces across the country. As he explained to Bill Goodfellow before a meeting of welfare ministers,

> I quite recognize the difficulty of the Federal Government in establishing a standard which would fit evenly across a great country like Canada with its varying conditions, [but] at the same time it is a matter which should be closely kept in hand by the Central Government because after all the Central Government contributes 50 per cent of the pensions. There are many extremely undesirable features of such a plan. It immediately places all of the 10 provinces in competition against the others and it means that the whole matter becomes the subject of pressures from various sources, with the result that what may be done in Ontario is forced upon the other provinces, in many cases against their better judgment. The converse is also true. The governments of Alberta or Saskatchewan may decide upon a certain course and then the Government of Ontario may be pressured into accepting this although in actual fact the policies in these western provinces might have little common to our conditions here. This is extremely unsound. For the protection of all, it seems to me to be better that the Federal Government and the provinces should agree to a common plan.[84]

Frost was personally opposed to the continuation of a means test for any age group, and he certainly gave every indication of wanting to get rid of the test in Ontario. Yet he also wanted it to be the policy across the country, and he was not in favour of provincial flexibility in the determination of how to deal with pensions for those under seventy. If the federal minister persisted, however, Ontario would be left with one of the more generous plans nationwide: a non-means–tested pension for all those over age sixty-five. His motives in pressing for a national plan, therefore, seemed based almost entirely on a two-part argument: first, means testing reduced productivity by encouraging the poorest in society to leave the workforce and simply collect a pension; second, the national interest was best served by a uniformity of program across the country, regardless of the different provincial motives for either wanting or rejecting a means test. In the end, Frost was unsuccessful in securing a uniform national program, as each province introduced its own variation, but his interest in promoting the national interest found another outlet in the area of tax agreements.[85]

Here too, the dominion-provincial conference of December 1950 had appeared close to agreement. The federal proposal, with its two different options for tax sharing, seemed designed to appeal to the widest number of provinces. As the Ontario officials calculated and recalculated the advantages of participating in the new tax rental scheme being proposed, they weighed several variables.[86] The financial factors were obvious, but others also played a role in determining Ontario's position. Months of analysis of the federal proposals pointed to two conclusions: in the details, there could hardly be a more attractive tax-sharing proposal than the one Ottawa had offered in December 1950, but in the broad strokes of the offer there was much to cause concern. The advantages of the tax rental proposal were multiple. Ontario would be able to count on $101.8 million per year in lieu of the income from its personal, corporate, and estate tax collections and would thus ensure "unrivalled" security by joining the agreement. The amount of the money provided by the scheme was considered "fair and just." Ontario would save money by eliminating the cost of collecting corporate taxes, and would simplify the system in the process. The "relatively stable revenue" the province would secure would facilitate the process of budget planning in the years ahead. And joining the scheme would "be one further step in mutual co-operation" between the federal and provincial governments, a long-standing goal of the Frost administration.[87] As the Ottawa designers had hoped, the new tax rental proposal was extraordinarily attractive to Canada's largest and wealthiest province.

It was not without disadvantages, though. Accepting the offer would mean that Ontario "would suspend its right to tax in at least two major fields of direct taxation" and would forfeit the ability to exercise much control at all over its own finances. By renting the direct tax fields from the provinces, the federal government was essentially providing grants instead of adequate tax room; Ontario officials expressed concern that these rental payments, or "subsidies," would "tend to reduce frugality and wise spending by governments" and would encourage the tendency to "look at a grant as something for nothing or, if not something for nothing, at least something that can be obtained at someone else's expense."[88] Moreover, acceptance of the offer would undermine the province's ability to design policy, and would compel it to search for additional revenue through "more various and onerous forms of taxation." Finally, the Ontario officials argued, perhaps disingenuously, the federal government itself would be harmed if Ontario signed on. As the report explained,

If Ontario does not enter into a tax agreement and yet obtains the sum of $14.7 million in personal income tax, the Federal Government will be better off financially to the extent of $36 million. If Ontario and Quebec both do not enter into an agreement, the Federal Government, even while paying these provinces the 5 per cent personal income tax, will be better off in its budgetary position to the extent of nearly $80 million in 1952–53. In other words, it will cost the Federal Government about $80 million annually to have these two provinces enter into a tax agreement.[89]

Ontario's reasons for considering remaining outside of the tax rental agreements were interesting. On the surface, at least, self-interest pointed to joining the scheme rather than rejecting the federal offer once again. The principles of provincial autonomy and fiscal manoeuvrability seemed to animate Ontario's views of the disadvantages of the plan. So too did a sense of what was fair and just across the country and in the national capital. Thus, the rents or "subsidies" might encourage an inappropriate sense of entitlement in the poorer regions, rather than the commitment to innovation and accomplishment achieved by providing adequate tax space in the first place. Further, the federal government would find itself financially weaker, albeit jurisdictionally stronger, if Ontario and Quebec opted to accept the generous tax rentals being offered. Regardless of whether the disadvantages Ontario officials identified with the federal proposals were considered by others to be either legitimate or accurate, they were unquestionably concerns regarding the entirety of the program, rather than simply its application to Ontario. Whether or not one agreed with the Ontario version of the national interest, the province was certainly advancing nationwide arguments for why the tax rental agreements should not be accepted.

There was one other, extremely important reason that Ontario was loath to enter into a tax agreement with the federal government, and that the officials identified it as problematic demonstrates the depth of their commitment to the national interest. Despite the financial attractiveness of the federal offer, "if the Province of Ontario should enter into a tax-rental agreement and the Province of Quebec is left as the only province to levy its own taxes, the effect would be to split Quebec off from the rest of the provinces and destroy the carefully nurtured amity which has been a feature of Federal-Provincial conferences for the past two years."[90] The 1952 federal proposals guaranteed a higher minimum payment, but in all other respects were virtually the same as the offer made in 1947; there seemed little hope that a Quebec government opposed to the earlier proposal would leap at the chance to sign on to the new one. If the views on the federal tax rental scheme unfolded as expected, "there is not the slightest doubt that if Ontario signs an agreement, many people in Quebec, and perhaps some French-Canadians in Ontario, will regard it as a defection ... What is needed is an agreement," the Ontario bureaucrats contended, "signed by all provinces ... which will enable all provinces to raise by taxes or receive by way of a rental a satisfactory revenue to carry out their function."[91] There was nothing less than national unity at stake.

Having identified the severity of the situation were Quebec to be the only province not to sign the tax rental agreements, Frost contacted the prime minister, who "saw the danger of Quebec's isolation immediately." With St. Laurent's blessing, Frost and Ontario Deputy Treasurer Chester Walters met with their counterparts Duplessis and Onesime Gagnon in Montreal in an effort "to try and reach some understanding which would place no impediment in the way of a friendly settlement of inter-governmental fiscal matters."[92] The meeting resulted in an agreement in principle that the two provinces would rent their corporate taxes to the federal government at a rate of 8 1/2 per cent and their personal taxes at a rate of 5 per cent calculated on the provincial yield in 1948, provided several conditions were met. In addition to agreeing to hold annual federal-provincial conferences, Ottawa would also have to recognize the provinces' right to statutory subsidies, and their right to levy mining and logging taxes. Succession duties would continue to be collected by the provinces if they wished, and would "be allowed as a tax credit up to half the Federal duties under the Federal succession duty law." Finally, Ottawa must agree to make up the difference between the 1950–51 yield on liquor and gasoline taxes and the amount collected in any year of the tax rental agreements "where the reduction ... is the result of Federal action designed to meet a national emergency."[93] Canada's two largest provinces were certainly not going to make it easy for the federal government to secure uniformity of rentals across the country.

Despite the inclusion of such an extensive array of conditions that had to be met before the central provinces were willing to sign onto the agreement, Ontario officials still thought that modifications would need to be made before the offer was suitably attractive to Quebec. Due to the lower personal and corporate tax yields in Quebec, it would not be advantageous to come in under the same terms as Ontario unless the federal government increased the per capita payment it was offering.[94] In mid-August, Premier Frost attempted to convince St. Laurent to change the offer he had made the previous year. The problem, he underlined, was not Ontario, which "can accept the terms of your tax rental proposal of last December or continue to collect its own taxes in its own way without substantial financial difference either one way or the other."[95] The problem was Quebec, which "does not, even for a short period, favour the rental of its corporation tax." The threat of Quebec once again remaining outside the tax rental agreements, this time alone, "is not a good thing for national unity"; Frost urged the prime minister "to revise your proposal to make it possible for all the provinces to march together in substantial harmony."[96]

Leaving nothing to chance, and certain that extensive discussions with Quebec politicians and officials had provided the Ontario delegation with a degree of expertise missing in Ottawa, Frost offered a possible third option for inclusion in the tax rental agreements. Option 3 stipulated that provinces would agree not to impose a corporate tax higher than 7 per cent, special business taxes higher than those already in place in Quebec, a personal income tax, or succession duties in excess of the present levels. In return, the federal government would agree that all of the provincial business taxes would be treated as credits and deducted from income for federal tax purposes, and they would agree to pay a rental fee equal to the yield of personal income tax at 5 per cent of the 1948 federal rates. Were Quebec to accept this offer, as Ontario officials believed it would, the total rental payment would be $7,743,000.[97]

Frost met privately with St. Laurent to press for the inclusion of a third option in the federal tax rental proposals. The Ontario premier argued the advantages of providing an alternative formula that Quebec could accept: in addition to not isolating the one francophone province, the federal government would "have full power to manage corporation and personal income taxes as it sees fit," and it would "save money and reduce the amount of revenue it would have to raise." Ontario's proposal did not increase the rental amount but rather provided the opportunity for the provinces "to raise their own resources and take responsibility for them," another feature of the plan that would preserve national unity. According to Frost, Ontario's reasons for proposing an alternative rental scheme were entirely external to its own provincial interests. Having not completely decided whether to accept the December 1950 tax rental offer, "Ontario seeks to avoid any rupture in its common interests with Quebec, in view of that Province's known desire to retain the exercise of its own corporation and succession duties."[98]

In the field of fiscal relations, Ontario politicians, with the support of their bureaucracy, attempted to reshape the national program of tax rentals. That they did this not to secure a better economic arrangement for their own province, but rather to ensure the unity of the national economic community and, more specifically, to guard against any further isolation of Quebec, is remarkable. Even more interesting is that the Ontario delegation undertook to identify the shape of a tax rental offer that would be palatable to Quebec with, apparently, the full blessing of the federal government. Far from usurping the role of the national government, Ontario had positioned itself as an interpreter of information between levels of government. The part was virtually neutral: clearly, Ontario could accept or reject the tax proposals with almost equal effect, so it really had no ulterior motive for pressing for a third option to entice Quebec's entry. Ontario's role as a mediator in this situation served to provide credibility for the future. No longer solely devoted to provincial gain, Ontario under Leslie Frost had developed a real capacity to consider and work towards the national interest.

Not that the national interest, or at least Ontario's version of what that might entail, was always possible. After considerable consultation with provincial politicians, federal Finance Minister Douglas Abbott offered a somewhat revised plan to rent tax fields from the provinces for the 1952 to 1957 period. While revising the manner in which payments were calculated, and in which provincial population was determined, and in which corporation taxes were counted in non-agreeing provinces, the federal government did not follow the Ontario officials' advice and present a third rental option.[99] This meant that, not only was Quebec's participation impossible, but also that there were considerable obstacles to the inclusion of other provinces as well.

Nova Scotia's Angus Macdonald proposed that a further federal-provincial conference be called to discuss the new proposals in detail and in a group. Frost thought that such a strategy would have little effect, but nevertheless suggested that "it might be all right to attend as we seldom come away empty handed."[100] Chester Walters agreed, but was "persuaded that progress is best made by separate discussions."[101] Accordingly, Ontario officials entered into several private discussions with their counterparts in Ottawa. During the first of these, Walters and his team announced that Ontario would not rent its succession duties, and they made arrangements for the possible re-entry of the province into the corporate tax field.[102] In repeated contact between officials of the two levels of government, Walters pressured the federal bureaucrats to

change the basis for calculating population upon which the rental figure was determined. On this issue, however, the finance minister ruled
against the Ontario population proposal.[103] There was nothing more to
be done.

Convinced that the provincial negotiators had extracted what concessions they could from the federal government, Frost wrote St. Laurent in
August 1952 to advise him that Ontario was willing to enter the tax rental
agreements. This move was not to be taken as a major shift in Ontario's
traditional approach to intergovernmental relations, however. "While a
tax rental agreement may be suited to the needs of an abnormal period"
which, the premier noted, was currently created by the situation in Korea, "we do not believe that an arrangement providing for the rental of
taxing rights from the Province to the Government of Canada affords a
satisfactory long-term solution to the Dominion-Provincial fiscal problem."[104] To this end, Frost pressed the federal government to reconsti-
tute the joint Economic Committee, and wrote to his old friend Angus
Macdonald to suggest provincial action. Frost was sure that "the time is
ripe for a general review of our tax structure … I think the provinces
have established themselves in the eyes of the public as being agreeable to dealing reasonably with the problem of making our constitution
work and allotting revenues to the various jurisdictions to enable them
to carry out their duties. A study such as I suggest would take some time
and indeed there should be time for consideration and negotiation and
it is not a bit too early to start this now having in mind that 1957 arrives
pretty quickly."[105]

Far from becoming "more comfortable within Ottawa's embrace," as one
commentator has suggested,[106] under Leslie Frost Ontario began reshaping the national interest in its own image. On matters that had been on
the books for some time, such as pensions and unemployment assistance,
the Ontario government pressed alternative policy approaches on both
the federal government and on other provinces. Although there was not
a great deal of success on these fronts, they showcased the Ontario approach to intergovernmental relations that emphasized alternatives to
the proposals offered by the federal government. On tax rental agreements, the provincial strategy was more nuanced, and it clearly reflected
Ontario's commitment to the national interest. Quebec's refusal to enter
into tax agreements with Ottawa threatened national unity, according to
Frost, and ought to be corrected when the next round of tax deals were

negotiated. Even St. Laurent recognized the legitimacy of Frost's position, allowing the province to play a central role in attempting to secure Quebec's signature on the 1952 arrangements. But if Frost's Ontario was playing a pivotal role in some key intergovernmental issues, it still had not seen much success in tilting the balance more towards the provinces. The rather unexpected appearance of the constitution on the agenda held out some hope for Ontario officials, who saw that amendment offered the possibility of correcting the balance of the federation structurally rather than in the piecemeal fashion that had dominated since the end of the Second World War. Moreover, the fact that the Ontario government devoted so much attention to offering constitutional alternatives during a period of already heavy intergovernmental negotiations suggests the beginnings of an obsession.

Chapter Four

"Ontario's Earnest Desire for National Unity": New Policies, New Approaches, 1952–1960

Leslie Frost's decision to rent provincial tax fields to the federal government was, in many ways, a monumental one. His government had given little indication in the early months of 1952 that there was anything more agreeable about the new offer than there had been about the old one, and indeed, apart from a slightly sweeter financial settlement it appeared that Ontario gained little in accepting the deal. Moreover, the central province appeared to reverse two key elements of its traditional position: Frost's agreement put an end to Ontario's insistence on not isolating Quebec, as well as to its long-standing argument that responsibilities and taxation jurisdiction had to be equitably and realistically divided between the two levels of government. Certainly, when viewed as an event in the trajectory of fiscal relations between Ontario and Ottawa, Frost's signature on the agreement marked the conclusion of a long battle "begun flamboyantly by Hepburn and continued stubbornly by Drew."[1] Moreover, the battle, from the perspective of Ontario's traditional defence of provincial rights, appears to have been won by the federal government. However, when viewed in the context of other ongoing issues of federal-provincial negotiation, it is clear that understanding Ontario's strategy needs a more nuanced interpretation.

Throughout the remainder of the 1950s, Frost pressed – privately, softly, diplomatically, and ultimately, ceaselessly – for a renegotiation of the relationship between the federal government and the provinces. Using his considerable charm and easy temperament, Frost built personal relationships outside the normal intergovernmental institutions. With a solid understanding of the national interest – better, at many times, than that of his counterparts in Ottawa – Frost shaped alternatives to national policy that reflected Ontario's interests. Far from being a period in which Ontario bent to the national will, the Frost era was one in which the national interest was massaged into conforming to Ontario's interest. Taxes and the fiscal relationship more generally were an ongoing issue, and one in which Frost had some modest success in directing the national agenda and drafting the national position. Old social policies, like unemployment assistance, and new ones, like health insurance, sometimes shifted to the top of the intergovernmental priority list, and they also gave Frost the chance to offer provincial alternatives or, more significantly, to take the initiative. What appeared to be a collegial relationship between the two leaders gave those in both capitals cause for hope that the intergovernmental warfare might finally have ended, but not because Frost had succumbed. In some instances, at least as it related to federal-provincial affairs, it appeared that Ontario and Ottawa were operating a quasi-coalition.

Ontario's National Economic Leadership

Frost's early suggestion that the Economic Committee be reconstituted provides a clear illustration of the premier's emerging role in the federation. The proposal was for an intergovernmental committee that would "undertake studies of fiscal problems"[2] outside of the confines of first ministers' conferences, where agendas were often "too heavy" to have issues adequately addressed.[3] Repeatedly, both in writing and in conversation, Frost urged the prime minister to address the issue of federal-provincial relations in such a way that future disagreements could be minimized, and the entire process could be "rationalized." The key to such pressure was the close personal relationship the two leaders shared, which, in essence, allowed Frost to write and speak in a manner that was simply "thinking out loud."[4] The prime minister's response to Frost's suggestion was telling. If Frost was interested in pursuing this sort of idea, St. Laurent wrote, he ought to discuss it "informally with other provincial governments" and then the two leaders could talk further "on a private basis whenever circumstances permit."[5] Frost's consistent strategy of advocating the national interest in intergovernmental affairs seems to have paid off: the prime minister was abdicating responsibility, however momentarily, for finding a long-term solution to the federal-provincial dilemma in favour of Ontario's first minister. Was this unprecedented magnanimity between the two prime ministers an indication that Ontario had reversed its decades-long position on provincial rights? Hardly. What had begun to happen, however, was the conflation of Ontario's interest with Canada's interest. Coordinating a provincial consensus on the need for a permanent Economic Committee was just the beginning, a task Frost accomplished through private conversation and persuasion.[6]

One of the things that Frost and his right-hand man in this endeavour, George Gathercole, discovered as they floated the idea of establishing a new Economic Committee in other provincial capitals was the variety of different provincial views of the fiscal situation in Canada. In early 1954, for example, British Columbia approached the federal government for financial aid on the basis of an increasing population, the high levels of current expenditure, and "the large Federal collections of corporation and personal income taxes and succession duties" which "were considerably higher than the average for Canada."[7] If Frost was going to speak with any authority, he would have to be familiar with the nature of the fiscal complaints in other provinces. British Columbia's financial situation underlined the dangers of the current tax-sharing arrangement. Quebec also obviously had concerns, evidenced by the fact that it had not signed onto the 1952–57 tax rental agreements, and Ontario remained as committed to bringing Quebec onside as it had been before the previous round. The Ontario team was increasingly adept at mediating between the provinces, and especially Quebec, and the federal government. Frost had already apparently convinced the new federal finance minister, Walter Harris, and his deputy Ken Taylor, that "there was merit in the holding of informal annual or semi-annual meetings between the advisors of the Federal and provincial governments."[8] Whether or not this would be sufficient to solve B.C.'s problems or to smooth the already rocky terrain that lay between Ottawa and Quebec on fiscal issues remained a question.[9]

In the autumn of 1954, a series of secret and not-so-secret meetings took place between, variously, representatives of the Ontario, Quebec, and the federal governments. The discussions began with a telephone conversation between St. Laurent and Frost that indicated the prime minister's willingness to engage in a debate "which would contribute to a solution of the Federal-Provincial fiscal problem."[10] After an unusually "pleasant meeting" between St. Laurent and Duplessis, during which "the important fiscal problem" was discussed, the Quebec premier retired to his province to consider his government's response.[11] Meanwhile, key officials in Ontario's Treasury Department travelled to Ottawa to discuss the same situation with their federal counterparts. While this too was "very cordial and friendly" with the federal team "genuinely eager to understand Ontario's position," the views of the other provinces were never far from the surface of discussions.[12]

From the perspective of the federal officials, the Ontario delegates seemed as concerned about finding a way to bring Quebec back into the fiscal fold as they were about getting a better deal for their own province. Recognizing "the need for a continuation of the present tax rental agreements in some form" because of the high revenues they provided to some provinces, the Ontario group was nevertheless concerned "that the Province of Quebec was completely opposed to suspending its taxing rights." As long as this was the case, "there would be a feeling of isolation and resentment if Quebec was under one fiscal system and all the other provinces were under another." In part because of its "close economic ties with Quebec," but more importantly because of "Ontario's earnest desire for national unity," Canada's largest province was "prepared to consider, and indeed, to participate in the devising of an alternative plan or plans" under which "Ontario and Quebec, and probably British Columbia, could operate effectively."[13]

It would be naïve to imagine that the provincial delegation, led by Gathercole, was only interested in securing Quebec's signature on an intergovernmental tax agreement. Clearly, the very special needs of Ontario could not be forgotten: with a booming economy and growth in expenditures for education, hospitals, and highway construction, Ontario needed a bigger piece of the fiscal pie to finance its growth.[14] But although the meeting was not without its points of disagreement, the atmosphere was remarkably pleasant and there was a decidedly pan-Canadian tilt to the discussion as both federal and provincial officials competed for the right to speak for the nation. Bringing Quebec on board, however, remained more elusive.

Maurice Duplessis was not an easy premier for any prime minister to deal with. His ultra-conservative Union Nationale government was committed to protecting Quebec autonomy to the extent that any sharing of jurisdiction with the vastly wealthier federal government was generally rejected. This was as true for social policy initiatives as it was for the ongoing fiscal arrangements. And yet securing intergovernmental agreements with Quebec remained the goal of successive prime ministers, who recognized the benefits of pan-national programs and the pitfalls of isolating one province from the others. The prime ministers of Ontario were just as eager as their counterparts in Ottawa to secure Quebec's participation. The price of such participation, however, was often high.

Despite the appearance of amicable discussion between Ontario, federal, and Quebec representatives over the best way to bring Quebec into the tax rental agreements, Duplessis finally made clear what he wanted from the federal government. Having refused to accept rental payments for the tax fields that Ottawa had been occupying since 1942, the provincial government found itself in need of cash. In 1954, Duplessis imposed a provincial income tax, thereby subjecting Quebeckers to double taxation and a heavier tax burden than people in other parts of the country experienced. What Duplessis now sought was that the amount of tax collected by the province be allowed to count against money collected by Ottawa in the same field. The result would be a sharing of income tax revenue in Quebec rather than an increase in tax levels. Ottawa would get less money, Quebec would get more, and individuals would pay the same amount. St. Laurent wasted little time in rejecting the proposition that the province, essentially, could set the federal level of taxation.[15] Of course, the federal government had already set the provincial levels of taxation, but this absence of equality in the fiscal environment was not of concern to the prime minister. After a good deal of discussion between the Prime Minister's Office and the Department of Finance, and with the apparent intervention of Toronto businessman Walter Gordon, St. Laurent accepted the wisdom of reaching a temporary agreement with Quebec.[16] The current law allowed taxpayers who paid provincial income tax to claim as a deduction 5 per cent of the federal tax. In 1955, the prime minister proposed to increase that deduction to 10 per cent, and allow all people living in a province that had introduced a provincial income tax to claim the deduction.[17] Further changes to the method by which taxes were shared between the two levels of government would wait until a full federal-provincial conference could be convened later in the year.[18]

The government of Ontario saw very real advantages to Ottawa's statement that taxes were being shared to ensure that all provinces could "perform their constitutional functions themselves."[19] Despite the fact that the move was regarded as a sop to St. Laurent's home province, it also represented the first step towards disentangling federal and provincial income taxes, something that the Ontario government had long been proposing. With its 90 per cent, the federal government was free to act as it saw fit; the same was true for the 10 per cent – or less or more if the province so desired – collected by the provincial government. Ontario stood to collect more money than it had in the past, and officials hoped that raising "the personal income tax to 10 per cent should, in time, tend to strengthen the case for allowing corporations under similar circumstances a credit of 10 per cent of their income instead of the present rate of 7 per cent."[20] All in all, the change was regarded as "a forward step in recognizing the rights of the Province to an effective field of taxation in which to operate."[21]

On the matter of the tax rental agreements, by the summer of 1955, federal bureaucrats had identified three different "lines of approach" for the upcoming round of fiscal negotiations. First, the federal government could strive to renew the tax rental agreements with all provinces except Quebec, which was essentially dismissed as unlikely to join any tax-sharing agreement. In this option, Ontario's acceptance was instrumental and, to secure it, Ottawa considered it "necessary to make concessions totaling close to $110 million for the other nine provinces."[22] A second solution would be to forget about Ontario, and offer to renew the agreements with the other eight provinces on the same rental basis as the 1952 agreements. This option would certainly not appeal to Ontario, but the lower cost to the federal treasury meant that Ontario's agreement was no longer necessary.

The Cabinet Committee on the Federal-Provincial Conference was most interested in the third approach, which came to be known as "Plan C." The side agreement with Quebec had pointed to a new way of dividing tax space. This new option abandoned entirely the principle of "renting" tax fields from the provinces, in favour of a system of "tax equalization payments to all provinces under conditions which could range from agreements with minimum conditions that Quebec might accept, to a completely one-sided commitment by the Federal government involving no provincial obligation."[23] The suggestion was for the federal government to back away from the income, corporate, and succession tax fields by, respectively, 10, 7, and 50 per cent, allowing provincial governments that tax room. Ottawa would then make up the difference between what the poorest provinces collected under this system and what the wealthiest province was able to collect.[24] The cabinet committee agreed that this "seemed to offer the most practical and desirable solution to the federal-provincial fiscal problem," but it planned to announce all three possibilities to provincial representatives in July "without ... giving any indication as to which ... was likely to be favoured by the federal authorities."[25]

When the Preparatory Committee of the Federal-Provincial Conference met in July, with Canada's Deputy Minister of Finance Ken Taylor in the chair, the provincial financial advisers were treated to an even more ambiguous glimpse of federal intentions. The first two tax rental possibilities were offered in a straightforward fashion, and debate raged around the calculation of the rental fees and the claims of have-not provinces to a bigger piece of the pie. Ontario's finance bureaucrats had made a great deal of progress in assessing the merits of different rental levels, for example, and George Gathercole's contributions were consequently considerably more specific than those of many other participants.[26] Provincial focus thus seemed to be successfully redirected to the first two federal alternatives, neither of which was the strategy that Ottawa intended to follow. The more attractive Plan C was offered up to the provincial representatives for consideration rather obliquely: Bob Bryce referred people's attention to an earlier article in the *Canadian Tax Journal* on tax equalization towards the end of the preparatory meeting, and Taylor then quickly outlined "the general theory of the tax equalization approach whereby the Federal Government would supplement the return to the Provinces from certain taxes."[27] From the provincial perspective, Ottawa was really only offering two possible approaches to fiscal arrangements. The closest that Plan C came to being discussed was in a proposal by British Columbia to re-enter the direct tax fields.[28]

The focus in Ontario had been on some kind of renewal of tax rental agreements, and not on a rethinking of the whole principle. When Plan C was finally discussed, due in part to a leak to Michael Barkway of the *Financial Post* on the matter, provincial representatives responded with some surprise. Most particularly, representatives from the wealthiest provinces expressed concern over the level of equalization anticipated. British Columbia's Fisher feared that this strategy would elevate all provinces "to a common average" which was beyond what the poorer provinces "should expect ... in attaining economic equality." Similarly, Gathercole had already complained that "equalization costs fell indirectly most heavily on Ontario residents." Once Plan C had been introduced, Gathercole also "thought this would remove incentive from provincial effort if it could always rely on being brought up to the highest."[29]

George Gathercole was enough concerned about the tenor of the meeting to write Frost a hasty note following the first day of discussions. Although the "jettisoning" of the existing tax agreements was the "principle revelation," what they were to be replaced with was what made Gathercole anxious. "You may well judge," he wrote to Frost,

> that there are some wild ideas on what these equalization grants should be and I have repeatedly emphasized that an industrial-urban province has to spend money to earn revenue that a subsidized province is not required to do. On this matter too there are divergences of opinion and it is to be hoped that in the end common sense will prevail. There is no doubt that sympathy for a completely equalizing federal tax payment is running strong

in some quarters and could become a source of concern. It is even suggested that the equalizing should bring everyone up to Ontario's yields and
that the adjustment cover all provincial tax fields. This is an extreme position, but if it were implemented it would mean that Quebec could collect
it [sic] own taxes and over and above its revenue, receive an 'equalizations'
payment from the federal government.[30]

The new approach to fiscal relations did not sit well with a Conservative government in Ontario, and new strategies for dealing with Ottawa
would have to be considered.

According to one well-placed insider, Frost agreed with Gathercole
and was "suspicious" of the federal scheme. Having for years argued for
the need to include Quebec in the tax rental program, he now feared
"a plot to buy off Quebec with Ontario's money."[31] Certainly, confusion
seemed to characterize the mood in the Ontario bureaucracy following
the close of the federal-provincial conference.[32] Other provinces had
concerns as well. Saskatchewan, for example, complained about the
method of calculating equalization payments and the low price tag on
renting tax fields to the federal government.[33] Manitoba, on the other
hand, was "already pretty firmly committed to the new plan 'C' or something close to it," as the provincial officials understood it to be a chance
to bring everyone up to Ontario's standards through the federal equalization grant.[34] Ultimately, however, "the key to success or failure" lay
not with these "minor figures" but with Leslie Frost.[35] Federal officials
therefore took every opportunity to assess the reaction to their proposals
in Toronto. Although R.M. Burns felt, in mid-November, that "Ontario's
attitude remains most cooperative and friendly," he nevertheless indicated that the government officials to whom he had talked informally
felt "very strongly that equalization to Ontario's level is not justified."[36]

After much communication between Ontario and the federal government – at the executive, ministerial, and bureaucratic levels – St. Laurent
clarified the national position. Ottawa's "definite proposal" included an
"unconditional tax equalization payment to the provinces" with a guaranteed floor, and an offer to share the three major direct tax fields with
any province not wishing to collect its own.[37] Later in the month, Frost
explained his objection to the offer: providing equalization payments
to all provinces except Ontario failed to "recognize the heavy financial
burdens that are imposed on this Province ... in servicing a rapidly growing population and industry which produce such a large proportion of
the Federal Government's revenues."[38] He was even more forceful at a

Premier George Drew made effective use of the radio on the campaign trail. Radio also allowed him the chance to make his displeasure with the federal government – particularly over the implementation of family allowances – more broadly known across Ontario. (Archives of Ontario, digital image I0005349)

Louis St. Laurent (left) was Mackenzie King's chosen successor, even though they followed different approaches to the intergovernmental relationship. (Library Archives Canada, C-023259)

Leslie Frost was the man next door, a genial "Old Man Ontario," but that public image hid a master political strategist. (Archives of Ontario, digital image I0005375)

Frost, Prime Minister Louis St. Laurent, and Quebec Premier Maurice Duplessis (left to right) were rarely on the same side, but it was not for lack of trying. (Archives of Ontario, digital image I0005392)

Federal provincial conferences were serious affairs for Frost's Ontario, offering opportunities for formal portraits both outside (opposite page, top, with St. Laurent seated third from the left and Frost seated third from the right) and in (opposite page, bottom, with a rather startled focus on the camera by Prime Minister John Diefenbaker, seated in the centre). By the 1960s, the mad men of politics allowed more casual photos (above), as they relaxed with John Robarts (third from right) and wandered on the lawn drinking and smoking cigarettes. (opposite page: Archives of Ontario, digital images I0005385 and I0005369; above: Library Archives Canada, Duncan Cameron fonds, E008300742)

The Confederation of Tomorrow Conference showcased the new Toronto-Dominion Tower and the luxurious 54th floor; whether the lofty location would parallel the outcomes of the conference, however, remained to be seen. (McCord Museum, M965.199.9614)

For Bill Davis, "bland" worked; here he is at his most charismatic. (Archives of Ontario, digital image I0005424)

The constitutional conferences of the 1970s were decreasingly productive. (McCord Museum, M986.289.16.1)

Davis's (left) contribution to constitutional success lay in his capacity to talk to all sides, and to keep a conversation on the constitution going when no one felt like it any longer. Alberta's Peter Lougheed (right) sometimes needed convincing. (Library and Archives Canada, MIKAN no. 400218)

Roy McMurtry, Jean Chretién, and Roy Romanow worked together to produce a constitutional deal in November 1981 that owed a great deal to the lobbying and dialogue-building that Ontario bureaucrats had been engaged in over the previous few weeks. (Library and Archives Canada, MIKAN no. 4002112)

While the deal pleased Davis (right), it was "the night of the long knives" for
René Lévesque (left) and a large portion of Quebec. (Library and Archives Canada, MIKAN no. 400214)

Constitutional negotiations with Pierre Trudeau were federal machinations with the provinces at arms-length. (Library and Archives Canada, MIKAN no. 3205978)

conference called a few weeks later, where he presented the Ontario government's alternative vision of tax sharing and equalization.

Frost was irritated by the "unfairness of the present formula," which offered an adjustment grant to Quebec of over $40 million. Surely, he argued, Ontario's needs were even greater given "our larger population and industrial structure."[39] Years of Ontario's advocacy of a tax-sharing system that would be palatable to Duplessis had finally been successful, but the pleasure in Toronto was seriously dampened by the realization that Quebec's windfall came at a cost to Ontario taxpayers. Frost's efforts to have the standard rates of taxation increased to 15 per cent of income tax, 15 per cent of corporate tax, and 100 per cent of succession duties, fell on largely deaf ears. Instead of simply attacking the federal proposal, however, Frost offered an alternative. The poorer provinces should certainly receive equalization payments, but those should be equivalent to the average of the taxation income in the four richest provinces. He also advocated an increase in the rental fees that the federal government would pay for the opportunity to occupy the direct tax fields and, because of their particularly precarious financial situations, a $10 million annual subsidy to each of New Brunswick and Nova Scotia.[40]

Frost's approach to the federal offer clearly reflected an increasing resentment over the division of fiscal resources, but despite that, he did not stray from the strategy developed over the previous decade. The Ontario premier resisted vitriol, responding instead with a provincial alternative. Still, it was disheartening that the easy camaraderie that he had shared with the prime minister had done so little to secure a bigger piece of the pie. When the fiscal arrangements were passed in the House of Commons in the summer of 1956, provinces received equalization payments equal to the average tax yield of British Columbia and Ontario. The Frost government continued its critique, arguing that the financial burdens of managing such a prosperous economy necessitated levying "special corporate taxes and, as in the past, have them treated under Federal tax law as an expense without any offset by the Federal Government."[41]

Frost had not been as successful at shifting the federal Liberals away from their commitment to some form of direct tax sharing as he might have hoped. Nevertheless, his relationship with the prime minister and his insistence on offering alternatives had borne some fruit: the new fiscal system incorporated both an equalization component, which Frost had championed, plus a recognition, beyond that given in previous agreements, that the provinces had a right to a share of the direct tax field. The federal government had certainly not gone as far as Frost or his colleagues wanted, but there had still been a shift towards accepting the provincial version of the national interest. Similar shifts were also apparent in the other fields that dominated the intergovernmental agenda in the 1950s.

Initiative and Responsibility in the Social Policy Field

While the fiscal relationship was being debated, untangled, and rearranged, provincial and federal politicians and their staffs were also concerned with other areas of shared interest. In the case of both unemployment assistance and health insurance, there was more at stake than simply constitutional jurisdiction. Ontario's Conservative government questioned at a rather fundamental level how far the state should go in providing social services to its population. This question of government responsibility muddled the issue of jurisdictional responsibility even more than usual. The alternative proposals that were crafted in the halls of Queen's Park clearly not only demonstrated a different way of dividing power between Ottawa and the provinces, but also they illustrated a different understanding of the role of the state.

In the area of social policy, no single issue had been hanging over the collective heads of the first ministers longer than the extension of unemployment insurance to those called the "unemployed employables." The Green Book proposals, debated during the reconstruction conference, contained the unfortunate federal acceptance of responsibility for assistance to employable people; Ontario, Quebec, and the Maritime Provinces had been doggedly refusing to assist this group of people ever since, instead holding Ottawa to the promise of the Green Book. The federal government had been equally insistent that, constitutionally, the jurisdiction remained with the provinces. When unemployment reached epic heights in British Columbia in 1954, and Premier Bennett was forced to ask for federal assistance in providing relief for those unemployed employables, the federal government was handed something of a solution to its quandary. This was the "first offer from a province that implies a clear acceptance of their responsibility" in the field, allowing the federal bureaucrats the chance to devise some sort of formula to share in the costs, without actually accepting responsibility.[42]

Although federal officials had anticipated that unemployment figures for the winter of 1955 would be low enough to buy them some time in coming up with a solution, the reality was a 7 per cent unemployment rate, higher than at any point since the end of the Second World War.[43] By spring, with pressure mounting from governments as well as from the Canadian Welfare Council, it was clear that the topic of unemployment insurance would have to be discussed at the preliminary meeting of the federal-provincial conference held later in the month.[44] This meeting provided the federal government with the opportunity to rather informally float a shared-cost scheme that had hurriedly and somewhat reluctantly been devised a couple of weeks before the start of the meeting. Based on the assumption that the normal percentage of people chronically unemployed was about 1 per cent of the population of any given province, Ottawa offered to contribute to the cost of assistance if this category of unemployed people rose above that normal level. The contributions would be offered on a sliding scale ranging from 30 to 50 per cent of the total cost of assistance.[45] It was a complicated proposal, it had been explained verbally rather than offered in writing, and it was parsimonious. The objections were quick to come, beginning with the point that this was "very different from the federal unemployment assistance proposals put forward in 1945" and "might not be adequate."[46]

Ontario had several complaints about the federal proposal. There no longer seemed to be any merit in pressing the case that the federal government was solely responsible for assisting the unemployed, regardless of their employability. However, given the relatively low unemployment rate in Ontario compared with other provinces, there were few formulations that would be particularly beneficial. Unless Ottawa agreed to take an absolute proportion of the responsibility for the unemployed – preferably 100 per cent, but barring that, 40 per cent was the figure discussed – the "cost to the Province and municipalities, which has averaged about $5 million a year, would be at least doubled, and probably far more than doubled."[47] The prime minister consistently maintained, however, that Ottawa was prepared to offer assistance "only above a certain level."[48]

There was a good deal of evidence that Ontario politicians were philosophically opposed to unemployment assistance as anything other than an emergency measure to address short-term problems. The Ontario program, unveiled at the April federal-provincial conference and hammered home in speeches leading up to the provincial election of 9 June 1955, dealt with unemployment as something other than simply a social policy problem. The real issue was maintaining "high productive employment";[49] unemployment assistance was only necessary when other measures failed. Discussions between officials of the various provincial and federal governments made it clear that "Ontario's system of poor relief and assistance has been more restricted than that in other provinces."[50] But despite the hesitancy about extending assistance coverage, if the federal government was going to contribute to the costs, then Ontario wanted some of the money. Frost used his standard line about the challenges facing Ontario. In an environment of rapid growth, expenditures for essential services "will surpass anything that has gone on before." And yet, Frost complained, "the proposed federal formula" forced the province "to take on a new burden, namely direct relief for the able-bodied workers ... It is a lamentable retreat from the position the Federal Government took ... in 1941."[51] If an agreement such as that proposed by the federal government had to be adopted, Frost maintained that the sliding scale of federal contribution was "unrealistic," and he argued instead for an equal sharing of costs between the two levels of government.[52]

The June negotiations resulted in some concessions on the part of the federal government. Ottawa offered to contribute half the cost of assistance to unemployed employables once that group represented more than 0.45 per cent of the provincial population.[53] St. Laurent argued that assuming the cost of anything more would "constitute a major departure from constitutional law and practice in this country."[54] As the federal government was prepared to go no further, the proposal was then "considered by the various provincial governments" with an eye to entering into individual agreements with Ottawa for sharing the costs of unemployment assistance.[55] Ontario could not be wooed in this half-hearted manner. Having completely back-pedalled on its earlier promise of assuming complete responsibility, Ottawa was now offering only a "limited" solution by not considering ways in which work could be provided for the unemployed. Ontario officials considered this "a most important point" highlighting the philosophical differences between the positions of the two governments.[56] Privately, however, Ontario official George Gathercole offered another explanation for Ontario's decision to reject the federal offer: forecasting "a much easier winter as far as unemployment is concerned than the last two have been," Ontario politicians opted to "preserve their freedom of action and ride the winter through." If unemployment rates rose higher than expected, the federal-provincial agreement could always be entered into late, at no cost to the provincial treasury.[57] Quebec, Alberta, and Nova Scotia also elected to remain outside the agreement offered by Ottawa, although presumably for different reasons.

Unemployment had been on the intergovernmental docket for years, but other social services were moving to the forefront of public interest. Governments were increasingly looked to for security against the exigencies of age, ill-health, and misfortune. In Ontario, sentiment had been building for years in favour of some kind of health insurance program, and the government seemed to be doing nothing to stop it. The provincial health minister had already claimed that Canada would have national health insurance by 1960, and Premier Frost had addressed British audiences about the possible ways of introducing comprehensive health care coverage in Canada.[58] Still, in preparing for the agenda-setting meeting at the end of April 1955, the federal government seemed oblivious to the events taking place in the provinces and to the possibility of including health insurance in the discussions.[59]

Instead, it was Frost who raised the topic in his rather extensive introductory remarks.[60] He was supported by his colleagues in British Columbia, Saskatchewan, and Manitoba, who agreed that since "the question of health insurance had been before the Canadian public for the last 35 years" the time had come to discuss it formally.[61] St. Laurent was visibly uncomfortable with Frost's efforts at manipulating the agenda,[62] but Ontario had snatched the initiative. Throughout the summer of 1955, both levels of government worked to lay the groundwork for the full federal-provincial conference in October. The assembled officials variously discussed the components of a full health insurance scheme, the types of additional services that might be added, and the existing programs of health grants offered by the federal government since 1948. Neither the federal nor the provincial representatives dealt in specifics, although Gathercole did make it clear that from Ontario's perspective, provinces "should not be bound by the standardizations of an overall plan."[63] While this did not cause any debate at the time, St. Laurent later indicated that "as long as the Federal Government gives health grants to the provinces, it is its responsibility to exercise some control and to make sure that the money is spent for useful purposes."[64]

But the broad statements Ontario officials made at formal meetings with their counterparts belied the work that was being conducted by health consultant Malcolm Taylor, and the information that was being conveyed through less formal avenues. Taylor had, the previous year, prepared a report for the Ontario government that outlined and evaluated six different ways of providing health coverage, ranging from full government administration to various forms of government subsidy. In the summer of 1955, he was charged with preparing a proposal to submit to the full conference in the fall. He noted that the "general strategy that emerged to guide Ontario's planning was (1) the most desirable plan for Ontario, modified by (2) the kind of program that would be acceptable to Ottawa, which would in turn by influenced by (3) the program or programs acceptable to the majority of the provinces."[65] To this end, Taylor's proposals were careful to combine the degree of flexibility that Gathercole had already stated was a necessity.

Taylor's work was far enough along by midsummer that Gathercole was able to talk knowledgably and at length with federal Deputy Minister of Welfare George Davidson about the various ways governments could go about achieving a national health insurance plan. Noting first "the importance of extending full radiological and laboratory services to cover the needs of the entire province," Gathercole went on to discuss at least four possible ways in which hospital insurance could be introduced. This was the area of health insurance on which the Ontario government was focusing its deliberations, clarifying for Davidson "that whenever Frost talks about health insurance he is thinking about hospital insurance and little else but that."[66] Still, the result of such single-minded focus seems to have been a comprehensive series of proposals for establishing a national system of hospital insurance. Ontario's work became the basis for discussions at the federal level, where there was no objection to the "suggestion that diagnostic services be undertaken as a first step." Instead, federal officials discussed how the federal contribution should be made, and how much it should cover.[67]

The federal and Ontario governments were working together closely. But the close relationship between the two first ministers, characterized by frequent telephone communication, did not mean that St. Laurent always knew what Frost had up his sleeve.[68] The most the federal representatives could glean was that "the situation regarding health insurance is as it was in early July," which meant that western provinces would likely participate in a national scheme, the Maritimes did not want health insurance but would probably accept it, Quebec was the big unknown, and "Ontario will be coming up with proposals, the details of which are not at all clear at this time."[69] All the intelligence indicated that Frost "has something in mind" in terms of health insurance, but it was thus far "something which Ottawa has been unable to find out."[70] Meanwhile, a reluctant St. Laurent was pressed by Health Minister Paul Martin to forge ahead, and cautioned by Finance Minister Walter Harris to avoid "committing the federal government to action regarding it."[71] As an issue that clearly would not go away, it was better for Ottawa to feign interest than to ignore health insurance entirely.

After at least one more telephone call from the prime minister, Frost finally relinquished an outline of what he intended to say about health

insurance at the intergovernmental conference. Noting that his government had been "engaged in an intensive study of this problem" for
months, Frost offered St. Laurent a confidential glimpse of Ontario's
study document. Should an evolutionary, national plan that had been
subjected to careful technical scrutiny be adopted, Frost intimated that
Ontario would be prepared to participate in it.[72] Before reciprocating by
sending Frost the comments he expected to make at the conference, St.
Laurent, his advisers, and Ministers Martin and Harris, worked on refin-
ing the federal statement. St. Laurent urged watering it down while the
team from National Health and Welfare pressed for a concrete proposal.
Clearly, the prime minister did not take the drafting and redrafting as
seriously as the others: when asked if "he wanted it shortened, the PM
laughed and said, 'No – it's only *verbiage* anyway, and the more of it the
better.'"[73]

Whether they were the remarks of a seasoned participant in federal-provincial conferences, a cynical elder statesman, or merely a quip
designed to lighten the mood of a frenzied bureaucracy, St. Laurent's
comments were prescient: the assembled first ministers did little more
than talk, and posture, and agree to further study and further thought.
The formal unveiling of the Frost proposal, which offered five different insurance schemes of increasing comprehensiveness, may well have
had "an almost electrifying effect on the conference,"[74] but it moved the
group only infinitesimally closer to achieving any kind of national health
insurance plan. Ottawa did not make a hospital insurance offer until
January 1956, and even then did so reluctantly and left the program dependent on six provinces signing on, which meant that there was a great
deal still to be negotiated with the provinces.[75] Similarly, the announcement of a new federal offer in regards to the tax rental agreements was
merely left on the table, waiting for the due consideration of provincial
officials that it would receive after the conference had adjourned. Those
hoping for more than verbiage would have been sorely disappointed by
the federal-provincial conference of 1955.

Old social policies, like unemployment assistance, and new ones, like
health insurance, played more of a role in the discussions leading up to
the 1955 meeting, and in the debates at the conference itself, than many
of the participants would have anticipated at the beginning of the year.
In the latter, Frost was able take the initiative, really shaping the national
policy conversation in a way that suited Ontario. The health insurance
program itself was far from a reality, but the province had played a leading role in getting it on the agenda and dictating the way other governments began considering the issue. On unemployment assistance, on the

other hand, Ontario preferred to press for federal control, an indication of the provincial wariness surrounding aid to the unemployed, in general, within the context of clear jurisdictional divisions.

Diefenbaker and the Possibility of Intergovernmental Accord

By 1956, the bonhomie that had characterized the relationship between Frost and St. Laurent seemed to have hit a wall. The federal government's refusal to budge on tax sharing was just one indication of a growing overconfidence with the responsibility of governing. Conservative organizer Harry Robbins mused that it was "not unlikely that the doctrine of provincial rights will have to again become a matter of paramount importance."[76] While that was not Frost's style, the increasing evidence that "fatigue and age had pretty well extinguished [St. Laurent's] reform zeal,"[77] made Frost impatient. He still had things to accomplish, not least of all a better intergovernmental deal for Ontario. With the new federal-provincial tax agreements destined to provide additional federal money in the form of equalization payments to every province except Ontario, and social programs looking like they would be equally spartan with Ontario, Frost began to look not just at alternative federal arrangements, but for the first time in more than a decade, at the possibility of an alternative federal government.

The apex of Liberal arrogance was reached during the pipeline debate of mid-May. Introducing contentious legislation that would provide financial assistance to the American builders of the trans-Canada gas pipeline, Minister of Trade and Commerce C.D. Howe immediately invoked closure, a rare device designed to severely curtail legislative debate. In the midst of the parliamentary crisis over the legitimacy of closure, Conservative MP Donald Fleming was expelled from the House of Commons, the Speaker reversed rulings and inexplicably consulted with government ministers about how to proceed, and the facade began to crumble from the Liberal fortress. According to one observer, "the government's image of competence and wise benevolence had evaporated, revealing, instead, a galling arrogance overlaid with a surprising maladroitness."[78]

Public sentiment began to turn against the Liberals, a response that could not but help the Conservatives' fortunes in Ottawa. Drew's stewardship of the party had not exactly lived up to either his or the party's expectations: he was too patrician, and too obviously central Canadian, to ever appeal to the voters in the way that was necessary. Even Frost had found it important to distance himself, and the Ontario Conservative party, from his former boss. Although his performance in the House during the pipeline debate was "the most exemplary of his career,"[79] Drew's days as leader of the Conservative party were numbered. Ill-health and doctors' orders, no doubt exacerbated by his election failures, led him to resign from the Conservative leadership in September 1956. While it was clearly a difficult decision for Drew and his family to make,[80] the opportunities it presented for the party in general, and leadership hopefuls specifically, as well as for the future of federal-provincial relations, were enormous.

The convention held in mid-December 1956 to replace George Drew had an important effect on Ontario's position on fiscal relations. Despite some concerns from his own advisers that he was simply "trying to enhance his own populist image," Frost quietly threw his support behind leadership candidate John Diefenbaker, widely expected to win the position.[81] He was, quite clearly, "the man that can win the next election," according to Frost.[82] Years later, Frost admitted to one of his cabinet colleagues that he and party president Alex Mackenzie and powerful *Globe and Mail* editor Oakley Dalgleish met with Diefenbaker in Toronto and committed the even more powerful Ontario Conservative machine to Diefenbaker's election efforts. From that point on, "his election as leader in December 1956 became assured."[83] Even Diefenbaker agreed, recalling that "no one did more than [Frost] did" to secure his first ballot victory at the Conservative leadership convention in December. Frost was "an amazing politician" and one whose support could not go unthanked.[84] Tax room might be the ideal place for gratitude: when provincial Treasurer Dana Porter introduced a new corporate tax of 11 per cent, more than the rate that the federal government would cover with its tax-sharing formula, but necessary given the high cost of government in Ontario, Diefenbaker responded.[85] He demanded a rethinking of the fiscal arrangements "now that the Government of Ontario has come out so strongly for Provincial taxation rights."[86]

When Parliament adjourned and the Liberal government called an election for 10 June 1957, it was with every expectation that twenty-two years of sound management of the economy would earn the Liberals another victory. From the outset, however, there were signs that things might turn out differently. For example, arcane intergovernmental tax arrangements became stump issues. Frost had been so effective at driving home his twin messages – more tax room for the wealthier provinces, equalization grants for the poorer provinces – that fiscal concerns became identified as a key battlefield in the federal election. Introducing Diefenbaker at a rally in Toronto, Frost reiterated that "it is not a matter of the Federal Government giving Ontario or the Provinces anything. That is the patronizing attitude in Ottawa. All that we ask is a reasonable part of our own."[87] This speech caught the attention of premiers in the Maritimes, who asked Frost "to appear at public meetings in Fredericton and Halifax with the respective premiers to discuss the subject of a fair division of the national tax dollar."[88] The result was a strange federal election campaign, according to Grant Dexter at least, who argued that in making "the tax agreements the vital issue in the campaign" the real Conservative leader was Frost. All appearances suggested that "Mr. Frost is in control of Federal Conservative policy."[89] He certainly played an extraordinary role in the national election campaign, and elevated tax policy to a staggering level of public interest. The price Diefenbaker paid for Frost's instrumental support in the 1957 election, at least according to one insider, was "a promise to revise the tax-sharing agreement" so that Ontario would come closer to receiving the $118 million that had been demanded in the provincial budget.[90] Never had tax arrangements played such an important role in the outcome of a national election.

Although it came as a surprise to the Liberal establishment, jaded after twenty-two years in office, Diefenbaker scored a clear, if minority, victory in the election of 1957, largely due to the impressive support he received not only from Leslie Frost, but also from his provincial machine. With a Conservative heading governments in both Ottawa and Toronto, Diefenbaker's election marked the beginning of an abnormal period in postwar intergovernmental relations, but also one in which expectations for agreement ran particularly high.[91] Diefenbaker would have to move quickly to address the tax concerns if he expected Frost's goodwill to last. Early in his mandate, therefore, Diefenbaker reopened the 1957–1962 tax rental agreements, calling a conference of first ministers for November "to review the present pattern of tax sharing arrangements."[92] Frost was instrumental in the decision to call the meeting, which opened with "an atmosphere more hopeful than that which has prevailed at any previous Dominion-Provincial conference."[93] This was, perhaps, premature. The conference turned into yet another fact-finding exercise, with Frost getting increasingly weary of the absence of any decisions on issues of federal-provincial concern.[94] There was only one tangible result of the conference in the fiscal area – an agreement to supplement the tax yields of the Atlantic Provinces by providing an adjustment grant. In addition, Diefenbaker announced that his government would lift the six-province requirement for federal participation in a shared hospital insurance plan, and immediately begin contributing to half the costs of direct relief for the employable unemployed. Both were welcome changes, and the "elimination of the objectionable .45 formula" was "described as a personal triumph for Premier Frost of Ontario"[95] but neither had been the purpose for calling the conference. Fiscal relations remained unsatisfactorily handled.

As other provincial premiers wrote letters of complaint to Diefenbaker, criticizing him for ignoring the "most basic matters" concerning the "broader questions of the general financial arrangements,"[96] Frost held his tongue. Certainly Gathercole, and probably Frost as well, agreed "that in some respects it might have been preferable to deal with the general tax-sharing arrangements before giving consideration to the special needs of the Atlantic Provinces," but both knew better than to say that in public.[97] In fact, at a conference characterized by a relative absence of support for the national interest, the fact that Ontario's premier had publicly supported adjustment grants earned him the position of the only "giver" present at the conference.[98] Instead, Frost spoke confidentially with the prime minister a few weeks after the conclusion of the conference, following that up with a letter outlining his position on the need to increase the existing 10–9–50 formula for provincial sharing of personal, corporate, and succession duties to a more generous 15–15–50 share.[99] Early in the new year, he sent Gathercole for a face-to-face meeting with Finance Minister Donald Fleming in Ottawa.[100] According to the federal finance minister, Gathercole's mission was designed to strong-arm Ottawa into increasing the formula. Fleming recalled that he was told that if Ontario's concerns were not met with some tangible action, Frost "would find it difficult to assist in a general election campaign as he had in 1957."[101] The fact that the following week Diefenbaker wrote to all provincial premiers advising them that "as an interim measure" he was immediately increasing the provincial share of income tax room from 10 to 13 per cent suggested that the efforts of the Ontario officials had been successful.[102]

But at what cost was Ontario's success in forcing the federal government to offer more generous terms in the tax-sharing arrangements? The political environment was changing rapidly, and Diefenbaker's debt to the Ontario political machine would soon be forgotten, if not erased. Early in January, the federal Liberals met in convention to select a new leader to replace the retiring, and defeated, Louis St. Laurent. Despite a rather shocking lack of preparation on the part of either of the two front-running candidates, Paul Martin and Lester Pearson, the latter's victory on the first ballot gave renewed confidence to the opposition Liberals. His acceptance speech assertively promised that the government would fall, "and soon."[103] The bravado of Pearson's convention performance undoubtedly led to his unwise acceptance of advice that saw him demand the resignation of the government – in favour of a Liberal government under his leadership – in one of his first performances in the House of Commons. Diefenbaker took full advantage of the arrogant misstep, offering a reply that was "so destructive to the Liberal Party that many said it virtually decided the outcome of the next election."[104] Although not offering to resign, Diefenbaker did shortly thereafter ask for a parliamentary adjournment, and was soon on the hustings again.

Diefenbaker had become more assured during his few months in office, and this election unfolded differently than had the one in 1957. No longer reliant on Ontario's "big blue machine," the Conservatives instead operated under the able stewardship of Allister Grosart's election management with a "pervasive feeling of confidence."[105] In the eyes of some, however, Diefenbaker seemed both unaware of the significance of the assistance that had led to his first electoral victory, and ungrateful to those in Ontario who had offered it.[106] His attitude had no discernible effect on the election outcome, however. The Conservative victory was understood as inevitable, to a certain extent – a rejection of the Liberals as they had become "under the old men" and a "healthy inclination" to give Diefenbaker a real chance to govern.[107] Unlike the results of 1957, this time around did not seem like a miracle orchestrated by the powers in Toronto. With the first Conservative majority in Quebec since 1887, and at 208 of the 265 seats the largest majority in Canadian history, Diefenbaker's Conservatives were poised to make their own mark on the political landscape, on their own terms.

Observers and participants alike certainly had reason to believe that federal-provincial fiscal arrangements would appear near the top of the priorities of Diefenbaker's new majority government. Not only were the provinces sharing taxes with the federal government using a formula that had already been described as an "interim" measure, but Diefenbaker himself had promised on the campaign trail an early resumption of the dominion-provincial conference and pledged his support for a formal equalization program.[108] Despite the expectations, however, the Conservative government lost little time in slipping into a kind of chaotic inactivity behind the "congenital caution, disorganization, and shallow intellectual focus"[109] of its leader. The initial optimism of Ontario's Tories at the prospect of dealing with a like-minded government in Ottawa quickly disappeared. Provincial alliances began to appear as Diefenbaker ignored or confused the intergovernmental issues.[110] By the end of 1958, with no sign of an interprovincial first ministers' conference being called, Tommy Douglas appealed to Frost. "Both Premier Roblin and I feel that there would be a good deal of merit in having the provinces meet for a day prior to a Federal-Provincial conference," he wrote. The pre-meeting would provide the opportunity to agree on a strategy before facing the federal politicians and officials. Apparently, both Douglas and Roblin thought that Frost was "the logical person to call such a meeting." Moreover, Douglas suggested that "if [the meeting] were confined strictly to the tax-sharing arrangements we could get all the provinces to agree on the 15-15-50 formula."[111] Without any sign of activity in Ottawa, and indeed merely the "temporary" continuation of the 10 to 13 per cent increase in the provincial share of income taxes,[112] a united front from the provinces seemed the only way Frost's desired formula could be achieved.

Diefenbaker clearly intended to rest on the strength of his huge parliamentary majority, and consistently ignored provincial entreaties to reconvene the meeting of first ministers. But Frost could not be pushed aside quite so easily. In correspondence, he noted his displeasure with the "terminal recalculation" of Ontario's portion of the tax rentals.[113] He made the relationship with the federal government a campaign issue in his own bid for re-election in the spring of 1959, making repeated allusions to a forthcoming conference which was "about to make a survey of Canada's tax structure."[114] Diefenbaker was not about to be embarrassed by Frost's election rhetoric, even after the Ontario Conservatives swept to what seemed to some another inevitable victory.

With it obviously no longer possible to push Diefenbaker into calling a conference he was not keen to call, Frost hoped that private discussions with the prime minister might yield the desired results. The two had shared a friendly relationship in the past years, although Frost was becoming increasingly irritated with the prime minister's unwillingness to consult on issues affecting Ontario.[115] Still, in a one-on-one meeting, the cracks in the relationship might be healed. The Ontario Treasury Department advised the premier to focus on fiscal relations in his discussion with Diefenbaker in the summer of 1959. The elusive 15–15–50 tax-sharing formula had yet to be achieved, the 1952–1957 tax rental agreements had been modified in a questionable manner that needed correction, and the whole issue of equalization and how exactly it would be calculated needed to be addressed. Premier Frost was sent on his way to Ottawa with a long list of complex issues he needed to discuss with the prime minister; past experience would presumably have suggested the unlikeliness of reaching a solution on much.[116] The prime minister was preoccupied with Bank of Canada Governor James Coyne, who was "one of the enemy within," determined to undermine the Conservative government with his tight-money policies.[117] In the summer of 1959, however, the developing crisis served only to derail Frost from his planned discussions of the tax rental system with the prime minister.

The fiscal relationship had also topped the agenda for the summer and fall meetings of finance ministers, but these discussions had only confirmed a continuation of the temporary three-point increase in income tax rentals, and the federal government's desire to open up discussions on a new five-year agreement sometime in mid-1960.[118] After an initial period of activity in intergovernmental relations following Diefenbaker's 1957 victory, Ottawa's attention to the issues waned dramatically. Intent on pursuing an agenda of their own making, the federal Conservatives were uninterested in attending to the recurring and more usual demands of federal-provincial relations. Opting to call provincial leaders together for frantic meetings on particular issues without having first laid the groundwork for the relationship led to unsatisfactory results. Ontario leaders were at a loss in dealing with this new chaos that characterized official Ottawa, and by the 1960s it was becoming apparent that dealing with the Liberals had been considerably more agreeable.

The meeting of first ministers held in late July 1960 was a good indication of the Diefenbaker style of management once he had secured a parliamentary majority. The gathering was the first of substance since the 1958 election, despite the issue of tax rentals and equalization having been left largely unresolved in the fall of 1957. Premiers from all the provinces had been pressing Diefenbaker for a resumption of discussions for years, although Frost's patience had perhaps worn most thin. Nearing the end of his own time in office, disgruntled with the lack of attention Ontario had been receiving under Diefenbaker, Frost entered the meetings in no mood for conciliation. On the opening day, Frost used "unexpectedly blunt language"[119] to renew his calls for provincial control of 50 per cent of the direct tax fields. His opening speech served as a strong reminder that Ontario was far from pleased with the current fiscal situation. In the in camera session the following day, Frost continued to press the case for a full recognition of Ontario's constitutional rights with an equal sharing of direct tax revenue with the federal government – a situation, he admitted, that "couldn't be done in one year or even five years."[120] After the other premiers made their cases for more tax room or more equalization dollars or both, Finance Minister Donald Fleming claimed that the provincial demands would cost the federal treasury $2 billion, a figure Frost and others questioned.[121] The federal government clearly was not entertaining provincial proposals, a shift that undermined the Frost approach.

Instead, it became clear that Diefenbaker was intent on charting new territory in the intergovernmental relationship. One long-standing goal, for example, was the achievement of a Bill of Rights, so the prime minister reopened constitutional negotiations. These proceeded awkwardly: the provincial attorneys general rejected Justice Minister Davie Fulton's suggestion that they begin by patriating the constitution and proceed to discuss an amending formula.[122] After Fulton agreed to the shift in strategy, he had trouble keeping his cabinet colleagues on side, especially with relentless pressure from Ontario's Kelso Roberts to clarify the amending clause.[123] No one made any headway, and the constitution remained unamended and unpatriated.

Despite the slow start, Diefenbaker was also eager to stamp his mark on the fiscal relationship. Unlike Fulton, however, he was more successful in setting the agenda. At the October 1960 meeting with premiers to continue discussions on the 1962–1967 tax rental agreements, Diefenbaker made it clear that he wanted to introduce a completely new way of sharing taxes between the two levels of government. He proposed two policies. First, Ottawa would vacate income, succession, and corporate taxes to the extent of the existing 14–9–50 per cent formula. Second, in recognition "that handing these rental fields back to the Provinces will not solve the whole problem of Provincial finance," he proposed a flat $220 million a year equalization payout to the poorer provinces.[124]

Diefenbaker's position was a surprising one to observers – and participants – in several different quarters. Federal bureaucrats, the finance ministers, and provincial representatives had all been under the impression that the current scheme would continue alongside some form of equalization. All negotiations had been undertaken with this in mind. After meetings with provincial finance officials, for example, federal bureaucrats Ken Taylor and Robert Bryce understood that the provinces wanted a greater portion of the tax room, and they were willing to consider a different model for determining equalization payments, while being generally committed to the concept itself. Ontario officials were particularly disenchanted with an equalization formula that brought eve-

ryone up to the taxing level of the two wealthiest provinces. In later conversations between George Gathercole and Ken Taylor, the latter made
clear that he understood "the injustices of the present [equalization]
situation" and promised to "intensify" his efforts to "evolve a solution."[125]
But Taylor apparently had little luck in transmitting the views of the provincial civil servants and of his own staff up the lines of communication to the Prime Minister's Office. Finance Minister Donald Fleming,
to whom Taylor reported, had had increasingly strained relations with
Diefenbaker over intergovernmental relations and other monetary matters. Taylor indicated that the "chasm between the minister of finance
and the prime minister is very costly to the public interest" and necessitated "strenuous efforts" on the part of his office to work out a policy to
match Diefenbaker's surprise retreat from the tax rental system.[126]

Politics played a huge role in determining the formulae: Diefenbaker
found it inconceivable for New Brunswick, with its new Liberal government, to get more from any new equalization system than the ever-loyal
Nova Scotia. Where that left Ontario in the Ottawa considerations was
difficult to determine, but it was an open secret that Frost had "come to
have a contempt and bitter hostility to Diefenbaker."[127] Frost's wrath was
not so much directed at the proposed system of vacating tax room for
the provinces, or equalizing to a national average rather than to the level
of the wealthiest two provinces, as it was at the content of the proposals.
To perpetuate the old 14–9–50 rates of provincial participation clearly
indicated that all of Front's clamouring for a true sharing of the tax fields
had fallen on deaf ears. The federal-provincial conference of February
1961, apart from addressing some technical matters, merely formalized
Diefenbaker's earlier offer.[128] Frost had had enough of Diefenbaker's
empty promises, and very close to enough of politics in general.

Rather than looking to renegotiate the federal-provincial relationship through bi- or multi-lateral discussions or meetings, the Ontario
government set off on its own. Pensions, a field in which Diefenbaker's
government had long considered action, moved to the top of Ontario's
agenda.[129] Spurred on by growing public interests in "the adequacy of
retirement incomes," the committee worked from the proposition that
"government has a positive role to play in encouraging appropriate initiative both on the part of the individual and institutions."[130] The conclusions of the committee were likely to be friendly to the insurance
community that the Ontario Conservatives had cultivated so carefully,
but they were also sure to establish a role for the provincial government
in the protection against the exigencies of old age. Ottawa would no
longer be the only public player in the field.

In a similar move away from negotiating with Ottawa, premiers resurrected a seventy-five-year-old tradition and met for a provinces-only tête-à-tête in Quebec City in the fall of 1960. Although in public the premiers were quick to stress that "in no sense could a Premiers' Conference substitute in whole or in part for a Federal-Provincial Conference,"[131] in private it was clear that more could be gained from purely provincial discussions than "a discussion of virtual platitudes." Leslie Frost's "charming and forceful leadership"[132] was clearly instrumental in guiding the premiers towards agreeing that such meetings were "a logical step in the collaboration required ... not only between levels of government but within the respective levels themselves."[133] The premiers' conference underlined the collective provincial sense that there was a need for a coordinated strategy, a provincialist position from which to confront the Diefenbaker government. That even Diefenbaker's allies in Ontario felt this way said volumes about the state of the intergovernmental relationship.

Just how the provincial position on the constitution, or tax sharing, or the increasingly important social policies was to be expressed was left to younger men than Frost. Premier of Ontario for twelve years, Frost had had enough. His easy relationship with Liberal Louis St. Laurent had allowed him an authority in the intergovernmental field that Ontario had not wielded since the nineteenth century and had afforded him the opportunity to articulate a "national" interest that was increasingly the same as the provincial interest. Social policies like health insurance emerged on the agenda because Frost introduced them, and the conversation about how they should be delivered began on Ontario's terms. The contours of the hospital insurance program did not follow Ontario's proposals particularly closely, but there was still much to discuss in the health care field; there was still an opportunity for the province to determine the shape of the program. On the bigger questions that Ontario was increasingly focusing on, there were other successes: taxes were shared more equitably, if not equally, and every conceivable effort had been made, through the office of the Ontario government, to bring Quebec into the fiscal family. Clearly, the provinces, with Ontario in the lead, were playing a bigger – if not yet determinative – role in the process of sharing tax revenue. On the constitutional debate, it was also to Ontario that the others, in both federal and provincial capitals, looked. But Frost's successes during the St. Laurent period hinted at a greater role for Ontario once a Conservative government was established in Ottawa, and when Diefenbaker failed to play the game the way Frost had come to expect, the disillusionment was palpable. Intergovernmental relations entered a period of drift, rather than the expected period of progress. Perhaps another premier would have more luck than Leslie Frost with the Conservatives in Ottawa.

Chapter Five

"A Lasting Effect on Confederation Itself": Robarts and the Realignment of Intergovernmental Relations, 1961–1964

Leslie Frost's decision to bow out of provincial politics in the summer of 1961 should not have come as a surprise to anyone. He had hinted at it for months, debating only the timing of his announcement. This he ultimately opted to make on the eve of the first national convention of the New Democratic party, skilfully taking the front page of the next day's newspapers away from his old colleague around the conference table, Saskatchewan Premier Tommy Douglas, who had just been elected as the NDP's first leader. Whether Ontario's Progressive Conservative party would be able to find as wily a political tactician as "old man Ontario" remained to be seen, but soon half a dozen of his cabinet ministers had offered themselves up as possible replacements. By all accounts, the leadership campaign was a close one, with front-runners Kelso Roberts, Robert Macaulay, John Robarts, and James Allan all attracting considerable constituency support.

These were interesting times for intergovernmental affairs. Frost's approach had served Ontario well for over a decade, but it was clear that more had been expected from the Diefenbaker government than had been forthcoming. The most recent tax-sharing arrangements, for example, still under discussion as Frost prepared to take his leave, were a "marked improvement" from the tax rentals but were still "not all that might be expected."[1] The same could be said of virtually all aspects of intergovernmental cooperation in the Diefenbaker years. Frost's sense of disappointment had implications for his approach to federal-provincial matters; another premier, unburdened by disillusionment over expectations not met, would be freer to pursue different strategies when dealing with the federal government.

There was much work to be done. Although the 1962–1967 tax-sharing arrangements were still being discussed, most of the principles had been agreed on. The flaws that remained in the way in which tax power was divided would have to be corrected in the next round. The constitutional conference, while still mired in debate over an amending formula was, nevertheless, still meeting. Furthermore, on the purely provincial scene – at least for the short term – the Ontario committee on portable pensions was coming close to tabling a report. Moving into the field of retirement pensions would surely mean a confrontation with Ottawa, as both the Diefenbaker government and the Liberal Opposition were conducting inquiries into the matter on their own. Finally, health insurance, the subject of the recently appointed royal commission headed by Justice Emmett Hall, would also undoubtedly bring the two levels of government into negotiations. With a new man at the helm in Ontario, there was hope that the strategy of offering alternative national policies might finally show some rewards; Frost had made some progress in massaging the national interest, but there was still a long way to go. In the short term, however, that progress was halted, thanks to the emergence, in the early 1960s, of another province as a linchpin in the federation and a dictator of national policy direction. The Quebec that emerged from the shadow of Maurice Duplessis and his isolationist Union Nationale government in 1960 was vibrant, energetic, and poised to make an indelible mark on intergovernmental relations. Ontario's successes in its relations with Ottawa disappeared as the province was essentially sidelined in discussions, but what emerged was an even greater resolve to play a key role in guiding the federal-provincial relationship.

The Roberts-Diefenbaker Dance

When Frost had replaced George Drew in 1949, the new premier of Ontario was already an experienced player in intergovernmental relations as a result of his work as provincial finance minister. Frost had guided his premier through the minefield of negotiations with Ottawa, and by the time he assumed the top provincial job, he already had a well-defined idea of how best to approach the relationship with his Ottawa counterparts. Frost was well aware of the need for forging provincial alliances and for offering viable alternatives to the federal economic or constitutional initiatives. He was able to put these ideas virtually immediately into action. None of the men vying to replace Frost had the same kind of intergovernmental experience. Whoever won would bring a fresh perspective to the table.

The leadership convention, held at Varsity Arena in Toronto, opened with a "rousing tribute" to Frost.[2] It could hardly have been otherwise after twelve years of prosperity and sound government. On the next day Diefenbaker addressed the delegates. He used the opportunity to attack the federal Liberals – including the "apostles of gloom and doom" like Paul Martin and Jack Pickersgill, who were attracting "a queer assortment of political bedfellows" as the party prepared itself for the next election.[3] Diefenbaker knew that Ontario would be key if he had any hope of winning again, although rumours suggested that so deep was the animosity between him and Frost that the latter would do nothing to assist in the next federal election.[4] Regardless, Diefenbaker wanted to use the Ontario leadership convention as an opportunity to shore up his political reserves.

Then the candidates for leader addressed the delegates, each delivering "much the same speech he had in his campaign." Education minister John Robarts even went so far as to suggest it would be "presumptuous" to talk about a policy platform before giving delegates the opportunity to express their views on the various candidates.[5] The vote on the first ballot, at least between the front-running four, was very close: Roberts, 352; Robarts, 345; Macaulay, 339; Allan, 332. To whom Leslie Frost gave his vote remained a secret, but there were some who believed that he favoured his education minister, and had quietly been "lining up support behind the scenes."[6] It took five ballots, with Robarts moving into the top spot on ballot number three, to secure an outcome.[7] The handsome forty-four-year-old, who ran for the leadership "not exactly as a lark but not quite with much forethought either," was poised to take over Canada's largest, wealthiest province. And with his "legendary charm,"[8] combined with what were clearly superior political instincts, he was going to take Ontario into its second century.

The federal government that Robarts faced was one increasingly seen to have lost its focus. Diefenbaker still commanded the largest majority to date, but he saw conspiracies at every turn. Finance Minister Donald Fleming, with whom Ontario politicians had close dealings on tax sharing and other issues, had already felt the sting of Diefenbaker's dissatisfaction. The prime minister's uncertainty on financial matters had cost the government a great deal in terms of both money and trust; intent on heavy spending despite warnings from the Bank of Canada and from Fleming himself, the Diefenbaker government careened towards crisis. Fleming took responsibility within cabinet and would pay the price for it after the 1962 election;[9] Governor of the Bank of Canada James Coyne was fired, but that decision ended up costing the government more than it did Coyne. No matter which way one turned, Diefenbaker seemed to be handling money matters badly. Combined with the ongoing debate over Canada's nuclear policy,[10] the result was profound government instability despite extraordinary electoral security.

Diefenbaker and Frost had shared something approximating a political friendship. Certainly the former had failed to come through on several matters that Frost had considered important, yet any disappointment between the two did not translate into public rebuffs. In fact, in his retirement Frost continually fielded requests for counsel, and offers of positions, from the prime minister.[11] But whatever had held those two leaders back from expressing the contempt that they occasionally must have felt was not present between Diefenbaker and Robarts. A month after Robarts's selection, Diefenbaker informed his secretary that "in letters written to Provincial Premiers he wished the form of address to be 'Premier of ...' in all cases."[12] Leslie Frost, and all those before him, had been "prime minister of Ontario." So too would John Robarts, just not in letters from the federal prime minister's office. It was a small slight, but one indicative of the threat Diefenbaker felt himself under, and the dim view he had of the new first minister in Ontario.

This was not the time to be unnecessarily angering the provincial government. The federal cabinet was reconsidering its "policies relating to old age and survivor benefits, portable pensions, the levels of benefits payments and public assistance legislation." Although it would be "difficult to justify" spending a great deal more than was being spent at present, the political attractions of increasing the old age pension were difficult for many cabinet members to ignore.[13] Many of the changes contemplated would need provincial agreement, however. And the idea of portable pensions, which had been gaining favour in government circles, would have to be shelved to "await the reaction of other provinces to the proposals of the government of Ontario."[14] Thus, the federal government was going to need Ontario's consent, and it was going to need Ontario's guidance; it could not risk raising Ontario's ire.

Having decided that pension reform was necessary, Diefenbaker appealed to the provinces for agreement. The 1951 amendment to the BNA Act had given Ottawa the power "from time to time to make laws in relation to old age pensions in Canada," but it did not allow the federal government to include benefits to widows and orphans as Diefenbaker envisioned. He thus wrote to the provincial premiers proposing an addition to include "pensions and other benefits incidental to, or conducive to the better operation and administration of, a scheme of old age pensions."[15] Such an open-ended amendment was bound to raise the hackles of the provincial governments, and Quebec Premier Lesage's response – that a full federal-provincial meeting would have to be called on the issue before any agreement could be reached[16] – should not have come as a surprise to anyone. The federal government's gambit on pension reform served to highlight two things. First, agreement had not yet been reached on an amending formula. The constitutional conference that had opened in 1960 with such idealistic hopes for quick agreement was still pondering the level of provincial agreement that would be necessary to change the BNA Act.[17] As Diefenbaker noted in his letter regarding pensions, he hoped that the changes to section 94A "would have been one of the first amendments made under the new arrangements."[18] Such was not to be the case. The second issue that this poorly conceived foray into pension reform indicated was just how much progress had already been made in Ontario on this topic. Figuring out what Ontario was intending to do following its inquiry into portable pensions became a topic of considerable debate in official Ottawa.[19]

The two levels of government seemed engaged in a strange, parallel, negotiation. When Diefenbaker introduced his government's pension amendment proposal in the House of Commons, he commented on "the desirability of the new plan taking into account private pension arrangements."[20] Gathercole regarded this as a sign that Ontario's "leadership in this field has not passed unnoticed."[21] In his opinion, Diefenbaker's plan would "be capable of dovetailing" nicely with the provincial proposals.[22] With its focus on regulating private insurance schemes, combined with compelling businesses with a certain number of employees to provide some form of pension, the work of the Ontario committee seemed likely to appeal to the federal Conservatives.[23] Thus, Robarts pledged his support for any scheme designed to make a "contributory social insurance program becoming a reality,"[24]

It would have been interesting enough watching the antics of two governments vying for a position in the highly contested – and very expensive – pension field, but there were other players rapidly moving into action. And the growing distance between Conservatives in Toronto and Ottawa came to be significant. The Liberals, in their efforts to return to power, were devising a new set of policies that would change the way they did business. In crafting a social policy platform, the Liberal party looked to outside advisers and to its own grassroots for inspiration. One of the most significant results of the massive Liberal Rally of January 1961 was a new interest in pension reform.[25] This drew Robarts's attention. "I learn with much pleasure," he wrote to Liberal leader Lester Pearson, "of your proposals to develop a contributory social security scheme for the aged."[26] Plans in Ontario, however, seemed much more advanced than those of either the Liberals or Conservatives in Ottawa. Tired of attempting to coordinate plans, Robarts was prepared to lead and hope that other jurisdictions would follow.

The federal Conservatives were no longer in a position to make Ontario an enemy. An election was looming for Diefenbaker, and his shaky management of the nation's finances, among other crises, left more than a few concerned about the chances of repeating his 1958 electoral performance. In this environment, it was important that Diefenbaker attempt to avert any conflict with Ontario over pensions. Donald Fleming noted in cabinet the incompatibility of contributory pensions, which were what the federal government was considering, and the portable pensions being discussed in Ontario. Cabinet agreed to give the whole question of portability consideration, which meant tapping into Ontario's thinking on the issue.[27] University of British Columbia economist Robert Clark, a member of Ontario's Portable Pension Committee and subsequently a member of the federal task force on old age security, was the perfect source for information on activities in Toronto. During visits to Ottawa, Clark met with Minister of National Health and Welfare Waldo Monteith, Hart Clark in the Department of Finance, and carried on a correspondence with Finance Minister Fleming. He used the opportunities to promote the Ontario approach to pensions as "a logical alternative to a contributory government pension program with graduated benefits."[28] According to Clark, there were two approaches to achieving portability of pensions. The first, in the process of being adopted in Ontario, was to pass legislation "requiring employers to adopt pension plans meeting specified standards"; the second, being considered in Ottawa, was to have a program with graduated benefits from which employers could contract out if they met certain qualifications. Either way, Clark predicted that "the Ontario Pension Benefits Act should have a substantial influence on the outcome."[29]

As the federal Conservatives bounced from one crisis to another in the early spring of 1962, Diefenbaker decided to play to his strengths and return to the hustings. An election was called for mid-June, and everything else ground to a halt. Progress on a national health insurance program, intentionally slowed by the appointment of the Hall Commission, now had to be made in consideration of the election. Commission member Wallace McCutcheon, a Toronto-based businessman and friend of Leslie Frost, sought to advise Premier Robarts on how to deal with the hearings scheduled for Ontario in May. Any brief that Ontario might present "would probably contain some policy statements … which might make headlines and be somewhat embarrassing." Why not just greet the commissioners, welcome them to Ontario, and tell them that the Government of Ontario will present a brief at some later date? Don't, he advised, do anything that would complicate the federal election.[30] Without a firm proposal on health insurance in hand, Robarts was more than happy to oblige.

By sidelining intergovernmental relations and delaying debate on potentially divisive issues, Diefenbaker was able to devote his attention to wooing the electorate instead of wrestling with the provinces. It was not an election the Chief was expected to win: his cabinet was in disarray, and the campaign seemed doomed to mishap. The Liberals and NDP made particularly advantageous use Diefenbaker's mid-election decision to peg the dollar at 92½ cents American.[31] But the Liberals under Lester Pearson, despite a heavy arsenal of policy proposals, were unorganized on the campaign trail. The leader lacked the charisma that Diefenbaker still seemed able to summon. When the votes were tallied, the Conservative majority was greatly depleted; Diefenbaker clung to control of the House of Commons with only 116 seats to the Liberals' 98, 30 for the Social Credit party and the NDP's 19. But he nevertheless did cling to power, returning to continue much of the work done in intergovernmental affairs in the previous few years.

The election of 1962 did nothing at all to strengthen Diefenbaker's position vis-à-vis the provinces or even within his own cabinet. He was severely shaken by the public's loss of faith in him, and struggled to pull himself out of a funk in the first few weeks after the election.[32] He sought advice from Leslie Frost again, who hammered home the view that Diefenbaker himself was the "one on whom the Government will stand or fall." Frost urged him to seek advice from the business community, whose confidence the prime minister had lost completely.[33] While Frost himself refused – repeatedly – Diefenbaker's offer of becoming the minister of finance, he suggested that McCutcheon be given the post.[34] An outsider, he would bring both business acumen and a clean slate to the cabinet table. With Frost facilitating the invitation, McCutcheon was made a senator and sworn in as minister without portfolio, the "only important new influence" Diefenbaker agreed to add to the old cabinet mix.[35]

In all matters, the federal government struggled to maintain the initiative. In health care, the Hall Commission continued its public hearings, returning to Ontario in the summer to hear the views of the provincial government, which were unsurprising in their calls for increased federal funding.[36] The federal government could still argue that it would delay action as long as the Commission had not yet reported; Ottawa's time would be up as soon as Hall issued his recommendations. Moreover, a three-week-long physicians' strike in Saskatchewan following the 1 July 1962 implementation of a public provincial health insurance program served to move health care closer to the top of the agenda. Diefenbaker could still afford to wait, but he couldn't wait for much longer. Constitutional amendment proved similarly plagued by questions of timing: clearly another intergovernmental meeting would be necessary, but calling one would highlight the disagreement over the federal government's power of unilateral amendment in section 91(1) and would likely require a modification of the long-standing federal position that individual sections of the constitution would not be amended until agreement was reached on an amending formula. To change tacks in a way that would "not unduly prejudice the Federal position and interests"[37] proved to be an impossible challenge, and the conference was not reconvened.

Delay on these fronts did not concern John Robarts: his government had not invested a great deal of attention in achieving immediate health or constitutional reform. Pension reform, however, was another matter. Here, Ontario was preparing to take a leadership role, and Diefenbaker's shaky re-election did nothing to derail those plans. The differences between the portable pension scheme being crafted in Ontario, and the less attractive old age insurance program advocated in Ottawa left the latter "in a very vulnerable position."[38] Ontario's pension legislation was already well along: the committee on portable pensions had made its report in the summer of 1961, a draft bill had been prepared and debated, a revised bill was submitted to the Legislature in the spring 1962, and one final round of public hearings would be held in September.[39] Ottawa had done only a fraction of the work that Ontario had, yet still maintained its desire to act in this field. Federal Deputy Minister of Welfare Joe Willard warned of the "confusion which will result" if both levels of government acted; the Ontario legislation would make it "very difficult" for the federal government to act.

From Robarts's perspective, Ontario was playing a leadership role in the provision of pensions; other provinces would follow suit, and the federal government would not likely be far behind. At a summer meeting of provincial premiers, Robarts explained the progress being made in Ontario to a receptive audience. Premier Lesage noted, somewhat disingenuously given events the following year, that in Quebec "we have not gone very far with this very complicated question [of portable pensions], but in Ontario they have been studying it." Alberta Premier Ernest Manning was grateful to the government of Ontario for having provided "lots of information," and Saskatchewan's Minister of Health Allan Blakeney proposed ways in which the provinces could act in concert in the pension field.[40] Enthusiasm for portable pensions was also high at home in Ontario, where the September hearings elicited a high degree of support for Ontario's "compulsory pensions by free enterprise means."[41] Ottawa had been usurped: Health and Welfare Minister Waldo Monteith was reduced to begging for as much information as Ontario politicians could provide on the details of the pension legislation and the nature of the support it had received from other provincial premiers.[42] When Robarts introduced the Pension Benefits Act in the Ontario legislature on 19 March 1963, it appeared that the province had captured the initiative with a major piece of social security.[43] It remained to be seen whether other jurisdictions would follow suit.

Diefenbaker, however, was in no position to calm the inherent instability of his minority government. While he might listen to Leslie Frost's advice, he couldn't hear the veteran politician urging the prime minister to adopt a stance of quiet confidence. Instead, he saw enemies everywhere. For once, this seemed accurate: over the weekend of 2–3 February 1963, Diefenbaker's cabinet staged a coup against their leader over his defence policy indecision. "Either you go or we go," the rebels, including both Wallace McCutcheon and Davie Fulton, declared. It was a standoff, but the Conservatives were in such clear disarray that two days later Pearson moved in Parliament a vote of non-confidence "because of lack of leadership, the breakdown of unity in the cabinet, and confusion and indecision in dealing with national and international problems."[44] The government fell, and back on the hustings once again, Diefenbaker's electoral stance was to cast blame. "Some have wondered why I didn't give up in face of some of the distortions of truth and some of the difficulties that faced me," he mused to a national television audience during the campaign.

> That was what the Opposition wanted.
> Well, the answer is very simple. I believe, and I am old-fashioned enough to believe, that the truth will out. The reason they wanted me out of the way is that they didn't want to be faced with the facts of the Canadian economy as they are compared with what the Opposition told you they were going to be. They didn't want you to hear the story of their obstructions in the last

Parliament. Day after day they put party politics above the business of Parliament and the Nation – your business. They paralyzed Parliament. They didn't want you to hear about the benefits that they denied you when they joined to end Parliament – to put it out of business before it could give effect to the 31 Bills which died on the Order Paper and many more matters which would have been available for action.[45]

"They" figured prominently in Diefenbaker's presentation of the facts, although their identity changed frequently. Sometimes, "they" were the Liberal brains trust of Tom Kent and others, sometimes the Liberal party as a whole. Lurking in the background of Diefenbaker's paranoia was the suggestions that "they" were even members of his own party, so disillusioned with his leadership that they would forfeit power simply to get rid of him. Whoever it was that the Chief thought "they" were, the public was not convinced. There was still something vaguely unsettling about the Pearson Liberals, however, and in 1963 the electorate returned a second minority government in as many years. This time, the Liberals were at the helm.

The change of federal government had important implications for politics in Toronto. On the one hand, the association of "Conservative" with "Diefenbaker" was a negative one, and "not a helpful association."[46] If Robarts intended to call an election of his own, and that was certainly a possibility, he would have to carefully distinguish his party from the Conservatives at the national level. On the other hand, a new adversary in Ottawa would certainly mean a different approach to intergovernmental relations, and perhaps one that was more beneficial for Ontario. Early on in the life of the Pearson government, Robarts pledged "to withhold nothing in the way of co-operation with the new Government at Ottawa." But he also saw no reason "for altering our course" in terms of economic and industrial development and social security. "In a word," he declared, "our Ontario program will be a very powerful assist to any forward-looking national plan and we are most eager to get on with the job."[47] Eyeing another minority government, this time with an untested leader and a House filled with novice Liberals, Robarts's prime ministerial tone was understandable, if somewhat premature.

Blindsiding Ontario

The single most important intergovernmental issue for the first year following the election of the Pearson government in the spring of 1963 was pensions. How Ottawa played its hand, how much of a leadership role Ontario would be able to take as a result of its three years of study and legislation on the matter, and how the other provinces lined up in the battle over pension rights would have a lasting effect on federal-provincial relations in Canada. Constitutional arrangements, other social security programs, and the inevitable negotiations over tax sharing all hinged on the highly politicized negotiations over pensions. That the outcome was a surprise to virtually everyone only served to enhance the importance of the lessons learned during the pension debates.

Pearson had campaigned on a platform promising "60 days of decision" as a way to distinguish the Liberals from the indecision that marked the Diefenbaker Conservatives in their last days of power. Once elected, however, the Liberals had to make good on that promise, and thus they hurried into existence an array of proposals that stretched the inexperienced government's ability to function. One of the early victims of such an enormous agenda was the new finance minister, Walter Gordon. His first budget was roundly condemned and had to be almost immediately overhauled, undermining confidence in his ability to manage the nation's finances.[48] The Canada Pension Plan resolution, passed on the sixtieth day of decision, came close to sharing the budget's fate. Introducing the resolution on 21 June 1963 was an act of bravado: the Liberals were not at all clear about what this new Canada Pension Plan would entail, apart from the broad platitudes that had been articulated in their campaign brochure "Better Pensions for All," but they were at least certain that the federal government was going to stake its claim on pension jurisdiction.[49]

There had been no such vagueness in Ontario. The Ontario Pension Benefit Act was already in place, if not yet in effect, and early appraisals were very positive. Representatives of the insurance industry were said to be "strongly in favour of it over the Liberal proposals"; editorials had "been surprisingly unanimous and favourable"; politicians in other provinces were continuing to seek assistance from Ontario in preparing their own provincial pension schemes.[50] All signs pointed to Ontario being able to exert considerable influence over the shape of the national pension plan. Yet, instead of leading, Robarts was forced to follow the lead of the federal government, however shaky that might be. Invited to Ottawa at the end of July for a discussion of pensions with other first ministers, there was little Robarts could do but attend.[51] He complained that "this matter will require more consideration than it could be given at a two-day conference," but he agreed to the meeting.[52] Pearson's advisers were well aware of the advances that were being made in Ontario, and were urging haste in large part in order "to have the conference precede the Ontario election campaign."[53] But while Ontario was dictating political strategy, it was not having the desired influence on the shape of pension legislation. The Ottawa plan, still in rough form, envisioned a $10 supplement to old age security, the collection of contributions at the rate of 1.5 per cent of earnings, and graduated benefits available at age seventy beginning in 1966.[54] The federal plan was compulsory; the Ontario plan was not. Clearly, the two governments would be at odds at the July meeting.

The Ontario bureaucracy put in as much work on preparing Robarts for his intergovernmental meeting as possible, although there was a clear "inability to review this complex subject with its variations and implications in the short time at our disposal."[55] Regardless of the preparatory work, the meeting was a failure – at least from Ottawa's perspective. Quebec's delegation made it clear, without wasting too much time in discussion, "that they were desirous of completely contracting out."[56] The Ontario delegation – which included insurance industry representative Laurence Coward and therefore immediately attracted federal distrust – stressed "confusion and duplication" that would result with the passage of the Canada Pension Plan, and pointed to the absence of actuarial reports. Ontario, like Quebec, was opposed to the federal proposals.[57] The new minister of national health and welfare, Judy LaMarsh, was sent back to the drawing board.

But the Liberal government was reluctant to alter the course that had been established in Opposition. A new approach to social security was one of the key goals of the group of planners and politicians who had arranged themselves around Pearson during the Opposition years, and few were willing to give up on those goals without a great deal more negotiation with the provinces. The one change that Pearson accepted before the next federal-provincial meeting in September was an to increase the existing old age security cheques by $10 regardless of whether agreement was reached on the new pension plan.[58] It represented a change in strategy, but not a change in the Liberal commitment to a public, contributory pension plan.

Robarts was just as dedicated to the Ontario version of pension reform as Pearson was to Ottawa's scheme, and felt that after three years of study and with the legislation already passed he had a great deal more reason to hold firm. When the premiers met at their annual summer conference, Robarts's main goal was to shore up provincial support. He reminded his provincial colleagues of the purposes of the Ontario Pension

Benefits Act, which included extending and improving benefits under private pension plans and providing for the portability of those benefits, and then underlined the "fundamental conflict between the private plan funded approach of the Ontario plan and the so-called pay-as-you-go approach of the Canada Pension Plan."[59] He raised the possibility of other provinces passing legislation similar to Ontario's, thereby establishing a degree of uniformity that would "reduce confusion and duplication."[60] It was all too much to decide so quickly, but at least there was another option available for those premiers unsettled by the federal proposals.

Progress on pensions was slow, but the show was worth watching. Rarely has such political intrigue been expended on such a dreary topic. The meeting called for September to continue the work of the July meeting of first ministers was intended to include the relevant ministers – usually health and welfare ministers – rather than their premiers. But coming as it did in the middle of a provincial election campaign complicated matters in Ontario. That the federal Liberal government kept feeding Ontario Liberal Opposition leader John Wintermeyer information about how it intended to proceed on the pension issue made things even worse.[61] There was no way that Robarts was prepared to stand idly by as Wintermeyer purported to have influence over the direction of pension reform at the national level; the premier decided to attend the September ministerial meeting and set the record straight. He and his entourage flew to Ottawa, declared Ontario's willingness "to co-operate with the Federal Government to the fullest extent," stressed Ontario's expertise on the subject of pensions, and hoped that the two plans could somehow be coordinated in such a way as to allow "integrating the new plan with existing employee-employer pension plans and contracts."[62] Then he departed, upstaging LaMarsh at her own conference. Other than agreeing to further technical studies, the ministers made no progress themselves on either coordinating existing plans or deciding on a course to follow.[63]

The jostling over pensions did nothing to help Wintermeyer defeat Robarts and the Conservative's "big blue machine"; Robarts won the election handily, and debate over pensions moved off centre stage and into the backrooms. Following the Ontario election, Pearson wrote to offer congratulations and propose a private "exploratory discussion" between the first ministers on pensions.[64] The Ontario premier was definitely interested: he would be "pleased" to meet with Pearson, and thought "that our interests might best be served if we were to meet in a completely informal manner and alone, at least in the beginning."[65] The private meeting between premier and prime minister was followed by more discussions involving officials. While the tenor of the former may have been pleasant and non-confrontational, the "negotiations" that the latter engaged in were fraught with tension. The notes on the 31 October meeting indicated that the Ontario officials were "rude" and "adamant," attitudes that their chair, Laurence Coward, thought were unintentional. There also seemed to be disagreement over what had been discussed at the meeting, and whether or not the Ontario officials thought "contracting out" was "essential." With the two sides so clearly drawn, even writing the minutes became a heavily negotiated task.[66]

Waiting for the next federal move left ample opportunity for rumours to spread. As vice-chair of the Ontario Hydro-Electric Power Commission, George Gathercole found himself in Montreal on business. But unable to wash his hands of the pension question after three years as chair of Ontario's Portable Pension Committee, he invariably ended up talking about pensions. He shared his reconnaissance with the premier. He learned that work being done in Quebec was "adapting the elements of the Ontario model." He learned from John Deutsch, chair of the Canadian Economic Council, that "an increasing number of the Federal Cabinet Ministers were now disenchanted with the proposed Canada Pension Plan." And he learned from the president of North American Life, Bill Anderson, that Walter Gordon "had a completely new receptiveness ... to work out a national pension plan which would be more acceptable all around."[67] From Gathercole's perspective, it was looking increasingly like Ontario would be successful in its efforts to mould the shape of the new national pension plan.

The November conference had a full agenda: discussions over pensions were only a small portion of the work the first ministers set for themselves. More importantly, the participants were scheduled to discuss the state of the economy, conditional grants and shared-cost programs, and fiscal relations in general. There was the potential that "what was done at this conference might have a lasting effect on Confederation itself."[68] When it opened – a day late due to the assassination of U.S. President John F. Kennedy and Pearson's attendance at the funeral – all of the participants indicated their willingness to get down to the onerous work of cooperation. The focus was clearly on the various elements of intergovernmental revenue sharing, which dominated discussion for much of the four-day conference. As with most meetings of this sort, little was actually finalized, but the perspectives of the various governments were clarified to a certain extent. The most concrete conclusion reached – over Roberts's mild objection to tinkering with an agreement "hammered out after months of discussion"[69] – was to change the method of calculating equalization. Instead of equalizing revenue to the national average tax yield, as had happened under the Conservative government, Pearson proposed a return to the original system of equalizing to the average tax yield of the top two provinces. In recognition of the destabilizing effects of different levels of natural resource revenue, the new Liberal proposals would see resource revenue that exceeded the national average being subtracted from the provinces' equalization.[70] Robarts later worried that, despite accepting equalization both in principle and in fact, the new proposal had its "limitations." If the growth of the Ontario economy was not protected, there would be "nothing to equalize to [and] nothing to equalize from."[71] Nevertheless, his objections at the time were muted.

On the pension front, which was where the Ontario delegation really expected to shine, there was a great deal of discussion but movement towards an agreement seemed to stall. Had there been any doubt, it was now abundantly clear that Quebec intended to opt out of the national plan in favour of its own scheme. Seemingly moved to concessions by the attractiveness of some of the features of Quebec's still-unfinished plan, LaMarsh intimated that some of the federal pension funds might be available for provincial investment,[72] but nothing was stated particularly authoritatively. Without a clear idea of the intentions of all the various players, Robarts noted that "we cannot be asked to go for or against the Canada Pension Plan until we have seen 1) what Quebec is doing and what deal is offered her; 2) [how the] integration of our present [plan is organized]; 3) future fiscal arrangements; 4) effect on capital creation and accumulation in Ontario – and therefore all of Canada."[73] The Ontario delegation was hopeful that rumoured January cabinet changes in Ottawa would lead to more fruitful pension negotiations. While there was some evidence that other provinces were following the Ontario example, most notably Manitoba and Quebec, where Premier Lesage said that "portable pension legislation on the Ontario model was needed," the federal government was still firmly committed to its draft Canada Pension Plan. Just exactly how to proceed with the Ontario Pension Benefit Act was becoming a more immediate question: according to Coward, "a 'point of no return' is approaching" although he advised Robarts to "wait for the new federal proposals before taking a final position."[74]

The two levels of government carried on a somewhat desultory correspondence over the next four months. When Ottawa released its proposals to the provincial premiers in January, they contained the non-negotiable points that the prime minister had identified at the November conference the previous year. Regardless of opposition, the Canada Pension Plan was going to be universal, "apply up to at least an average level of earnings," provide "modestly adequate" pensions for older Canadians, have a "moderately short maturation period," and be available at age sixty-five.[75] Following those guidelines, Pearson then explained the revised federal pension proposal. Ontario advisers were not impressed: in particular they noted "the adverse impact on private pension plans and on capital savings in this province."[76] Robarts made clear to Pearson that the changes that had been made "fall far short of what he had hoped" and "are little in accord with the representations that we have made."[77] The prime minister's five-page reply indicated that Robarts's complaints had fallen on deaf ears.[78]

The relative intransigence of the federal government left Ontario in the position of either accepting the plan in principle or contracting out. Following the former option would not necessarily mean "endorsing the federal plan" but would be taken "in the interests of some degree of national unity and in order not to delay matters further."[79] Contracting out had the advantage of ensuring provincial control over future changes to the plan, the investment of the plan's funds, and would allow the integration of private pension plans. Its disadvantages included the administrative costs, the need to negotiate portability with other provinces, and most importantly, a separate Ontario plan would "break up national unity, although," Coward noted, "the exclusion of Quebec from the Canada Pension Plan means that national unity has been impaired in any event."[80]

The place of Quebec in the federation continued to be a pressing interest in the province of Ontario. Just as the isolation of Quebec had concerned Frost as he contemplated tax rental agreements, Robarts was guided in his intergovernmental calculations by what was going on in Quebec. With the Quiet Revolution well underway, Quebec was even higher on everyone's agendas than it had been in the previous two decades, and Robarts was keen to take Quebec into consideration in his own decision making. That meant understanding what was happening in Quebec. There had been off-the-record seminars on French Canada so that English-language journalists could grasp the extent of the separatist threat and meet the new generation of players such as René Lévesque;[81] there had been a well-publicized and well-received visit by Robarts to Quebec City where the premier had spoken eloquently (although in English) about the long-standing relationship between the two provinces. "The mere discovery," he said, "that there are some cracks and crevices in the edifice of our Confederation should not cause us to flee in panic and abandon our century-old home. Rather, let us proceed as good craftsmen and overcome these defects and make it a more durable dwelling. For I am certain that we are capable of better political leadership and I am equally certain that the two great people who first established our Confederation are ready to make a greater effort to make it work and succeed."[82] Lesage indicated that his government was also willing to embark on the task of upgrading the "century-old home": it would be "a very delicate task" but from Quebec's perspective "the province of Ontario is probably the Canadian province that is in the best position to understand our situation."[83]

But however close the relationship between the two provinces had been historically, and however committed to rebuilding Confederation together the two premiers might be, Robarts was hearing a great deal of advice that pointed towards ignoring Quebec and pursuing Ontario's own interests on the pension front. Coward was leaning towards contracting out of the Canada Pension Plan and following through with what had been started by the Ontario Pension Benefit Act. George Hogan, a prominent young Conservative, media personality, and informal Robarts adviser, argued in favour of "going our own way" and producing a "plan which is demonstrably superior to that offered by the Federal Government."[84] George Gathercole also offered up "a few notes" for the premier "to try out on your pension piano." His suggestion to opt out of the federal plan was justified on the grounds that without Quebec, the Canada Pension Plan would have none of the advantages of a national plan.[85]

Going into the federal-provincial conference of 31 March to 2 April 1964, Robarts had a clear idea of the issues at stake, if a somewhat less-than-clear view of how Ontario intended to proceed. His legal advisers had assured him that there was nothing prohibiting Ottawa from passing its pension legislation or prohibiting both federal and provincial plans from operating simultaneously.[86] The question for Robarts was whether to contract out for the sake of implementing the scheme that had been studied for four years in Ontario, or stay in for the sake of national unity. In his opening statement to the conference, Robarts thus took aim at the convention that was causing him so much difficulty – contracting out itself. If the new Pearsonian approach of cooperative federalism implied "a system under which some provinces with Federal approval can stay out of programs, while against others that also elect to stay out is levelled the accusation that they are 'breaking up Confederation'" then Robarts could not support it. "It is imperative," he said, that each province be "able to reach its own decision" about participation.[87] As for what Robarts intended to do regarding the pension plan, that remained to be seen.

In the end, it didn't really matter. On the second day of the conference Quebec Premier Lesage began conciliatorily by pointing out the high degree of similarity between the proposed Canada and Quebec pension plans, which would mean that portability would not be a problem.[88] But after some whispering with his ministers René Lévesque and Paul Gérin-Lajoie, he decided to drop his bombshell and announced the details of the Quebec Pension Plan legislation that was about to be introduced to the Quebec legislature.[89] The Quebec plan would be compulsory for all employees and self-employed persons; its benefits would begin at age sixty-five; contributions were to be based on that portion of a person's income between $1,000 and $6,000, making them more generous than the federal proposal, and were graduated within that range; and survivor benefits were included, as was legislation for the preservation of rights existing under private pension schemes. It thus contained all of the features that Ottawa hoped to maintain, plus those that were important in Ontario. But the best was yet to come: the reserves built up under the plan were at the complete disposal of the provincial government.[90] Joey Smallwood, the outspoken premier of Newfoundland, summed up the surprise and enthusiasm of the assembled first ministers when he asked whether it would be possible for a province to sign onto the Quebec Pension Plan.[91] According to federal adviser Tom Kent, there was "just no question at that moment the Canada Pension Plan was dead."[92] For the federal delegation, that had built an election campaign around pensions, the conference was a disaster.

Somehow, the crisis had taken Ontario completely by surprise. In the days following the conclusion of the intergovernmental conference, Pearson's advisers went to work salvaging something out of the pension muddle. Tom Kent and Secretary to Cabinet Gordon Robertson both drafted memoranda that recommended modifying the federal plan so that it meshed more neatly with the Quebec plan. A few days later, they flew to Quebec City to meet with Quebec's Deputy Minister of Intergovernmental Affairs Claude Morin to hammer out the deal face to face.[93] In the midst of all the intrigue, Pearson telephoned Robarts. According to the premier, the prime minister called "to inform me that this Government was negotiating with the Government of the Province of Quebec in regard to the relationship between the Canadian Pension Plan and the

Pension Plan, as proposed by the Province of Quebec at the recent Federal-Provincial Conference. Mr. Pearson did not tell me the details but wished me to be aware that these negotiations were being carried on."[94]

There was little question that Ontario was out of the loop now. Finance Minister Walter Gordon worried about this, urging the prime minister to "telephone Robarts again today to make him feel he is being kept in the picture."[95] Gordon had had a particularly long and friendly relationship with Leslie Frost, and it was to the former premier that he turned to discuss matters of federal-provincial interest on a more personal level. Frost took it as a sign that "there is a very considerable change of opinion at Ottawa" and advised the finance minister "not to try to bring all of the provinces into one plan."[96] But a national plan was what the Pearson Liberals wanted, and having more provinces than Quebec opting out was not desirable. The revised federal proposal would allow each province, if it so chose, to administer its own scheme, but there was a "strong attempt to reach agreement on a uniform plan."[97]

Ontario bureaucrats also felt stymied on the whole issue of contracting out of shared-cost programs. At the initiation of the government of Quebec, representatives of the eleven governments had hammered out an interim guide to opting out that guaranteed the non-participating province compensation in the form of income tax abatements or lump sum payments equal to the value of the federal contribution to the shared-cost program.[98] From Ontario's perspective, the provision of full compensation meant that "the question of whether a province does or does not contract out of the proposed arrangements is one of principle, for no other considerations are involved during the interim period."[99] Some of Robarts's closest advisers urged him to pull out of the Canada Pension Plan on principle. In a situation "whereby Quebec runs her own plan and the rest of the provinces join in a centralized Ottawa plan," George Hogan argued, "we are ... paving the road to separatism." More tangibly, he suggested that Ontario was surrendering control over pensions by joining the federal scheme, and not gaining anything substantial in return.[100]

Although discussions over the details of contracting out, terms of payouts, and opportunities for amendment continued through much of 1964 and beyond, it was clear from the first of April onward that Ontario had been outmanoeuvred by Quebec. Taking out their frustration on the future of the pension plan was not an option, and Ontario remained a participant in the quasi-national plan. But from that moment on, Robarts resolved to "build a base of new competence in the Ontario government" as a means to combat the forces in Quebec and "the 'Tom Kent Liberalism' prevailing in the nation's capital."[101] Adopting the Quebec plan, by and large, for the rest of Canada was a "veritable landmark in federal-provincial financial relations." As a subsequent deputy minister of finance for Ontario recalled, "a province suddenly moved to centre stage on a very complex national issue, and the so-called mysteries of governmental finance – previously the exclusive domain of federal civil servants – could be understood by a province with the will to do so."[102] Ontario definitely had the will.

The Lure of the Constitution

While the pension negotiations occupied Ontario officials first as active participants and then as somewhat miffed observers, there was relatively little other activity on the federal-provincial landscape. But the scuffle over pensions had laid bare some of Canada's more serious constitutional impediments. Federal activity in fields, such as pensions, where provincial legislation was also possible complicated an already muddy relationship between the two levels of government. The possibility of Ottawa moving even more dramatically into health, an area that was unquestionably within exclusive provincial jurisdiction, as suggested by the first volume of the Hall Commission Report in 1964, pointed to the need to sort out the constitutional issue once and for all. Pearson hoped to take advantage of the symbolism of the Charlottetown first ministers' conference, to be held in early September 1964 to commemorate the one hundredth anniversary of the conference that led to Confederation, to "reach an agreement in principle" on the question of constitutional amendment, much as the founding fathers had in the nineteenth century.[103] At the premiers' conference in Jasper earlier in the summer, the topic of patriation had also been discussed, and the consensus appeared to be in favour of "the formula [that] emerged from the Constitutional Conferences of 1960 and 1961."[104]

Constitutional discussions had been in abeyance for some time; bureaucrats and politicians at both levels of government needed to remind themselves of what had been agreed to during negotiations with the Diefenbaker government. The "Act to provide for the amendment in Canada of the Constitution of Canada" laid out the proposed formula: all provincial legislatures had to agree to any amendment that affected the distribution of power or education; if a law related to one or more but not all of the provinces, it had to be accepted by all the affected provinces; any other constitutional amendment would need the agreement of "at least two thirds of the provinces representing at least fifty percent of the population."[105] There was also a "delegation" clause whereby either level of government could delegate to the other authority to make laws in areas under its jurisdiction.[106] Ontario's main objection to the recommendations as they stood was the continued inclusion of the 1949 amendment undertaken unilaterally by the St. Laurent government that allowed the federal government – again, unilaterally – to amend the constitution "with respect to matters exclusively within [its] legislative power."[107] In this, Ontario's concerns were mirrored in both Alberta and Quebec.[108] Otherwise, however, the formula seemed to hold out the promise of actually securing provincial agreement.

Gathering in Charlottetown in the "historic Confederation Chamber" on the one-hundredth anniversary of the meeting at which colonial politicians had met "to establish the principles of Confederation," the twentieth-century first ministers seemed moved by the circumstances.[109] The next day, the Halifax *Chronicle-Herald* rejoiced, under a red banner headline, that the "Constitution [was] 'Coming Home'"; the *Globe and Mail* similarly enthused that "Change Likely within a Year."[110] Convening the constitutional conference in such an auspicious location almost guaranteed success, but there remained points of disagreement that would have to be worked out by a more expert group of participants at a future intergovernmental conference. Behind the bonhomie of the maritime meeting lurked the same problem that had plagued the earlier constitutional discussions: without an agreement to include a discussion of section 91(1) – the federal power to amend federal matters unilaterally – many of the provinces were reluctant to continue discussions of a more general amending formula.[111] Although some provincial premiers were quick to point to Quebec as the source of intransigence on the amending formula, there was no doubt that Ontario was similarly reluctant to proceed without reconsidering section 91(1).[112]

Thus, despite the appearance of progress, there was still much to be done at the next intergovernmental meeting. In Ontario, Attorney General A.A. Wishart began to "reactivate" the 1961 committee on constitutional amendment.[113] In Ottawa, Justice Minister Guy Favreau led the debate over how far the federal government was prepared to go on changes to section 91(1), whether or not to allow provinces to initiate constitutional amendments, and how many provinces would be required to delegate legislative authority to Ottawa.[114] Most seemed to be in agreement that Ottawa's right to unilaterally amend the constitution should be reconsidered but, as Bob Bryce pointed out, it should be presented as "a major concession to the views of the provinces as expressed in the last 20 years."[115] In Ottawa, discussions of constitutional strategy were wide-ranging, including active participation from Gordon Robertson and Tom Kent in the Prime Minister's Office, Walter Gordon and his staff in the Department of Finance, as well as all of the members of Favreau's Justice Department.

In Toronto, in contrast, the staff in the Attorney General's office hammered out the provincial position, leaving others to fret about the final details of the pension plan, which seemed to occupy more attention than the constitution.[116] Of all the issues that bedevilled federal-provincial relations in Canada, it was the constitution that seemed to cause the fewest waves in the provincial capital. Even after the meeting of the attorneys general had to be adjourned and reconvened following the collection of more information by the various governments, officials in Toronto remained calm. "The revision" that was introduced by Favreau "meets Ontario's request quite fairly and," according to Wishart, was "acceptable." The attorney general was concerned, however, about the "reservations and even dissent" that seemed apparent between the federal government, Quebec, and British Columbia that had necessitated "the further meeting." The disagreement revolved around amendments to the Senate, which were currently possible under section 91(1). From Wishart's perspective, Ontario could afford to be flexible and support the position at the conference that "would most assist the acceptance of the amending formula."[117]

The federal politicians were also in an agreeable mood. In accordance with Guy Favreau's recommendations, cabinet approved of a strategy that would see the federal government open by being "reluctant to agree to changes in the powers of the Senate" – the key issue as far as changes to section 91(1) were concerned – but to be prepared, if "no agreement is going to be possible without some limitation," to bow to provincial pressure for a reconsideration of the power to make unilateral changes to the Senate.[118] The path was clear to realizing a made-in-Canada amending formula, and with all the goodwill they could muster, the first ministers reached "an historic" agreement in mid-October 1964. According to the *Toronto Daily Star*, "Canada cut her constitutional ties with Britain yesterday. For the first time in 97 years, this country is to have a constitution she can call her own and the means to amend it without asking permission of the British Parliament." The red headline implied "hurrahs" were in order, despite the need for legislative and parliamentary ratification, and denunciations of the deal by those committed to maintaining a strong central government.[119] The agreement on the amending formula – what would become known as the Fulton-Favreau formula, after the two justice ministers who worked towards its acceptance – was a great feat for Prime Minister Pearson. As Joey Smallwood was reported to have said the day after the agreement was reached, "in another country on a day like yesterday, there would have been dancing in the streets."[120] It was just as well there wasn't, as the celebration would have proven to have been about twenty years premature.

In Ontario, however, the aftermath of the pension issue cast a long shadow over any great enthusiasm there might have been for an agreement on the constitution. On the one hand, the fall of 1964 marked the inaugural meeting of the Tax Structure Committee, a group agreed on at the federal-provincial conference at which Lesage's pension scheme had been announced, and which promised to "undertake a synoptic study of the whole field of federal-provincial fiscal relations."[121] Although this might prove useful for Ontario, it was fraught with difficulty. The information gathered by the Tax Structure Committee would be used to determine future equalization payments, but the choice of Al Johnson as secretary of the committee was problematic in Toronto. "With his Saskatchewan experience," complained George Gathercole, "[Johnson] has been indoctrinated with the idea of pooling revenue, and greater equalization."[122] The idea was unsettling to the bureaucrats in Queen's Park.

But the pension issue itself had still not been finalized. Throughout the fall of 1964, Robarts and several of his cabinet ministers had been attempting to change the details of the pension agreement. Specifically, Robarts sought a concession whereby "the province of Ontario should be able to enact its own legislation establishing the pension plan in the same terms as the federal plan but appoint the federal government as agent to administer the Ontario legislation along with the federal legislation."[123] Robarts wanted to secure the appearance of control over the delivery of contributory pensions in Ontario, while still not upsetting the national quality of the scheme agreed to in the spring. Pearson did not accept Robarts's arguments, and the pension legislation remained largely the same as it had been when accepted originally.

Robarts's first few years in office had been more difficult on the intergovernmental relations front than anyone would have had any reason to expect. He inherited a province that, under Leslie Frost, had made great strides in both smoothing the relationship with Ottawa and dictating the direction that that relationship would go. Robarts brought a managerial temperament that seemed well suited to guiding the provincial strategy of offering clearly conceived, attractive alternatives to federal policy, and manipulating the national interest in a way that conformed with provincial goals. Pensions clearly fit easily into the Ontario model: while the federal government was slow to act, the Ontario government was conducting serious research, preparing proposals, and consulting among the various interest groups. The resulting pension proposals were careful alternatives to the more hastily cobbled-together Canada Pension Plan scheme. But this carefully established approach that Ontario had been following since the end of the Second World War was upset by the unexpected appearance of Quebec as a player, rather than a roadblock, in the intergovernmental arena. Following the pension debacle, Robarts made it clear that this would not be allowed to happen again: Ontario, he argued, "will recognize no further deals between Ottawa and Quebec in which the other provinces are not consulted."[124] In arguing for the need to lift the veil of secrecy on intergovernmental negotiations, Robarts was – unwittingly – taking the first step towards constitutional transparency. He was also positioning Ontario to play a much different role in future intergovernmental issues. Sidelining Ontario over pensions had irritated Robarts to the point of action, and while there was little he could do about the Canada Pension Plan, there were other avenues of negotiations just opening up. Robarts would not soon let another opportunity pass.

Chapter Six

"Profound Changes in the Character of Canadian Federalism": Ontario Charts a New Course, 1964–1966

The mid-1960s marked a turning point in Ontario's relations with the federal government. For most of the postwar period, successive Ontario governments had been attempting to articulate an alternative interpretation of the national interest on particular issues, whether it was in proposing new tax-sharing arrangements or ensuring that discussions of national health insurance were placed on the intergovernmental agenda. This was a strategy that was in contrast to the head-on confrontations that characterized premiers' approaches to Ottawa before the Second World War, but it was also one that was experiencing little success. Too often Ontario's version of the national interest was seen by other provinces as being primarily in Ontario's interest; even more frequently, governments in Ottawa took the Ontario propositions as starting points and then went off in their own direction. The final program or agreement was often widely divergent from the one that had originally been proposed by the Ontario government. Even after a change in leadership in Toronto, with John Robarts replacing Leslie Frost, and unambiguous attempts to design policy in areas like pension reform, the Ontario government experienced little success in dictating the national agenda. Worse still, other provinces – less interested than Ontario in designing national policy and more interested in securing a better position for themselves within the federation – were making better progress in affecting the design of intergovernmental policy. Ontario's failure to take advantage of the perceived vacuum in leadership at the national level made the lack of progress all the more disappointing.

The issues that confronted the two levels of government in 1965 were very similar to the sorts of topics that had been discussed for the previous two decades. Fiscal arrangements between the two governments were paramount, and in many ways determined the positions on social policies and other shared-cost measures. The constitution had been a nagging problem since before the Second World War, but the desire to agree on a domestic amending formula had increased exponentially with the end of judicial appeals to Britain and the establishment of the Supreme Court of Canada as the court of last resort. Still, despite the unchanging nature of the intergovernmental topics themselves, the tenor of the debate was in the process of a profound alteration. The tactics – and the success – of the Quebec government during the pension negotiations had had a dramatic effect on Ontario players.

It no longer seemed feasible – and, in fact, it probably never had been – for Ontario to function as the voice of Canada. A Quebec in the midst of its Quiet Revolution had little time for the national interest, whether it was articulated by Ottawa or Toronto. Instead, the divide between the national and the provincial interest seemed to be widening, and by the mid-1960s finding a compromise position between the two looked increasingly necessary. Ontario was well positioned to facilitate that compromise. Therefore, in addition to dealing with the nuts and bolts of health insurance, and welfare policy, and tax rental agreements, Ontario bureaucrats under the able guidance of Premier Robarts began to shift their interest towards foundational, fundamental issues and away from the minutiae. That approach meant that constitutional reform moved to the top of Ontario's agenda, but it also meant a subtle shift away from promoting one version of the national interest towards facilitating dialogue between the component parts of the Canadian national state.

Several factors affected Ontario's shifting approach to intergovernmental relations. The implications of the Quebec Pension Plan were particularly far-reaching, as Ontario bureaucrats were forced to confront their own lack of preparedness on the pension issue. With its "carefully designed proposals ... [Quebec] was effectively setting the agenda for federal-provincial discussion,"[1] taking that role over from Ottawa, but more importantly also from Ontario.[2] The pension issue highlighted for Ontario that the intergovernmental field was getting increasingly cluttered, and suggested to bureaucrats the possibility of playing a more useful role in the establishment of a coherent intergovernmental framework. The work of the Tax Structure Committee was one possible step in that direction; the formation of the Ontario Advisory Committee on Confederation was even more clearly designed to address broad issues of federal-provincial relations. In declaring its intention to host the Confederation of Tomorrow Conference, however, in the fall of Canada's centennial year, the Ontario government firmly announced itself as dedicated to finding a solution to the intergovernmental impasse rather than simply blasting through it.

The Spread of Advice in Intergovernmental Affairs

The federal-provincial conference of April 1964 that had witnessed the shocking announcement of Quebec's pension scheme and had unsettled the intergovernmental equilibrium also produced, less dramatically, an agreement to investigate the fiscal basis of the country.[3] What would become known as the Tax Structure Committee was "dreamed up" by Bob Bryce in finance, Clerk of the Privy Council Gordon Robertson, and Tom Kent from the Prime Minister's Office.[4] It was, according to Kent, a sop to the provinces as it "would result, a year or two hence, in some realignment of taxes favourable to the provinces."[5] But because its mandate was more sweeping than that of the first ministers' meetings regularly dedicated to negotiating tax-sharing arrangements, there was a sense that the Tax Structure Committee could explore intergovernmental affairs in a general manner. The Ontario bureaucrats, for example, hoped "for a declaration of what Canada's needs are from 1967 on"; these would include investigations into "the programs that must be developed to meet these needs," how they would be financed, and "what national priorities should be set."[6]

In its conception, the Tax Structure Committee was designed to create an environment within which the entire fiscal basis of Confederation was examined. While dealing with slightly different but nevertheless related subject matters, it paralleled the later developments in constitution making that have been called "mega-constitutional politics" or a shift towards dealing with the British North America Act in its entirety.[7] No longer piecemeal or ad hoc, the Tax Structure Committee envisioned mega-fiscal change. Participants recall meetings of the committee as quite unlike other intergovernmental discussions. Donald Stevenson was a relatively new recruit to the Ontario Department of Treasury and Economics, and he remembers that "there was a deliberate attempt to stay away from Ottawa" and hold meetings instead in convivial locations where "everyone got together in the evenings and common approaches were worked out to many issues."[8] The Tax Structure Committee was an ambitious and somehow good-spirited undertaking that the Ontario government embraced as it shifted its intergovernmental approach towards facilitating fundamental change.

The fiscal and monetary tools, including taxation, that were available to governments offered a unique opportunity to achieve economic objectives such as high levels of income and stable prices. In Ottawa, new recruits from the Saskatchewan bureaucracy like Al Johnson and Tom Shoyama were especially interested in pursuing the policy potential of taxation, and the Tax Structure Committee was the key body through which to explore the intergovernmental issues. Quickly, however, problems such as "how to achieve a consensus" and whether to share "classified information" became apparent. Subsequently, the "problem of harmonizing national objectives with the needs of the provinces arises."[9] In Ontario, it was clear that these sorts of problems were having an effect on the usefulness of the Tax Structure Committee. Despite the division of labour that had been agreed upon regarding studies on capital markets, for example, Ontario officials nevertheless duplicated the work of federal authorities to ensure their accuracy.[10] With concern over figures, Robarts's attention focused on how the Ontario delegation should behave at the December meeting of finance ministers. The initial Ontario submission was "a broad statement of the economic goals of the Government," designed to steer discussion away from the details that had bogged down discussions of the Tax Structure Committee already. But the premier "wondered if this was the place to say this" and thought "the proposed statement was the kind that should be given in the Legislature or at a public forum."[11]

After considerable discussion with bureaucrats from the departments of Economics and Development and the Treasury, Ontario's Treasurer John Allan was "authorized by the Prime Minister of Ontario to discuss the economic problems of Confederation rather than conditions and prospects."[12] He proceeded to explain to the assembled finance and treasury ministers that the "heart of the economic problem facing Confederation" was that provinces bore the majority of the responsibility for the increasingly costly fields of education, welfare, and the "provision of most social capital." In contrast, the federal government collected the "bulk of the revenue." This discrepancy between revenue and responsibility, combined with the fact that Ontario politicians believed "that a strong Federal Government is needed in order to achieve objectives such as enlarged immigration, greater mobility of labour, availability of foreign capital, appropriate trade policy, and suitable monetary policy," led to the current crisis.[13]

The solution was complex. The Ontario delegation underlined the necessity of "a better matching of revenue resources with constitutional responsibilities," a solution that had been proposed at least since the Rowell-Sirois Commission had reported in the early years of the Second World War.[14] Both levels of government needed to better coordinate their economic activity and "reach agreement on the goals and priorities involved in our common interest." They also needed to "refine" their respective understandings of the "nature and role of monetary and fiscal policies."[15] On the basis of the experience to date with the Tax Structure Committee, the Ontario submission proposed an "agreement on the type of machinery and procedures required for the exchange of information and the discussion of goals, priorities and policy co-ordination."[16] In sum, Allan argued for "a complete exchange of views at the political level [and] as little conflict as possible among federal and provincial" representatives. But he also noted contentiously that the federal government had an important leadership role to play, and that "the efforts of the provincial governments to improve their economic potential must fit into a framework of national priorities."[17] The suggestion, by Ontario, that provincial priorities needed to fit within a larger national context was directed explicitly at Quebec, as was noted in the margins of Allan's text of the submission.[18] According to Ontario's Chief Economist Ian Macdonald, who was also present at the meeting, the federal officials "certainly welcomed our initiatives as did Quebec for different reasons." Informal discussions between Ontario and Quebec bureaucrats suggested that the Ontario submission "caught Quebec slightly off balance" and forced the Quebec delegation to broaden their perspective beyond their "own introspective concern." Macdonald predicted that "for Quebec to confront strong, positive but reasonable and understanding positions in Ontario will, I believe, shift the whole balance of present discussions and, perhaps, even save the day."[19]

The discussions in preparation for and during meetings of the Tax Structure Committee point to a new direction in the thinking of the Ontario government regarding federal-provincial relations. Macdonald knew that and predicted "in the next few months, Ontario must demonstrate not only tactical but strategic initiative in the conduct of federal-provincial fiscal affairs as a contribution to profound changes in the character of Canadian federalism."[20] The Ontario view had shifted away from a focus on the details, and towards a more comprehensive articulation of both the challenges and the solutions that the two levels of government were facing. But despite taking the broad view, and embracing platforms like the Tax Structure Committee, there remained details that needed attention. The federal decision to move on a system of national health insurance was one of the more important "details" of intergovernmental relations in the 1960s, although the script had largely been written already.

Ontario's activity in the field of health insurance paralleled, in many ways, its earlier activity on pensions. In April 1963, Ontario's Health Minister Matthew Dymond had introduced a medicare bill that would provide government assistance for individuals who were unable to pay the premiums for voluntary provincial health insurance provided through private insurance companies. Physicians would be free to deal with patients and insurance companies as they chose, and members were protected against insurance companies cancelling contracts due to old age or poor health. Although a decision to provide some degree of government assistance in securing insurance was a step forward from Frost's position on the matter a decade earlier, and was no doubt a response to Saskatchewan's implementation of full health insurance the previous year, the Ontario scheme was nevertheless roundly lambasted by both the Liberals and the NDP.[21] In response, Robarts appointed University of Waterloo President Gerald Hagey chair of a committee to investigate the health insurance proposals and possible alternatives.

When the Hagey Committee reported a year and a half later, early in 1965, it endorsed the broad elements of the government scheme, offering a few suggestions for amendments to the premium system. The labour representative on the committee, however, disagreed strongly enough with the findings to write his own dissenting opinion which "undoubtedly indicates that the position of the NDP will be for a fully-governmental plan à la Saskatchewan."[22] In fact, when the report was made public in February 1965, there was quite a bit of opposition: the *Toronto Star* called it "medicare for insurers, not for the public," and argued that "never before ... has a scheme to benefit private business masqueraded so brazenly as a social welfare plan."[23] Robarts immediately set up an internal government committee to investigate how best – or indeed whether – to implement the recommendations of the Hagey Report. After more than twenty hours of meetings, the group proposed covering low-income families under the auspices of the Ontario Hospital Services Commission.[24] The change would go part way towards addressing the concerns that had been voiced, but the left was not likely to be completely mollified. Of far greater immediate concern was what was happening in Ottawa.

Diefenbaker had been responsible for the appointment of the Royal Commission on Health Services, and for the selection of his friend and fellow private-insurance advocate Justice Emmett Hall as its chair in 1961. It was to the Pearson Liberals, however, that the report was submitted, in two pieces, in the summer of 1964 and in January 1965. The final component of the Hall Report was released at about the same time as the Hagey Report, and rendered the provincial report moot. When the Hall Commission recommended the immediate introduction of full, government-sponsored health insurance, the question of medicare moved firmly to centre stage of the intergovernmental agenda. Given the coincidence of the timing of the federal and provincial reports, and that the Ontario recommendations did "not have a broad enough socialistic base to satisfy current editorial and public thinking," there was ample reason for the Robarts government to delay legislating on provincial health insurance.[25] However, there was evidence that the federal Liberals found the timing of the Hall Report just as irksome: Minister of National Health and Welfare Judy LaMarsh called the timetable for implementation of full health insurance as proposed by Hall "unrealistic and precipitate."[26] One of the unexpected consequences of the Hall recommendations for the Ottawa Liberals was the heating up of a power struggle between the left and the right of the party that left lasting scars.

As the head of the Liberal party, Prime Minister Pearson faced some difficult decisions about election timing and the role that health insurance ought to play in the spring of 1965; as the leader of the federal government, he faced a mounting intergovernmental agenda. The chorus of concerns over shared welfare programs, the constitution, financial arrangements, and most enormously, health insurance that Pearson heard in response to a proposal for a meeting at the end of May forced the two levels of government to postpone their meeting until mid-July.[27] The delay had to do with the quantity of material on the agenda and the difficulty in making arrangements around eleven first ministers' schedules; nevertheless, the extra six weeks of preparation time gave the federal civil service the chance it needed to "solve" the problem of medicare. Or, as far as Deputy Finance Minister Bob Bryce was concerned, the opportunity to "stall our way through" medicare for the short term.[28] But mere days before the convening of the intergovernmental conference, Assistant Deputy Minister of Finance Al Johnson came up with "the kind of solution that, once you have heard it, you kick yourself for having failed to think of."[29]

Instead of following the tradition formula, based on agreements signed with participating provinces, administered by the provinces, and financed by some form of either federal taxation or transfer payments,

Johnson proposed that the whole system be simplified. The key to his suggestion was that there no longer be any formal agreements with the provinces, but rather "they would simply have to enact legislation which established a plan in conformity with the principles enunciated by the Federal Government after, and as a consequence of, consultation with the provinces."[30] The Liberals quickly confirmed the health insurance principles. To receive federal monies, the cabinet agreed, provinces would have to introduce their own legislation that established a health insurance scheme that was universal in coverage, comprehensive in the medical services to be covered, portable across provincial boundaries, and publicly administered. "In order to make the services available to a national standard in all parts of Canada," cabinet concluded, Johnson's strategy "seemed to be the only reasonable plan which could be put forward by the federal government."[31] When Prime Minister Pearson introduced the topic at the federal-provincial conference on 19 July 1965, he did so in a lengthy opening address that left little room for discussion with the provinces. By announcing principles rather than objectives, there was no need to reach any kind of consensus with provincial premiers. As Pearson noted, "discussions of our officials ... lead me to hope that these four principles will command general approval."[32] Moreover, there simply wasn't room for provincial manoeuvring. Robarts might complain that the federal government was just using medicare for electoral advantage, but by the time the four principles were announced they were already a fait accompli.[33]

A full national health insurance system was another of a long line of programs that necessitated federal and provincial cooperation. That the Pearson Liberals had devised a strategy that minimized coordination with the provincial level of government and at the same time preserved what could be argued was a high degree of provincial autonomy meant that the road to securing this program might be smoother and straighter than had been the case with pensions just the previous year, or with any of the tax rental agreements that had littered the postwar landscape. Robarts responded to Pearson's conference announcement of principles with more sanguinity than some might have expected. The Ontario premier's thinking on intergovernmental issues had shifted fundamentally in the previous six months or so, and one simple policy or agreement was hardly cause for upset, even one as major as national medicare. Robarts, and the rest of the Ontario team, had started thinking about the big picture.

The formation of the Tax Structure Committee marked a move in the direction of mega-planning, but it had been undertaken at the instigation of the federal government, and moreover, was in some ways doomed to a lengthy cycle of planning and report sharing between the eleven governments. Within the Ontario government itself, however, a different sort of process of evaluation was commencing. Early in 1965, the government established an Advisory Committee on Confederation to assess the provincial position "within the framework of Confederation." The terms of reference noted the extent of the changes that had gone on in the intergovernmental relationship since Confederation, and that Robarts's government sought "continuous advice" on issues that affected "its part in maintaining and strengthening Canadian unity."[34] To this end, the committee would offer advice on both specifically constitutional issues, but also on "matters in relation to and arising out of the position of Ontario in Confederation."[35] It was a broad mandate.

The advisory committee was really the brainchild of the premier himself. The letter inviting participation was personal, suggesting a fairly intimate relationship between Robarts and the committee members. It was to be a "private committee" with deliberations held in camera and reports and recommendations made only to the government itself, being made public only "if the Government feels that this is desirable." It was, significantly, "a completely non-partisan" committee, designed with broad but somewhat amorphous goals.[36] Its membership was drawn largely from academia, highlighting the "think-tank" quality of the enterprise and Robarts's own desire to establish something of a "brains trust." Eleven of the advisory committee members were university professors, most of them from departments of political science and law, two were university presidents, and four were either lawyers or worked in public institutions like the hydro commission. All were men and only two of the seventeen were French, but in the Ontario of the mid-1960s it was nevertheless an impressive experiment in government advising.[37]

Robarts himself did not attend meetings of the group, which were held once a month in Toronto, but he often joined them at the end of their day of discussion for drinks and dinner. Its format reflected John Robarts's style: while the group might be heavily male, it was relatively young and hard-working and potentially innovative in its thinking. And despite its seemingly informal structure, in some ways, it had the potential to be even more influential than the more traditional advisory body of the royal commission. Commission reports could be ignored, as could the advice of the advisory committee, but as the latter met monthly for over two years, its discussions would have to be ignored in a more concerted and systematic manner. There is little evidence that Robarts sought to ignore their advice; rather, he seemed to enjoy his regular meetings with the professors.[38]

The chair of the committee was the new chief economist in the Department of Economics and Development, H. Ian Macdonald, a young economist lured from the University of Toronto. The secretary was Donald Stevenson, who had developed a reputation as a keen observer of intergovernmental affairs in general, and Quebec in particular. Both were close to the premier and able to bring Robarts's concerns to the group. At an early meeting, as the advisers struggled to figure out how best to undertake their work, Macdonald indicated the premier's thinking on the matter: Robarts felt that "this is the time in the reconstruction of Confederation, that the Prime Minister of Ontario should be in a position where from day to day he does not have to take a position or take a stand without the best advice, without the best counsel, without the best guidance he can muster."[39] The group must have been pleased with the endorsement of the premier of Ontario as they set about "interpreting the concern of Ontario," which the Ontario government viewed the same "as the concern of the country as a whole."[40] More than any other initiative, the formation of the Ontario Advisory Committee on Confederation signalled that the Robarts government was taking its approach to intergovernmental relations in a new direction, building on the progress of the Drew and Frost governments before it, but shifting the agenda towards the very framework of the relationship and away from the details.

It was a propitious moment to begin an examination of the place of Ontario in the federal system. Although not all of the advisers had been selected because of their expertise in the fields of constitutional history or law, it quickly became clear that the details of the amending formula – heralded only a few months earlier as successfully concluded – were still under debate. The Fulton-Favreau formula had raised nationalist suspicions in Quebec, forcing Premier Jean Lesage to tread carefully. Union Nationale leader Daniel Johnson took advantage of the opposition by labelling the formula "une camisole de force" (a straitjacket), and members of Lesage's own cabinet – including René Lévesque – were privately uncertain about the logic of Quebec's acceptance of the amending procedure.[41] Reflecting the ambivalence in Quebec, Lesage wrote to the prime minister to outline his "conception of the purport and effect of the proposed enactment."[42] Lesage's understanding raised several questions for the federal government, and would ultimately affect the other provinces as well. The Ontario Advisory Committee on Confederation would by necessity become involved in the background of the continuing discussions, whether or not individual members were especially competent in the field.

The premier of Quebec argued that the amending formula as he understood it would require unanimous consent for either any reduction in the powers granted to the provinces under section 92 of the British North America Act or for "any amendment of section 91 for the purpose of enlarging the powers of the Parliament of Canada." To *expand* provincial powers, however, he argued that it was only necessary to secure the consent of two-thirds of the provinces representing 50 per cent of the population.[43] It was a view that raised "very real difficulties indeed" from Pearson's perspective.[44] In his effort to publicly argue that the Fulton-Favreau formula did not "impose a 'strait-jacket on Quebec,'" Lesage had instead argued that "the strait-jacket is really on Ottawa." And in truth, it was now the federal government that found itself severely constrained: according to Gordon Robertson, if Pearson's "reply negates Mr. Lesage's argument, it will be extremely difficult, if not impossible, for him to go ahead in the Quebec legislature to get the plan approved."[45]

The renewal of opposition in Quebec led to some structural changes in the way that each level of government dealt with constitutional issues. In Ottawa, Pearson endeavoured to establish "a Constitutional Consultant" to avoid leaving "this field to the Provinces by default, and later to be thrown entirely on the defensive."[46] In Ontario, Robarts also indicated his interest in considering the institutions of constitutional negotiation. As Macdonald reported to the Advisory Committee on Confederation, the premier had identified four points that "he considered of first priority" for their deliberations. These included "the status and power" of first ministers' conferences, interprovincial agreements, and the "institutions of Dominion-Provincial relations" including the efficacy of a Dominion-Provincial Secretariat.[47]

The new approach that Ontario was taking required careful consideration of policy goals and outcomes. To that end, the work of the advisory committee provided "a central focus."[48] It was not, however, speedy work. The issues that the group examined were complex and often unclear, and the implications of the work potentially profound. Had there been any doubt, as the year wore on there was increasing evidence "of the importance of Ontario taking leadership" in intergovernmental matters and "that strong positions by Ontario are in fact welcomed by Ottawa as a means of counterbalancing some of the stresses that they are exposed to in a Federal-Quebec sense."[49] Stevenson suggested that "Ontario had perhaps a more important role than any of the other English-speaking

provinces."[50] The work of the advisory committee, therefore, was presented as of pressing interest not only for the Ontario government but
also, perhaps, for the state of the federation.

With such responsibility and such a volatile mix of academic ego and
potentially divergent opinions, it is not surprising that the work of the
committee was slow and sometimes acrimonious. Younger observers of
the discussions found the talk thrilling – like being in a senior gradu-
ate seminar[51] – but the participants themselves were sometimes less
generous about their colleagues' abilities. Eugene Forsey, for example,
found it necessary to comment on a paper prepared by fellow committee member Alex Brady. The latter, according to Forsey, was dead wrong
about the position of the provinces at the time of Confederation, and he
thought it important to fill the chair in on what really happened. "Like
Donald Creighton," Forsey argued, "I do not like the frequent modern
implication that the poor old Fathers of Confederation really had no eye
to the future … I feel that this particular passage in Alex's paper comes
too close to the 'Victorian plumbing, let's throw it out and get a new
unit' school of oratory (I will not say 'thought'), against which Donald
Creighton has broken so many valiant lances, and against which I here-
with fling my small dart also."[52] The work of chair was as much to keep
tempers even as it was to direct the advisers in their discussion of the
pressing matters of the day.

Health and Welfare Wrangling

While the academics debated the big issues, even if they sometimes
seemed to get mired in minutiae, the bureaucrats and their political
masters had to tackle their own problems. Despite a shift in thinking in
Ontario towards a more foundational approach to intergovernmental
relations, the necessity of dealing with individual programs did not stop.
Two particular policies occupied the attention of policy makers in Ontario in the mid-1960s. Welfare reform had plagued federal-provincial
relations since the Second World War, with memories of the Depression
colouring the desire of both levels of government to avoid taking complete control of assistance. By the 1960s, however, a solution seemed to
be in sight, despite some reluctance on the part of Ontario. Even more
troublesome, however, was health insurance, and the almost continuous
attempt on the part of Ontario officials to untie the knot of medicare as
announced at the July federal-provincial conference. Between welfare
reform and health insurance, there was more than enough work on details to keep the Ontario civil service occupied.

The issue of welfare reform returned to Ontario early in 1964 with U.S. President Lyndon Johnson's announcement in his January State of the Union address that he was about to embark on a "war on poverty." The public suggestion that a wealthy nation like the United States could be plagued by pockets of poverty pointed to the possibility of trouble at home as well. The Ontario Federation of Labour's careful, statistically based study of the extent of poverty in Ontario provided the facts for the arguments that the left had been hammering Robarts's Conservatives with all year: 11 per cent of Ontarians were living in destitution; 19 per cent were living in poverty; and 32 per cent were living in poverty, destitution, or deprivation. The figures, according to the report, "paint a picture of the poor that staggers the imagination."[53] Although there was some doubt within the government as to the accuracy of the figures, there was little question that action would need to be taken in this direction.

The initial response was to investigate the workings of the war on poverty in the United States. A group of officials, headed by provincial Deputy Minister of Welfare James Band, travelled to Washington in the winter of 1964–65. They were not impressed. The program was still "very much in the planning stage," and Band regarded the architects as "impossibly naïve." As he saw it, "the elimination of poverty may be accomplished in the remote future by evolutionary methods; if it is to be done in our day, the methods would have to be revolutionary."[54] But while there was reluctance in Ontario to move very quickly in the direction of a war on poverty, in Ottawa the political merits of such a scheme were immediately apparent. The minority government circumstances meant that an election was never far from the minds of the federal Liberals. Pressure in favour of an early election from Finance Minister Walter Gordon made it even more imperative that the government have some politically popular successes under its belt as quickly as possible. Piggybacking on the popularity of President Johnson's announcement seemed an ideal strategy.

The 5 April 1965 Speech from the Throne, therefore, contained a commitment to ending poverty in Canada, and provided the impetus for the federal ministers to begin to act on several different fronts. Among them was the consolidation of a variety of different categorical assistance programs into one coherent intergovernmental plan. It was to be called the Canada Assistance Plan, and it came into being with the realization that there were several social and economic programs "spread around among various departments" that required detailed provincial planning but nevertheless would benefit if Ottawa could "provide a broad push."[55] As the minister of national health and welfare outlined to her provincial counterparts following a preliminary ministerial meeting, the new scheme would cover "needy mothers," health care services for welfare recipients, and would provide for "new expenditures for administration and the provision of social services."[56]

The conversation about assistance was scheduled to continue at the mid-summer federal-provincial conference but, in the meantime, LaMarsh sought some clues about provincial thinking on such matters as work-for-relief, and the relationship between this new Canada Assistance Plan and other benefits available under existing programs.[57] She expected that Ontario would be generally supportive of the proposal, as Welfare Minister Louis Cecile had already indicated that it was time for "all-inclusive legislation" that would provide a basis for sharing costs. The Ontario officials did not disagree with LaMarsh's version of the province's position; not only did Band remind the premier that Ontario "has pressed the federal government for such a program," but also he guestimated an $11 million increase to the provincial treasury as a result of participation in the new arrangements.[58] But despite the inclusion of the new rationalized system on the agenda for the full intergovernmental meeting, welfare ministers were not expected to attend; in contrast, health ministers were supposed to be there, suggesting to Ian Macdonald that "health questions will command the principal attention of the meeting."[59]

Both the Canada Assistance Plan and medicare were announced at the July intergovernmental meeting, and yet it was only the latter that elicited much interest at the conference itself, or generated much activity on the provincial scene in the months that followed. In fact, devising a provincial response to the federal medicare conditions occupied much of the Robarts government's attention for the remainder of the year and beyond. Meeting with his cabinet colleagues and their officials shortly after the conference adjourned, Robarts laid out some of his concerns. Most revolved around the relationship between the Ontario health legislation that had originally been announced in 1963, and the new federal health care proposals. The first step, the premier announced, was to determine "whether we take our present plan and implement it as of June 1, 1966 as planned." Next, he wanted to understand how welfare cases figured into the federal proposals. Finally, and most significantly for the course of Ontario's position on national health insurance, was to determine "the effect on our present arrangement if [the] Federal Government says [the] medicare plan is compulsory."[60] The key questions, then, revolved around whether to go ahead with the provincial plan – amended or as it was originally introduced – in light of the federal proposals, and whether to worry about the idea of "compulsion" contained in the federal principles.

Having first agreed that there was little use in arguing over what the federal proposal meant ("it was agreed it meant exactly what it said"[61]), the Ontario government moved on to poking holes in the details. The first point was the extent of the coverage the federal scheme envisaged. "You will recall," Robarts wrote to Pearson, "that the magnitude and importance of the problem of patient care for tuberculosis and the mentally ill were given recognition and are mentioned in the report of the Royal Commission on Health Services." That being the case, he postulated, these two items "might very well be considered to have priority over the provision of physician services."[62] It was, perhaps, a feeble attempt on Robarts's part to open up a line of argument with the federal government, but it was psychologically necessary. With so little room for manoeuvring, the Ontario government snatched at whatever possibilities there might be for staking out a provincial position on the question.

The more important debates were destined to occur within the province rather than between the two levels of government. The two main areas on which there was a significant discrepancy between the federal and provincial proposals – the conditions on the carrier and the nature of compulsion – left the Ontario government particularly susceptible to entreaties from the insurance industry. That the Robarts government had so often curried favour with that particular group made the requests all the more plaintive. But by the mid-1960s, the days of private insurance domination in either pensions or health seemed to be numbered. Even Laurence Coward, chair of the Pension Commission of Ontario and a private insurance dealer, admitted that "Ontario accepts the principle that public money from taxation should not go to private insurers."[63] The medical community also had to be considered. While the Ontario government had engaged in extensive consultations with the Ontario Medical Association and its constituent parts in the design of their own health insurance plan, the new situation created by the federal proposals opened the field up for further negotiations. This allowed the government to correct some of the errors of the previous round of negotiation. As Robarts noted to his subcommittee on health insurance, "the Government had made a horrible mistake in going for 100% of the Ontario Medical Association schedule of fees." Luckily, the federal proposal was based on payments up to 85 per cent of the physicians' fee schedule, providing a logical "out" for the provincial government.[64] The Ontario government faced considerable opposition from both the insurance and the medical communities; neither, however, could count on public opinion swinging to their side, and in that, at least, Robarts's team had the upper hand.

In the short term, there was relatively little that the provincial government could do besides figure out how best to introduce a bill that would be acceptable as enabling legislation under the terms of the federal medicare proposals. Perhaps there might be some movement on the inclusion of tuberculosis sanatoria or mental institutions, although Pearson had not sounded enthusiastic about the suggestion.[65] Perhaps there might be a way of including private insurers or of addressing the financial concerns of the doctors,[66] but in general the Robarts government looked on the federal proposals as something of an avenue of escape from being too closely tied to private interests. That the federal Liberals had decided to call an election and were using the health care proposals as one of their chief arguments in favour of being returned with an enlarged mandate placed Ontario "in a delicate position. Because of the November 8th Federal election, the Federal Government might want to jockey Ontario into a position of opposing medicare,"[67] and despite minor opposition to the timing, the details and the manner in which it was introduced, Robarts's Ontario was not about to oppose national health insurance: at least not yet. As Ian Macdonald concluded after an intergovernmental meeting of health ministers, "the scheme would appear to be a fait accompli," with even Alberta moving onside.[68] From the federal perspective, the decision to identify principles, the adherence to which would result in federal funding for a provincially legislated program, was ingenious.

Social policies, in fact, did not play much of a role in the election campaign of 1965. Rather, the press and the public both paid more attention to the scandals that had plagued the government – particularly those involving Guy Favreau's acceptance of campaign funds and how much the government knew about the existence of Soviet spy George Spencer. The result was another minority government for the Liberals, a significant restructuring of cabinet, and a suddenly uncertain future for medicare. Because Gordon "had advocated the election more strongly than anyone" he shouldered "a large share of the responsibility" for the failure to win a majority. His offer to resign from cabinet, vacating the important finance post, was accepted. Gordon was well aware that Pearson "was taking advantage of" his offer to resign in order "to make a change at Finance – despite his promises" to the contrary.[69] Pearson put the much more conservative Mitchell Sharp in charge of finance, leading Gordon to fret about the apparent "move to the right" and others to wonder whether health insurance would still be possible in what was expected to be an environment of fiscal restraint.[70]

The election proved that there might be room for manoeuvring on shared-cost programs, and suggested to Ontario politicians and bureaucrats the importance of being prepared for any eventuality. One of the interesting questions of the health insurance debate revolved around Quebec. There had been some attempt to figure out what the Quebec government was intending to do about medicare but, like Ontario, its position remained in a preliminary state. Early reports suggested that "Quebec was opposed to per capita grants" and preferred compensation through tax points or "fiscal abatement"; and unlike Ontario, "Quebec tends to favour a compulsory tax-supported plan rather than a voluntary premium-supported plan for political reasons."[71] Although it was too early to develop a uniform approach to medicare by Ontario and Quebec, there was no question that such a possibility was being considered by officials in Ontario. The ties between the two provinces were traditionally strong, and there was growing interest in Ontario in making them even stronger.

Impasses, Delays, and an Uncertain Future

The goodwill and guiding principles that were established during a visit to Quebec City from an Ontario parliamentary and press delegation in June of 1963 continued throughout the decade. During his first visit to the Quebec capital, Robarts had indicated his intention to be a strong ally to Quebec. It was not surprising, then, that the Advisory Committee on Confederation was also concerned about maintaining the relationship with Quebec. As the cultural subcommittee reported to Premier Robarts during one of their regular dinners, "the survival and viability of the federation" depended on creating "a stronger sense of community or collective will between English-speaking and French-speaking Canadians." Suggesting that Canada adopt official bilingualism, and in addition that Ontario engage in cultural exchanges with Quebec and designate French an official language in the province, the advisers were proposing a "role [that] is in harmony with views that you have publicly expressed, that have been promptly commended by the French-Canadian press, and aroused expectations both inside and outside Quebec."[72] It was a compelling proposal for saving Canadian unity, and one to which Robarts would return again and again, but in light of more pressing issues was shunted to the background for the immediate future.

Events in Quebec made the question of intergovernmental cooperation even more troublesome than usual in the winter of 1966. Under
pressure at home to assert greater independence from Ottawa, Lesage
indicated to the prime minister that his government would "postpone
indefinitely the consideration of the proposal for constitutional amendment."[73] The prime minister was shocked: he had been certain that Quebec would ultimately endorse the Fulton-Favreau amending formula
because it had been unanimously agreed on, because a subsequent federal white paper on the subject had been endorsed by all ten provincial
governments, and because there had been allusions to the amending
formula in Quebec's most recent Throne Speech.[74] But it was not to be.
Lesage's about-face on the issue left a chasm of uncertainty hanging over
intergovernmental relations in Canada.

The attitude in Quebec City over constitutional amendment, which
intimated serious questions over how Quebec intended to proceed on
medicare, combined to heighten concerns about the economic arrangements in Canada. The Tax Structure Committee was still hammering out
an agreement, but shared-cost programs such as medicare contained fiscal redistributive qualities that confused what was already a complicated
arena of tax sharing. The economic and fiscal subcommittee of the Advisory Committee on Confederation had some thoughts on this matter,
suggesting a shift towards block grants that provided provinces largely
unallocated funds to use at their discretion.[75] Wanting to ensure that the
federal government retained enough fiscal power "to preserve a national
economy," the advisers also thought "Ontario need not be taking a pas-
sive role in federal-provincial economic negotiations but should be leading the way."[76] Concerns that Quebec was "moving in the direction of
unconditional fiscal authority" placed Ontario in an even more delicate
position. "Are we to follow the same path," asked Ian Macdonald to the
advisory group, "or should we suggest some alternative?"[77]

After first suggesting that any agreement on a new tax-sharing formula
be delayed for a year,[78] the various Ontario committees responsible for
negotiating taxation issues got down to work. In preparing for the final meeting of the Tax Structure Committee, the Ontario officials were
aided, consulted, and watched by their federal counterparts. Assistant
Deputy Finance Minister Al Johnson visited Toronto at the conclusion
of a cross-Canada tour, leaving Ontario to the end, according to Macdonald, "because they regard our judgment as being critical to the [fis-
cal] proposals."[79] A subsequent meeting brought Robarts into the mix.
Taxation issues were too important for the premier not to be involved

personally, so unlike the first exploratory meeting led by Johnson, the follow-up included Finance Minister Sharp and his deputy Bob Bryce, as well as Johnson, and on the Ontario side included Robarts and senior bureaucrats Keith Reynolds, Macdonald, and Stevenson. This time, Ontario's position was made clearer. On equalization, Robarts acknowledged that Ontario was in favour of the general principle, but was "very interested in the total amount of equalization payments since Ontario would, in effect, be paying for a large proportion of them."[80] Included in the total, Robarts reminded the federal finance officials, would have to be the "equalization component of shared-cost and other programs." Tax sharing, which had never been straightforward, was made immeasurably more complex when questions of both equalization and social policies were taken into consideration. Robarts pressed for more clarity on the issues, but he also worried about the "erosion of the federal government power."[81]

From Ontario's perspective, the whole process was a "frustrating exercise." Without any clear sense of the intentions of any government – federal or provincial – regarding the tax-sharing arrangements for 1967–72, the Ontario civil service was at a loss to know how to advise.[82] As the lone "strongman in the Canadian political battlefield," Robarts had heavy responsibilities not only to his own province but also, in some eyes, to the country as a whole as the fiscal agreements were cobbled together.[83] With the surprising defeat of Lesage's Liberals in the Quebec provincial election, and the return to power of the Union Nationale under Daniel Johnson, "John Robarts was suddenly carrying a new and weightier responsibility, and a strength he had not anticipated."[84] Moreover, what would happen in Quebec now that the much more assertive Union Nationale was in power was anyone's guess. The medicare bill was suddenly less certain: Daniel Johnson had apparently told journalist Peter Newman that "he was not going to be pushed by Ottawa on medicare, and he didn't like Ottawa trying to jiggle provincial priorities in matters within provincial jurisdiction."[85] And the next round of tax agreements were on just as shaky footing.

The atmosphere in Ottawa was one of "doubt and uncertainty" which was "proving detrimental to the settlement" of any of the intergovernmental issues. The situation in Quebec "provided the federal government with a ready rationalization for postponement of discussions"; Ian Macdonald warned Robarts against encouraging delay in any way. The longer issues were postponed, the more likely it was that "final decisions will ... be taken at a single meeting, in quasi-emergency conditions, rather than on the basis of reasoned discussions."[86] But despite pressure from the premier on his provincial counterparts, and repeated entreaties by Ontario bureaucrats, the federal government nevertheless opted to put off the next meeting of the Tax Structure Committee. Rather than meeting in August, as Robarts had advocated, a September gathering was called. While not the preferred date, it left ample room for a summer of perfecting the Ontario position on tax sharing, equalization, and medicare, which both Al Johnson and Ian Macdonald agreed was "now more a financial and a federal-provincial matter than a health matter."[87]

The Treasury Department officials made very clear Ontario's interest in the three areas that were under discussion: of greatest importance was tax sharing itself. Following the negotiation of an acceptable tax-sharing arrangement, Ontario sought agreement on cost sharing by rationalizing the expenditures related to existing programs, and equalization, which could only be "fruitfully" considered after "the other areas of federal-provincial arrangements have been settled."[88] This integrated approach to the fiscal issues was in contrast to Ottawa's position that the problem should be attacked in two distinct phases,[89] a strategy that did not bode well for the conclusion of the tax agreements.

By the time the Tax Structure Committee met in mid-September, the various government positions were both reasonably well known and increasingly hardened. Ontario's position remained the same: to deal with the fiscal situation in the country, it was essential to address the issue of tax sharing first, leaving equalization until later. The federal position also remained the same: open with equalization, in order to "announce its generosity on the first item," then announce its intention to "opt out" of hospital insurance, the Canada Assistance Plan, and national health grants, followed by an offer of tax sharing, by which time the federal treasury would be dry and Ottawa could "plead no ability to share taxes."[90] Quebec's position was just as difficult, and also not surprising. Johnson advocated beginning a shift to 100 per cent provincial control of direct tax fields, although not so quickly that it would "jeopardize its favourable situation on equalization over the next five years," and the elimination of cost-sharing programs altogether, or at least the intention to opt out of all that existed and all that were proposed in the future.[91]

Having made their positions clear, each of the delegations returned home to consider any changes that they were prepared to make before the anticipated conclusion of the Tax Structure Committee's work at the final meeting in October. Al Johnson in Ottawa was reportedly "despondent about the results of the meeting."[92] The positions seemed so entrenched that any movement – especially on the part of either the federal government or the Quebec government – would be seen as "backing down." But Robarts was beyond despondent and seemed not to care about losing face. He was angry. First, with the federal government, for attempting to buy the goodwill of the provinces by handing them seventeen tax points in return for pulling out of some long-standing shared-cost programs. Robarts was sure that "Ottawa would set up new programs that would cost Ontario money," so therefore the province would not accept the seventeen points. He said that it simply was not "good enough for Ottawa to say, 'We'll go our way, you go yours.'" Working up to a final rant, Robarts told his closest advisers that "he had no choice but to 'scream' if Ottawa went ahead with equalization and did not give anything to Ontario."[93] The premier's anger was, however, tinged with disappointment at the apparent failure of leadership within the federal government. He "thought Ottawa should be the Federal Government, take a stand and say 'No' against further encroachments on its tax power. Ontario would be prepared to help Ottawa to say 'No,'" although Robarts wasn't clear how that help was going to be offered.[94]

Second, Robarts's anger was directed at Quebec. When considering the question of how to deal with Quebec's notion of Canada being comprised of two nations, an English one and a French one, Robarts again seemed to lose his composure. Perhaps, he said, the time had "come to tell Quebec to 'get with it.' He was tired of Quebec's continual demands. If Premier Johnson comes to the Conference with a political attitude, then perhaps all the provinces should talk politically. He did not think Quebec would have any chance of leaving the federation. He thought Quebec will take everything she can get. He thought Ontario should say what it thinks. He did not think Ontario would lose in an economic fight."[95]

The level of antagonism at the meeting that followed, the one that left only a few hours before the deadline for agreement for the fiscal year 1967–68, was therefore not particularly surprising. It was "an acrimonious meeting," according to one New Brunswick official, "a disaster" according to another from Ontario.[96] Ian Macdonald spent some time in the weeks following the conference attempting to dispel "any implication that Ontario was being unco-operative";[97] nevertheless, the conflict that characterized the meeting left deep scars. The federal government refused to depart from its initial proposal, and the provinces refused to budge from their stated positions. The conference dissolved without a formal end, and the premiers returned home empty-handed.

There was, however, one interesting development at the conference that was to have lasting implications for Canada. Months earlier, the Advisory Committee on Confederation had suggested that Ontario should host a conference on the future of Canadian federalism as a way to mark the centenary.[98] More recently, at a conference sponsored by the New Democrats in Ontario, editor of *Le Devoir* Claude Ryan advocated tighter ties between Ontario and Quebec as a solution to the current problems.[99] Either of these two suggestions might have been playing in the back of Robarts's head while he sat through the final meeting of the Tax Structure Committee, or perhaps he was just "in a pretty nasty mood." Regardless of the genesis, Robarts took the opportunity to suggest that perhaps the time had come for the provinces to take the initiative since the federal government seemed incapable of solving any component, fiscal or otherwise, of the intergovernmental dilemma. Robarts introduced the idea of a Confederation of Tomorrow Conference, and Canadian constitutional history changed course abruptly.[100]

As Ontario approached Canada's centennial year, it confronted the intergovernmental relationship with a nuanced strategy, a sort of Robartsian amendment to the tactics that had been employed by successive Conservative governments since George Drew. The earlier approach of presenting policy alternatives to the federal agenda, and attempting to win support in other provincial capitals, had been paying slim rewards. Thus, having failed to dictate national policy, or even to convince a majority of other provinces to adopt an Ontario-designed policy on tax sharing or welfare services or health care, Robarts began in the mid-1960s to shift his attention more keenly towards mega-intergovernmental projects like the work of the Tax Structure Committee and the negotiations over the constitution, and towards facilitating dialogue rather than dictating the agenda. There had always been an element of these twin goals in Ontario's postwar approach to dealing with Ottawa: continuing an inclusive conversation had animated Drew's position on the Dominion-Provincial Conference on Reconstruction and Frost's on the tax rental agreements, for example, and the big constitutional question of how to shape the intergovernmental framework had always been less contentious and more alluring in Ontario than some of the details of social policy. Even in the 1950s, the constitution had offered an attractive way for the Ontario delegation to begin to address first principles. But facilitating dialogue about foundational issues had never been quite so clearly the raison d'être of the Ontario approach to federal-provincial relations as it was becoming in the late 1960s.

Chapter Seven

"See if We Can't Amend the Marriage Contract": The Confederation of Tomorrow Conference and Beyond, 1967–1971

The year 1967 was Canada's centennial year, which meant that there were innumerable schemes for celebrating the success of the young nation, from the spectacle of Montreal's Expo to the transnational canoe pageant that was meant to repeat the accomplishments of the explorers of the sixteenth and seventeenth centuries. In Ottawa, there were the usual plans for fireworks and 1 July celebrations, but there was also a push to complete several projects that would secure Canada's position as a mature nation. The year was certainly one for commemorating past triumphs, but it was also an opportunity for rejuvenation, for house cleaning, and for setting the nation on a new course. It marked a turning point for the Conservative government in Ontario, too. In Canada's centennial year, Ontario politicians and bureaucrats alike shifted their attention almost completely to mega-intergovernmental issues of infrastructure and away from the nuts and bolts of the relationship that had been causing so much difficulty in the preceding twenty years. The Confederation of Tomorrow Conference represented the debut of Ontario as a facilitator of constitutional dialogue, a mediator between divergent interests, and a province with a real stake in securing and protecting national unity. The framework of Confederation became, in the centennial year, an obsession with those in Ontario, where short-term goals in the intergovernmental playing field were forsaken in the interest of long-term harmony. The Robartsian strategy stemmed naturally from George Drew's attempt to offer alternative solutions to the problems of reconstruction, but in focusing so intently on the big picture, the provincial rewards were markedly more difficult to count. That was of small concern in a province where the game of intergovernmental relations itself had begun to outshine the score; as long as there was the possibility of big rewards through constitutional reform, Ontario politicians would stick with their obsessions.

Ontario Takes Charge

For the national Conservative party, 1967 marked both a death and a rebirth. A "deep and profound split" in the party had led its president Dalton Camp to openly question the continued leadership of the aging and increasingly paranoid John Diefenbaker, and to force a leadership convention. It was, according to one commentator, "the night of the knives."[1] Seeing "no way of that Party continuing, by way of inheritance or legacy from the so-called Diefenbaker forces,"[2] Camp was successful in orchestrating a national convention that swept the old guard out of office and brought new enthusiasm to the party.[3] No Canadian Conservative remained entirely unscathed by the spectacle of the dethroning, but John Robarts was careful to stay as far out of the fray as possible. His unfortunately late arrival on the podium at the spring meeting at which the leadership review was first proposed nevertheless earned Diefenbaker's ire, probably completing the break between the two men that had been evident since Robarts first assumed the premier's office.[4] By the close of 1967, Conservatives finally had something to celebrate in the choice of the popular Nova Scotia Premier Robert Stanfield as leader.

The introduction of social policies, always popular with the public, was a far better way of marking Canada's centennial than in ousting a national party leader. The Ontario government had announced its new welfare program – the Family Benefits Act – to considerable fanfare in April 1967. Federal Health Minister Allan MacEachen's displeasure with the attention that the Ontario measure received, however, and the later concerns in Ontario that other programs "get all the credit for [being] positive, poverty-prevention programs, while welfare has a negative image"[5] suggested that the chief concerns about welfare arrangements were political. Ottawa's Medical Care Act, which would make it possible for agreeing provinces to receive federal money for their health insurance plans, was a far more important centennial project. Scheduled to begin operation on 1 July 1967, medicare was designed to be a feather in the cap of the Pearson government, but the high costs that were associated with such a program caused concerns at both levels of government. Ontario Health Minister Matthew Dymond was particularly worried about how his province would be affected by the federal offer:

the federal proposal used a formula for cost sharing that "placed a heavy penalty on high cost provinces such as Ontario," where Ottawa would only contribute about 40 per cent of the costs of implementing health insurance.[6] Although MacEachen argued that the simplicity of the federal offer clearly demonstrated that the Medical Care Act was not designed to be another shared-cost program,[7] the question of potentially skyrocketing costs would not go away. Provincial premiers rarely missed an opportunity to complain about "the imposition of medicare expenditures on them when they need money for other things."[8] And that reluctance on the part of the premiers gave support to the growing federal sentiment, especially among the more conservative members of Pearson's cabinet, that medicare was too expensive to introduce very quickly.[9]

The centennial celebrations also pointed to a need to put federal-provincial administrative matters in order. Two royal commissions – the Carter Commission on Federal-Provincial Financial Relations and the Bilingualism and Biculturalism Commission – both completed years of work in 1967, and their respective reports had implications for the way the two levels of government would interact in Canada's second century. Both were broad-ranging inquiries, although it was the so-called B and B Commission that generated more public interest than the much drier recommendations of the Carter Commission. It was the latter, however, that interested the Ontario bureaucracy the most. On the one hand, Ian Macdonald wrote Robarts, "the Report is thorough and imaginative" but it failed to address the problem of different expenditure requirements for the two levels of government. To point out such a serious shortcoming, Macdonald warned, might put the premier in a position of being "accused of taking a 'dog-in-the manger' attitude or an unduly provincial view in the face of serious national requirements."[10] It was a classic Ontario dilemma: how to ensure that the province's rights were respected without upsetting the ship of state.

The Carter Commission had offered an overview of and recommendations for revising the existing taxation system in Canada, and federal Minister of Finance Mitchell Sharp intended to use it as the basis for government policy.[11] Ontario bureaucrats had already expressed their concerns over the failure to include discussion of expenditure requirements, but in an effort to avoid being "locked into a position against which we can only react,"[12] the Department of Finance had prepared a substantial response to the Carter Report. It underlined Ontario's concerns about the "ramifications of the Carter Report in the field of tax sharing at the federal, provincial and municipal levels of government."[13]

Other provincial delegations had not come to the meeting as well prepared as the Ontario representatives, and in general seemed to adopt a "negative and even narrow approach." Western provinces, particularly concerned over the Carter recommendations regarding the abolition of exemptions for corporations in the extractive industries, seemed committed to impeding the progress of the federal tax reforms. According to Ian Macdonald, "the Report has tended to stiffen *regional* concern and regional outlook; in turn, the importance of a province such as Ontario taking a fair and sensible view becomes more apparent than ever."[14]

The Carter recommendations, which were discussed at continuing meetings of the Tax Structure Committee, quite clearly had important implications for a broad range of intergovernmental issues, and the various views on the report tended to stir up regional differences. The same was also true of medicare, still being hotly debated at federal-provincial meetings. The program was clearly going to be expensive, and as a result would have an effect on provincial spending priorities and provincial tax distribution. As Provincial Treasurer Charles MacNaughton complained, the federal position was "contradictory: on the one hand, it wishes to control expenditures and reduce inflationary pressures, and, on the other hand, it pushes the provinces to increase expenditures very substantially, by undertaking medicare."[15] The B and B Commission Report was potentially even more troublesome for federal-provincial relations, as it dealt with matters of culture rather than costs. Few of the issues that were supposed to be resolved in Canada's centennial year were clear-cut; all seemed to have far-reaching implications; all seemed to warrant a more exhaustive discussion of intergovernmental relations than had yet been undertaken. Ontario's very own centennial project thus seemed extraordinarily well timed.

When Prime Minister Lester Pearson learned that Ontario Premier Robarts had every intention of making good on his promise – or threat – to host a Confederation of Tomorrow Conference in Toronto in 1967, he immediately put pen to paper. "I think I am right," he wrote, "in saying that there is no precedent for a Federal-Provincial conference being called by a provincial government." That didn't mean, of course, that it couldn't happen, but Pearson thought it was not "wise, or desirable, to move to a situation in which the Premier of any province might initiate a Federal-Provincial Conference that could be awkward or untimely for one of the other provinces, or unhelpful to the country as a whole." In this particular situation, perhaps the whole problem could be avoided by Ottawa scheduling a conference and Ontario making some agenda suggestions.[16] Robarts was not about to be moved from his position, and while he attempted "to allay any feelings of disquiet and alarm" that the prime minister might have held, he nevertheless insisted that his invitation did "not infringe, nor was it intended to infringe, upon the jurisdictional authority of the Federal Government."[17] Although the exchange continued, Robarts had won his point. The Confederation of Tomorrow Conference would proceed, and federal-provincial relations in Canada would take a dramatic turn.

So too would the capacity and approach of the Ontario civil service. A conference that had been called "for the purpose of examining the present status of Confederation in Canada and our federal system" had the potential to be extraordinarily broad ranging.[18] To effectively host such an event, the Ontario bureaucrats involved in intergovernmental affairs issues had to have a full understanding of what could be expected from each of the other participants, and they had to prepare Premier Robarts for facilitating free, open, and useful discussion. It was a tall order, and one that made full use of the new Federal-Provincial Affairs Secretariat within the Treasury Department, as well as the advice of the Advisory Committee on Confederation. It also demanded a clear articulation of goals on the part of the Ontario government: what exactly was Ontario trying to achieve in moving the intergovernmental discussion away from the details of tax agreements or health insurance, and towards the much less certain territory of the future of Confederation? The process of answering that question took some considerable introspection on the part of the Ontario participants, but the result was worthwhile not only from the provincial perspective but also from the vantage point of the achievement of constitutional reform in Canada. As all governments in Canada embarked on a process of constitutional amendment, shifting the federal-provincial debate permanently from the details of individual agreements to big-picture, or mega-intergovernmental, change, Ontario assumed an important position as facilitator. The experience of the Confederation of Tomorrow Conference served as an important initiation into this role.

In keeping with the Ontario commitment to full preparedness for any intergovernmental meeting, the civil servants charged with spearheading the organization of the Confederation of Tomorrow Conference gleaned as much information as possible from their counterparts in other provinces. Quebec was on board immediately. Premier Daniel Johnson wrote Robarts soon after the formal declaration of Ontario's intention to host the conference was made public in the Legislature's

Throne Speech, congratulating him on his "province's willingness to face Canada's problems, present and future, with courage and clear sightedness."[19] His Deputy Minister of Intergovernmental Affairs Claude Morin echoed that sentiment and added some suggestions for organizing the event. He hoped that it could be the first of many intergovernmental meetings to maintain the spirit of compromise at the outset: "the Quebec people would feel compelled to present a complete statement of their desires at any one-shot conference," he argued, "which might result in a breakdown of any constructive work."[20]

After considerable internal debate, the planning committee responsible for organizing the Confederation of Tomorrow Conference opted for a relatively informal series of presentations and discussions with relatively full access for the press.[21] Armed with at least some sense of direction, various members of the Ontario bureaucracy scattered across the country to meet with both their civil service counterparts and, in some cases, ministerial representatives in the various provincial capitals. Their goal was to determine how Robarts's formal letter of invitation had been received, and how each of the premiers intended to respond to the invitation and to behave at the conference. These were all eye-opening excursions. In Winnipeg, Keith Reynolds of the Attorney General's Office and Ed Greathed from the Federal-Provincial Affairs Secretariat learned that "little, if any, thought about the [conference] had been given by anyone in the Manitoba government."[22] It was not an uncommon response to the arrival of the emissaries from Ontario. In Regina, none of the officials had seen Robarts's letter of invitation, which did nothing to stop them from identifying problems with the proposed agenda that the Ontario delegation presented to them.[23] On the British Columbia tour, Reynolds once again met with officials who "appeared to be disinterested in the conference."[24] In Alberta, the reception was quite different. Premier Manning himself met with the Ontario visitors, and talked at length "in a forthright and vigorous manner."[25] He expressed serious reservations about the inclusion of "linguistic and cultural duality" on the tentative agenda, and stressed instead his understanding of Confederation as "a union of provinces" and his own "doctrine of variety." In no way did he support "special status" for Quebec. While the Ontario delegation was no doubt pleased with the amount of thought that Manning had given to the forthcoming conference, in marked contrast to bureaucrats and politicians elsewhere, it was a bit more unsettling to realize "that he has reached a number of firm positions on these issues and that he is fully prepared to discuss them with zest and candour next month."[26]

Bad luck followed the Ontario emissaries to the Maritimes, postponing a meeting in Nova Scotia and forcing the Ontario contingent down to one for the final meeting in New Brunswick. They were pleased to learn, however, that the initial opposition of Joey Smallwood of Newfoundland had "undergone a complete change for the better" and that the officials in Prince Edward Island were "sympathetic to the Conference and are fully prepared to participate in it."[27] In New Brunswick, however, the provincial civil servants were perhaps emboldened by the appearance of only one Ontario representative, and they took it upon themselves to present "a federalist point of view and [state] that a province should not call a confederation conference." Deputy Minister of Economics and Development S.W. Clarkson, the lone Ontarian in the room, remarked upon his return to the safer environment of Toronto that the "the main point was very clear – Ontario should not be holding a Confederation Conference."[28] He thought that the upcoming provincial election might have made the situation even more tense, and suggested that it would be best to postpone further work with New Brunswick until after the election.[29] Luckily, when the meeting with the Nova Scotia representatives was finally able to be rescheduled, it was clear that in Halifax at least, there was some sympathy, if not much knowledge, "about Quebec's aspirations." The Nova Scotians had given enough thought to the proposed conference that they were ready to discuss logistics rather than get embroiled in debates about the merits of a province taking the lead on constitutional discussions.[30]

Clearly, the views of the politicians and bureaucrats in Quebec were more important to the Ontario organizers than those of the other provincial delegations; consequently, the job of feeling out the Quebec delegation was reserved for those with the most seniority, and the most experience with Quebec – Ian Macdonald and Donald Stevenson. Similarly, Daniel Johnson's Union Nationale government was represented by senior officials Claude Morin, Louis Bernard, and Jacques Robichaud of the Department of Intergovernmental Affairs. The discussions revealed Quebec's eagerness for "as much public exposure" as possible. The first draft of Johnson's opening statement already ran to forty pages, and Morin and his team hoped that the hour and a half it would take to read the statement could be squeezed into the agenda: "there was a reluctance on the part of some of the Quebec people to see such a major statement summarized briefly and then tabled or distributed."[31] Increasingly, the Quebec delegation was coming under public pressure "to outline a clear-cut Quebec position" and regarded the conference as an opportunity to uncover the reactions of other provinces to their presentation. Although Ontario officials were hesitant to proceed with the discussions quite as formally as Quebec seemed to want,[32] it was nevertheless evident that the Confederation of Tomorrow Conference was going to be primarily about figuring out what Quebec wanted out of Confederation, and determining whether anyone else could live with those demands.

While members of the planning committee on the Confederation of Tomorrow Conference were most intimately involved in the day-to-day organizational work, the Ontario Advisory Committee on Confederation was also kept in the loop and consulted regularly. The views of the group were rarely unanimous and frequently at cross purposes, but they were useful in providing a range of responses that better prepared the planning committee for the actual conference. In the final weeks before the conference's opening, advisory committee members outlined potential problems around who would occupy the chair (Robarts himself was finally forced to play both host and chair); the implications of the federal government's decision not to participate in the conference ("John Meisel said that at some point someone will have to speak for Canada and since Ottawa will not be represented by Ministers, the Hon. Mr. Robarts will have to do so"); and what would happen after the conference concluded (Harvey Perry worried that if the conference shifted to another provincial venue for round two, "then Ontario would lose control").[33] Although the various views of the members of the advisory committee were taken into consideration, the planning committee seemed preoccupied in these final days with decisions about seating arrangements and no-smoking sections.[34] The combination of advice from the practical bureaucrats and from the cerebral academics may not always have been easy, but the conference itself was well served by its twin planners.

In the meantime, Ottawa seemed to have been left behind by events taking place in Ontario. After battling with Robarts over the right to hold the conference in the first place, Pearson chose to allow federal participation only to the extent of sending observers. For some, like the increasingly disillusioned Walter Gordon, this retreat was simply a further sign of the prime minister's weakness. Gordon maintained that it was Pearson's "understanding of Quebec" and his "efforts to hold the country together" that were his "single most important contribution … as Prime Minister"; but all that was in jeopardy with former Liberal cabinet minister "Rene Levesque's unequivocal espousal of separatism" and the absence of any real attack against it in Quebec itself. "It seems to me," wrote Gordon, "that in view of this confused situation and the vacuum that seems to exist at present, the federal government should be prepared to step into the breach and give a lead."[35] But Pearson was, for the time being at least, in a wait-and-see mood. If Robarts wanted to "step into the breach," then Pearson was prepared to see where that might lead. The relative lack of action at the national level only served to increase the anticipation leading up to the opening of the Confederation of Tomorrow Conference.

Although the members of Ontario's planning committee, as well as most of the Federal-Provincial Affairs Secretariat, were well aware of the difficulties that the conference would face in finding common ground between the provincial premiers, there was nevertheless a high degree of enthusiasm in the days leading up to the conference.[36] The spirit that had motivated holding the meeting was positive, so there was no reason to imagine that the results should not also be so. It was lucky, however, that the conference was scheduled to last three days, as accord was certainly not immediately apparent. In his opening remarks, Premier Daniel Johnson painted a picture of Canada that would sit uneasily with many of the premiers present: "Canada is not merely a federation of ten provinces. It is also home of ... two nations in the sociological sense," he stated. But "while our present constitution still contains elements which are valid for organizing Canada as a partnership of ten, we are forced to conclude that much of this other two-partner Canada remains to be invented."[37] This process of "invention" would demand a thorough constitutional overhaul, and the line was drawn. Interestingly, it was a line that for the most part had already been drawn in 1867: the original provinces in Confederation tended to agree that constitutional change was necessary, while the "newcomers" held firm that "adjustments could be made within the framework of the existing Constitution."[38]

On the second day of the conference Robarts and Johnson disagreed over whether amendment of the constitution was sufficient to solve the problems of Confederation or whether a complete rewriting of the document was necessary. Although Robarts's statement that Ontario "was not necessarily anxious for a complete revision" aligned him with Ernest Manning and Joey Smallwood and against his traditional ally Johnson, it was nevertheless a negotiation strategy that bore results. When Johnson relaxed his "hard line" policy, it went further than merely mending relations with Ontario. By insisting that a solution could be achieved through a series of amendments that "could later be consolidated," Johnson was essentially stating that rewriting the constitution was unnecessary; when he offered a metaphor, the tension broke with laughter. "Some people in

Quebec want to divorce Canada and then remarry the same woman with a new marriage contract," he declared. "I want to see if we can't amend the marriage contract, rather than take the chance of a divorce and having the woman meet someone else."[39]

Despite having very different conceptions of both the problems that were facing Canada as it entered its second century and the solutions that might be necessary, it was clear that each of the provincial premiers had arrived at the conference in a positive frame of mind and with a willingness to make this new kind of constitutional discussion work. Without the usual antagonist of the federal government present, there was a sense that the premiers were more conciliatory, more willing to work together on a solution to their collective concerns. As Don Stevenson wrote after the delegates had returned home, "the conference was noteworthy because of the spirit of compromise that was evoked with regard to an approach to" constitutional questions.[40] Observers also noted the cooperative tone of the conference: federal civil servant Carl Goldenberg was one of many who wrote to Robarts to "congratulate" him on his "expert handling of the Conference ... There is general agreement," he wrote, "that you deserve the credit for the feeling that with goodwill and continued effort Confederation may yet be saved."[41]

The official federal observers were less glowing in their praise for Robarts, but the reports that made it back to Ottawa about the results of the conference were nevertheless still positive. The federal contingent was pleased to see that provinces were "awakening to the seriousness of the problem" facing the country and that there was a clear "willingness ... to open up the whole constitutional issue for discussion."[42] But most interestingly, the federal observers found reason for the federal government to rejoice: not only had the premiers "managed to identify a number of national goals" including economic growth, equalization, and equality of French and English, but "some provinces, at least, appeared to come to the conclusion that there is a need for the federal presence in such considerations."[43] Even in the midst of a provincially initiated conference on the future of Confederation, they seemed to say, there was evidence of the need for Ottawa. All was not lost. While there were still reasons for concern, including "failure of policy and leadership" that seemed to be implied in the fact that the Confederation of Tomorrow Conference was necessary at all, in general the federal representatives saw much that was heartening about the way the conference unfolded.[44]

Most significantly, the federal officials saw an opportunity to move directly from the Confederation of Tomorrow Conference into a formal federal-provincial conference on the constitution. Long before the Ontario conference Pearson had proposed meeting to reach an agreement on the enactment of the Bill of Rights in each province; gradually this idea had been transformed and upgraded as the constitutional issue seemed to become both more important, and controlled by the federal government. Building on Pearson's original invitation, Justice Minister Pierre Trudeau proposed that the Canadian Bill of Rights be entrenched in the constitution. This would open up the question of the amending formula, as well as calling into question the role of the Supreme Court as final adjudicator and the current federal powers of disallowance and reservation. The result of starting with the Bill of Rights would be that "constitutional reform would be raised by [the federal government] in some sort of controlled manner in order to prevent the entire situation from escalating out of federal control."[45] But the federal reconceptualization of the constitutional conference did not stop there: in October 1967, it was broadened to include "any and all suggestions of the participating provinces with regard to constitutional problems" and, with the publication of the *Report of the Royal Commission on Bilingualism and Biculturalism,* "Mr. Pearson suggested that the conference consider its recommendations" as well.[46]

As the proposed February 1968 conference loomed closer, its agenda became increasingly cluttered and less focused. A general discussion of constitutional issues might have been fine for the Confederation of Tomorrow Conference, which was not designed to reach conclusions, but in a formal first ministers' conference this was another matter altogether. The Ontario bureaucrats fretted about the implications of the "lack of clarity" that seemed to characterize Ottawa's approach to the agenda. Gary Posen and Bob Metcalfe of the intergovernmental affairs division of Ontario's Treasury Department were particularly perplexed and exasperated:

> Is the federal Cabinet so divided that it has been unable to prepare a clear approach to the Conference? Have the events of the last eight months forced it to keep changing its mind as to its nature? Or is the federal government planning to seize the initiative at the Conference by suddenly presenting it with a series of concrete proposals? The provinces will again be forced into the position of 'reacting' with the federal government in the driver's seat. I fear that if this is the case only Quebec will have prepared counter-proposals and will be in a position to challenge the federal initiative. Ontario might then be nothing more than a bystander in an Ottawa-Quebec struggle.[47]

Robarts clearly expected that the Confederation of Tomorrow Conference would simply be a prelude to a more official intergovernmental meeting; in the Ontario Legislature he declared that "we believe that our decision to call the Confederation of Tomorrow Conference made it possible for the federal government, if it chose to, to resume its primary role in these matters, and I think that events have proved us to be correct."[48] Nevertheless, to have moved so quickly from hosting discussions to being at the mercy of a bafflingly unorganized federal government gave some cause for concern in the halls of power in Ontario. As had been the case so many times in the past, the uncertainty about Ottawa's intentions gave rise to the fear that "Ontario may be driven into the position of simply reacting to Federal proposals, or else, watching an Ottawa-Quebec confrontation."[49] The situation in Quebec was certainly paramount. The prime minister indicated to his cabinet that the timing of the constitutional conference was critical: "the balance between unity and secession may depend on what the Conference does or fails to do."[50] Citing French President Charles De Gaulle's "Vive Québec libre!" speech, the split between federalists and separatists within the Quebec Liberal party, and the pressure Réné Lévesque's brand of separatism had placed on Premier Daniel Johnson, Pearson impressed upon his colleagues the need to tread carefully. Moreover, the publication of the first volume of recommendations of the B and B Commission pointed to the inequality of French and English across the country and raised issues that had implications for the proposed Bill of Rights and the structure of the Supreme Court.[51] But despite rumours that the federal government intended to drop the text of a brand new constitution on the first ministers assembled at the February conference, what was prepared was a broad outline of "the goals of Canadian federalism ... and the kind of constitution these goals call for."[52]

When the federal-provincial conference opened on 5 February 1968, Robarts was armed not only with the advice of a civil service that had devoted considerable time over the previous several months to the future of Confederation, but also the conclusions of the Continuing Committee on Confederation. The somewhat informal committee of the premiers of Alberta, Nova Scotia, Quebec, and Ontario that had been struck at the conclusion of the Confederation of Tomorrow Conference had met a few weeks before the opening of the full first ministers' conference, and concluded that they would have a continuing role to play regarding "matters ... which could be dealt with most efficaciously at the inter-provincial level" such as official languages.[53] When Robarts stood to address his colleagues at the constitutional conference, then, it was not surprising that he noted the key role that the Confederation of To-morrow Conference had played in "creating an attitude conducive to the discussion of change."[54] On the issues that had been raised by the B and B Commission regarding official languages, however, Robarts was more circumspect. "Although Quebec will always be the heartland of French Canada, we reject the view that Quebec is the nation state of French Canadians," he stated. And although the Ontario premier had "no intention of forcing anyone to become bilingual," there were several steps that the government had already taken, and more that would follow in the future, that would make French a more welcome language in Ontario.[55] By the end of the conference, Robarts was being praised for his move towards making Ontario bilingual and his willingness to make "spiritual or financial" sacrifices to keep the country together.[56]

In what was heralded as an important step in the direction of constitutional change, Robarts continued to play the role of statesman, carefully building bridges between various positions. Daniel Johnson invariably stood at one end of the spectrum, arguing that Quebec did not want bilingualism forced upon the rest of Canada but instead wanted the premiers to work towards fundamental constitutional change, while Ernest Manning stood at the other, where meeting Quebec's demands would come to be seen as a "constitutional Munich" wherein "reasonable concessions were made in good faith" now, only to "precipitate a more serious situation" in the future."[57] Three days later, the disparate views had been at least cobbled together to the extent that all were willing to continue the process of federal-provincial dialogue.

New Players on the Constitutional Front

Constitutional review was never expected to happen overnight; the meeting in February 1968 was just the beginning. To facilitate the process, a Continuing Committee of Officials on the Constitution (CCOC) was struck at the conclusion of the February conference and would meet dozens of times over the next three years. The first strategy that the CCOC employed was to require that all provinces submit a series of constitutional propositions and explanations as a way "to discover areas of agreement and disagreement among various governments."[58] Ontario duly submitted twelve propositions dealing with the objectives of Confederation, official languages, and fundamental rights.[59] With its fifty propositions, it quickly became clear that Quebec's "purpose is ... a wholly new constitution for Canada based on a set of principles that would explicitly recognize a country of two nations as well as ten provinces." What seemed manifestly less clear was anyone else's purposes.[60] The review process was destined to drag on a long time.

While the CCOC met over the course of 1968, however, much changed in the political world around it. Having earned the attention of English-speaking Canada with his performance at the 1968 constitutional conference, where he displayed a "magnetic television presence,"[61] Pierre Trudeau moved on to the Liberal leadership convention a month later. Pearson's two minority governments had worn him down, and by the end of the centennial year he was ready to move into retirement. Several members of his cabinet manoeuvred to replace him, but after a short campaign and a long leadership convention, Trudeau emerged from the fifth ballot victorious. The change in personnel in the prime minister's office was bound to have important consequences on the outcome of constitutional review. So, too, would events in Quebec City. Daniel Johnson left the 1968 conference tired, not surprising given the tenor of the discussions. But he soon became ill, and was dead by September. Robarts was not alone in feeling both shocked and saddened by the sudden departure of his colleague: whatever his constitutional position may have been, Johnson and Robarts had grown very close in the few months of their association. It was a heartfelt personal note that Robarts sent Johnson's widow calling the late Quebec premier "a great Canadian, a great Quebecois, and a true personal friend of mine" and promising to "always treasure the memory of our association through the years."[62] With Trudeau in the prime minister's seat, and new Quebec Premier Jean-Jacques Bertrand representing the alternative vision, in was hard not to imagine constitutional reform changing pace.

Not only did the people change, however, but also strategies changed. Trudeau moved quickly to end the uncertainty surrounding the implementation of national medicare, which had plagued the last months of the Pearson government. With conservative members of cabinet seeking to delay implementation and the legislation's backers seeking to push it through on schedule, combined with the confusion of leadership politics, the future of medicare itself seemed in question. At root was whether Ottawa had enough money to honour its commitment to pay half the cost of medical insurance in a province that passed legislation satisfying the federal government's five criteria – that it be portable, universal, comprehensive, publicly administered, and compulsory. With Trudeau at the helm, and Edgar Benson in finance, Ottawa moved quickly to pass a 2 per cent social development tax that was designed to raise the money necessary to cover the anticipated costs. Robarts, among others, was furious.

The second meeting of the constitutional conference, held in December 1968, was characterized by uncertainty, caused largely by the "uneven" quality of provincial representation to the CCOC. As a result, the committee "had to travel slowly and has made little headway in reaching a consensus on the issues before it."[63] With little reason for enthusiasm, Robarts thus moved into the next meeting of the constitutional conference, called for February 1969, angry about the methods that had been used to finance medicare, and uncertain of what to expect from either Trudeau or Bertrand. A few days before the opening of the conference, the premier and some of his officials met with the new Justice Minister John Turner, in an effort to convey Ontario's thinking on the constitution and the approach the provincial delegation intended to take at the upcoming first ministers' meeting. Over the hour and a half of the meeting, Turner heard some pretty blunt views; Robarts seemed to agree with the normally calm former premier of Ontario, Leslie Frost, who advised that Ontario should "be brutal" with a federal government prone to "meddling in provincial business."[64] The first issue was the social development tax, about which Robarts was "genuinely angry." Having suggested that the provinces raise their own taxes as a way of financing medicare, the federal government's own 2 per cent tax hike ate into the existing tax room. It was, according to Robarts, "the action of an insensitive and centralizing federal government."[65] At root was Robarts's anger over the pressure to introduce medicare despite clear provincial opposition, which he saw as an indication "that the Government of Canada has no real sense of what federalism means." According to Ottawa official Al Johnson, who was by now the "economic advisor on the constitution" in the Prime Minister's Office, Robarts argued "that [Trudeau's] attitude constitutes a real threat to federalism just as the Government of Canada considers the failure to act on bilingualism as a threat to Canadian unity."[66]

This anger on Robarts's part seemed to colour his intended approach to the constitutional conference as a whole. As Al Johnson reported, the premier "clearly intends to take a very rough, very critical line at the Constitutional Conference" based on a criticism of Ottawa's "approach … to federal-provincial relations." In this, Robarts expected the support of many of his counterparts in other provinces. On the issue of official languages that had been raised at the first conference, Robarts repeated his earlier argument that Ontario had already made great strides in the direction of accommodating French-speaking Ontarians and would "stand on his record of bilingualism" which, he underlined, had the support of "virtually all the Franco-Ontarians."[67] In fact, the topics that fell under the rubric of constitutional review – the enumeration of human rights, the language issue, and the reconsideration of the division of powers themselves – were of little interest to Robarts, and had it not been for Quebec's concerns, Robarts indicated that he "would be quite satisfied with the BNA Act as it is."[68]

What the Ontario team wanted was for Trudeau to back away from medicare, and away from the invasion of both provincial jurisdiction and provincial tax room. If that didn't happen, Robarts made it clear just how far he was prepared to go: "If I am forced to I will set up a state within a state. I don't want to," he said, "I don't think it would be a good thing for Canada; but if Ottawa goes on treating the provinces as they are ... then I will do it. And Ontario has the muscle to do it."[69] Robarts's "state within a state" would imply contracting out of existing programs like the Canada Pension Plan and "imposing a separate Income Tax Act with a different tax base." But in addition to defending Ontario's interests in the face of what appeared to be an increasingly centralist federal government, Robarts maintained a position as defender of all provinces: more than once, he reportedly said, "Don't drive us into a corner; above all don't take advantage of Premier Bertrand's weakness." And later, "don't try it with the other provinces either."[70]

The process of preparing for intergovernmental meetings of the constitutional conference was enormously time consuming and demanded the attention of a large number of civil servants in Ontario. While the Federal-Provincial Affairs Secretariat of the Department of Treasury and Economics spearheaded Ontario's efforts, there were still five ministerial committees, plus the Tax Structure Committee, the Study Committee on the National Capital, the Distribution of Powers Committee, *and* the Continuing Committee of Officials on the Constitution that needed staffing.[71] As discussions became more sophisticated, advice from experts in other departments seemed necessary as well.[72] Other intergovernmental issues were falling by the wayside, although Robarts was surely heartened to learn that the majority of the letters received by the government as a result of the February 1969 constitutional conference were written in support of his stance on medicare.[73] Yet despite the attention and personnel devoted to the constitution, progress remained unsettlingly slow. In June, for example, the first ministers met for another round of negotiations. The Ontario team had already prepared extensive working papers on the spending power and intergovernmental finance and had participated in various ministerial committees.[74] And yet, the first ministers' meeting itself quickly became mired in debate over innumerable small and esoteric issues. At root, Robarts consistently advocated postponing the constitutional discussions until the question of tax sharing had been settled, while Trudeau consistently argued the opposite, and little headway seemed to be made.[75]

What had become quite clear was that the government at Queen's Park and the government in Ottawa had markedly different agendas when it came to the constitutional conference. Trudeau had come to office with what seemed to be very specific goals: he wanted to secure an entrenched Charter of Rights, and he wanted to establish Canada as a bilingual nation. He had also earned a reputation – whether deserved or not – as being able to quash Quebec separatism before it got off the ground, and so expectations in English Canada in particular were running high.[76] Robarts, on the other hand, had initiated the entire constitutional review process by hosting a broad-ranging discussion of the very nature of Canadian federalism. He viewed Trudeau's agenda as too specific, and ultimately not specific enough on the issue that was of fundamental importance to Ontario – the division of money and jurisdiction between the federal and provincial governments. Committed as he was to making the constitutional review process work, he was reluctant to follow the course that Trudeau was setting.

There were other matters to discuss apart from language and rights, in Robarts's opinion. In the fall of 1969, he suggested to Trudeau that the time had come to open new discussions, separate from the constitutional review series, dealing with tax reform, pollution, First Nations, and housing.[77] The prime minister had also earlier announced measures that the federal government intended to take to curb inflationary tendencies; while there were few obvious implications for Ontario at the time, it was nevertheless a topic that the Federal-Provincial Affairs Secretariat intended to watch.[78] By 1970, the economy was threatening to overtake constitutional review as the topic of discussion at the increasingly frequent federal-provincial conferences, and Ontario officials had to advise Robarts not "to be stampeded by inflation hysteria." Instead, they suggested, "Ontario could usefully redirect the emphasis of the inflation debate from the narrow short-run emergency view to the more fundamental issue of long-run economic growth without inflation."[79] But these sorts of issues, regardless of whether they were considered in the long or short run, served to confuse the already confusing intergovernmental agenda. In addition to first ministers' meetings, there were also regular meetings of civil servants with the Continuing Committee of Officials on the Constitution in preparation for the more political gatherings, meetings of finance ministers and welfare ministers and health ministers, and, since February 1969, further meetings of the Tax Structure Committee. The federal-provincial program was in danger of becoming overloaded, unfocused, and incapable of reaching conclusions on the issues of constitutional change that had prompted the series of meetings in the first place.

Those outside the conference rooms had little interest and less say in what was going on. According to NDP leader Tommy Douglas, by adopting "a very dull and pedestrian approach," the federal Liberals had succeeded in "throw[ing] a smokescreen of boredom around the subject [of constitutional review] and have really turned the people off."[80] As Ontario bureaucrat Gary Posen saw it, there were three ways out of this morass: first, the politicians could be removed from the process, decreasing public expectation of tangible constitutional results, and the bureaucrats could continue with a "long-term study of the constitution to assess its contemporary strengths and weaknesses"; second, the process could simply be ended on the grounds that "it is progressing slowly, is increasingly a source of dissension, and is deflecting energies away from the important day-to-day problems of the federation"; or finally, everyone could agree that what was needed was the complete rewriting of the constitution, rather than the piecemeal reconsideration that was currently being undertaken. Posen advised that Ontario follow the last course.[81] It was slightly more abrupt than Robarts was prepared to countenance, but he was set to move the process ahead more aggressively than he had in the previous two years. At the September 1970 meeting of first ministers, Robarts pushed for immediate agreement on an amending formula, which was the key step in constitutional reform, and the early conclusion of the meandering review process in which all had become bogged down.[82]

Bilateral Confrontation and Constitutional Collapse

This strategy also had its weaknesses, as the Ontario officials were to discover. Discussions surrounding the amending formula were clearly a minefield, and although the federal bureaucrats superficially seemed to be prepared to take part in a discussion of the formula by the constitutional conference as a whole, a careful parsing of the federally drafted minutes of the September 1970 meeting proved otherwise. In what Ontario's director of the Federal-Provincial Affairs Secretariat Ed Greathed termed "the richest example to date of a federally-drafted and totally meaningless communiqué which obfuscates political meaning,"[83] Ottawa appeared to be endorsing an open discussion of the amending formula but in reality was pushing for "high level bilateral discussions with two or three of the key provinces to find out how much room for compromise there was."[84] While this infuriated the Ontario officials, causing confusion over what tactics they should employ in dealing with Ottawa over the constitution and begging the question "are the mandarins at it again?" there was no way around the new reality.[85] Bilateral discussions became the de facto approach to constitutional change.

There were several reasons that more private discussions between federal representatives – either officials or ministers – and their provincial counterparts had become, by 1971, a more appropriate way of handling the constitutional issue than through multilateral intergovernmental conferences. The strategies that had worked during the 1960s were no longer practical given the changed environment at the beginning of the 1970s. Trudeau's arrival on the scene was partly responsible for the changing tenor of constitutional debate. As Robarts noted as he considered Canada's prospects, the 1960s could be characterized by a "continual raid on Ottawa – confrontations with Quebec – eternal necessity to return to Quebec 'with something' – to satisfy the Quebec position." There had been, however, a "shift in emphasis with Trudeau Gov't" that could be seen as a "battle between French Ottawa and French Quebec," and that meant that Ontario's "role has changed."[86] Bilateral conversations with federal representatives were a useful way for the Ontario government to make the transition from one role to another.

Similarly, there were changes in the provincial actors that had clear implications for the future of constitutional renewal. In 1970, the young Liberal Robert Bourassa had ousted the Union Nationale in Quebec, which many observers heralded as bringing a stronger federalist perspective to the intergovernmental table. With the kidnapping of senior politicians in Quebec by the Front de Libération du Québec (FLQ) in October 1970, and the murder of Pierre Laporte, however, Bourassa's political credentials were tarnished. Not only did the events indicate a strong grassroots support in Quebec for a separatist option, but Bourassa's reliance on federal military support during the crisis led many to question his strength as a leader.[87] The October Crisis, as it has come to be known, pushed Bourassa into a position of having to prove his independence vis-à-vis the federal government, and constitutional negotiations were one obvious place for such muscle flexing.

In Ontario, the long reign of John Robarts was also coming to an end. The field of leadership hopefuls included five cabinet ministers, although it became quickly evident that the men to beat were Education Minister William Davis, the front runner, and Mines Minister Allan Lawrence, who had earned a reputation as being something of a maverick within the Conservative party. The party convention, held in mid-February 1971, was almost a disaster: voting machines failed in the first round and were rejected in favour of the old-fashioned pencil and ballot card for the following four rounds of balloting. Davis, whose campaign approach had been "low-key and bland," nevertheless eked out an 812 to 768 vote victory over Allan Lawrence thanks to the "overwhelming support of members of the legislature." It was an inauspicious continuation of the Tory dynasty in Ontario, and early analysis focused on why it was that Davis almost lost the premiership at the convention.[88] Although Davis had been a key player in the Robarts government, there were obviously going to be differences between the approach each took to intergovernmental relations. Where Robarts had been a mediator, fully aware "that the strength of Ontario comes not solely from the efforts of the people of this Province but, in good part, from the markets we enjoy throughout the rest of the country," Davis was initially more concerned about protecting Ontario's economic position within the federation.[89] The economic downturn of the early 1970s demanded such a view, but the effects on constitutional negotiations might prove to be substantial. Changing personnel, then, at all levels of government suggested that bilateral conversations might better secure progress on the constitutional front than round table debates where the characters were different at each new meeting.

The basis of Ottawa-Ontario talks before the resumption of the constitutional conference was a provincial draft, or "grid," of its proposed division of powers, listing items as either falling under federal, provincial, or shared jurisdiction. Although the Ontario civil service had had a draft prepared "for some time ... the Federal government could not submit such a document for some time to come."[90] As a result, conversations continued on an informal basis, with the grid informing the Ontario representatives' position but not laid on the table for federal scrutiny. John Turner, the federal finance minister, was Ottawa's point man in discussions with the provinces. He, and a powerful collection of bureaucrats including Gordon Robertson, Bob Bryce, Gerard LaForest, and Barry Strayer, met with Ontario officials in January and again in April. In between, there were numerous phone calls back and forth between the two capitals, resulting in the sharing of both official and unofficial news on the constitutional front.[91]

After Turner's initial cross-Canada tour, Gordon Robertson in the Prime Minister's Office was able to conclude that "there was general unanimity that real progress must be achieved, at this juncture, in the Constitutional discussions" and that "all provinces indicated a better and more sympathetic realization of the situation in Quebec and, in particular, of Mr. Bourassa's position."[92] Apart from those general conclusions, however, there was little consensus across the country: British Columbia "objected strenuously" to an amending formula that privileged Ontario and Quebec; there were provincial questions about the language rights that Ottawa proposed be included in a new constitution; Nova Scotia wanted the provinces consulted about Supreme Court appointments; and social policy was threatening to become a serious roadblock, with Quebec pushing for "important constitutional changes ... which Ottawa will simply not accept."[93] Turner acknowledged that there were "important problems still to be surmounted," but he thought it was "not unrealistic to hope" that the next round of discussions would "disclose significant agreement."[94]

On the basis of these bilateral meetings with federal officials, the Ontario civil servants were able to focus their strategy a little more clearly. This meant greater attention to "the distribution of powers in the context of matching expenditure requirements" and the formation of task forces to study social policy, the amending formula, and patriation.[95] But discussions with the federal government not only identified areas in which more work needed to be done to reach agreement, they also pointed to potential problems with Trudeau's new approach to intergovernmental relations. Without a clear statement of federal intentions, and no way of knowing the position that other provinces were taking in these bilateral conversations, rumours and suspicions were bound to grow. By early April, Ian Macdonald was convinced that "the evidence grows every day ... that the federal government is bent firmly on a course of greater centralism in our federation and ... that Ontario is marked out for particular exclusion from this process."[96]

Any serious discussion of the constitution that had occurred in the period since the Second World War had happened within the large intergovernmental environment: all provincial premiers had been present and were allowed to consider each other's positions in light of their own strategy. With this sort of approach, successive Ontario premiers, but most clearly John Robarts, had been free to play the statesman, attempting to balance provincial and national interests insofar as that was possible and serving as a moderator between positions that were particularly far apart. This was nowhere more apparent than with the Confederation of Tomorrow Conference, the event that precipitated the current round of constitutional discussion. By first learning everyone else's position on the future of the federation, the Ontario delegation was in a position to try to bring the various sides towards a consensus. But by the spring of 1971, Ottawa had effectively eliminated that role for Ontario in its shift to bilateral discussions. Unable to contemplate any other role than that of conciliator, Ontario officials tried to glean as much as they could about what Ottawa was learning in other provincial capitals before committing the new Davis government to a constitutional position.

Clearly, social policy was going to be a key topic of debate. The federal government's use of the spending power throughout the previous decade, and Quebec's exercise of its right to opt out of national social programs, had put the two levels of government on a collision course. However, Quebec regarded social policy as integral to a discussion of constitutional review, while the federal government consistently sought to separate the two issues – this much the Ontario observers knew. But apart from recognizing the differences of opinion on the matter, and hearing that meetings had occurred in Quebec City specifically dealing with social policy, even Ontario's best-informed bureaucrats remained pretty much in the dark.

When Ontario cabinet ministers Allan Lawrence and Darcy McKeough – along with a handful of their top bureaucrats – met with Turner and his aides again in April, they pressed him for as much information as they could, but it was clear that the federal government was in the position of being able to regulate just how much information was shared. On the meeting the previous week with Quebec officials, Robertson simply allowed that the "problems with [Quebec were] not too serious" and the sticky question of social policy, on which Ontario officials had hoped to glean "some impression of the difficulties which this issue could create in June," seems not to have been raised at all.[97] In a later meeting between Trudeau and Davis in April, for example, Ian Macdonald pressed for a clarification of "what the federal government expects from the June meeting."[98] As the date of the Victoria conference loomed, it increasingly seemed that the two levels of government were tumbling into a constitutional abyss. Not only were the Ontario advisers finding that they knew little about what was going on in other capitals, most particularly in Quebec City, but also this meant that they were susceptible to suggestions that agreement had to be immediate or any hope of it would collapse. Despite the fact that "constitutional review was initiated" at least partly as a result of "Ontario's sympathy with the grievances underlying Quebec's demands" and "Ottawa's late and reluctant entry into the arena ... did not match the concerns, priorities or objectives of Ontario or Quebec," it was unsettling to reach the conclusion that by 1971 the federal government had clearly taken the upper hand.[99] There was also an increasing sense that Ontario was moving into a position of watching what was going on rather than determining the course of events.

A few weeks before the opening of the Victoria conference, John Turner was able to submit a federal draft of the constitutional changes to all of the provinces. He explained that the federal government had "revised and consolidated the texts with a view to accommodating, to the greatest extent possible, the points made during our [bilateral] discussions."[100] Finally, the Ontario officials had something concrete – a draft that incorporated many, but not all, of their suggestions and that gave the provincial team something from which to work. Ontario's proposed preamble was included as an option; some of the Ontario wording was used in the section dealing with rights and freedoms, which was of particular interest to Trudeau; and Ontario's concerns had at least been considered in the sections dealing with appointments to the Supreme Court, regional disparities, future first ministers conferences, and the amending procedure. But even with a draft in front of them, Ontario officials were not satisfied with the progress that was being made on the constitution.

The key problem stemmed from different understandings of what was driving constitutional renewal. From Trudeau's perspective, the need for an entrenched Charter of Rights was essential, but in Quebec the most pressing issue was jurisdiction over social policy, which had increasingly come to be treated as the arena in which the larger jurisdictional battles would be fought. And in Ontario, where Robarts had perfected a cautious approach to formal constitutional change that relied on a "studied vagueness about the details of what reform should encompass,"[101] and where Davis had already staked his claim to the lowest key, it was not entirely clear just how much reform was desirable. Three things were certain, however: ultimately, Ontario ministers and politicians wanted "a full-scale review of the distribution of powers" to begin to address fiscal and jurisdictional problems that had plagued generations of Ontario officials; there was general agreement that this could only be undertaken if it was agreeable to all governments involved; and in the spring of 1971, no one in Ontario seemed to have the capacity to steer events that were being directed either by Ottawa or by Quebec City.[102]

Thus, unable to dictate the terms of discussion, and unsure of what had transpired in other provincial capitals, the Federal-Provincial Affairs Secretariat prepared a strategy for Victoria. Having decided that "social policy is the principal and most crucial issue" and that all of the other issues remained "well within the realm of resolution," the Ontario delegation agreed that the "worst possible outcome" of the Victoria conference would be a failure to reach agreement on the constitutional package as "all-out recrimination would likely follow."[103] It was the next stage of constitutional review, however, in which the distribution of powers were determined, that would address Ontario's concerns, and therefore Victoria seemed simply a hurdle that needed to be cleared – a hurdle that might mean "agreeing to include a Canada-Quebec accord on [social policy] as part of the charter and for recommendation, with the rest of the charter, to the Legislature." So be it.[104]

While Bill Davis and his advisers could afford to consider Victoria with some composure, biding their time until it was possible to make real progress on issues such as tax sharing, Quebec's Bourassa was in no such position. He was faced with extraordinarily high expectations from all sides: the nationalists "regard the constitutional meeting as crucial for Confederation in the sense that its outcome represents the crucial test of the federal system's ability to satisfy cultural and regional aspirations."[105] Similarly, the federalists, who normally counted Bourassa among their numbers, looked to Victoria for evidence that Confederation could be redesigned to satisfy the needs of Quebec, most particularly through the crucible of social policy. When the conference opened on 14 June, all eyes – both in Victoria and across the nation, where viewers tuned into the televised opening statements – were on Trudeau and Bourassa. Bill Davis was left to offer the "emptiest"[106] address and sit back and watch what had unfolded in the private bilateral discussions of the previous two months.

For months, if not years, Quebec had been pressing for a restriction on the federal use of the spending power to access provincial jurisdiction in the social welfare field. These calls only became clearer and more pointed with the release, early in 1971, of the report of the Castonguay-Nepveu Commission into health and social welfare. Here, Quebec Minister of Social Affairs Claude Castonguay detailed the provincial position: social policy was too important a field for the cultural preservation of Quebec to be shared with the federal government and therefore the provinces should be given "overriding responsibility for the social policy framework and objectives."[107] This was too much for

National Health and Welfare Minister John Munro and the rest of the federal cabinet, where the decision was made to try to win Quebec over to constitutional reform with more money. Just days before the conference got underway in Victoria, Ottawa dumped $150 million into the family allowance program in an attempt to buy Quebec's agreement to the Victoria Charter.[108] Moreover, discussions were held at a private dinner between Trudeau and Bourassa, at about the same time, at which the federal government offered to make legislative changes to social programs that would go part way to meeting Quebec's demands.[109] Only the full intergovernmental meeting, however, could determine whether the bilateral discussions had been sufficient to secure constitutional reform.

Following the opening remarks of each of the first ministers, the group retired to "begin a long, and amazingly secret, debate."[110] Thirteen hours of closed-door discussion concluded the two days of in camera sessions, and when the premiers and prime minister finally appeared, they had the Victoria Charter in hand. In addition to the amending formula, political and language rights, and statements on regional disparities and continuing federal-provincial consultation, it included a revised section 94A dealing with the crucial matter of social policy. The new section gave Ottawa the power to "make laws in relation to old age pensions and supplementary benefits including survivors' and disability benefits irrespective of age, and in relation to family, youth, and occupational training allowances, but no such law shall affect the operation of any law present or future of a Provincial Legislature in relation to any such matter." Moreover, the section also detailed the responsibility of the federal government to consult with each province regarding the substance of any proposed new social welfare legislation and elicit its views on such changes.[111] Precisely how the agreement was reached, how much strong-arming was necessary, and which provinces – if any – were reluctant to sign on is unclear; Davis, at least, was in an agreeable mood when the conference opened, stressing that in Ontario "we are anxious to proceed on agreements reached at this Conference as quickly as possible." On social policy issues in particular, Davis underlined his province's desire that "income security and income distribution policy should be an integral part of taxation policy"[112] but presumably he agreed to the change to section 94A as a first step towards more complete integration.

The mood was hardly elated at the close of the conference as the Victoria Charter was introduced to the public: governments had until

28 June to secure legislative agreement on its terms, and Premier Bour-assa was already showing signs of discomfort with the agreement. They were well founded. Commentators in Quebec were quick to pounce on Bourassa's agreement to "La Charte à Trudeau," and by 23 June the pre-mier was forced to withdraw his support, torpedoing the Victoria Char-ter and leaving the eleven ministers with nothing to show for their years of work.[113] Although Ontario civil servants saw in Victoria's collapse the possibility that Premier Davis could offer "a relatively neutral corner for continued discussion and arbitration of any current dispute"[114] by recon-vening the Confederation of Tomorrow Conference, there was "almost a sense of relief" to move away from constitutional negotiation for the time being.[115]

Ontario's successes in the mega-intergovernmental field were mixed. There can be no question that the Confederation of Tomorrow Con-ference was an enormously triumphant gambit: against much advice to the contrary, a province convened an intergovernmental confer-ence that managed to frame an important discussion on the future of the federation. The terms – vague though they may have been – of the constitutional conversation had been set by Ontario. Constitutional change in Canada would be inclusive, and would consider the position of each province in the final calculation. In essence, this meant a re-turn to the sort of conversation that had been held during the original constitutional discussions in the 1860s, where provincial actors debated how their regional needs could be accommodated within the larger na-tional framework. There too, perhaps, Ontario played a pivotal role in opening the conversation in the first place and ensuring that the larger purpose was not forgotten in the myriad of regional concerns. But fol-lowing Robarts's success with the conference, an empowered Ontario was pushed to the sidelines by new federal and Quebec governments, where a bilateral conversation began to dominate the constitutional field. The Confederation of Tomorrow Conference had ensured that the constitutional debate would be, at its heart, about Quebec; that was a discussion in which Ontario had for decades played a role. Brokers were not a part of the continuing constitutional conference, although that might have secured a more successful outcome. The failure of the Victoria Charter was the failure of a constitution negotiated in private, in an era when the terms – set by Ontario – dictated that multi-lateral dialogue was expected. It was also the failure of Trudeau's brand of bilateral, confrontational negotiations, which had important consequences for the way that the issue of patriation was addressed in the future and suggested the continuing relevance of Ontario's intergovernmental strategy. While the participants may have been keen in the summer of 1971 to take a break from constitutional reform, they were not prepared to do so for long.

Chapter Eight

"Disentanglement" and Mega-intergovernmental Politics in Ontario, 1971–1978

The collapse of the Victoria Charter was a significant setback for inter-governmental relations in Canada, ending, as it did, the momentum towards constitutional change that had been gathering since Ontario convened the Confederation of Tomorrow Conference in 1967.[1] Exhaustion, cynicism, and defeatism overtook most of the participants, and they turned their attention to other, more pressing, matters of state. But failure overshadowed Ontario's approach to federal-provincial relations throughout most of the 1970s, colouring the strategy that the Davis government pursued over the next half-dozen or more years. The Victoria situation seemed to point to the failure of the Robartsian tactic of keeping the intergovernmental focus on the big picture, emphasizing large-scale, foundational change rather than piecemeal, ad hoc amendments to the relationship. In the 1970s, therefore, we see the Ontario government flirting with a complete strategic turnaround. Perhaps the time had come, thought many of the politicians in the Davis government, to pursue ends that were specifically in the provincial interest and would have short-term rewards, rather than continuing to reflect on the national interest and pursue long-term goals. The crisis over Alberta's energy reserves pushed many Ontarians in the direction of a new, less collegial approach to intergovernmental relations. But within the bureaucracy, mega-intergovernmentalism still had an appeal; rather than focusing so intently on the constitution, however, as had been the case since 1967, the new focus in the 1970s was on "disentangling" jurisdiction. The tension between the two possible approaches – a return to Ontario-centrism, on the one hand, a rebranding of mega-intergovernmentalism, on the other – was a clear result of the collapse of the Victoria Charter. But when the constitution reappeared on the agenda, Ontario politicians and bureaucrats alike were quick to grab the opportunity to play a role in reshaping the federation.

Oil, Gas, and "Raising Hell"

After the exhausting run of constitutional negotiations, the locus of activity on the intergovernmental front following the collapse of the Victoria Charter shifted from the first ministers to the finance ministers. The tenor of the meetings also changed, as Ontario Finance Minister Darcy McKeough adopted a more provincialist stance than had been seen for some time. Meetings in November 1971 and again in January 1972 inevitably raised several issues that were particularly important to the province of Ontario, which continued in its position as the most populous province with the largest tax base. Tax sharing was the perennial problem, its "inadequacy" having "been documented extensively" since the formation of the Tax Structure Committee in 1966.[2] Matters had only gotten worse with the implementation of a "new income tax system [that] will restrict provincial ability to use this field," complained McKeough to his counterparts in early 1972. "In fact," he continued, "in the very process of reforming the national income tax structure the federal government has confronted the provinces with a *de facto* loss in income tax sharing."[3] The only solution, according to McKeough, was to "recognize that federal-provincial financing has already moved substantially out of balance" and to ensure that future tax revenue was divided equitably between the two levels of government.[4]

While tax sharing had been a contentious issue since early in the twentieth century, cost sharing was a relatively new source of irritation between the two levels of government, and one that was raised repeatedly by finance ministers in the early 1970s. In making the move into social programs that were constitutionally within provincial jurisdiction, the federal government had used its spending power, or its ability to finance programs and force provinces to comply with a set of nationally determined objectives. That meant that since the 1960s, both levels of government had been sharing the cost of financing programs like health insurance and the Canada Assistance Plan, and the relationship wasn't getting any easier with the passage of time. Meetings between Ontario and federal officials over CAP, for example, made clear "that Ontario's scope to develop and implement new programs is severely constrained by existing cost-sharing arrangements" and that the province "should strongly resist the use of federal financial leverage to prevent rationalization of provincial programs."[5] Two of the specific problems that arose in the early 1970s related to Ontario's administrative decisions to train juvenile delinquents under Correctional Services rather than Social and Family Services and to reorganize daycare facilities within the Department of Education, both of which resulted in losing CAP funding for these programs.[6] Thus, although recent discussions over CAP had brought the issue of cost sharing to a head, at root were long-term questions of fiscal fairness that had plagued the Ontario bureaucrats for decades. Health insurance was equally irksome for the provincial politicians and civil servants. Late in 1971, the federal government proposed a new basis for sharing the cost of health care between the two levels of government and, after months of consideration, a "number of provinces expressed reservations" about that basis. In particular, the provinces objected to using the 1970–71 GNP as the base for calculating federal contributions, rather than a formula based on actual health costs. Finance Minister McKeough had some strong words for his federal counterpart John Turner when the two met in July: Ontario was not interested in the "seed money" that Ottawa seemed to be throwing in their direction vis-à-vis health care. Opting out might be the only reasonable alternative, and in August 1972 Ontario seemed ready to do so.[7] Ultimately, the Ontario people backed down from this position, and the "interim step"[8] of federal cost sharing became a more permanent solution for sharing the cost of health care, but it had not been without something of a battle.

In early March 1972, McKeough had a much more "candid, wide-ranging and … fruitful discussion" with John Turner, where the topics covered tax sharing, cost sharing, and coordinated planning between the two levels of government.[9] On the first two topics, the two finance ministers enjoyed a general airing of views, bringing each other up to date on what was being done by their respective governments. When the discussion turned to economic planning, the two perhaps showed more of their hand than expected. According to McKeough, he "emphasized that what Ontario was looking for more than anything else was what [Turner] called consultation and what I chose to call discussion and/ or argument." But the Ontario minister's suggestion that "we should more often kick all the officials out and just leave ministers and deputies to try and really get down to discussing things" left Turner somewhat concerned. He "worried that [Ontario] is trying to run the show."[10] McKeough resisted this characterization, but must surely have recognized some truth in it. For his part, McKeough was also interested in assessing whether the current ad hoc arrangements and consultations were, in fact, alternatives to direct constitutional negotiation. Don Stevenson, the key Ontario bureaucrat on the constitution file, pressed his minister to find out whether Turner saw "some of the deliberations on long term policies envisaged by the Finance Ministers to be a partial substitute for distribution of powers discussions."[11] Turner made clear that "Constitutional talks were dead for the time being," but he was also "rather strong on by-lateral [sic] discussions with Ontario and, for example, BC and Alberta, who were the only provinces that care."[12]

Those were precisely the provinces embarking on a collision course. In the spring of 1972, the Alberta Energy Resources Conservation Board began hearings on natural gas field pricing; there was "no doubt that Ontario, as a major user of Alberta's natural gas, has a keen interest in the level of field prices."[13] The Board's report was adopted virtually in its entirety by Peter Lougheed's Conservative government, including a commitment to increase field prices by 10 cents per 1,000 cubic feet from an average of 15 cents, and to impose annual base price increases of between 3 per cent and 4 per cent. Even more gallingly, the province announced that it would introduce a two-price system that would ensure Albertans the lowest fuel costs in the country.[14] The announcements from Alberta suggested to McKeough that "the whole situation is deteriorating rather quickly." With oil and gas costs for Ontario bound to increase, while costs in Alberta remained artificially low, McKeough's staff continued to urge him to enter into discussions with his counterparts in Ottawa and in Alberta to "sort out just where Ontario should be going."[15]

In the summer of 1972, McKeough resigned his cabinet position following conflict-of-interest allegations revolving around a provincial development project;[16] that did nothing to dampen his interest in energy. After consulting with representatives from the oil and gas industry in Ontario, as well as with members of his former staff, McKeough was prepared to advise four courses of action. All involved Premier Davis sitting down with people – in industry, in Alberta, in other provinces, and in the federal government – to either "get the lay of the land" or "get their back up." McKeough was particularly "hepped that we should be down seeing Ottawa on a number of things right now."[17] Whereas two months earlier the provincial committee of advisers had agreed "that there are a large number of major issues which require a carefully planned provincial strategy for negotiation with the Federal Government," they had also thought that the relationship already established by McKeough's department had "established good working liaison with the operating Ministries" in Ottawa.[18] By December, however, the tone of intergovernmental relations had changed: McKeough pressed Davis about "raising hell on some things, playing other things softly, and going for the jugular on a few others. I would hope," McKeough continued, "that there is a well-thought-out plan of just what we hope to achieve, or could try to achieve in the next few months while we still have a minority government who presumably would be prepared to do a few things for Ontario. I think of such things as energy, opting out, tax points, correctional service problems, etc. etc."[19] The looming energy crisis spurred Ontario to action on several different intergovernmental fronts.

In addition to raising multiple points of irritation, the oil situation also pushed Ontario to renew old federal-provincial strategies, most significantly its relationship with Quebec. McKeough had specifically urged Davis to "line up support"[20] from Quebec vis-à-vis Alberta, and throughout the fall of 1972 officials from the two provinces met to discuss their common interests. Despite a general sense that Robarts had been more receptive to the needs of Quebec within the federation than was Davis,[21] there were still opportunities for establishing a united front against the federal government. Both provinces, for example, were interested in moving into the tax space created by the anticipated federal income tax cuts. Other matters might be more problematic, however: Ontario's interest in possibly opting out of established programs threw into disarray the manner in which Quebec had calculated its fiscal equivalents, or tax points, and a new five-year equalization equation was threatened by Quebec's desire to include municipal revenues in the formula, and Ontario's desire to keep equalization costs, which it financed to a considerable degree, to a minimum.[22] Tax sharing provided the real point of connection between the two provinces.

In the absence of any real interest on the part of the Quebec government in resuming constitutional talks, officials in Ontario's Intergovernmental Affairs Secretariat argued that by opening up an interprovincial dialogue on fiscal matters, the two might come to some agreement on a strategy regarding the division of powers.[23] This in turn might benefit Ontario's case against Alberta, which while ostensibly about the price of fuel, laid bare some key differences between the views of the two provinces regarding jurisdiction over natural resources. The major point on which representatives of the Ontario and Quebec governments agreed was regarding "a net transfer to the provinces of four points of the personal income tax." In dollar terms, that would mean an estimated $200 million for Ontario and $115 million for Quebec; although the provincial people agreed to make the request "for the 1973–74 year, the point would be made that this was just symptomatic of a longer-term problem which would require a longer-term transfer of tax room from the federal government to the provinces."[24] By building bridges with other provinces, Ontario officials hoped to secure some future goodwill in the brewing battle with Alberta.

But efforts to present an Ontario-Quebec front in appeals to the federal government on tax sharing went nowhere: Turner's budget of early 1973 did roll back taxes, as expected, but it failed to outline a new division of tax points with the provinces. Although Conservatives tended to see the budget as creating a "tax jungle" that would be "the Achilles heel of the Trudeau Government,"[25] it nevertheless passed, ending any real threat to the life of the federal minority government. And determining a response to Alberta's bellicose position on oil pricing was equally difficult. Darcy McKeough's efforts in the energy field earned him a return to favour as Davis's parliamentary assistant on energy policy, but repeated junkets to Edmonton failed to secure a change in Alberta's position, and equally failed to clarify Ontario's position to the oil barons. By midsummer, with McKeough's key role in the unfolding saga solidified by his reappointment to cabinet as minister of energy, the sides seemed to be even more starkly drawn. In addition to announcing a version of a provincial energy policy, Davis also announced that he would challenge Alberta's price increases in court.[26]

More than a year after Davis first pressed for a first ministers' meeting on the question of energy, the premiers and prime minister met in Ottawa in January 1974 to begin a conversation that had thus far been waged largely in the media. There, Davis pushed for a national energy policy, arguing that "economic disparity among provinces and regions works to Ontario's ultimate disadvantage." The Ontario version of a national policy held as its "first principle" a guaranteed supply of energy for domestic use.[27] Premier Lougheed then criticized the export tax that had been slapped on Alberta oil exports to the United States as discriminatory and "contrary to the spirit and the intent of confederation": other sources of energy, such as Ontario Hydro, were not similarly taxed, and the federal export tax undermined Alberta's capacity to sell its resources at a fair price.[28] The meeting decided nothing, leading instead to months of largely bilateral discussion between Trudeau and the premiers of the two provinces most affected by energy prices – Saskatchewan and Alberta.[29]

While Trudeau and Lougheed and Blakeney traded thinly veiled threats through Canada Post and their respective legislatures, Ontario's

Davis could afford to sit back and await a decision that would benefit the central province's economy. This was not a battle that Ontario could enter directly, and so instead the strategists in intergovernmental affairs busied themselves preparing to host the annual premiers' conference in September 1974. York University's Glendon College was the location, and the bureaucrats hoped that the meeting would "act as a catalyst" to fixing the federal system. In this regard, the Ontario-hosted premiers' conference was being designed as a second Confederation of Tomorrow Conference. From Ian Macdonald's perspective, the conference could be used as an opportunity to "look at broad national objectives as viewed by different regions of the country" and as a forum for disabusing people (presumably particularly those in the federal government) of the idea "that prov[inces] can only fight among themselves."[30]

Macdonald was unsuccessful in selling the idea of a second Confederation of Tomorrow Conference to the other provinces; it was quite likely that the energy situation had divided the provinces sufficiently to warrant viewing Ontario with even more suspicion than usual. Whereas in 1967 Ontario could make an honest claim to being interested in ensuring a fair deal for the provinces in a renewed confederation, by 1974 it was becoming increasingly clear that the province's interests were Ontario-specific. That was even more apparent in the few weeks before the opening of the premiers' conference, when Ontario Energy Minister Darcy McKeough made a surreptitious visit to Ottawa to discuss the situation with his federal counterpart, Donald MacDonald. The two discussed electricity, uranium, and coal, with McKeough generally requesting federal support in his proposed negotiations with private companies. On the topics of oil and natural gas, however, the discussions became more heated. After learning that the federal government intended to index natural gas prices to oil prices, with the intention that both would reach world prices by 1979, McKeough "expressed Ontario's unhappiness" with Ottawa's position. He pressed for "keeping the price of flowing gas ... low, with the price of new gas at a level which would bring new reserves into production." In response, the federal deputy minister of energy "gave an impassioned defence of market pricing, expressing the philosophy that high prices with excess profits taxed away by government were preferable to low prices in which there was an implicit subsidy to consumers encouraging distortions in energy consumption."[31]

This put Ontario in a difficult position. According to MacDonald, the federal government was shortly going to propose to Alberta indexing natural gas prices; if Lougheed did not agree, the federal energy minister said that Ottawa "will seek support for federal control of gas prices." Without benefit of cabinet consultation, McKeough "reluctantly" had to agree to support the federal position as "federal regulation would protect the interests of Ontario consumers better than Alberta control of gas prices, which would likely mean an almost immediate increase to international price levels."[32] But there was no way that Ontario actively supported the idea of indexing gas prices: as the deputy minister of treasury, economics and intergovernmental relations in Ontario noted later, "each increase in oil prices produces a windfall in gas revenues, or, conversely, an additional loss of jobs and income in Ontario."[33] The proposed increase in the price of natural gas in Alberta was estimated to cost Ontario consumers about $131 million in 1974–75, a situation that everyone in Davis's government was anxious to avoid.[34]

By the end of the year, it was clear that Ontario was finding itself in unfamiliar intergovernmental territory. In its pursuit of "equality of economic opportunity across Canada," the federal government had shifted from its late-1960s emphasis on social policy solutions to its new 1970s focus on "resource-related matters" and the design of "policy levers to deal with these problems."[35] With the western provinces undergoing rapid economic development through oil and gas exploration and sales, it was clear to Davis that this presaged a shift in economic power away from the central provinces. While he could claim that this decentralization "was important to Ontario as a means of strengthening Confederation and as a means of reducing growth pressures in Southern Ontario," it was equally clear that Ontario wanted some control over the "rate of change" in the economy.[36] Ontario's quandary, then, came as a result of the sense that Ottawa's position on taxing oil and gas revenues, and securing below-market prices domestically, "has been relatively much more favourable than that of the provinces."[37] Would it be appropriate – let alone possible – for Ontario, in the post-1975 years, to abandon its traditional concern with "reducing the forces of centralization that had developed in Canadian federalism since World War II" and instead support what amounted to an increase in federal authority over the national economy?[38]

Ontario was supportive of federal efforts to rein in inflation, agreeing to wage and price controls, but the same could not be said of the province's response to the continuing oil and gas saga. Throughout 1975, Davis adopted a hard line in his approach to the federal government. Already irritated with the Trudeau government's move to cut contributions to shared-cost programs, combined with its desire for "more recognition for the programs and services to which it is financially contributing,"[39] Davis and his bureaucrats were in a combative mood. Federal-provincial meetings in the spring saw Davis arguing "that the economy of Ontario carries a great part of the federal load and must be in a solvent position to do so for the good of Canada";[40] it was a more "inflexible position" than his colleagues were used to from Davis, and one that was "not easy for the Premier of Ontario to have to adopt."[41] Robert Nixon, the Liberal leader of the Opposition in Ontario, was not pleased with the tone Davis had taken: "instead of negotiating," Nixon complained, "he was grandstanding."[42] In the days leading up to the federal budget, Davis pressed his point further, voicing "Ontario's strong opposition to any increase in the domestic price of crude oil until such time as inflation is brought under control and unemployment is substantially reduced."[43] But both Davis's grandstanding and his almost plaintive opposition to price increases went unheard; the budget of 23 June 1975 announced a 15 cents per gallon increase in the price of crude oil, to the annoyance of Davis and the Ontario consumers.

Disentanglement and Mega-intergovernmentalism

The oil and gas crisis laid bare one of the key components of Ontario's postwar intergovernmental strategy. Clearly, as successive governments in the central province attempted to offer an alternative national vision on issues of social, economic, and constitutional policy, they were doing so from a position of dominance within the Canadian federation. As soon as that began to crumble, as it did in the mid-1970s when Alberta's resource-based wealth began to be equated with greater power in the federation, Ontario's strategy for dealing with Ottawa came into question. Reports from Ontario expressed exasperation with the federal government, which under Trudeau seemed to be pursuing an increasingly centralized agenda, so it was clear that Ontario politicians and bureaucrats were not moving willingly into a position of supporting Ottawa's manoeuvres in the intergovernmental arena. And yet, as the provincial officials repeatedly proclaimed, they were marginally more comfortable in following Ottawa's lead than they were in following Alberta's – at least in terms of the national economy. As Deputy Minister Don Stevensón put it, "by supporting the federal government, Ontario may be able to protect its economy from the immediate effects of further oil and gas price increases ... but if it relies too much on the federal government, it may have to accept a shift in the balance of federalism."[44]

It was clear that intergovernmental relations were in chaos, and that both troubled Davis and occasioned reflection within his relevant ministries. In May 1973, the premier had stressed the need for "a new national consensus" on constitutional jurisdiction;[45] officials subsequently outlined the situation in terms that indicated frustration with both the federal government and with provincial counterparts. By mid-1973, the report claimed, intergovernmental relations in Canada could be characterized by "a persistent unwillingness" in Ottawa to undertake meaningful fiscal or constitutional reform, as well as "a growing tendency by the federal government to use its increasingly surplus revenue position and its constitutional spending power to move more aggressively into new priority areas." Furthermore, the officials pointed to "a lack of significant consensus among the provinces on almost any issue" and a "deliberate effort" by the federal government to use this division to its advantage. Perhaps worse still, the current round of federal-provincial debates had led to "a swelling tide of criticism directed at Ontario" which was posing "a tempting target."[46] Although the Ontario bureaucrats had long recognized that "other Provinces are prejudiced by history and training to dislike and distrust Ontario,"[47] it was nevertheless imperative that Ontario adopt a strategy that would put an end to "the federal government being able to do pretty much as it pleases" in an environment of provincial dissension.[48]

There were several possible responses to the situation, as the Office of Intergovernmental Affairs saw it. Ontario could "go it alone" by taking "an extremely aggressive stance on all federal activity." Alternatively, the provincial politicians could opt for the "more conventional piecemeal approach to problems in the federation" and deal with each crisis as it arose. Finally, the provincial players could "go to ground [and] be far less visible in public."[49] Settling on the final option, officials began the task of identifying the "major federal-provincial and interprovincial issues" with which they would deal over the next few years, prioritize them, and "design a strategy for achieving each of the Government's priorities."[50] The key problem was that the policies and priorities had become hopelessly confused with few clear lines of authority. Pulling the threads apart – or seeking "disentanglement" in the language of the Ontario bureaucracy – became so central to the purpose of the government that it was code-named "alpha."[51]

At the same time, an increasingly aggressive Ottawa continued in its centralizing ways to introduce policies that were seen as interfering in provincial jurisdiction. Thus, while those in Queen's Park sought to disentangle the threads of policy and operation that had become knotted over several decades of shared, stolen, and relinquished jurisdiction, Trudeau's government offered even greater confusion. Among the tangled threads were health care cost sharing, which Ontario wanted to see shifted to a system of tax points rather that cost ceilings; the Canada Pension Plan, about which McKeough "had written a nasty letter to [National Health and Welfare Minister Marc] Lalonde ... oppos[ing] the new ventures in guaranteed income"; the Anti-Inflation Act, which was being challenged by public service groups in Ontario and which Ontario Attorney General Roy McMurtry requested Ottawa refer to the Supreme Court for adjudication; and all elements of the Fiscal Arrangements Act, including equalization, revenue guarantees, and tax credits. And this particularly confusing array of intergovernmental issues did not begin to address Ontario's continuing opposition to the increase in oil and gas prices, which "galled" McKeough by going "directly into the revenues of the federal government and the producing provinces."[52]

Hoping to learn from their neighbours in Quebec, where "delegations are generally aware of what has been taking place in other fields of federal-provincial relations," deputy ministers from the two provinces met repeatedly in late 1975 and early 1976 to share notes and, perhaps, develop a strategy to deal with Ottawa. André Saumier, a recent addition to the Quebec bureaucracy, was particularly enlightening on events in Ottawa: he saw "a determined federal effort to become heavily involved in what might be termed 'glamour' issues ... regardless of the normal distribution of responsibility." He also worried that the provinces, and Ontario in particular, had too quickly agreed to the Trudeau's government's anti-inflation program. Quebec legal advisers were "concerned that the precedent might be used in future situations where an area within provincial jurisdiction had national overtones even though it might be even more difficult to term the problem a national emergency."[53] Clearly, suspicions seemed to be a great deal higher in Quebec City than they had been in Toronto, but the meeting of deputies, which was "more candid and less formal" than previous meetings,[54] resulted in a general agreement that it would be "useful" to try to "understand each other's positions in advance of major federal-provincial negotiations."[55] While it was a long way from an Ontario-Quebec axis, the Trudeau government had so upset the balance of intergovernmental relations that the normally confident bureaucrats in the province of Ontario were struggling to get some control over the situation, and renewing relations with Quebec was a good place to start.

This was particularly so as the prospect of reopening the constitutional conversation began to loom ever closer. In October 1974, Trudeau had announced in Parliament that he intended to secure the patriation of the constitution within four years;[56] in response, Davis "noted that Ontario was the first province to endorse the Canadian Constitutional Charter in 1971, and stated that Ontario would cooperate fully with the federal government in this matter."[57] Following on Trudeau's announcement, in the spring of 1975, Gordon Robertson had toured most of the provincial capitals in his new position as secretary to the cabinet for federal-provincial relations, discussing the various views on constitutional reform, presumably preparatory to another round of intergovernmental negotiations. Again, Ontario representatives stated their agreement "in principle" with the federal proposal, "but expressed the concern that Quebec should not be isolated in the current process."[58] Other provinces, meanwhile, were less supportive. Quebec's Bourassa indicated that he would not agree to patriation without guarantees in areas of immigration and communications, the premiers of Manitoba and Alberta expressed some concern over the proposed amending formula, and Alberta and Saskatchewan both wanted "a clearer definition of provincial control over natural resources."[59] But after Robertson's round of discussions in provincial capitals, "nothing much happened";[60] the constitutional issue was, perhaps, again on the back burner.

But early in February 1976, Trudeau moved the issue right back into the middle of the tangled mass of intergovernmental issues by raising the possibility of the federal government pursuing patriation unilaterally. As he stated in a detailed letter to all of the provincial premiers, "if unanimity" on a variety of alternatives – ranging from simple patriation to a combination of patriation, a revised amending formula, and changes to those parts of the BNA Act on which agreement had already been secured – "does not appear possible," the federal government would have to consider a joint address of the Senate and House of Commons "to the Queen, requesting appropriate legislation by the British Parliament to end its capacity to legislate in any way with respect to Canada."[61] Trudeau's parliamentary statement followed by his letter to the premiers immediately renewed the constitutional negotiations that had stalled in Victoria, and begged the question of how Ontario should respond.[62]

The early reaction was hesitant. Unilateral patriation and the adoption of the amending formula that had already been accepted at Victoria posed no risk for Ontario, and if the federal government chose to act in this manner, it would be the last unilateral act possible given the structure of the amending formula. Therefore, on the basis of Ontario's earlier support for both the amending procedure and patriation, and the fact that neither politicians nor bureaucrats in Ontario had ever raised any concerns about these issues, plus the conclusion that it was impossible to set a precedent for unilateral federal action, there was a strong inclination to support Ottawa's position. However, there were political effects to consider, including "the danger of isolating Quebec," the "public perception of the issue," and "the element of bluff in the Prime Minister's statement." Intergovernmental affairs officials, used to federal strategy, wondered "to what degree was it designed either to get the provinces into line or to show the impossibility of getting unanimous provincial agreement?"[63] Ultimately, they recommended "a further, and hopefully final, discussion among the First Ministers to secure the desired unanimity," despite a strong desire to proceed by "saying nothing at this time."[64]

The federal strategy seemed to be to let the threat of constitutional negotiations, and in particular the possibility of unilateral action on Ottawa's part, hang over the other intergovernmental issues that occupied first ministerial attention. In early April 1976, Trudeau invited his provincial colleagues to two discussions, one to consider oil and gas prices, and the other to deal with shared-cost programs. Ten days after receipt of the telex, only half the premiers had responded to the invitation, only two had suggested that the two topics were so closely related that they should be dealt with at the same time, and none "had raised the question of the Constitution for discussion by the First Ministers."[65] Patriation was clearly the elephant in the room. Moreover, from Ontario's perspective, the federal government was obviously trying to push its ideas about both energy and shared-cost programs onto unprepared provinces: in attempting to combine two topics into one meeting, and then suggesting that both might be discussed at "a brief private luncheon at Sussex Drive,"[66] Trudeau was seizing the initiative on all of the major intergovernmental files, leaving the provinces scrambling.

In Ontario, the idea of disentanglement provided some structure within which to approach the multiple proposals and suspected policy plans of the federal government. A provincial strategy of pressing for lines of administrative responsibility to be clearly defined or, in other words, for the knotted mess that had developed in the postwar years to be disentangled, "might well form an integral part of the provincial position" at the first ministers' conference in mid-June, argued Don Stevenson.[67] By focusing on a mega-intergovernmental problem – in this case, that the lack of clarity over jurisdiction had led to confusion, overlap, and, most significantly from Ontario's perspective, federal interference in provincial priorities – the Ontario officials could devise a strategy that would deal with both the constitution and shared-cost programs. In each case, the provincial contingent was simply guessing as to federal plans or motives. Minister of National Health and Welfare Marc Lalonde was "difficult" to read, and despite some suggestions that piecemeal changes were likely in the financing of health services, his officials "exercised subtle but firm pressure in favour of an early global review of health financing."[68] This would open the door for a discussion of disentanglement.

Similarly, the constitutional gambit that Trudeau had taken, threatening to act unilaterally, could also open up the possibility of discussing how jurisdiction might be disentangled. It was clear that "Trudeau's initiative posed a political dilemma for each province," however. "To oppose the federal threat to act unilaterally ran the risk of seeming to oppose patriation per se. While patriation is not a matter of great public concern," Gary Posen pointed out, "the provinces have been put in the position of appearing to be against motherhood."[69] The solution to this was for the provinces to agree on a patriation package among themselves, perhaps disentangling as much as possible, and then presenting the federal government with the way forward. Posen was clear that while disentanglement might animate Ontario thinking, it should not be mixed into the patriation issue; it would be "something that is pursued with the federal government over the next few years whether patriation is achieved or not."[70]

The federal proposal regarding health care, announced at the intergovernmental meeting in mid-June, went part way towards solving the problems that Ontario officials had identified. Preparatory to the first ministers' conference, Trudeau tabled a proposal on "established program financing" which acknowledged Ottawa's intention to continue "to pay a substantial share" of the costs of health care and education, while allowing provinces greater independence to design their own programs and use funds within the context of a more nationally equitable system based, at least in part, on the transfer of tax room to the provinces rather than cash.[71] Davis was guardedly optimistic about the program, which represented "a commendable start to resolving some long-standing difficulties." He noted with considerable pleasure that the proposed shift from conditional federal grants to unconditional federal grants, and the use of tax transfers, represented the acceptance of "ideas which Ontario has put before these conferences and the federal government over the

[past] decade." Although he warned of potential problems created by excluding welfare from the agreement, and by not easing the transition from one form of sharing to another, in general Davis seemed to suggest that the new proposal for established programs financing went a long way towards disentangling financial arrangements of the two levels of government.[72]

However, as long as the folks in Ottawa kept offering up new policies – a new way of financing health care and education through the Established Programs Financing Act, an ultimatum on the constitution, ongoing tax reform – the tasks of the two levels of government were becoming more entangled, not less. The Trudeau governments seemed to simply steamroll over any calls from Ontario to untie the knots of federal-provincial relations as constitutional initiatives dominated federal thinking in a way that baffled the Ontario ministers. After meeting privately with the Clerk of the Privy Council, Michael Pitfield, McKeough complained that he "still can't make the connection between why patriation is necessary in terms of all our other problems but they really are going to bull ahead." And when the federal government decided to "plunge ahead,"[73] then the rest of the governments had to simply follow suit. Disentanglement went onto the back burner while the constitutional negotiations threatened to entwine the two levels of government even further.

In addressing the ultimatum that the federal government had issued earlier in the year – agree on patriation or face unilateral action on the part of Ottawa – the provinces first sought agreement among themselves. Ontario's "preferred" or "minimum" position was to achieve provincial agreement on patriation and an amending formula. Other provinces, most particularly Quebec, Alberta, and Saskatchewan, would only accept the federal demands for patriation if other items were also agreed on. Thus, essentially Ontario's "'maximum position' was to consider these items insofar as this contributed to the achievement of an interprovincial consensus."[74]

Starting, then, with proposals from Ontario and Alberta, the premiers met at their annual conference in Edmonton in the summer of 1976 and came away with some significant constitutional accomplishments. Language rights, the protection of French culture, equalization, permanent mechanisms for intergovernmental agreements and constitutional review, and the creation of new provinces were all agreed to by the assembled premiers. Some big issues remained outstanding, however, including the amending formula, the Supreme Court, and the taxation of corporations and natural resources.[75] The provincial leaders were far from dejected about their failures, focusing instead on their irritation with the federal government's insistence on "pursuing policies which were seriously straining the negotiating climate."[76] The premiers resolved to continue their discussions later in the fall.

The key bone of contention among the provinces was the amending formula. Lougheed proposed that distribution of powers amendments should require unanimous consent, a proposition that seemed to the Ontario officials to be a "tactic designed to force serious consideration" of natural resource ownership and control.[77] When all was said and done, it appeared "that the major interests of all regions *except Ontario* are represented in the discussions."[78] The Atlantic region had been assuaged with agreement over equalization, an initiative spearheaded by the Ontario delegation; Quebec had put its cultural autonomy on the table; the Prairies were pressing for control over natural resources, and British Columbia was in the throes of requiring a veto in the amending formula. The Ontario approach was to seek "possible accord" on all three remaining issues of conflict – cultural autonomy, natural resources, and the amending formula. From the perspective of bureaucrats in the offices of the Attorney General and Treasury, Economics, and Intergovernmental Affairs, "the fall-back for Ontario" if agreement on the three remaining issues fails "is unilateral federal patriation with provision for an amending formula which can be adopted when all provinces have agreed to it. This would meet Ontario's minimum position of patriation with an amending formula, but with neither the desired form of patriation nor the substance of a practical amending formula."[79] As early as 1976, Ontario officials were establishing the terms under which they would agree to the federal government proceeding with patriation unilaterally.

Provincial meetings of premiers and officials in the summer and early fall of 1976 were animated by a comment Trudeau made at a dinner with the premiers in June. At that point, the prime minister made a "general observation that he would accept the unanimous views of the Premiers." The provincial leaders ran with the idea of achieving unanimity, opening discussion on the division of powers at their annual meeting in August. This was clearly not what Trudeau had in mind, but according to Rendell Dick, rather than "restrict[ing] his earlier observations [he] relied upon the Premiers to recognize that any change in the jurisdiction of Parliament would require the approval of the Federal Government."[80]

By the time Lougheed, chair of the premiers' conference, wrote to Trudeau regarding the outcome of his colleagues' deliberations, the premiers had gone too far towards achieving agreement on matters that Trudeau thought beyond their scope, and not far enough towards agreement on the one issue that mattered. While "all the provinces agreed with the objective of patriation," they had failed to reach agreement on an amending formula. Eight provinces remained committed to the formula agreed to at Victoria; British Columbia wanted its own veto, as indicated earlier, and Alberta wanted to ensure that no changes could be made to the constitution without "the concurrence of that province."[81] But regardless, the provinces had pressed ahead, and agreed – unanimously – to such things as "a strengthening of jurisdiction of provincial governments of taxation in the areas of primary production from lands, mines, minerals and forests" and a limitation on the federal use of the "declaratory" power.[82]

Trudeau was not impressed. In a hastily written telex sent before leaving the country on an official visit to Japan, the prime minister noted his "disappointment" that the premiers had failed to bring "matters much closer to a solution." More than a year and a half earlier, Trudeau reminded Lougheed, and all of the premiers who were copied the correspondence, "that we would see if 'patriation' with an amending formula, could be achieved without getting into the distribution of powers. Your letter suggests to me that the premiers, at their meetings, seem to have turned the process upside down and to have concentrated on increasing provincial powers *without* agreeing either on a basis for 'patriation' or a procedure for amendment."[83]

Constitutional Strategy after the Election of the Parti Québécois

Events in Quebec, to some extent, overtook the constitutional negotiations, threatening to derail them even further according to the pessimistic view, but perhaps offering a way forward, at least in some of the areas in which agreement had not been achieved. By mid-summer 1976, Ontario officials were hearing troubling news from Quebec: an air traffic controllers' strike, in part over language issues, "had created many new separatists." Ontario Treasurer Darcy McKeough took the threat seriously, and asked Davis whether there was anything the province of Ontario could be doing. Not only should Davis be wary of doing "anything which might fan the flames of divisiveness" but also, McKeough warned, "we should be taking every opportunity to show some degree of solidarity with Quebec in intergovernmental matters."[84] But while Ontario ministers might have seen cause for concern in Quebec, apparently Quebec politicians did not. Calling a snap election in the fall of 1976, Premier Robert Bourassa expected to make quick work of a Parti Québécois that had recently had to shut down its separatist newspaper.[85] It was a monumental miscalculation.

The 15 November 1976 election of a majority government for René Lévesque's Parti Québécois came as a surprise to all concerned, including the Péquistes themselves. Less than a week before the election, Ontario observers still predicted "a fairly narrow Liberal majority."[86] Such was not the case, and the resulting election of Canada's first separatist government was cause for much concern in other capitals. The advisers and bureaucrats knew so little of what to expect in Quebec City that their advice sounded frenzied, almost hysterical.[87] While the initial anxiety was stilled somewhat by reports that the new Péquiste ministers had, at their first cabinet meeting, decided to adopt a "cooperative approach" to intergovernmental relations "in the interests of economic stability and good government," in the long run, of course, the intention remained to hold a referendum on the question of sovereignty-association.[88] Although the first meeting of PQ politicians and their counterparts across the country was a bit rocky, with Lévesque responding unnecessarily violently to the established programs financing negotiations, relations soon settled into a relatively comfortable zone.[89]

That certainly did not mean that Canadians outside of Quebec had become complacent about the future of the country – far from it. In Ontario, Bill Davis struggled somewhat under the shadow of his predecessor, earning less-than-positive commentary in Quebec newspapers for his treatment of the Franco-Ontario minority.[90] But perhaps in an effort to recall the glory days of Robarts's relationship with Quebec, Davis resurrected the defunct Advisory Committee on Confederation, keeping some of the old players such as Ian Macdonald, and adding new ones such as Rosalie Abella, Richard Simeon, and Ken Dryden to the roster. Half of the members "would be experts on Canadian federalism" while the remainder were "general citizens of proven sensitivity on these matters."[91] With the same name as the group that had inspired the Confederation of Tomorrow Conference, it should come as little surprise that the new ACOC also sought to host an event that would serve as a starting point for a renewed federalism.[92] Times had changed, however, and little became of either the committee or its initiatives.

Outside Ontario, there were other efforts to address the threat of Quebec separatism. For Senators Eugene Forsey and Carl Goldenberg, the election of the PQ pointed to an immediate need to establish an informal advisory committee for Trudeau. Seeking to include a variety of academics – Donald Smiley, Arthur Lower, Ramsay Cook, Peter Leslie, John Saywell, Marcel Hamelin, and Jacques Monet were among those named in the correspondence – there is little evidence that much advice was either offered or taken.[93] But there were other forms that advice could have. In the summer of 1977, Trudeau appointed John Robarts and Jean-Luc Pépin, a defeated member of Trudeau's cabinet from Quebec, to head an inquiry in response to the new situation in Quebec. The two co-chairs thought that it was best to describe their mandate as "to help develop the processes for strengthening Canadian unity and be a source of advice to the government on Canadian unity issues." Moreover, Robarts liked the idea of calling the group a task force, as that "implies an advisory position and a determined duration (one year)."[94] Thus was born the Pépin-Robarts Task Force on Canadian Unity.

For once, it seemed, neither the federal nor provincial decisions to appoint advisory bodies or task forces were designed to buy time in the race towards a renewed federalism. The letters continued to fly between Ottawa and various provincial capitals as Lougheed and others responded to Trudeau's criticism of the provincial efforts at achieving a constitutional consensus. The Ontario strategy, much discussed beforehand, was to express disappointment with Trudeau's response to the Alberta premier. Pointing out that it was Trudeau himself who "broadened" the focus of constitutional discussion from simply "patriation and an amending formula," Davis argued that the provinces' objective had "remained consistent" and was far from comprehensive – an accusation that Trudeau had first made in the Lougheed letter. "In the interests of consensus," Davis stressed, Ontario had "put forward no proposals of its own."[95] But since the provincial discussions had taken place, the landscape had changed dramatically with the election of the Parti Québécois, and for Davis the idea of moving forward with "simple patriation" was "an even more unrealistic option to consider."[96] Governments at all levels would need to rethink "the fundamental purpose of Confederation" before proceeding any further.[97]

In Ontario, this seemed to be one way of pressing again for disentanglement. Since the fall of 1976, the provincial intergovernmental bureaucracy had been working towards this goal – largely covertly given the relative lack of interest in any of the other provincial ministries, and largely independently of other provinces. Disentangling responsibilities was apparently too complicated to trust with other provinces mired in a constitutional impasse. "While disentanglement and constitutional review are two different matters," explained Gary Posen and Ed Greathed, "our concern is that the distinction will be lost on the other provinces or at the very least hard to make with them." Worse still – and perhaps even more illuminating – many of the other provincial bureaucrats "think we are a bit crazy in this area."[98] With little support from either provincial colleagues or counterparts in other capitals, the proponents of disentanglement in the Ontario government suggested that no time be wasted convincing "our provincial brethren to see our viewpoint," and that all focus should turn to Ottawa. "If the principal concern is to clarify federal and provincial roles and responsibilities," Posen and Greathed stressed, "bilateral discussions with Ottawa make the most sense."[99]

But entangled relations were surely part of the federal government's long-term constitutional strategy. As the two Ontario bureaucrats pointed out, it was difficult to distinguish between constitutional and disentanglement issues – perhaps impossible, they thought, for some of their weaker provincial counterparts. But Ottawa counted on the confusion. As long as jurisdiction, as long as tax room, as long as social welfare responsibilities remained knotted and unclear, the only possible avenue towards a solution was constitutional review. Trudeau, by the mid-1970s, was more committed than ever to patriating the constitution and making his mark on Canada's evolution as a nation state. With little going right for the federal Liberals, and even less going right in his private life, Trudeau grasped at old ideas to rejuvenate the government's fortunes.[100] There was no way that the federal Liberals would consider disentangling anything until the constitutional impasse was broken, and Ontario's obsession with untying the existing knots played exactly into the ambitions of the Trudeau government.

Moreover, it was hardly as if Ontario politicians were not also obsessed with the constitution, but not because of a long-standing commitment to either patriation or to an entrenched Charter of Rights, as was the case with the Trudeau government. In Ontario, the constitution was the ultimate mega-intergovernmental project, and it appealed to the same people who found disentanglement such a panacea. Lévesque's election only encouraged the Ontario advisers to think in more innovative ways about how to achieve constitutional progress. Increasingly, for example, both officials and arm's-length advisers were coming to the realization that "an eventual solution to maintaining Quebec in the federation is going to have to involve some form of special status for Quebec."[101]

Private discussions between representatives of the Ontario and Quebec governments suggested that handling Quebec would probably require more than simply recognition of its status as a distinct society. Not only was "sovereignty/association … the best deal that English Canada can expect" but it was probably better from the Quebec perspective for the country to "aim for a friendly divorce" as it was already too late for "marriage counselling."[102] The introduction of Quebec's Bill 101 in the summer of 1977 confirmed the seriousness of the situation. The so-called Charter of the French Language limited the use of any language other than French in public in Quebec, raising important questions of constitutionality for both the federal government and for all interested provincial governments. While Ontario Attorney General Roy McMurtry expressed a cautious opinion that, for the most part, the bill was "not in excess of the legal powers of the province as a whole," there was no question that the sentiment behind the enactment caused the proponents of federalism grave concern.[103] The key to Ontario's constitutional strategy was to find an approach that had "appeal to Quebec" but also "(a) doesn't wind up looking like today's arrangements; (b) doesn't give the country away; and (c) presents an 'accommodation profile' that all concerned, including Quebec, would find hard to turn down."[104] It was a tall order.

Although there seemed to be absolutely no interest in addressing the issue outside of Queen's Park, "entanglement" was an appropriate way to understand the intergovernmental relationship at the end of the 1970s. The Quebec election and Trudeau's insistence on achieving patriation meant that the constitution remained at the top of the agenda, especially given Ontario's long-standing commitment to both understanding and accommodating Quebec interests. But there were other matters that needed attention. Ontario's Conservatives had, for some time, been operating under the assumption that they can't "lose by spending a lot of time and effort on the constitution" and achieving a "national solution with Ontario taking a truly national viewpoint and outlook."[105] The weakness of the federal government suggested that the time was ripe for a "third option" in intergovernmental relations, namely, a massive decentralization of the existing structure. That, then, would provide the provinces with the opportunity to play a greater role in economic and social development and, as a result, untie the knots of entanglement.[106]

The federal government was not so easily sidelined. Ontario officials might be contemplating a third option, and the Pépin-Robarts Task Force might be travelling the country stressing the "rigidity in the Federal Government that is a cause for worry" and the need to "formalize" provincial "initiatives" or "options and packages of ideas,"[107] but this was not in line with federal thinking. After months of rumours about its imminent arrival, Trudeau finally released *A Time for Action*, a succinct summary of Ottawa's plans for constitutional renewal, in the summer of 1978.[108] The prime minister was convinced that Lévesque's election had emboldened the premiers, who "were only too happy" to use the threat of separatism "as a foil to get more for themselves." Wanting to appear "flexible rather than obstinate,"[109] Trudeau's constitutional proposals offered a two-part timeline for the achievement of, first, patriation and an amending formula and then more complicated questions of the division of powers. The first phase would be completed by 1 July 1979; the second was to be in place by 1 July 1981.[110]

The Ontario goal was "to be positive in reacting to the Federal proposals" and to Bill 60, which was the legislative iteration of *A Time for Action*, and perhaps to bide time until after the next federal election. Trudeau was weak, his Conservative counterpart Joe Clark had endorsed the idea of a more decentralized federation, and perhaps a better constitutional deal could be struck at a slightly later date.[111] Immediately, the provincial premiers agreed that the target dates for agreement were too rushed, that the two-part approach would inappropriately separate rights, institutions, and the division of powers that "should not be treated in isolation from each other," and that the possibility of the federal government acting unilaterally in the first phase would set an unacceptable precedent.[112] The strategy, then, from Ontario's perspective, was "an interprovincial one" relying on "co-operation [that] is based on shared concern over scope and timetable of federal proposals."[113] Securing Quebec's status in the federation had been one of the driving factors in determining Ontario's position on the constitution; that the province should confront Trudeau's federal position within the context of a provincial alliance was somehow fitting. It was not, however, lasting.

* * *

The provincial commitment to stand together in the pursuit of constitutional change was sorely tested and ultimately broken in the next few months. First, at least from the perspective of those working towards change in Ontario, was the realization that other matters had been lost in the blinkered drive towards patriation and disentanglement. In public statements of priorities, Davis and others had always been careful to underline the province's primary commitment to maintaining a strong economy, but the truth of the sentiment was coming into question by the end of 1978. Without intergovernmental agreement on tax sharing, measures to combat inflation, or delivery of social services, there was little that the provinces could do to manage the economy independently. As Davis commented to his fellow premiers at a gathering in Regina in the summer of 1978, "the speedy timetable which the Prime Minister has set to deal with the constitution is in sharp contrast to the slow and uneven pace in dealing with basic reform of Canada's economy."[114]

Particularly irritating had been the process of reform of the Social Services Act, over which provinces had been engaged in more than two years of "intensive discussions" before being "suddenly ... presented with a block funding proposal which is then arbitrarily reduced in size before it can even be accepted in the appropriate federal-provincial forum."[115] But the reduction in the size of the federal contribution to social services was hardly the end of it; by September 1978, Trudeau offered premiers "the distinct possibility that established services to the public will be unilaterally disrupted."[116] While the first ministers debated the constitution, the economy was suffering and the tools that the leaders used to affect it – fiscal levers and social services – were left in disarray in the no man's land between Ottawa and the provinces. The Trudeau government's confrontational approach to intergovernmental issues, and its frequent "take-it-or-leave-it" strategy, did not leave much room for Ontario, let alone the other provinces.

The collapse of the Victoria Charter had slammed closed one important chapter of Ontario's evolving strategy of offering intergovernmental policy alternatives, forging alliances, and keeping the participants engaged in the conversation. In its aftermath, Ontario's rhetoric became more confrontational – especially in regards to energy issues – but the dominant tendency in Ontario had been to focus on the mega-intergovernmental issues that had seemed to offer the provincial bureaucrats something of a panacea. Fixing the structure, they argued, would inevitably correct the details of fiscal or social policies. Constitutional amendment was certainly a foundational, structural arena for attention, but the idea of the constitution had become something of a non-starter in the mid-1970s. Instead, the Ontario civil servants shifted their language, if not their thinking, to embrace the idea of disentanglement, also a mega-intergovernmental strategy that envisioned untying the knots of federal-provincial relations in an almost *constitutional* manner. But focusing almost exclusively on disentanglement or the constitution had not achieved anything; the intergovernmental playing field was as littered as it had ever been, the rules still had not been agreed on, and now the economy was showing signs of distress. The work of successive Conservative governments in Ontario was at risk, as there had been little progress made and increasingly real costs associated with a strategy that depended on Ontario's ability to forge allies, design alternatives and keep the participants engaged in conversation.

Chapter Nine

"The Hot Gospel of Confederation": Securing a New Constitution

Once the conversation about constitutional renewal began, it was extremely difficult to stop. There were certainly other matters on the intergovernmental agenda, including the direction of the economy and the future of social policy arrangements, but the constitution continued to obsess Ontario bureaucrats and politicians. By the end of the 1970s, Ontario had spent at least a decade, first informally and then more officially, pursuing a first-principles approach to the federal-provincial relationship: rather than getting mired in the minutiae of the individual intergovernmental deals and programs, the provincial actors had tried to focus on fundamental issues of equitable monetary and jurisdictional divisions. And as became increasingly apparent, nothing was more fundamental than the constitution, the reform of which held out the possibility of righting the existing imbalances and disentangling the entangled jurisdictions. Had there been a moment at which to forget about the constitution, and shift back to an ad hoc, piecemeal approach to federal-provincial relations in Canada, that time was at the end of the 1970s. That it did not happen owes a great deal to the twists and turns of Pierre Trudeau's political life; it also, however, owes more than has been acknowledged to the commitment of Ontario politicians and bureaucrats to a particular approach to intergovernmental affairs.[1]

In the years leading up to an agreement on constitutional change, all of the various intergovernmental lessons that the people in Ontario – both the political masters and their advisers – had learned in the years since George Drew sat down to his first intergovernmental meeting were pulled out and used in the interest of achieving patriation. The lessons had been cumulative, but each strategy had an important role to play in Ontario's approach to constitutional negotiations in the late 1970s and early 1980s. First, Ontario offered provincially designed alternatives, both to the constitutional policy of the federal government but also to Trudeau's constitutional tactics; second, as had been a key component of Ontario's intergovernmental stance since the Second World War, the province tried to build bridges between competing interests. Unlike in other periods, however, the bridges were not merely necessary between Quebec and the federal government, but rather were required between several different interest groups. Third, Ontario continued its determination to keep the focus on mega-intergovernmental issues; discussion of the nuts and bolts of the relationship would surely lead to acrimony, and Ontario's strategy was to deal with the fundamentals first. Finally, Ontario's intergovernmental team strove to keep all lines of communication open. The conversation had to continue if there were to be any results at all.

Provincial Positioning and the Conservative Interlude

Trudeau's constitutional initiatives of the late 1970s failed, although they did so with a whimper rather than a bang. Having inferred from remarks that the prime minister had somewhat indiscreetly made that provincial consensus would secure federal agreement on constitutional change, provincial premiers – including the pseudo-separatist Lévesque – busied themselves trying to reach agreement on a satisfactory division of powers. From Trudeau's perspective, however, provincial consensus would be sufficient to secure a new amending formula, but on the division of powers he demanded full intergovernmental agreement, not simply provincial agreement. That particular misunderstanding probably ensured that the two levels of government were always approaching the problem from a different perspective and never able to completely engage the opposite government in fruitful discussion.

Despite the election of the Parti Québécois in 1976, an event that had the potential to establish a new consensus on the constitution as the country faced its own break-up, the distances between the federal and the provincial governments were too significant to bridge. Having struggled to reach provincial agreement on jurisdiction, the premiers were hardly in a mood to trim their demands; likewise, Trudeau's increasing unpopularity suggested that the federal government was weak and, with an election imminent, perhaps not long in power. When, in the fall of 1978, Trudeau wrote to all the premiers and reminded them of his previously stated goal to reduce transfers to the provinces by about $370 million, and reiterated his commitment that "the remaining $220 million in federal transfers would be recovered," he certainly did not engender any goodwill from the provinces.[2] The decision to find this money by "adjusting" the escalator used in the Established Programs Financing Act was, according to Ontario Treasurer Frank Miller, a poor one. "We feel very strongly that the EPF arrangements should not be tampered with," he wrote to Davis, "given the length and intensity of negotiations that were necessary to achieve the agreement – and the uncertainty it would bring to all subsequent discussions on disentanglement."[3] Offering legal advice, Michael Gough reiterated Miller's concerns, suggesting that the changes Ottawa was proposing would require provincial consent before they could be made.[4]

Late 1978 was hardly the time for the Trudeau government to be proposing changes to federal-provincial shared-cost programs. Unpopular with voters, suffering from the collapse of his marriage and thus preoccupied with non-governmental conflicts, and facing an election within months, Trudeau was a marked man. The decision to call fifteen by-elections for October, which resulted in thirteen Liberal defeats, underlined the weaknesses of the Trudeau government.[5] The Alberta government took a page out of Ontario's intergovernmental playbook and offered an alternative to the federal proposal – published as *Harmony in Diversity* – although this was designed specifically as a "confrontation document."[6] When the full intergovernmental conference on the constitution met later that month it ended, predictably, without agreement but with promises to "identify the problems, develop possible solutions," and attempt to come to agreement by early 1979.[7] The prime minister later maintained that his strategy of making a relatively generous offer on the division of powers at the conference was designed to lay bare the greediness of the provincial premiers and the tensions in their alliance.[8]

By January 1979, the recently struck Continuing Committee of Ministers on the Constitution (CCMC) had met three times and outlined a list of "best effort" draft proposals on resources, tax sharing and the spending power, the Supreme Court, and equalization and regional development.[9] The CCMC conclusions did not exactly satisfy Ontario: "our initial reaction is negative," wrote the executive director of Ontario's Fiscal Policy Division of the Treasury Department. "We get an overwhelming impression that the proposed changes would have little substantive impact and could lead to confusion and divisiveness."[10] Still, in keeping with Ontario's general position to "follow a positive and constructive approach" and "attempt to get other provinces to soften the shrillness of their anti-Ottawa stance," he proposed that it might be "wise to treat the issues gently at the officials level."[11]

At about the same time that the CCMC was concluding its first round of meetings in preparation for the February first ministers' conference, the Pépin-Robarts Task Force issued its report. *A Future Together* proposed – much to Trudeau's disapproval – that the provinces retain responsibility for protecting minority language rights, opening the commissioners up to criticism "for being decentralist."[12] Although some heralded the report as a "stunning" accomplishment that "should be studied in the schools," it felt out of step with the Trudeau approach to constitutional reform.[13] It was a poor introduction for the federal government to proceed with intergovernmental negotiations, although it perhaps played more effectively into the hands of the provincial premiers. When the first ministers met again in February to discuss the "best efforts" draft, they did so having logged an enormous amount of time on the process, and with a fairly intimate familiarity with the goals, alliances, and agendas of each of the various governments involved. Although there was significant agreement, it was not sufficient. The conference, like all the ones that had preceded it, ended without a new constitution. It also left matters up in the air; Ontario's reconnaissance in Ottawa's Federal-Provincial Relations Office suggested that "it is obvious that they have yet to finalize their ideas."[14]

Suddenly, however, the situation changed dramatically. Joe Clark's minority victory in the general election of May 1979 opened up a whole new realm of possibilities. Not only was the election in many ways a rejection of Trudeau's constitutional vision, but it also suggested that the nation – or at least that part of it west of Quebec, where the Liberal collapse was most apparent – was ready for Clark's new province-friendly approach to intergovernmental relations.[15] The Conservative leader had campaigned, in part, on establishing a new "community of communities" approach to Canadian federalism, and the premiers, not surprisingly, had high hopes for what this would mean for provincial powers. Clark seemed to speak the language of cooperation and conciliation: writing to the premiers to indicate when he intended to call Parliament, Clark underlined that "the Government of Canada neither can, nor should, attempt on its own to resolve the problems and develop the opportunities before us. My colleagues and I," he wrote, "are convinced that we must involve, much more deeply than in the past, both the provinces and the private sector in developing approaches."[16] He immediately struck a different tone than that which had characterized the Trudeau government of the previous decade.

But consultation inevitably led to balancing competing interests, and having established his government as prepared to shift the balance of power towards the provinces, provincial premiers were quick to start demanding even more. Energy moved back to the top of the agenda. In addition to "external pressures for price increases," and the "stated policies" of both Ottawa and the crude oil–producing provinces to move towards the world price, the Clark government moved into negotiations with Brian Peckford of Newfoundland over the control of offshore resources.[17] Energy-using Ontario was not about to let the energy-producing provinces dictate the future course of Canadian policy, and officials pointed to the implications for equalization, fiscal balance, and ongoing constitutional discussions in a paper released at the end of the summer. For Ontario, energy was the issue that brought centralization versus decentralization into greatest relief. Although the province "supported provincial ownership of natural resources and control of pricing," it did so only until "cases of compelling national interest [arose] when the federal government should have the authority to act."[18] Rising energy costs in Ontario would, presumably, be considered a crisis of compelling national interest.

A tour of the Atlantic Provinces quickly confirmed that there was little support for Ontario's position. Economic policy and intergovernmental affairs officials met with their stiffest opposition in Newfoundland, where "they are feeling quite confident that the oil and gas discovery scene is going their way and they want to make quite sure that they have immediate and full control of the resource revenues." Not surprisingly, the argument of the Ontario officials that the central province, "without complaint, had made its contributions to Confederation through equalization," went nowhere. In general, Ontario's intervention was regarded as having been undertaken "on behalf of federal powers," while "Newfoundland's position was identical to Alberta's."[19] Clark's decision, entered into orally with the premier of Newfoundland, ensuring provincial control of offshore resources demonstrated his government's willingness to consider provincial positions on jurisdictional issues. It also raised the question of whether the Davis government's centralist energy paper position was in fact more in line with the Trudeau government than it was with the current Clark administration.

On other matters, too, Ontario officials were concerned about the direction the Clark government was taking. The federal decision to review medicare, for example, was sprung on the provinces without the consultation "on matters of mutual interest" that was to be the hallmark of the "new face" of federalism.[20] But Davis and his advisers had little opportunity to worry or complain about the failures of the Clark regime with which they had, at best, "mediocre relations."[21] The hand-lettered sign that Trudeau's staff had left for Clark in the Prime Minister's Office – "we'll be back" – proved prophetic, and after only nine months in power, the Liberals resoundingly defeated the Conservatives and resumed their place in Ottawa.[22] Trudeau had only the briefest flirtation with resignation, announcing his intention in November and precipitating not only the usual race to replace him but also the announcement of the Quebec referendum on sovereignty-association, a much more straightforward event with Trudeau out of the picture. But the surprising defeat of the Clark budget on 13 December 1979 necessitated an election and paved the way for the return of Pierre Trudeau.[23] Although not confronting the constitution head on in what was a campaign vague on policy,[24] there was no question that the implication of Trudeau's return was that the constitutional portfolio would be reopened. The results of the Quebec referendum, called under entirely different circumstances than now existed, would play a big role in determining Trudeau's larger constitutional strategy.

The Unilateral Gambit

In Ontario, Trudeau's return was greeted with something more than resignation, but perhaps less than enthusiasm. Despite the colour of their respective parties, the Davis Tories had had a far better intergovernmental relationship with Trudeau than they had had with Clark during his brief stint in office. In an attempt to downplay the apparent attraction of opposites, Don Stevenson suggested putting "together a list of issues on which [the Ontario government] could reasonably claim that the Conservative federal government had made progress by adopting a different style." He also noted how the geographically skewed election results – only two Liberals won seats west of Ontario – might affect Ontario's approach to Ottawa: "While in a number of recent statements the Ontario government has been strongly supportive of a strengthened federal role, particularly in economic areas, I think we will have to be very cautious in the next two or three months in getting too far into bed with a centralist federal government ... The Ontario government should be more sensitive to western interests than it needed to be when the federal government was in many respects a spokesman for western interests."[25] Like so many others before him had done, Stevenson's tone suggested a certain conflation of the interests of Ontario with those of the federal government.

The Liberal election platform had included a national energy policy and a proposal to adopt the "blended price for petroleum ... [that] was urged by Ontario in its 1979 position papers on oil and gas pricing."[26] Davis's congratulatory letter to the incoming prime minister, in fact, began by pointing out that a national energy policy would be "a prime focus of our attention."[27] But while energy was clearly going to be a key issue on the intergovernmental agenda in the early 1980s, there was little reason to imagine that it would result in conflicts with Ontario; Trudeau had already given early indications that his approach might be more in line with that of Ontario politicians. On the constitution, however, everything seemed to hinge on the referendum. Scheduled for May 1980, the question Quebeckers were asked was whether they would give the PQ government of René Lévesque the authority to negotiate a new relationship – called sovereignty-association – with the federal government and the rest of Canada. In Quebec, provincial Liberal leader and former *Le Devoir* publisher Claude Ryan had issued a "beige paper" outlining his party's position on a new decentralized federalism. The Ryan position offered an alternative to sovereignty-association. Although observers in both Ottawa and Toronto were "happy to see a federalist paper from Quebec," the specific recommendations provided a lot of room for debate and left those outside Quebec pondering how they should best deal with the referendum.[28]

Although the federal bureaucrats "did not have a lot of specific ideas" about how to handle the referendum when the Liberals first returned to power and welcomed Ontario's "input," ultimately the results set the stage for "these forthcoming constitutional discussions becoming a battle between two Quebecers."[29] Some missteps by the Péquistes hindered the "oui" side: Claude Ryan's wife was called an "Yvette," a derogatory Québécois term implying a subservient housewife, and Lévesque himself tried to make hay out of Trudeau's anglophone middle name. Neither of these personal jabs went over well with the voters, although polling suggested that throughout the spring of 1980 the "oui" side commanded a fairly convincing lead.[30] Then in April, Trudeau stepped into the fray. He made three major speeches in Quebec in support of Claude Ryan and the "non" side; in the first and second, he linked a "non" vote to a renewal of the federal system. In the final speech, delivered six days before the referendum, he was even more explicit:

I know that I can make the most solemn commitment that following a No vote, we will start immediately the process of renewing the Constitution, and we will not stop until it is done ... We are putting ourselves on the line, we Quebec MPs, because we are telling Quebeckers to vote NO, and we are saying to you in other provinces that we will not accept that you interpret a No vote as an indication that everything is fine, and everything can stay as it was before. We want change, we are putting our seats [in Parliament] on the line to have change.[31]

The defeat of the sovereignty-association option just days later, by almost 60 per cent of the vote, was a humiliation for Lévesque, but opened the door for Trudeau's renewed federalism. To that end, the Continuing Committee of Ministers on the Constitution travelled across the country, picking up the "best efforts" draft where it had been left in 1978 and attempting to come to agreement on the outstanding issues. But that seemed more elusive than ever. On resource ownership, for example, "Alberta is now joined by Quebec" in rejecting the original "best effort" draft as "an insufficient limitation on the federal powers"; on the other hand, Ottawa, Ontario, and Prince Edward Island "consider the 'best effort' draft too decentralist." Disagreements were also evident on changes to the Senate, the Supreme Court, the amending formula, and virtually every other topic that had been under discussion.[32]

With a frustrating lack of consensus at the intergovernmental level, the Ontario bureaucracy turned inward and began the process of establishing a clear constitutional position for the province. A document on "priorities for the early eighties" stated that since 1978 Ontario's intergovernmental strategy had been "aggressive and focused" in its commitment to "a genuinely balanced pro-federalist approach to the constitution." But should, or even could, that approach be continued?[33] With the national press "determined to portray Ontario as increasingly ineffectual in intergovernmental terms,"[34] the civil servants in the ministry began working on "the hot gospel of Confederation."[35] In a long, often fervent, document entitled "To Renew and Strengthen Confederation: The Ontario View," the officials laid out a plan for a stronger federal government, a stronger national economy, and greater cooperation between the two levels of government. The soaring rhetoric of the draft document needed "a dispassionate eye and a firm hand," but the executive director of intergovernmental affairs still thought "we can be both moral and statesmanlike without risking a further caricature of Ontario as not just Upper but Only Canada."[36]

However, when the first ministers met in conference in the early autumn of 1980, four days of discussion on the topics that had been identified by the CCMC over the summer led only deeper into disagreement.

By the end of the conference, the premiers of the bigger, more power-ful provinces – those with perhaps the strongest opinions on what the outcome should look like – were uniform in their expressions of disap-pointment. But their displeasure stemmed from different issues. For On-tario, the problem was "that constitutional reform would not be achieved unless the pursuit of provincial goals was moderated by a concern for the national good." Lévesque, on the other hand, complained that the federal government "supported a concentration of power at the centre" in contrast to the decentralization favoured by "most provincial govern-ments."[37] Alberta's Premier Lougheed wondered aloud about how the existing constitution would withstand the pressure that energy negotia-tions over the next few months would put it under. Nor was the prime minister himself pleased with the outcome. He closed the conference by listing the concessions that the federal government had been pre-pared to make in order to achieve agreement, as well as the demands that provinces were continuing to make in terms of Senate reform and the amending formula. It was, according to observers, "one of the most acrimonious [constitutional conferences] on record."[38]

So bleak was the outcome that Davis wrote to all Conservatives serv-ing in an official capacity in Ontario – members of the federal and pro-vincial caucuses, party executives, nominated candidates – to explain that "last week in Ottawa, we sustained a very meaningful setback in ef-forts to achieve for Canada a new constitution and a truly renewed fed-eralism."[39] He explained Ontario's objectives at the conference, which included securing the role of the Crown, patriation, entrenching the Charter, and "preserving a strong economic union for all Canadians."[40] But more importantly, he explained the motivation behind Ontario's position: "Ontario did not go to Ottawa for the purpose of reducing the capacity of our National Government to deal with … national issues," he explained, underlining that "Ontario's nationalism is seen by some to be self-serving, but … the record of our province through equalization … constitutes a significant investment in the well-being of all Canadians."[41] The letter was almost apologetic in tone, less so for the outcome of the conference than for the position that the Ontario government had tak-en. Coming across as such a stalwart supporter of the Trudeau approach to constitutional reform clearly warranted an explanation, but it was one that the Davis government had been successfully defending for months. It was important that the Ontario position was firm; Trudeau's next gam-bit tested the resolve of all the provinces, regardless of their position on the current state of negotiations.

At the beginning of October, Trudeau made it clear that he was done negotiating with the provinces. Perhaps his announcement that the federal government was going to proceed unilaterally on the constitutional file had been the plan all along. Trudeau had already raised the possibility of unilateral action in 1976, although that had come to naught; a memorandum leaked just days before the opening of the 1980 conference indicated that the federal government should be again prepared to act unilaterally if no agreement could be reached with the provinces. This time, Trudeau made good on the threat. Just as importantly, Davis made good on his equally long-standing promise to support the federal government as it attempted to secure constitutional changes in Westminster without the prior agreement of the provinces.[42] Although there was modest pressure from the group in Ontario to secure some small changes to the Trudeau strategy, for the most part, the prime minister had himself a strong ally in Bill Davis.[43]

Such support seemed to warrant concessions in other parts of the intergovernmental mix, but Ontario had precious little opportunity to use its constitutional position as a "lever," despite considering increasing "its public support for the federal package through even stronger – and perhaps more frequent – statements, and by enlisting the voice of the Premier."[44] The work of the deputy ministers of finance on tax sharing, the established programs financing arrangements, and equalization, in addition to the wrangling over a national energy program, remained largely separate from negotiations and posturing over the constitution.[45] At root, all were problems of equitably and fairly sharing costs. The health care and education policies that were the heart of the EPF issue were expensive, for example, and Ottawa wanted to trim its spending. The provinces, however, wanted the original deal honoured. Any changes to the Established Programs Financing Act, however, would affect fiscal transfers and the determination of equalization. This, too, was a key concern for Ontario officials, who had been openly critical of the formula for determining payments ever since "Ontario began to show up as 'eligible' for equalization around 1978."[46] Especially troublesome in the equalization debate had been the position of oil and gas revenue, pointing to the national inequalities that resulted from Alberta's – and latterly Newfoundland's – natural resource bonanza. In some respects the National Energy Program, announced in the Trudeau government's fall 1980 budget, was designed to address not only "supply and energy self-sufficiency" but also "fairness of pricing and sharing of revenues."[47] But in Ontario, the increased revenue that the federal government was going to get from the oil and gas sector led to concerns about where the windfall would be spent – perhaps on "deficit reduction, [their] own account spending and a western economic development fund." Moreover, energy revenue created "revenue imbalances among the provinces" that were "different in kind rather than in degree, from anything experienced in the past," and that would ultimately have serious implications for both tax sharing and equalization.[48]

It is easy to see why the Ontario bureaucrats devoted so much attention in the 1970s and early 1980s to the idea of disentanglement. The issues that plagued the intergovernmental relationship were all interconnected; changes to one – even the signing of a satisfactory agreement in one area – had consequences for other issues. Untying the knots of decades of overlapping agreements and competitive jurisdiction seemed like an appropriate, even necessary, step towards a more workable federal system. But ironically, by the 1980s it was appearing as if the entangled jurisdiction itself was what allowed the system to function. The intractability of the entangled problems forced political attention onto the bigger canvas of the constitution, where there might be some real hope of achieving meaningful change. In Ontario, where a great deal of attention was still being paid to the specifics of the intergovernmental relationship, there is no question that these issues seemed like a house of cards – one false move and the whole structure might come tumbling down. The constitution offered the possibility, at least, of building a brick structure. And so it was that the constitution came to dominate the thinking of Ontario politicians and advisers alike throughout much of the 1980s.

Court Challenges and Constitutional Lobbying

The first step in Trudeau's constitutional strategy was to have the House of Commons pass his proposed legislation, including the Charter of Rights and Freedoms and the amending formula. This was hardly a hurdle with such a strong Liberal majority, but the debate proved instructive in that it resulted in changes to both the constitution as designed in 1980 and foreshadowed revisions that were attempted later in the decade. Because he was arguing over the heads of the premiers that this unilateral constitution was in reality a "people's package," Trudeau, the unlikely populist, had to avoid the image that he was ramming his constitution through a tame Parliament. Therefore, following a brief debate in the House of Commons, the constitutional package moved on to a joint parliamentary committee, where the hearings were televised and the proposals for modification were taken seriously. The hearings became another indication that the prime minister was pursuing a real, workable, rights-based constitution, rather than simply another notch in his belt in the war against the provinces. The committee introduced several changes, including entrenching rights for both women and Aboriginals, which ultimately became key components of the new constitution. Engaging the public in the debate also became a requirement of all future attempts at constitutional change.[49]

Optics aside, however, Trudeau was relatively uninterested in what was going on in Parliament and knew that the real fight over the constitution was going to have to be waged with the premiers, even if the shift to unilateral action had temporarily removed them from the equation.[50] Three provinces – Manitoba, Quebec, and Newfoundland – began court proceedings at the provincial appellate level on the constitutional viability of unilateral patriation in the fall of 1980. By the spring, the results were in. The courts of the first two upheld the federal government's right to unilateral action, holding 3–2 (in Manitoba) and 4–1 (in Quebec) that provincial consent was not a requirement for patriation. The Newfoundland court, on the other hand, held that provincial consent *was* necessary.[51] Once the Quebec court issued its decision in April 1981, the stage was set for an appeal of the three provincial court decisions to the Supreme Court of Canada.

In the House of the Commons, the Conservatives had been filibustering the bill as the only means at their disposal to prevent Trudeau from proceeding immediately to London. With the Supreme Court now engaged in the process, the Conservatives, New Democrats, and Liberals agreed to call something of a truce until after the Court had rendered its decision.[52] In Ontario, the reference to the Supreme Court offered an opportunity to intervene, a course of action that Davis indicated was "consistent with our view that the Parliament of Canada has the competence and right to make constitutional change on behalf of the citizens of Canada, without the unanimous agreement of the provinces."[53] Having just secured his first majority government in a decade, Davis was in a better position to show his support for the federal government than he had been during the election, when he came under "great pressure" to "distance himself" from Trudeau.[54] The Supreme Court intervention clearly marked Ontario as behind the federal gambit "one hundred per cent," although the intergovernmental advisers expected "more pressure" to "move off our current position ... in order to try to develop a greater federal-provincial consensus."[55] Davis hadn't seen a lot of partnership building to date, however. He had neither been invited to a meeting that those provinces opposed to unilateral patriation had called, nor had he "received a response to my request for a written outline of the agreement allegedly reached between the eight provinces."[56]

Yet despite the divide that seemed to be growing between Ottawa, Ontario, and New Brunswick, on the one hand, and the so-called Gang of Eight, on the other, the Ontario politicians and bureaucrats alike continued to try to build a consensus by whatever means. For example, senior intergovernmental affairs mandarin Don Stevenson thought it might be "worthwhile seeing if there is a possibility of the federal government accepting some changes in the amending formula." He argued that such a move might have the effect "of breaking up the gang of eight and adding somewhat more cross-country legitimacy to the entire package." Surely, he contended, there must be a way to continue working "towards a greater degree of consensus."[57] But clearly a consensus could be built only if some form of discussion continued, and in early 1981 each side seemed more interested in determining the parameters of agreement within the group rather than the opportunity for bridge building between the groups. Unable really to approach the Gang of Eight head-on, the Ontario strategy remained one of creating an atmosphere that might force the two sides back to the bargaining table. This was what was behind the search for changes to Ottawa's amending formula; it was also what compelled Ontario politicians and officials alike to lobby their counterparts in England.

Several Ontario officials made the trip to England in the winter of 1981, as had their counterparts from other provinces and representatives from Canada's First Nations, in an effort to influence British parliamentarians on whether they should be passing patriation legislation that had only the support of Canada's federal government. The strategy of the dissenting provinces was to "wine and dine British MPs" in an effort to convince them to either delay or vote against the Canadian bill.[58] Interestingly, Ontario's strategy was not much different. As the Supreme Court announced its decision to hear the appeals from the three provincial courts, Ontario adviser Hugh Segal set out the results of the various conversations he and others had had in London over the course of the winter and early spring. In general, they had detected "a strong anti-Trudeau bias," not surprising in the middle of the Thatcher era, but also that the absence of "any Tory pro-package presence … has hurt the overall perception of the package."[59] Whether that was a problem, however, remained debatable. Ontario's Attorney General Roy McMurtry, one of those who went to London, later expressed some doubts about the wisdom of the British Parliament debating the Canadian legislation – at least before the Supreme Court had had its say. "Each day as I read the Canadian press," he wrote to his British counterpart Sir Michael Havers, "it becomes increasingly apparent that the Federal Government's proposals are not as generally accepted by either Canadian citizens or their political representatives in Provincial Legislatures as political changes of this magnitude ought to be."[60] Perhaps, he suggested, it was premature for such a debate to be occurring in Britain.

This seemed to be the sentiment in London as well. From the British perspective, the Supreme Court hearings put any parliamentary decision onto the back burner, at least for the short term. Ontario politicians – McMurtry in particular – shifted their attention from London to Ottawa. At the end of April and the beginning of May 1981, the Supreme Court heard five days of oral arguments from federal lawyers, including the formidable J.J. Robinette and the future Newfoundland premier Clyde Wells, and provincial lawyers, who counted in their ranks the future separatist premier of Quebec Lucien Bouchard.[61] Attorney General Roy McMurtry acted for Ontario. Having already advised the federal government that the reference to the Supreme Court should be on legal grounds only, and not open up the question of whether political convention held that the provinces needed to be consulted on constitutional amendment, McMurtry devoted most of his attention to the legal aspects of the issue. But while the points of his oral arguments were on black letter law, he nevertheless strayed repeatedly into the realm of convention. "Internal Canadian political realities might well require consultation with the provinces," was one of the points of his Supreme Court argument, he later recalled. So, too, was the invitation "to take judicial notice of the political stalemate" which moved the deliberations rather further outside the law than McMurtry might have intimated was his intent.[62] It was a well-reasoned argument, but one that nevertheless left the door open to a ruling on the conventions around unanimity; unwittingly or not, McMurtry had presented a case that helped the jurists send the issue right back into the hands of the politicians.

But they took their time doing so. Although there were clear "reports that UK interest [was] flagging," delegations from the Gang of Eight continued to lobby members of the British House of Commons in the late spring and summer of 1981. From the federal perspective, however, the longer it took the Supreme Court to render a decision, the better.

The Court was not expected to deliver a decision until at least September, which was in the middle of the British parliamentary recess; there was no reason, then, "to rush the process in Canada." Moreover, Michael Kirby seemed to think that any "extra time provides opportunity for the group of eight alliance to weaken."[63] It also provided time for the federal government to shift attention away from the constitution, and onto the economy. With perhaps a greater degree of consultation with Ontario – and perhaps even more anomalously, with New Brunswick – than was usually the case, Ottawa embarked on a series of ministerial-level meetings on general economic questions. Not only were there one-on-one meetings between Allan MacEachen and his counterparts across the country, but Trudeau also wrote to the premiers initiating several meetings – building towards a first ministers' meeting in September – aimed at identifying "what constructive steps we might take together to resolve the critical problems now facing us."[64] But, apart from some manoeuvring around energy in Alberta, and around anticipated federal cuts to education through the Established Programs Financing Act, provincial attention was firmly fixed on the progress of the constitution.

A sense of "what next?" seemed to hang over virtually all that the various governments in Canada undertook through the summer and fall of 1981. With the Supreme Court still considering its verdict, there was room for strategizing. According to some observers, the Trudeau government's approach was based on "planning," "obsessively" pursued with a "Jesuit-like simplicity" and designed to "manipulate the events."[65] Ontario politicians and bureaucrats took a different approach. Their goal was to keep the options for compromise open and to encourage a continuing "dialogue" about the constitution. To that end, then, Ontario actors were less interested in planning than they were in maintaining the goodwill of participants on both sides of the issue. At the annual premiers' conference in mid-August, for example, "Davis explained in emotional terms that his stand was based on strong personal conviction and not a result of any sordid deal with the federal government." According to Don Stevenson, one of the bureaucrats most closely associated with Ontario's constitutional strategy, the "presentation appeared to be more accepted by the other premiers than anything said by Ontario to date."[66]

Keeping options open proved to be important in the months that followed. So, too, did earning the respect of players on both sides of the divide. Here, the understated "bland" qualities of Davis's Ontario were indispensible. Having not issued fiery statements about its position, the Ontario government could be seen as the one possible bridge between the provinces and Ottawa.[67] It was a mediation position that Ontario had frequently played in the previous decades between Quebec and the federal government; now there was an opportunity to play the same role in a bigger venue. There was evidence in the summer of 1981 that Ontario's brokering skills were still intact. A non-political Cambridge debate on the Canadian constitutional question was the occasion for many of the participants to once again make the trip to England. In addition to Chief Justice Brian Dickson and Mr. Justice 'Bud' Estey of the Supreme Court, Roy Romanow, Jean Chrétien, and Roy McMurtry all attended the conference. Although the debate obviously did not settle the real issue in Canada, while they were in England the latter three participants "appeared to have reached a tacit understanding that some further political compromise was required."[68]

The three were well placed to work towards a compromise. Saskatchewan Attorney General and Deputy Premier Roy Romanow was the leader of the moderate provinces.[69] Justice Minister Chrétien had begun his baptism in constitutional politics by reiterating the hard-line position of Trudeau and Pitfield, but after weeks of talking to premiers across the country he had become increasingly sensitive to their concerns.[70] By this time, McMurtry had also become personally convinced that recourse to Britain was no longer an option. The parliamentarians there had "become increasingly judgmental" and irritatingly "paternalistic" in their attitude towards Canadian constitutional affairs, so much so that the attorney general determined to devote his energies to securing a negotiated deal.[71] But despite Ontario's dogged defence of Ottawa's right to patriate the constitution unilaterally, a political solution had always been Ontario's main objective. Whether the sides would be pushed together by threats – like those of Trudeau – or drawn together by promises of a better deal remained to be seen.

Throughout much of September, the Ontario group held fast to its original position of supporting the federal government while acknowledging the complications that the Supreme Court ruling could introduce. The other provincial premiers, in meetings towards the end of the month to discuss the state of the economy, also stuck to their constitutional positions.[72] But on 28 September, the Supreme Court issued its historic ruling, in an historic manner. Before a live television audience, and with an Ontario delegation of ministers and advisers in Ottawa to hear the ruling, the justices announced their decision. It was a complicated one. On the question of the legality of whether the federal government could unilaterally initiate patriation of the constitution, the Supreme Court declared, in a 7–2 decision, that the answer was yes. But the Court also chose to answer the question of whether convention allowed the federal government to seek patriation without the agreement of the provinces, and on this question, a majority of 6–3 found that the answer was no. The simple explanation of the Court's forty-five-minute decision was that while it was legal for Trudeau's government to act unilaterally, it wasn't nice.[73] Ontario's Minister of Intergovernmental Affairs Tom Wells and Attorney General Roy McMurtry were quick to offer the province's opinion on the decision at a press conference that afternoon: they asserted that "the legal question has now been settled," and as far as the issue of convention was concerned, "it was always known that this was a departure from general precedent in order to break a logjam."[74] No one was immediately forthcoming, however, on what would happen next.

Securing a Compromise

Not only did the Gang of Eight regard the Supreme Court decision a victory, but also "some of [the] Ontario delegation [was] beginning to agree that it would be impossible to bull ahead without change." What was clearly the danger, however, was that "no one will take the first step to put together compromise proposals."[75] Within a few days of the judicial ruling, the phone lines were buzzing between provinces as advisers discussed the likelihood of compromise, and their political masters began to lay their cards on the table. Most of the discussions in which Ontario officials were involved were with other provinces; it was not until the middle of October that news of discussions between Trudeau and Davis began to trickle down through the Ontario intergovernmental civil service. Apparently, there was "room for a fair bit of flexibility on the charter, on timing, and some room for change on the amending formula."[76] A similar message was being quietly issued from British Columbia and Saskatchewan on the Gang of Eight side, and from New Brunswick on the "federalist" side. Another attempt at political compromise seemed increasingly likely.

Both sides remained wary, however. Trudeau was "pleased" that the Gang of Eight "accepted my invitation to attend a first ministers' conference on the constitution"; on behalf of his provincial colleagues, B.C.'s Premier Bennett in turn was gratified that the prime minister accepted the proposed dates.[77] Each side jostled for the upper hand. But during this period of Court-encouraged transition from the unilateral gambit of the federal government to the negotiated agreement that would be attempted at the November first ministers' conference, the Ontario politicians and bureaucrats played a key role. Conversations were virtually non-stop, as Davis, McMurtry, and Wells gathered information and noted areas where there might be some more flexibility on the political side of things; and Stevenson, Posen, and Segal worked in the same way on the bureaucrats and advisers across the country. In the very few days before the opening of the 2 November conference, meetings were even held in Toronto, despite Trudeau's refusal to convene a "preparatory meeting of ministers."[78]

In the lead-up to the November conference, Ontario officials were kept busy, fielding calls from other provinces, making sense of rumours that individual premiers were prepared to move on one or another part of the patriation package, and assessing how their intelligence on the position of the various members of the Gang of Eight might fit in with what they knew first-hand about the federal position. While many commentators have focused attention on the events of the period 2–5 November, calling it "the week that was"[79] or other titles suggestive of the centrality of the work done in Ottawa that week, it was really the period between 19 and 26 October over the telephone, and between 28 October and 31 October in various hotels in downtown Toronto, that the outline of the constitutional deal first began to appear. With Ontario representatives as point people, key conversations were held between Saskatchewan, British Columbia, and New Brunswick officials, with input from Alberta's team. A Quebec presence was notably non-existent in the back-and-forth over what might be possible in the context of a first ministers' meeting; instead, Quebec was "lobbying with other members of the seven [provinces] to hold tough."[80]

British Columbia officials seemed to be the most amenable to change, agreeing on the possibility of compromises on the amending formula, equalization, natural resources, linguistic rights, and opting out.[81] It many ways, it seemed too good to be true, but word from New Brunswick was that "Bennett is sincere in seeking compromise."[82] As the leader of the Gang of Eight, it was important that British Columbia showed some willingness to move, and by the week before the opening of the conference, B.C.'s point man Jim Matkin could report to Stevenson that British Columbia, Saskatchewan, Nova Scotia, and Prince Edward Island were all willing to make substantive compromises. That left Manitoba, Alberta, and least surprisingly, Quebec all "sticking to the confrontation." While the Toronto meetings were being held, Quebec's Minister of Intergovernmental Affairs Claude Morin expressed his concern about the conversations to his Alberta counterpart, making it "clear that if even one more province broke with the Accord then Quebec would no longer be bound by it and would move independently."[83] From Quebec's perspective, then, any willingness to compromise was regarded as a betrayal of the original alliance of the Gang of Eight.[84]

On the other side of things, however, the federal government sounded like it was less and less interested in "any exercises in cooperative federalism."[85] With evidence that at least some of the players on the provincialist side were willing to bargain, and a Trudeau government with both a reputation for intransigence and no evidence of altering that attitude in the short term, it was particularly important that Davis's Ontario could offer ways to bridge the divide. The one area in which Ontario usually excelled, however – interpreting Quebec for the rest of the country and bridging a linguistic divide within the federal system – seemed to be missing almost entirely. Still, skills gained over several decades of bridge building had come into play in a different, but perhaps just as useful, way as Ontario shuttled back and forth between the two sides of the constitutional divide. Interestingly, there was perhaps more evidence in the days leading up to the first ministers' conference of the contours of the deal to come than participants noticed at the time.

In many ways, then, the events of the week of 2 November should come as little surprise. The eight provinces began by trying to "'smoke out' Mr. Trudeau" in an effort to figure out whether he was just "going through the motions ... so that he could present the case to the British Parliamentarians saying that he had tried his best."[86] For those on the Ontario team, not only was it clear very early on that there was an "atmosphere [of] ... determination to reach a consensus" but also that the prime minister was well aware of the problems he would face in Westminster if he were to try to patriate unilaterally at this juncture.[87] Whether this was as clear to any of the members of the Gang of Eight is unlikely. The first three days of the meetings disappeared in the usual way, with arguments circulating about the amending formula and the Charter of Rights – the two components of a constitutional agreement that posed the most difficulty for one side or the other – and little progress being made on either. There were compromise possibilities in the air, as Ontario officials agreed that they could accept the so-called Alberta amending formula that eliminated their traditional 'veto' over constitutional change, and Trudeau was persuaded by Davis to accept a limitation on his Charter of Rights.[88] Still, with no real movement on the part of either side, the conference was threatening to end like the dozens that had preceded it with a lot of talk but no action.

Trudeau's brinksmanship broke the impasse. The prime minister suggested a referendum to decide the fate of both the amending formula and the Charter of Rights, thereby "letting the people decide," and Lévesque took the bait. Looking "enthusiastic" about the possibility, the Quebec premier seemed to break with his English-speaking colleagues in considering a mechanism that had long been opposed by the Gang of Eight because it eliminated the important role of provincial legislatures in constitutional amendment. The stage was set for a middle-of-the-night agreement between seven of the dissenting provinces and the three governments on the federalist side. Where in this, the "night of the long knives" as it would come to be known in Quebec mythology, did strategy end and luck begin? Had Trudeau all along been planning to break apart the alliance of provinces in this manner, marginalize Quebec, and achieve his long-sought goal of patriation? Probably not, despite the dramatic climax that dangling the possibility of a referendum in front of Lévesque gives to the retelling of the tale.[89]

Was the final work the result of the long conversations, over many months, between Roy McMurtry, Roy Romanow, and Jean Chrétien, or the short one in the kitchen of the conference hotel that has been glorified in the behind-the-scenes accounts? Certainly, they have received the lion's share of the credit – or the blame – for the after-hours agreement that was reached, and their efforts at securing a compromise should not go unnoticed. But lost, somehow, in most of the accounts of the constitutional conference is the role of the Ontario delegation as a whole – from premier through to intergovernmental affairs office bureaucrat – in defining the contours of what was possible, in keeping avenues of communication open and, ultimately, providing the template for the agreement that was reached.[90] When agreement was finally reached, it was on a variation of a proposal floated by Davis on the second day of the conference. Both sides would lose something. Trudeau would have to accept a limit, the notwithstanding clause, to his Charter of Rights, and he would have to let go of his insistence on entrenching a referendum mechanism; the Gang of Eight would have to accept an amending formula based on population and region rather than on provinces. When ten of the eleven governments finally agreed to a new constitution, it was a version of what Davis and his advisers had proposed; they were able to agree to it because Davis and his group of advisers had paved the way through days, years, arguably decades of careful intergovernmental management, dialogue, and bridge building.

It certainly seemed that Ontario's strategies of mega-intergovernmentalism and maintaining open lines of communication had worked: the Constitution Act, 1982 not only brought the BNA Act home with a domestic amending formula, but also it entrenched fundamental rights and clarified jurisdiction. But Ontario remained no better off – in terms of control over taxation or social programs or equalization – than it had been before the final round of constitutional negotiations had begun and, as the 1980s unfolded, quite possibly worse off. When the normal course of federal-provincial relations resumed after the fall 1981 agreement on the constitution, for example, all the old sore points remained. The federal budget laid out plans to use Ontario as the "benchmark or 'standard'" for the determination of national equalization grants, "an arbitrary and discriminatory approach" in the views of the Ontario economic bureaucrats.[91] It also announced a change in the way the Established Program Financing contribution would be determined, and the elimination of a revenue guarantee component that had helped to offset the costs of health care and post-secondary education. Both changes were, again, to the detriment of Ontario.[92] In public, the Ontario response had been "tempered," but its "criticisms had been rigorous in private."[93] The irony of the timing of these proposed cuts and policy changes was not lost on those in Ontario; on the issue of equalization, the bureaucrats noted that "Ontario is 'so important' in Canada that its service level is set up as the benchmark for the entire country, yet only a few days ago Ontario had to give up its claim to be 'so important' as to deserve a constitutional veto."[94]

In the aftermath of the successful constitutional negotiations, there is little evidence that either Ontario politicians or officials expected any kind of recognition or reward for the key role that the province had played in patriating the constitution. There was, however, clearly some bitterness that the intergovernmental agenda returned so quickly to the petty battles over money and jurisdiction that had characterized much of the pre-constitutional era. But initially at least, the Ontario strategy remained much the same as it had always been. That meant, primarily, striving to keep the intergovernmental focus on the big picture. The Ontario bureaucrats moved to "a more corporate approach" to the portfolio, "with Cabinet level approval of new policies, major initiatives and strategies for realizing them."[95] To this end, Hugh Segal was appointed as the key point person on intergovernmental affairs, charged with overseeing not only the relationship between the Ontario and federal governments, but also the interprovincial network. It was a task he was going to undertake "orally" by "maintaining close and frank contact" with his counterparts in other governments.[96]

But the intergovernmental relationship was becoming increasingly bitter. Quebec's refusal to participate in *any* intergovernmental meetings in the aftermath of their perceived exclusion from the constitutional agreement certainly shifted the dynamic.[97] However, the real vitriol in the federal-provincial relationship stemmed from Ottawa's withdrawal from social spending. The cutbacks to EPF transfers led those in Ontario to seriously contemplate a court challenge, and prompted a normally taciturn Premier Davis to express deep frustration at the "inflexible and intransigent" position of the federal government regarding established program financing and equalization.[98] The Ontario group seemed stymied at every turn, ultimately even "flirting" with "offering to surrender Medicare."[99] The absence of any economic cooperation was also infuriating for Davis: "coordinated approaches to economic recovery are not options," he wrote to Trudeau, "they are imperatives."[100] For a province that had devoted so much attention to mega-intergovernmental problems, the easy return to having the terms dictated by the federal government and to then bickering over the details of various programs was unsettling.

The quick slide into this version of normalcy points to the failure of Ontario's postwar strategy in intergovernmental relations. While succeeding in achieving national objectives, Ontario proved surprisingly incapable of securing provincial goals. For the most part, however, those goals remained unarticulated; although there was clearly an expectation of some correction of the intergovernmental relationship, this is really only evident in the mounting frustration of Ontario's civil servants and politicians with the way business was conducted between the province and the federal government. But in Ontario, as Bill Davis had said, "Confederation has always been a justifiable obsession,"[101] and its continuation was thus enough of a coup to ensure that the province's intergovernmental strategy was not immediately discarded.

On the big questions, then, Ontario was prepared to play the role of statesman, seeking compromises from other governments, facilitating conversations, attempting to ensure the continued functioning of the federal system. On the smaller issues – the terms of agreements, the division of tax room or points or dollars, the daily grind of federalism – the provincial position was much less coherent and sought largely to benefit from the perceived generosity of its statesmanship. Ontario was far less successful at winning the small victories than it was at meeting the more fundamental objectives of its mega-intergovernmentalism. That had been why, in the 1960s, the Ontario strategy had shifted towards embracing the reform of structural elements of the intergovernmental relationship, rather than continually getting mired in the minutiae. But the change to mega-intergovernmentalism had not meant a rejection of the idea of securing a larger place in the federation for Ontario, it had simply meant a different approach. An approach that seems clearly to have failed by the mid-1980s, as little seemed to be coming Ontario's way in the wake of the successful patriation of the constitution. It could not be long before Ontario's bureaucrats and politicians began rethinking their tactics, but it continued a surprisingly long time after it had become apparent to the Davis crew that there would be little in the way of kickbacks for their role in securing the Constitution Act, 1982.

Epilogue

In the spring of 1985, after forty-two uninterrupted years in power, the Conservative party in Ontario was finally ousted from office. The arrival of David Peterson in the premier's office, on the strength of an agreement with the New Democrats, brought a new approach to intergovernmental relations in the central province. Or, at least, it brought an opportunity for a new approach that had not existed since the Second World War, when the Conservative domination of the political environment meant that successive administrations may have operated as much out of inertia on the federal-provincial front as out of any real commitment to the strategy of the government it replaced. Similarly, the government in Ottawa had changed since the conclusion of the last major round of federal-provincial negotiations: Trudeau had finally retired, and after a brief interlude under John Turner, the Conservatives swept into office on the power of Brian Mulroney's new agenda. Thus, Peterson's Liberal government could quite freely chart a new course, not indebted in the least to either the Davis or the short-lived Miller regimes it replaced. The bureaucracy remained the same despite the change in party, however, and Peterson's early advice came from those who had crafted the intergovernmental strategy of the Conservatives before him.

Heading into his first series of intergovernmental meetings in the summer of 1985, Peterson received exhaustive briefings. Not only did his advisers need to explain the background to such events as the Halifax first ministers' conference or the trajectory of Quebec's position on a particular issue, but also they had to lay out "issues which must be addressed" and give advice on how Peterson should proceed.[1] In general, Peterson was advised "to avoid commitments" in this early period and "gauge the response of the other Premiers" to various proposals.[2] In his first bilateral meeting with the prime minister, however, the bureaucrats suggested a more assertive position that highlighted both the strengths and the weaknesses of Ontario's intergovernmental agenda since the Second World War. It was clearly an important meeting that would attract "significant media attention" and would establish "the tone for Ontario-federal relations."[3]

The staff of the Office of Intergovernmental Affairs advised the new premier that "the meeting should try to achieve three fundamental goals." As laid out, these goals were remarkably similar to those that had been pursued during the Davis period. They included setting the "tone" for the relationship, addressing "specific areas of current concern," and opening "channels of communication." Within this rubric, Peterson should "make it clear that Ontario will speak with a new and stronger voice in federal-provincial relations" which suggested that there would be a somewhat new approach emanating from Queen's Park. The remainder of the advice, however, followed well-worn tracks: the premier was to "assert Ontario's role and interest in maintaining a healthy system of federalism and a strong federal government" and make clear his "commitment to cooperative federalism."[4] As Deputy Minister of Intergovernmental Affairs Gary Posen later pointed out, "even where interests and views differ, Ontario wants to keep the lines of communication open and the relations among governments positive."[5] Federalism might have been a "justifiable obsession" for Bill Davis, and the bureaucrats were clearly encouraging Peterson to view it in the same light.

Only this time, it didn't work. The key intergovernmental issues in the Peterson period were the negotiation of a free trade deal and the reopening of the constitution to secure Quebec's participation. On the former, Ontario sought a voice in a negotiation that remained firmly bilateral, underlining that on economic issues the provinces – and even Ontario – were clearly second tier. On the latter, the negotiations around the Meech Lake Accord, Ontario played a determinative role, with Peterson donning the mantle of Bill Davis and working feverishly to keep an often fraught conversation going. But despite securing the initial agreement of all eleven governments, the clock ran out on the Meech Lake Accord when neither Manitoba nor Newfoundland managed to ratify it before the three-year deadline. This time, too, the price was high. Peterson had staked too much on an agreement that was not to be, and had spent too little time managing a province that was less of an economic engine than it used to be. In an election called too soon, and regarded as opportunistic, Peterson was kicked out of office in the fall of 1990. For him personally, and for the Ontario Liberal party, there was a high price to pay for having put so much effort into the Meech Lake Accord. But there were also lessons about the way the intergovernmental relationship had developed, and about how it would unfold in the future. Throughout much of the postwar period, successive Ontario governments had pursued their own interests under the cloak of making the federal system more functional; when it came to big questions of constitutional reform, Ontario had consistently shifted to a more clearly nation-building, brokerage-politics sort of stance. What the Mulroney government in general, and the Meech Lake Accord in particular, made clear was that there was no longer any space for a nation-building Ontario. As the deputy minister of intergovernmental affairs in Ontario said, "the federal government has adopted the role of broker of provincial and regional interests" and "in this environment, Ontario often becomes a reference point for unfavourable comparison and sometimes an object of attack."[6] Having failed to achieve the constitutional accord, and now pushed out of the role of broker, the Ontario strategy in intergovernmental affairs began an inexorable shift towards a protection of self-interest in the 1990s and beyond.

In the years between 1943 and 1985, successive generations of Ontario politicians and bureaucrats had devised a way of dealing with the federal government – and, both incidentally and integrally, of dealing with the other provinces – that had served them well. Never was that more clear than in the negotiations that secured the Constitution Act, 1982. It was a strategy based on offering alternatives that ultimately came to focus on the very roots of the intergovernmental relationship, the fundamental, foundational components of the interaction between the two levels of government. As these came to be defined in the 1970s and 1980s, these mega-intergovernmental issues were almost always constitutional in nature. Furthermore, the Ontario approach was rooted in building bridges between different governments and, again as it came to be defined towards the end of the period under consideration, keeping a multi-government conversation going despite the sometimes profound desire to simply walk away from the talks.

But if this had been the approach, and one that the province followed through to the successful patriation of the Constitution Act, where can we find the tangible results for Ontario? What was in it for Canada's largest, wealthiest, most Canadian of provinces?[7] Was the achievement of federal-provincial agreement enough? The answer is a cynical "of course not," tempered by a somewhat more generous interpretation of Ontario's motives in the years following the Second World War. When Ontario offered alternatives to the policy prescriptions emanating from Ottawa, they had generally been designed in such a way as to more equitably address what were regarded as Ontario's concerns. But as time progressed, and Ontario moved towards addressing intergovernmental issues at the level of first principles, it became more and more likely that the only thing in it for the central province was a functioning federation – a federation in which it retained its keystone position.

In the early era of premiers Drew and Frost, the provincially designed solutions to intergovernmental problems were quite clearly in Ontario's interests. Drew's alternative to the Green Book proposals, for example, began with the termination of the Wartime Tax Rental Agreements, which Ontario had opposed from the moment they were first raised. Other provinces had benefited from the rental of the direct tax fields, but not Ontario. The return to a system that allowed provinces to set their own tax rates was clearly in Ontario's interests, but not necessarily of great benefit to those provinces with smaller tax bases. The Ontario alternative to the Green Book did not completely ignore the needs of the smaller, poorer provinces: a form of equalization was included in the scheme, and a role for the federal government in the delivery of expensive welfare measures was included. For the most part, however, it was easy to identify the proposal as an Ontario document, and one that was unlikely to have been written in any of the other provincial capitals.

Social policy was an area where it was surprising to see Ontario taking such a leading role, given the dominance of the Conservative party at the provincial level for more than four decades following the Second World War. Nevertheless, the Ontario government played an important role in initiating discussion of a health insurance program in Canada in the 1950s, and by the early years of the 1960s had gone a long way towards introducing a contributory old age pension scheme that it was hoped would be emulated across the country. The form that the Ontario proposals took, however, differed significantly from the principles that were being embraced by the federal Liberal party.

In both the health insurance proposals, that ultimately led to the introduction of hospital insurance, and the pension proposals that were made public during the negotiations over the Canada Pension Plan, Ontario envisioned a key role for private industry. That was not what either the St. Laurent or the Pearson Liberals imagined when they embarked on discussions with the provinces over social policies. The federal approach was public; the Ontario approach was private. The latter was popular in a province where the insurance industry was influential, but it would certainly be less popular in a province that did not stand to gain by throwing business at insurance companies. In the case of hospital insurance, and later full health insurance, the federal proposal for a publicly administered scheme won out; in the case of pensions, it was Quebec's alternative proposal that essentially established the blueprint for a national contributory pension system. In neither case did Ontario's alternative, clearly devised with an eye to the local benefits, form the basis of the final national program.

On the fiscal front, Ontario was almost always offering alternatives to the federal proposals. At root, of course, Ontario politicians argued for an entirely equal division of the direct tax fields. Having wisely given up any hope that the federal government would vacate the fields permanently, and recognizing that the 50–50 split of true equity was probably little more than a pipe dream, successive Ontario governments pressed for increasingly more tax room. Proposals ranged from 10–10–50 splits of income, corporate and succession duties, to 15–15–50 divisions. Any proposal that would see the provinces getting more room within which to tax, and less paid as either a rental or a tax-point abatement, was in the interest of wealthy Ontario. It was not, however, in the interest of a province with a poorer population or fewer corporations. While Ontario was more successful winning its points in the regular renegotiation of the tax-sharing agreements than it was in other areas of intergovernmental contact, it was still clear that the particular interests of Ontario were what was motivating the shape of the province's proposals.

Ontario's record in federal-provincial negotiations during the 1940s, 1950s, and 1960s was decidedly mixed. Although there is little doubt that the province pursued a strategy based on offering alternatives to the federal proposals, and furthermore tried to secure the support of other provinces by addressing their concerns within the context of those alternative proposals, the new tactic did not result in tangible gains for Ontario. Ontario's scheme for postwar reconstruction remained undone (although, in fairness, the same was true of the Green Book itself); its proposals for combining public and private insurance for both health care and old age did not come into being; and if true equity of tax resources was the ultimate goal, Ontario fell far short of the mark. The province was successful, however, in shaping the terms of the debate in both social and economic policy. In some cases, Ontario initiated debate over a particular issue; in others, the Ontario position represented the one alternative to Ottawa's proposal. Still, perpetually offering up the alternative that is rejected was hardly reason to continue to pursue a particular approach to intergovernmental affairs.

Events of the 1960s, however, underlined the fragility of the federation. The Quiet Revolution in Quebec pointed to the possibility of the breakup of Canada, and convinced otherwise complacent governments at both the federal and provincial levels to take federalism more seriously or risk it entirely. In Ontario, that meant both the convening of the Confederation of Tomorrow Conference, and a shift towards a different strategy in intergovernmental affairs more generally. Rather than focusing on the design of alternatives to federal-provincial logjams that either overtly or covertly addressed the particular needs of Ontario, the provincial civil service began concentrating on maintaining a functioning federation. To this end, the Ontario corps pursued two parallel strategies: the first was to address mega-intergovernmental problems, such as the constitution itself, rather than getting tied up in debates over details, and the second was to keep the intergovernmental lines of communication open at all costs. Holding the Confederation of Tomorrow Conference itself was the first real foray into a tactic that sought to save the federation rather than simply offering a provincialist perspective on how to solve the dilemmas of federalism.

Throughout the 1970s and into the 1980s, the Ontario team continued to follow a strategy of securing a functional federation. This meant that both levels of government needed to retain clear powers and responsibilities, which pushed the Ontario team into supporting Ottawa in more than one debate. The benefits to Ontario were somewhat more subtle than was the case with some of the earlier alternatives the provincial politicians had proposed, but they were nevertheless still apparent. Ontario had profited from being part of the federal system: the rest of Canada had been a willing market for Ontario products and produce, national programs and national standards had kept the population spread throughout the country and ensured that people could continue to support the Ontario economy, and as a result the central province thrived through much of the postwar period. Less tangibly, but perhaps even more importantly, the Ontario public – and even more so its elected officials – seemed to care deeply about the preservation of the country. It was at least in part because there seemed to be little difference in anyone's mind between *Ontario* and *Canada*, that the intergovernmental strategy shifted in the 1960s, 1970s, and 1980s towards simply saving federalism. That, from the perspective of Ontario, was enough.

Notes

Introduction

1 Macdonald to Mowat, 25 Oct. 1872, quoted in Evans, *Sir Oliver Mowat*, 147. A great deal has been written about the Mowat-Macdonald battles, in part because they occupied the attentions of so many at the time and in part because they did so much to shape the BNA Act in the first century of its existence. See, especially, Armstrong, "The Mowat Heritage in Federal-Provincial Relations," 93–119, and *Politics of Federalism*; Hodgins and Edwards, "Federalism and the Politics of Ontario," 61–96; Vipond, *Liberty and Community*; Saywell, *Lawmakers*, 78–113; Stevenson, *Ex Uno Plures*, 48–76.
2 Quoted in Armstrong, "Mowat Heritage," 94.
3 Quoted in Saywell, *"Just Call Me Mitch,"* 460–1.
4 The literature on Quebec, in particular, is vast. Some recent examinations of intergovernmental issues include Béland and Lecours, *Nationalism and Social Policy*, and Poliquin, *René Lévesque*, although it is really the constitution that has attracted the most attention. See: Monahan, *Meech Lake*; Cohen, *A Deal Undone*; and the essays in Behiels, ed., *Meech Lake Primer*. On Alberta, see Connors and Law, eds., *Forging Alberta's Constitutional Framework*; Gibbons, "Alberta and the National Community"; Richards and Pratt, *Prairie Capitalism*. Other relevant recent studies include Henderson, *Angus L. Macdonald*.
5 In understanding the shape of federalism, scholars fall into either societal or institutional schools. The former emphasizes the cultural, geographical, and ethnic diversity of a federation as determining factors in the shape of the federal structure; the latter, in contrast, emphasizes the role of institutions – like the constitution, the courts, and the state itself. In Canada, institutionalism is the dominant framework, although important works (e.g.,

Cairns, "The Judicial Committee and Its Critics") have pressed for a more nuanced view.

6 Bakvis, Baier, and Brown, *Contested Federalism*, 14–15.

7 Graham, *Old Man Ontario*; McDougall, *Robarts*; Paikin, *Public Triumph, Private Tragedy*; Hoy, *Bill Davis*.

8 Manthorpe, *Power and the Tories*; McCormick, "Provincial Political Party Systems," 152–85.

9 This was the project that Peter Oliver was working on at the time of his death in 2006. I have benefited enormously from some of the papers he collected for that study, but the full-length examination of the internal functioning of the Big Blue Machine continues to await its historian.

10 Lower, "Does Ontario Exist?" 65–9.

11 On political culture, see Haddow, "Ontario Politics"; Morton, "*Sic Permanent*"; Nelles, "Red Tied"; Noel, "Ontario Political Culture"; Wiseman, "Change in Ontario Politics," and *In Search of Canadian Political Culture*, esp. chapter 8. A few important shorter works consider Ontario political culture within the framework of intergovernmental relations. See Cameron and Simeon, "Ontario in Confederation," and Stevenson, "Ontario and Confederation."

12 Dion, "My Praxis of Federalism," 114–27.

13 Mendelsohn and Matthews, "The New Ontario."

1 "The 'Keystone' Province"

1 "Canada: Mitch," *Time*, 20 Sept. 1937; "Canada: Mackenzie King Wins," *Time*, 8 Apr. 1940.

2 Saywell, *"Just Call Me Mitch,"* 340 and 339.

3 See Dion, "Ontario and Canada: Loyal Forever."

4 Legislative Assembly of Ontario, George Alexander Drew biography.

5 Saywell, *"Just Call Me Mitch,"* 436–7.

6 Archives of Ontario (AO), MU 4543, Latimer Papers. "Minutes of a Mtg of the Executive Cttee of the Ontario Conservative Association, held at the Albany Club, Toronto, 9 Nov. 1942."

7 Private Collection, Drew Papers, file 520. Frost to Drew, 15 July 1942.

8 Brownsey, "Opposition Blues," 290–1.

9 Stursberg, *Last Viceroy*, 62.

10 Private Collection, Drew Papers. "George Drew, Speaking over a Province-Wide Network, July 8, 1943."

11 "Says Ontario Liberals Can't State Opinion," *Globe and Mail*, 31 May 1943, 15.

12 Trent University Archives (TUA), 77-024, Leslie Frost Papers, Frost to Drew, 26 June 1943; quoted in Saywell, '*Just Call Me Mitch,'* 508.

13 AO, RG 3-18, Office of the Premier: George Drew, Letterbooks. Drew to Horace Hunter, 21 Sept. 1943, and Drew to Richard Stapells, 25 Sept 1943.

14 Ibid. Drew to Hunter, 21 Sept. 1943.

15 Ibid. Drew to Stapells, 25 Sept. 1943.

16 AO, RG 3-24, Office of the Premier: Frost Premier's Correspondence, box 3, file Dom.-Prov. Conference (hereafter D-PC) II. Walters to Frost, 29 Sept. 1943. Despite the "transcendent importance," there was a long hiatus in premiers' conferences between 1926 and 1960, a period of immense importance for intergovernmental relations in Canada. See Meekison, "Annual Premiers' Day," 144–5.

17 AO, RG 6-41, Department of Finance (hereafter DoF): D-PC, 1935–55, box 3, file Inter-provincial Conference (hereafter I-PC), 1945. Drew to King, 6 Jan. 1944.

18 Ibid.

19 Petter, "Myth of the Federal Spending Power," 450–1.

20 Library and Archives of Canada (LAC), MG 32 B34, J.W. Pickersgill Papers, vol. 1, file Federal-Provincial Relations (hereafter F-PR), 1943–53. "A Dominion-Provincial Conference," n.d.

21 AO, RG 6-41, box 3, file I-PC, 1945. A.D.P. Heeney to Drew, 28 Feb. 1944.

22 House of Commons, *Debates*, 27 Jan. 1944, 2. On the initial debates over family allowances, see Blake, *From Rights to Needs*, 89–124.

23 LAC, MG 32 B5, Brooke Claxton Papers, vol. 141, file D-PC, 1944, Corr. A.D.P. Heeney to T.A. Crerar, 14 Feb. 1944. See also, Slater, *War, Finance and Reconstruction*, 221–8.

24 Rea, *Crerar*, 221–4.

25 AO, RG 6-41, box 3, file I-PC, 1945. Drew to King, 14 March 1944.

26 LAC, Claxton Papers, vol. 141, file D-PC, 1944, Corr. Cabinet Committee on D-PC: Agenda for Mtg in Mr. Crerar's office on Thursday, 17 Feb. 1944.

27 LAC, Pickersgill Papers, vol. 2, file Reconstruction memoranda. H.R. Kemp memo, 23 June 1943.

28 LAC, MG 28 I10, Canadian Council on Social Development, vol. 70, file 518 (1941–46). George Davidson to Harry Cassidy, 7 Oct. 1943.

29 LAC, MG 26 J1, William Lyon Mackenzie King Papers, vol. 341. Godbout to King, 1 Dec. 1943.

30 Ibid. "Secret: Family Allowances – Comments on Mr. Godbout's Letter," 10 Jan. 1944. See, e.g., LAC, MG 28 IV 1, Cooperative Commonwealth Federation (hereafter CCF)/New Democratic Party (hereafter NDP), vol. 154, file Research: Family Allowances, 1941–56. Committee on Public Welfare of the

Montreal Branch of the Canadian Association of Social Workers, "Children's Allowances," 20 Jan. 1944.

31 LAC, King Papers, vol. 559. A.A. Dunton to cabinet, 7 Feb. 1944.

32 LAC, MG 27 III C15, Gordon Graydon Papers, vol. 11, file F-100, Family Allowance Material. H.H. Stevens to Gordon Graydon, 16 May 1944. LAC, MG 28 IV 2, Progressive Conservative Party (PCP) Papers, vol. 323, file Whitton, Charlotte. Whitton to Graydon, 16 June 1944.

33 LAC, King Papers, vol. 359. A.A. Dunton to cabinet, 10 July 1944. The view was erroneous: opinion polls indicated that 81% of respondents in Quebec, and 57% of those in the rest of Canada, thought that that family allowances proposal was a "good idea." "Public Opinion Polls," *Public Opinion Quarterly*, 446.

34 LAC, Drew Papers, vol. 64, file 572. Graydon to Drew, 18 July 1944.

35 LAC, MG 27 III C16, John Bracken Papers, vol. 81, file Family Allowance. Memo from Dr. R.P. Vivian, 19 July 1944; Memo from George Drew, 19 July 1944.

36 Ibid.

37 AO, RG 3-24, box 3, file D-PC II. Walters to Frost, 31 July 1944.

38 LAC, Drew Papers, vol. 64, file 572. Graydon to Drew, 20 July 1944.

39 Ibid., vol. 305, file 182. "Premier George Drew, speaking to a Progressive-Conservative Rally at Richmond Hill, Aug. 2, 1944."

40 LAC, MG 32 A4, Roland Michener Papers, vol. 88, file Drew, Hon. George, n.d., 1941–47. Drew to Michener, 3 Aug. 1944.

41 AO, RG 3-24, box 4, file D-P Re: Taxation D-P Co-ordinating Cttee, 1942–45. "Premier George Drew Speaking over Ontario CBC Network, Aug. 9, 1944."

42 Ibid.

43 *Toronto Star*, 10 Aug. 1944.

44 Ibid.

45 LAC, Drew Papers, vol. 54, file 473 (1a). C.E. Silcox to Drew, 10 Aug. 1944. *Ottawa Journal*, 11 Aug. 1944.

46 Toronto *Telegram*, 11 Aug. 1944. *Globe and Mail*, editorial, 11 Aug. 1944.

47 *Globe and Mail*, 11 Aug. 1944.

48 House of Commons, *Debates*, 11 Aug. 1944, 6276.

49 Ibid.

50 *Winnipeg Free Press*, 18 Aug. 1944. Garson later tried to find out from Ontario officials the basis of their calculations of tax revenue, not wanting to "quote or publish any figures at variance with those of Premier Drew's." Any good will that might have been felt between the two provinces had quickly disappeared, however, and Frost refused to release any of Ontario's figures. AO, RG 3-24, box 3, file D-PC II. Chater to Frost, 5 Sept. 1944.

51 *Winnipeg Free Press*, 21 Aug. 1944.

52 *Globe and Mail*, 23 Aug. 1944.

53 Ibid.

54 LAC, Michener Papers, vol. 88, file Drew. Drew to Michener, 24 Aug. 1944.

55 LAC, Drew Papers, vol. 305, file 1893b. "Address by Premier George Drew, Eastern PC Assoc., Gen. Mtg, Ottawa, Sept. 29, 1944."

56 LAC, Bracken Papers, vol. 81, file Family Allowance. "Remarks on PC public relations ..." 4 Oct. 1944.

57 See, e.g., *Winnipeg Free Press*, 21 Aug. 1944, and "Family Allowance Feud," *Canadian Forum*, vol. 24, no. 284, Sept. 1944, 123–4.

58 There is considerable debate over the intentions of the family allowance program. The most complete argument for understanding family allowances as a tool designed to increase levels of consumption is contained in Christie, *Engendering the State*, chapter 6, although her gendered analysis of the goals of social welfare more generally has not been entirely accepted. See, e.g., Finkel, "Welfare for Whom?" 247–53. For other interpretations, see, e.g., Marshall, *Social Origins of the Welfare State*, and Blake, *From Rights to Needs*.

59 See Bryden, "Beyond the Green Book," 136–41.

60 LAC, Drew Papers, reel M-9025. "Telephone Conversation between Premier George Drew and Dr. Charlotte Whitton, Feb. 20, 1945."

61 Ibid., vol. 64, file 572. Gordon Graydon to Drew, 27 Dec. 1944.

62 LAC, MG 30 E256, Charlotte Whitton Papers, vol. 4, file Corr., General, 1945 (March). Whitton to Drew, 28 March 1945.

63 On Whitton's role within the social welfare community, see Struthers, "A Profession in Crisis," 169–85; on her developing views on family allowances, see Christie, *Engendering the State*, 186–91.

64 In a telegram to Tommy Douglas of Saskatchewan, e.g., Drew noted that after having "raised questions about several things which have been done" and still facing inaction on the part of Ottawa, he concluded that "it is of vital importance that if a conference cannot be held there should be at least a preliminary of premiers without delay to settle certain fundamental principles which will guide future dominion-provincial relations." LAC, Drew Papers, reel M-9047, telegram, Drew to Douglas, 15 Feb. 1945.

65 AO, RG 3-24, box 3, file D-PC II. Telegram, Frost to Drew, n.d. (ca. mid-Nov. 1944).

66 Ibid. Telegram, Drew to Frost, 18 Nov. 1944.

67 LAC, Drew Papers, reel M-9047, telegram, Douglas to Drew, 9 Feb. 1945; telegram, Drew to Douglas, 15 Feb. 1945.

68 AO, RG 3-24, box 3, file D-P Negotiations concerning reciprocal agreements, 1944, 1945. Frost to Duplessis, 26 Jan. 1945.

69 Ibid. R.L. Crombie to Drew, 23 March 1945.

70 Ibid. Garson to Frost, 29 Dec. 1944.

71 TUA, Frost Papers, box 4, file 6. Frost radio broadcast, 18 May 1945.

72 LAC, Drew Papers, reel M-9047. King to Drew, 21 June 1945.

73 King had tried to outmanoeuvre Drew on the timing of the election. When the provincial Conservatives were finally defeated in the Legislature, Drew called an election for 11 June 1945; in an attempt to minimize the harmful effect to the national Liberals should Drew be handed the widely expected majority, King called a federal election for the same day. Drew countered by moving the Ontario election forward a week to 4 June and, as predicted, swept to victory. See Granatstein, *Canada's War*, 399–400.

74 AO, RG 6-41, box 3, file I-PC, 1945. "D-PC 1944: Memo of Suggestions for the Agenda and Procedure," 15 May 1944.

75 LAC, Pickersgill Papers, vol. 2, file Reconstruction memoranda. Skelton to Pickersgill, 6 Feb. 1945.

76 LAC, Drew Papers, reel M-9047. King to Drew, 21 June 1945.

77 AO, RG 3-24, box 4, file D-P Re: Taxation, D-P Coordinating Cttee. "Memo of Conversations between Hon. Maurice Duplessis … and the Hon. L.M. Frost … July 4, 1945."

78 AO, RG 6-44, DoF: Policy Division Subject Files, box UF 22, file Dominion-Provincial Relations (hereafter D-PR). Ontario Bureau of Statistics and Research, "Facts Pertinent to D-PR," 16 July 1945, 44, 46.

79 Ibid., 48.

80 LAC, MG 26 J13, William Lyon Mackenzie King Diaries, 30 July 1945.

81 LAC, Bracken Papers, vol. 16, file D-1100. Summary of points raised in letter from Robert M. Clark, 30 July 1945.

82 AO, RG 3-24, box 4, file D-P Re: Taxation and D-P Coordinating Cttee, 1945–46. "The D-P Tax Conference: Ontario's Role," 31 July 1945. See also ibid, "The D-PC," 2 Aug. 1945.

83 *Globe and Mail*, 7 Aug. 1945.

84 LAC, King Diaries, 6 Aug. 1945. On the PM's version of the conference, see also, Pickersgill and Forster, *Mackenzie King Record*, vol. 2, 449–56.

85 Quoted in Bercuson, *True Patriot*, 140.

86 LAC, King Diaries, 5 Aug. 1945.

87 AO, RG 3-24, box 4, file D-P Re: Taxation and D-P Coordinating Cttee. "The D-PC," 19 Sept. 1945.

88 Ibid., D-P Coordinating Cttee, 1942–45. "An examination of the Financial Proposals of the Government of Canada with Ontario's alternative plans," n.d.

89 Queen's University Archives (QUA), Grant Dexter Papers, box 15, file 100.

Dexter to George Ferguson and Bruce Hutchinson, 26 Sept. 1945. According to Marc Gotlieb, the Ontario Treasury Department was "shocked" by the federal government's use of population to determine subsidies. "Drew and the Conference on Reconstruction," 35.

90 AO, RG 3-24, box 4, file D-P Re: Taxation, D-P Coordinating Cttee, 1945–46: "D-PR," n.d.; box 5, file D-PC, British Columbia, 1945, Telephone Conversation between Colonel George Drew and Premier Hart, 1:30 pm. 16 Nov. 1945.

91 AO, RG 3-24, box 4, file D-P Re: Taxation and D-P Coordinating Cttee, 1942–45. "An examination of the Financial Proposals of the Government of Canada with Ontario's alternative plans."

92 AO, RG 6-15, DoF: Inter-Ministerial and Intergovernmental Correspondence, 1924–58, vol. 27, file PM no. 18, Canadian Club. "Speech by Premier George A. Drew before the Canadian Club, Toronto, Oct. 1, 1945."

93 QUA, Dexter Papers, box 15, file 100. Dexter to Ferguson, 6 Oct. 1945.

94 *Globe and Mail*, 27 Nov. 1945. Nova Scotia Archives and Records Management (NSARM), MG 2, Angus L. Macdonald Papers, vol. 898, file 19 1/2 D, "Preliminary Statement of the Province of Nova Scotia," 28 Nov. 1945. Wilfrid Eggleston, "Ottawa Letter," *Saturday Night*, 8 Dec. 1945.

95 AO, RG 3-24, box 3, file D-PC I, 1945. Frost to Chater, 11 Dec. 1945.

96 Public Archives of New Brunswick (PANB), RS 414, John McNair Papers, box C5, file Background Material for N.B. Delegation to D-PC, 1944–46. W.B. Trites, Dep. Provincial Sec.-Treas., to Hayes Doone, Provincial Sec.-Treas., 19 Dec. 1945.

97 QUA, Dexter Papers, box 15, file 100. "D-P agreements – first piece," 10 Oct. 1945.

98 Saskatchewan Archives (SA), R 33.1, T.C. Douglas Papers, file XXIII.749 b, F-PC, Other Provinces. "Premier George A. Drew speaking to the Empire Club, Jan. 8, 1946."

99 Wilfrid Eggleston, "Ottawa Letter," *Saturday Night*, 26 Jan. 1946.

100 QUA, Dexter Papers, box 15, file 102. Dexter to Victor Sifton, 7 Jan. 1946.

101 AO, RG 3-24, box 3, file D-P General, 1945, 1946. H.M. Robbins to Drew, 26 Jan. 1946.

102 PANB, McNair Papers, box C5, file Background material, FitzRandolph to McNair, 14 Jan. 1946; and file Corr. relating to D-PC, 1946, W.B. Trites to J.J. Doone, 21 Jan. 1946

103 AO, RG 6-41, box 7, file From PM's "red book," vol. 2. "Summary of the Minutes of the D-P Economic Cttee," n.d. PANB, McNair Papers, Fitz-Randolph to McNair, 14 Jan. 1946. King Diaries, 25 Jan. 1946.

104 NSARM, Macdonald Papers, MG 2, vol. 903, file personal and confidential. Macdonald to Alex Johnson, 18 Jan. 1946. On Macdonald's relations with the federal government more generally, see Henderson, *Angus L. Macdonald*, 90–149.

105 AO, RG 6-41, box 7, file From PM's "red book," vol. 2. "Summary of the Minutes."

106 National Archives and Records Administration (NARA), Washington, Ottawa Post Files, Ottawa Conference File 1946, box 1514, vol. 116, memo of conversation, 8 Jan. 1946; quoted in Bercuson, *True Patriot*, 144.

107 *Globe and Mail*, 8 Jan. 1946.

108 LAC, MG 26 L, Louis St. Laurent Papers, vol. 5, file Minutes of the Economic Cttee of the F-PC – received while the minister in England. "Comment on the Ontario Submissions by the Prime Minister of Canada," n.d.

109 LAC, Claxton Papers, vol. 139, file Province of Ontario. "The D-PC: Refuting the Ontario Case," n.d.

110 Ibid.

111 LAC, King Diaries, 23 Jan. 1946.

112 PANB, McNair Papers, box C5, file Minutes of Mtgs of D-PC Coordinating Cttee, 1946. Minutes of 29 Jan. 1946. *Globe and Mail*, 30 Jan. 1946.

113 LAC, Drew Papers, reel M-9047. Memo, "Re: D-PC, Ottawa, Jan. 28th to Feb. 1st, 1946," n.d.

114 Ibid. See also, PANB, McNair Papers, Minutes of 29 Jan. 1946, and *Globe and Mail*, 30 Jan. 1946.

115 LAC, King Diaries, 29 Jan. 1946 and 31 Jan. 1946.

116 On King's reluctance to proceed with the plan for reconstruction, see Finkel, "Paradise Postponed," 120–42.

117 QUA, Dexter Papers, box 15, file 104. "Proposed leader for Monday," 2 Feb. 1946. Legislative Assembly of Ontario, *Debates*, 19 March 1946, 800.

118 AO, RG 6-41, box 7, file From PM's "red book" notes and statements. "Notes on Statements of Premiers at Coordinating Cttee Mtg, April 25th and 26th," n.d. LAC, King Diaries, 25 April 1946; see also 23, 24, and 26 April 1946.

119 LAC, Drew Papers, reel M-9047, Drew to King, 16 April 1946. LAC, King Diaries, 25 April 1946.

120 QUA, Dexter Papers, box 15, file 105. Dexter to Ferguson, 29 April 1946.

121 LAC, King Diaries, 29 April 1946.

122 LAC, Drew Papers, box 428, file 6. "Draft Submission of the Government of Ontario to the D-PC, April 1946."

123 On Keynesian ideas and the federal bureaucracy, see Barnett, *Keynesian Arithmetic, War Budget* and *Keynes's* "How to Pay for the War," and Owram, *Government Generation*, chapters 11 and 12. Most scholars contend that

Drew was profoundly anti-Keynesian, although there is no real evidence to support this. See, Struthers, *Limits of Affluence*, 126, and Gotlieb, "Drew and the Conference on Reconstruction," 47.

124 QUA, Dexter Papers, box 15, file 105. Dexter to Ferguson, 1 May 1946. LAC, Bracken Papers, vol. 81, file D-PR. "D-PC," 2 May 1946.

125 PANB, McNair Papers, box C5, file Background Material. McNair, hand-written memo, 2 May 1946. LAC, King Diaries, 2 May 1946.

126 LAC, Drew Papers, reel M-9047. "Statement by Premier George Drew," 3 May 1946.

127 LAC, King Diaries, 3 May 1946. On Duplessis's role at the conference, see Black, *Duplessis*, 424–7.

2 "As Long as We Define the Terms"

1 LAC, King Diaries, 6 May 1946.

2 AO, RG 6-44, box UF 22, file 6, "S" Speeches: G.A. Drew. "Speech by Premier George Drew to Canadian Club, Winnipeg, June 17, 1946." Stuart Garson was responsible for most of the public attacks on Drew and Duplessis [*Globe and Mail*, 4 June 1946], although New Brunswick's J.B. McNair also blamed "the greed of Tory Ontario" for the failure of the conference [Young, "Reconstruction in New Brunswick," 145].

3 King had been terribly worried about the twin strains that the dominion-provincial conference and the budget preparation were putting on Ilsley, and had already spoken to him about retirement; Ilsley would stay through August, but felt that he would have to relinquish the finance portfolio then. LAC, King Diaries, 24 April 1946.

4 LAC, Drew Papers, reel M-9047. Ilsley to Drew, 28 June 1946. House of Commons, *Debates*, 27 June 1946, 2908–10.

5 LAC, Drew Papers, vol. 429, file 42. "Chronological Review of the D-PC 1945–46," 51; Perry, *Fiscal History of Canada*, 40; Simeon and Robinson, *State, Society and Canadian Federalism*, 120.

6 House of Commons, *Debates*, 18 July 1946, 3595.

7 AO, RG 3-24, box 4, file D-PC, letters and memos, 1946, 1947. Frost to Jim Macdonnell, MP, 24 July 1946.

8 Ibid. Frost to Bracken, 24 July 1946. Frost was perhaps alone in believing that the two levels of government had been close to reaching agreement prior to the delivery of Ilsley's budget: political commentator Wilfrid Eggleston saw "few signs of success in another Dominion-Provincial Meeting," and believed that for the premiers "the time to have bestirred themselves was in that fateful week in late April and early May." "Ottawa Letter," *Saturday Night*, 7 Sept. 1946.

9 LAC, Drew Papers, reel M-9047. Frost to Drew, 15 July 1946.

10 Ibid.

11 LAC, Claxton Papers, vol. 143, file D-PR, 1946. Drew to King, 2 Oct. 1946.

12 AO, RG 6-41, box 3, file D-PC, 1945. King to Drew, 10 Oct. 1946.

13 Ibid., box 6, file D-PC, 1945–46. Drew to King, 12 Oct. 1946.

14 Ibid., box UJ 3-4, file D-PC, Original letters from and to Mr. King and Col. G.A. Drew, 1945. Drew to King, 16 Oct. 1946.

15 Public Archives and Record Office, Prince Edward Island (PARO-PEI), RG 21, Federal-Provincial Affairs (hereafter F-PA): Conference Files, Series 1, subseries 8, file 9. King to Drew, 18 Oct. 1946. LAC, Drew Papers, reel M-9047. Drew to King, 21 Oct. 1946.

16 AO, RG 6-41, box 36, file Original letters. King to Drew, 22 Oct. 1946.

17 LAC, King Diaries, 22 Oct. 1946.

18 AO, RG 3-21, Office of the Premier: George Drew Election Material, box 1, file 76G. H.G. Gray, M.D. to Drew, 30 Sept. 1946.

19 Ibid., and Gray to Drew, 11 Oct. 1946.

20 AO, RG 4-2, Office of the Attorney General: Attorney-General's Corr. Files, 1926–64. C.R. Magone, "Memo for the Hon. the AG," 9 Oct. 1946.

21 PARO-PEI, RG-21, Series 1, subseries 8, file 9. Angus L. Macdonald (ALM) to King, 16 Oct. 1946, and King to Ernest Manning, 14 Oct. 1946.

22 NSARM, ALM Papers, vol. 898, file 19 1/2 D. Drew to Macdonald, 20 Sept. 1946. Henderson, *Angus L. Macdonald*, 150–66.

23 NSARM, ALM Papers, vol. 899A, file 1. Drew to Macdonald, 26 Oct. 1946.

24 AO, RG 6-41, box 6, file D-PC, Statistics and Tables, 1945–47. Manning to Drew, 28 Oct. 1946.

25 NSARM, ALM Papers, vol. 898, file 19 1/2 D. Macdonald notes on telephone conversation with Drew, 31 Oct. 1946.

26 Ibid. Macdonald notes for 4 Nov. 1946.

27 Ibid. AO, RG 6-41, box 6, file D-PC, Statistics and Tables, 1945–47. Drew to Manning, 18 Oct. 1946.

28 AO, RG 3-24, box 4, file D-PC, Letters and Memos, 1946, 1947. Henry Chater, "Memo to the Hon. the Treasury Board," 26 Oct. 1946.

29 AO, RG 4-2, box 19, file 20. Chater to Drew, n.d. (ca. mid-Nov. 1946).

30 AO, RG 6-14, DoF: Deputy Minister's General Corr., 1924–71, box 50, file Conferences No. 12C, April–May 1946, D-PC. "Memo Respecting Alternative Proposal for Settlement of D-P Fiscal Arrangements," 14 Nov. 1946.

31 NSARM, ALM Papers, vol. 1503, file 394. Macdonald diary, 17 Nov. 1946.

32 Ibid., vol. 899A, file 1. Drew to Macdonald, 23 Nov. 1946.

33 Ibid. Manning press release, n.d. (ca. 23 Nov. 1946).

34 AO, RG 6-41, box 6, file D-PC on Statistics and Tables of other Countries re: Tax Systems. Manning to Drew, 23 Nov. 1946.

35 AO, RG 3-24, box 4, file D-PC, letters and memos, 1946, 1947. Manning to Drew, 23 Nov. 1946.

36 Ibid. Frost to Manning, 3 Dec. 1946.

37 Ibid. "Memo respecting modification of the proposal contained in the memo prepared by the Treasury Dept. on Nov. 14th, 1946," 27 Nov. 1946.

38 QUA, Dexter Papers, box 15, file 109. J.R. Stirrett, "The Meaning of the Problem of D-PR," 26 Nov. 1946.

39 NSARM, ALM Papers, vol. 898, file 19 1/2 D. Macdonald notes for 11 Dec. 1946 and 12 Dec. 1946.

40 AO, RG 6-14, box 50, file Conferences No. 12C, April–May 1946, D-PC. George Gathercole to Chester Walters, 12 Dec. 1946.

41 PANB, McNair Papers, box C5, file Corr. Relating to D-PC, 1946. Press release, 31 Oct. 1946, and press release, 6 Jan. 1947.

42 LAC, Pickersgill Papers, box 1, file F-PR, Memos, 1943–53. Pickersgill to King, 5 Jan. 1947.

43 PANB, McNair Papers, box C6, file Corr. Relating to F-PR, 1946–49. "Capital Report" transcript, 12 Jan. 1947.

44 NSARM, ALM Papers, vol. 898, file 19 1/2 D. Macdonald notes for 19 Dec. 1946. Notes on telephone call from George Drew.

45 LAC, Pickersgill Papers, box 1, file F-PR, Memos, 1943–53. Memo for the PM, 5 Jan. 1947.

46 LAC, Claxton Papers, vol. 143, file D-PR, 1946. Abbott to Drew, 21 Jan. 1947.

47 Ibid. Drew to King, 23 Jan. 1947. See drafts, LAC, Drew Papers, vol. 239, file 306, pt. 1, 1945–48.

48 LAC, Claxton Papers, vol. 143, file D-PR, 1946. King to Drew, 27 Jan. 1947.

49 AO, RG 3-24, vol. 5, file D-PC, Discussions and Memos, 1947. "Draft Proposed Letter to PM of Canada," 29 Jan. 1947.

50 Ibid. Frost to Drew, 29 Jan. 1947.

51 NSARM, ALM Papers, vol. 920, file 31-2. Macdonald to Bill Macdonald (brother), 25 Feb. 1947.

52 Ibid., vol. 898, file 19 1/2 D. "Conversation between Drew and Wm.C. Macdonald at Toronto," 5 Feb. 1947.

53 Ibid. Macdonald to Bill Macdonald (brother), 25 Feb. 1947.

54 Ibid., vol. 899A, file 2, Drew to Macdonald, 9 May 1947.

55 Letter of 10 May 1947, Macdonald to Drew (ibid.) makes clear that ALM is going to agree to federal offer, but that he's going to give a speech in Ottawa that will "set them on their heels." See Henderson, *Angus L. Macdonald*, 164–5; Bickerton, *Politics of Regional Development*, 124.

56 See AO, RG 6-41, box 7, file From PM's "red book" vol. 2. "Summary of the Minutes of the D-P Economic Cttee," n.d. (ca. Jan. 1946).

57 AO, RG 3-21, box 1, file 76G, K.G. Gray to Drew, 30 Sept. 1946; file 19.20. C.M. Magone to Blackwell, 9 Oct. 1946. For an overview of part of the early history of health insurance in Canada, see Boychuk, *National Health Insurance in the United States and Canada*, 31–7.

58 AO, RG 3-21, box 1, file 76G, Gray to Drew, 30 Sept. 1946; file 19.20. Magone to Blackwell, 9 Oct. 1946.

59 LAC, Bracken Papers, vol. 58, file P-305. Drew to Bracken, 27 April 1948.

60 AO, RG 3-21, box 1, file 76G. Telegram, Col. Young to Drew, 15 May 1948.

61 AO, RG 10-5, Department of Health (hereafter DoH): Dominion Council of Health (hereafter DCH) Files, box 3, file RG 10-05-0-12, DCH, 1948. "Minutes of the 54th Mtg of the DCH, 7–8 June 1948."

62 AO, RG 3-21, box 1, file 76G. Gray to Drew, 10 June 1948.

63 LAC, MG 32 B39, Donald Fleming Papers, vol. 32, file 9, "Memo re statement by Mr. Bracken at [PC Party] D-PC May 21st" [1947].

64 See AO, RG 10-5, "Minutes of the 54th Mtg of the DCH," 39–86.

65 AO, RG 75-12, Cabinet Office, vol. 1, file Cabinet Agendas, 1947 no. 3. B.W. Heise, DM Public Welfare to L.R. McDonald, Dept. of the Provincial Sec., 19 Aug. 1947.

66 LAC, Bracken Papers, vol. 58, file P-305. Frost to Bracken, 12 March 1947.

67 LAC, Fleming Papers, vol. 34, file 1948 Election, Ontario, Provincial. "Address of L.M. Frost to PC Businessmen's Club of Toronto, 27 April 1948."

68 LAC, Drew Papers, vol. 239, file 306, pt. 1, 1945–48. "Rental Payments under the D-P Tax Agreements and Source of Dominion Government's Tax Collections by Province," 25 Nov. 1947.

69 Manthorpe, *Power and the Tories*, 36–7.

70 LAC, Pickersgill Papers, vol. 1, file F-PR, Memos, 1943–53. Cadieux to Pickersgill, 19 July 1948.

71 Wilfrid Eggleston, "Ottawa Letter," *Saturday Night*, 13 March 1948.

72 LAC, Drew Papers, vol. 239, file 1945 F-PR. Ontario Govt. Press Release, 15 April 1945.

73 TUA, Frost Papers, box 15, file 15. Gagnon to Frost, 23 Aug. 1948.

74 LAC, Fleming Papers, vol. 35, file 1948 Election, National Convention, Corr., file 1. Fleming to Marcel Beauregard, 9 Aug. 1948. Courtney, *Do Conventions Matter?*, 13.

75 It might be more accurate to say that it was widely hoped that Bracken would resign; he was being increasingly criticized from all sides as lacking "aggression in debate" and failing to advance Conservative policy. See, Kendle, *Bracken*, 228–37.

76 See, Graham, *Old Man Ontario*, 132–4; Brownsey, *Tory Life*, 136–46.

77 White, *Ontario, 1610–1985*, 270–1.

78 AO, RG 3-21, box 1, file PCP Copy's [sic] of Draft Letter. Draft letter for High Park, n.d. (ca. June 1948).

79 LAC, Fleming Papers, vol. 35, file Corr., Nov.–Dec. 1948. A.R. Gobeil to Fleming, 4 Sept. 1948.

80 J.B. McGeachy, "Progressive Conservatives in Convention," *Globe and Mail,* 1 Oct. 1948.

81 LAC, PCP Papers, vol. 244, file Convention 1948. Official Report, 1 Oct. 1948, 245–7. "Canada Must Be Free of Centralized Power, Premier Drew Stresses," *Globe and Mail,* 2 Oct. 1948.

82 LAC, Fleming Papers, vol. 35, file 1948 Election, National Convention, Corr., file 1. George Little to J.M. MacDonell, 10 Aug. 1948.

83 Ibid. George Little, "A Lost Leader," n.d.

84 "Margin Given PC Leader All-Time High," and "The New Leader," *Globe and Mail,* 4 Oct. 1948.

85 LAC, Fleming Papers, vol. 35, file 1948 Election, National Convention, Corr., file 1. "Acceptance Address of the Hon. George A. Drew … Oct. 2nd 1948."

86 AO, Latimer Papers, Minutes of the Ontario PC Leadership Convention, 25–27 April 1949, Royal York Hotel, Toronto, 20.

87 For a discussion of the events surrounding Drew's resignation, see Brownsey, *Tory Life,* 150–61.

88 AO, F 2094-1, Clare Westcott Papers, VP Ontario PCP: Corr., 1946–59, file Loose Corr. Memo of conversation, Dave Sleesor to Clare Westcott, 24 Nov. 1987.

89 Ibid., F 2094-2-0-10, file Memos from Macauley. "Detailed chronology of LMF and Politics 1940 to 1964," no author, no date.

90 Ibid., F 2094-1, file Loose Corr. Memo of conversation, Dave Sleesor to Clare Westcott, 24 Nov. 1987.

91 Graham, *Old Man Ontario,* 151.

92 AO, Latimer Papers, Minutes of the Ontario PC Leadership Convention, 51.

93 This is in contrast to the argument made by Ibbitson, *Loyal No More,* 86–90.

94 TUA, Frost Papers, box 5, file 1. Leadership Convention, 1949, minutes.

3 "Know and Understand the Problems"

1 On St. Laurent's selection as leader of the Liberal Party and prime minister, see Thomson, *St. Laurent,* 231–40; Pickersgill, *My Years with Louis St. Laurent,* 45–55. On the wartime charges against Drew, see Williams, *Duff,* 255–61.

2 See http://www5.statcan.gc.ca/access_acces/archive.action?l=eng&loc= Y75_198b-eng.csv.

3 Quoted in LAC, Claxton Papers, vol. 138, file D-PC (1949). Memo, R.G. Robertson, 26 July 1949.

4 Robertson, *Memoirs*, 83. Interestingly, Robertson makes no mention of having prepared the July memorandum.

5 LAC, Claxton Papers. Memo, R.G. Robertson, 26 July 1949. See also, Hurley, *Amending Canada's Constitution*, 27–9.

6 LAC, Claxton Papers. Memo, R.G. Robertson, 26 July 1949.

7 LAC, St. Laurent Papers, vol. 84, file Conference, D-P, vol. 1, Personal and Confidential. St. Laurent to Pickersgill, 19 Aug. 1949. This is, in fact, an extraordinarily badly written memorandum and while it may be true that the PM gave a great deal of thought to the idea, he clearly gave next to none to its articulation. Pickersgill, however, was quite clear on its "revolutionary" meaning: "that before a federal-provincial conference was held, Parliament should act to transfer the jurisdiction to make amendments to Canada." Pickersgill, *My Years with St. Laurent*, 113.

8 LAC, St. Laurent Papers. St. Laurent to Pickersgill, 19 Aug. 1949.

9 LAC, MG 31 E87, Gordon Robertson Papers, vol. 29, file Constitutional Conferences, 1949–50. St. Laurent to Frost, 14 Sept. 1949.

10 *The Legislative Competence of the Parliament of Canada to Enact Bill No. 9, entitled 'An Act to Amend the Supreme Court Act,'* [1940] S.C.R. 49.

11 *A.G. Ontario* v. *A.G. Canada*, [1947] A.C. 127. On the abolition of appeals, see Saywell, *Lawmakers*, 228–32.

12 LAC, Robertson Papers, vol. 29, file BNA Act, Amendments to, n.d., 1935–52. Gordon Robertson to Norman Robertson, 17 Sept. 1949.

13 Ibid., file Constitutional conferences, 1949–50. Duplessis to St. Laurent, 21 Sept. 1949.

14 Ibid. Frost to St. Laurent, 7 Oct. 1949.

15 AO, RG 3-24, box 5, file D-P, BNA Act (Amending) I, 1949, 1950. Frost to Garson, 6 Oct. 1949.

16 Ibid., BNA Act (Amending) II, 1949, 1950. Duplessis to Frost, 20 Sept. 1949.

17 LAC, MG 32 B12, Paul Martin Sr. Papers, vol. 38, file 3. D-PC on Constitutional Amendment: Procedure at Opening Session, 16 Dec. 1949.

18 Ibid. Minutes of the Cabinet Cttee on the D-PC, 20 Dec. 1949.

19 Pickersgill, *My Years with St. Laurent*, 117–18.

20 LAC, Martin Papers, vol. 38, file 3. Cabinet Cttee on the D-PC: Possible Provisions for an Amending Procedure, 3 Jan. 1950.

21 LAC, Claxton Papers, vol. 138, file Constitution. Cabinet Cttee on the D-PC, 5 Jan. 1950.

22 "It Need Not Take Years," *Globe and Mail*, 10 Jan. 1950.

23 "Duplessis Is in Accord with Conference Aims, Will Argue Some Points," *Globe and Mail*, 10 Jan. 1950.

24 AO, RG 6-41, box 3, file Constitutional Conference of FandP Govts., 1950. Notes on proceedings, 10 Jan. 1950.

25 LAC, St. Laurent Papers, vol. 222, file Constitutional Conference, 1950. "Notes on the Mtg of the Cttee of AGs of the Constitutional Conference of the FandP Govts. – Jan. 12, 1950." Martin Papers, vol. 13, file 3. R.E. Curran (Legal Adviser) to Martin, 11 Jan. 1950.

26 LAC, Martin Papers, vol. 38, file 3. Frost, "A suggestion for Discussion Regarding a Procedure for Amending the BNA Act in Canada," 11 Jan. 1950.

27 "The Discordant Note," *Globe and Mail*, 13 Jan. 1950. While this is a fairly low threshold for provincial agreement, Frost offered it as a simple starting point, knowing that constitutional negotiations invariably move towards more complex formulae rather than in the opposite direction.

28 Warren Baldwin, "PM Agrees to Widen BNA Act Discussions: Provinces in Accord on Principle," *Globe and Mail*, 11 Jan. 1950; Warren Baldwin, "Premiers' Parley Sees New Spirit of Unity," *Globe and Mail*, 12 Jan. 1950.

29 LAC, MG 32 B44, Walter Gordon Papers, vol. 6, file Constitutional Amendment, 1964–68. "Resolutions adopted by the Constitutional Conference of Jan. 10–12, 1950, regarding principles to guide Standing Cttee of AGs in devising amending formula," 12 Jan. 1950.

30 Warren Baldwin, "Ottawa-Provincial Conference Ends on Calm Waters," *Globe and Mail*, 13 Jan. 1950. SA, Douglas Papers, file XXIII.770, Constitutional Conference, Corr., 1949–61. Douglas to C.L. Coburn, 30 Jan. 1950.

31 AO, RG 3-24, box 5, file D-P Ottawa Conference, 10–12 June 1950. Frost to St. Laurent, 3 Feb. 1950.

32 Stanley Knowles, quoting King, in House of Commons, *Debates*, 23 Feb. 1950, 170.

33 See, Struthers, "Shadows from the Thirties," 9–21.

34 Ontario Legislative Assembly, *Debates*, 17 March 1950, 8–9.

35 Ibid., 33–6.

36 AO, RG 6-115, DoF: F-P Relations Corr. Files, 1950–62, box 1, file 13, Fed. Collection of Ontario Income Tax. Abbott to Frost, 27 March 1950.

37 White, *Ontario, 1610–1985*, 276; Richmond, *Economic Transformation of Ontario*, 13–14.

38 AO, RG 6-41, box 10, file F-PR, c. 1945–50. Chater to L.R. McDonald, 20 June 1950.

39 LAC, Claxton Papers, vol. 146, file D-PC, 1950, part 2. Govt. of the Province of Ontario, "Draft proposal to be submitted for discussion to the Cttee of AGs of the Conference on Constitutional Amendment." 1 March 1950.

40 Ibid.

41 Ibid.

42 LAC, St. Laurent Papers, vol. 222, file Constitutional Conference, 1950. Robertson to Pickersgill, 8 March 1950.

43 LAC, Robertson Papers, vol. 29, file Conference of FandP Govts., Dec. 1950, Planning (1 of 2), n.d., 1946–50. Memo for Robertson, no author, 5 April 1950.

44 AO, RG 3-24, box 5, file D-P, BNA Act (Amending) I, 1949, 1950. Frost to Porter, 14 Sept. 1950.

45 Government of Canada, *Proceedings of the Constitutional Conference*, 25–8 Sept. 1950. Frost opening statement, 25 Sept. 1950, 15–16.

46 Ibid., 17.

47 George Kitchen, "Procedures for Altering Canada's Constitution Snag at Quebec Talks," *Globe and Mail*, 26 Sept. 1950.

48 *Proceedings of the Constitutional Conference*, 48–52.

49 AO, RG 6-115, box 1, file 13, D-PC, Autumn, 1950. R.G. Robertson and Paul Pelletier, Minutes of the Mtg of the Cttee of the Whole of the Constitutional Conference of FandP Govts., 28 Sept. 1950.

50 A full discussion of the fiscal negotiations leading to the 1952 tax rental agreements can be found in Burns, *Acceptable Mean*, 92–106.

51 LAC, St. Laurent Papers, vol. 222, file C3-32. Norman Robertson to St. Laurent, 6 Oct. 1950.

52 LAC, Robertson Papers, vol. 29, file Conference of FandP Govts., Dec. 1950, Corr. re: Agenda. St. Laurent to Frost, 12 Oct. 1950.

53 Ibid.

54 LAC, RG 19, Department of Finance, vol. 4765, file 5600-03(47)-1. A.S. Abell to R.B. Bryce, 20 Sept. 1950.

55 LAC, Pickersgill Papers, vol. 1, file F-PR, Memos 1943–53. "Memo," no author, 16 Oct. 1950. Document edited in Pickersgill's office and sent to the PM. [LAC, St. Laurent Papers, vol. 84, file C-10-1, Conferences.] Pickersgill recalls that "there was a strong hint that Premier Frost was interested in an agreement for Ontario." [*My Years with Louis St. Laurent*, 138.]

56 LAC, St. Laurent Papers. "Memo," no author, 16 Oct. 1950.

57 LAC, Martin Papers, vol. 4, file 9. Cabinet Cttee on F-PR, 25 Nov. 1950.

58 Ibid.

59 AO, RG 3-24, box 4, file D-PC, Dec. 1950, 1951. Frost to Goodfellow, 22 Nov. 1950.

60 Ibid. B.W. Heisse to Frost, 29 Nov. 1950.

61 LAC, Robertson Papers, vol. 29, file BNA Act, Amendments to, pt. 1 of 2. "Establishment of the Canadian Constitution as a Canadian Document," 16 Nov. 1950.

62 Ibid., original emphasis.

63 Ibid.

64 AO, RG 4-2, file 47.9. Mtg of the Continuing Cttee of AGs, 23 Nov. 1950.

65 SA, Douglas Papers, file XXIII.767, F-PC: Constitution and Constitutional Amendment, 1949–54.

66 Ibid.

67 Ibid.

68 Frost opening statement, *Proceedings of the Conference of Federal and Provincial Governments*, 4–7 Dec. 1950, 22–3.

69 Ibid., 21.

70 Quoted in Bryden, "Money and Politics"; Frost opening statement, 4 Dec. 1950, 24. See also, Graham, *Old Man Ontario*, 177–80.

71 Frost opening statement, 4 Dec. 1950, 24.

72 Ibid., 19.

73 AO, RG 6-41, box 3, file untitled, F-PC, Dec. 1950. Unofficial proceedings of the Cttee on Old Age Security, 6 Dec. 1950.

74 Ibid. Unofficial proceedings of the Cttee of the Whole, 5 Dec. 1950. See also Unofficial proceedings of the Cttee on Old Age Security, 6 Dec. 1950.

75 Bryden, *Old Age Pensions*, 117–24.

76 Pickersgill, *My Years with St. Laurent*, 138.

77 LAC, Robertson Papers, vol. 29, file Conference of FandP Govts., Dec. 1950. Unofficial proceedings of the Cttee of the Whole, 7 Dec. 1950.

78 AO, RG 3-24, box 4, file D-PC, Dec. 1950, 1951. Frost press release, 7 Dec. 1950

79 LAC, Robertson Papers, vol. 29, file Conference of FandP Governments, Dec. 1950. Unofficial proceedings of the Cttee of the Whole, 7 Dec. 1950.

80 AO, RG 4-2, box 47, file 9. "Address of the Hon. Stuart Garson ... Toronto, April 27th, 1951."

81 See Bryden, "Ontario's Agenda in Post-Imperial Constitutional Negotiations," 222–3. According to subsequent accounts, "the third session of the Constitutional Conference to be held in Dec., 1950, was suspended pending consideration of the tax agreements and related matters." See, AO, RG 6-41, box 8, file D-P Financial Arrangements c. 1949–61. "Proceedings of the Constitutional Conference, Jan. and Sept. 1950, and the Mtgs of the AGs, Oct. and Nov., 1960, on Constitutional Matters," n.d.

82 LAC, Claxton Papers, vol. 138, file Constitution, Gen D P-1-9. Minutes of Cabinet Cttee on the D-PC, 3 Jan. 1950.

83 AO, RG 3-23, Office of the Premier: Frost General Correspondence, vol. 37, file D-P (Old Age Pensions), Hon. Stuart Garson, 1951. Garson to Frost, 3 April 1951. Claxton Papers, vol. 146, file D-PR, Memo re: proposal change.

Memo to the Cabinet Cttee on F-PR, re: Constitutional amendments, 5 May 1951.

84 AO, RG 75-42-1-85, Cabinet Office: L.R. MacDonald, Sec. to Cabinet, vol. 9, file F-P, Old Age Pensions. Frost to Goodfellow, 10 May 1951.

85 Bryden, *Old Age Pensions*, 124–8; Martin, *A Very Public Life*, 76–103.

86 On the calculations and recalculations, see AO, RG 75-42-1-85, vol. 9, file F-P, Old Age Pensions: "Some Comments on the Federal Proposals of Dec. 1950, as they concern Ontario," n.d.; "Observations on Proposals Relating to F-P Fiscal Relations, Dec. 1950," 10 Jan. 1951; and "Secret: Memo Re F-P Fiscal Relations," 22 Jan. 1951.

87 AO, RG 6-41, box 8, file D-P Fiscal Relations, 1941–52. "F-PR: Advantages and Disadvantages of Tax-Rental, Dec. 1950," 29 June 1951.

88 Ibid.

89 Ibid.

90 AO, RG 3-24, box 6, file D-P Memos, 1951. "Note on Tax Rental Agreement with Reference to Quebec," 9 July 1951.

91 Ibid.

92 AO, RG 6-41, box 8, file D-P Fiscal Relations, 1941–52. "Mtg at Montreal on July 17, 1951 between the Prime Ministers and Delegates of Ontario and Quebec," 23 July 1951.

93 Ibid.

94 Ibid. "Comments on the Foregoing Report of the Mtg at Montreal on July 17, 1951 and Alternative Suggestions on Formulae," 23 July 1951.

95 AO, RG 3-24, box 6, file D-PC, Abbott, Hon. Douglas. Aug. 1951. "Draft Outline of Statement to the Right Hon. Louis St. Laurent," 14 Aug. 1951.

96 Ibid.

97 Ibid.

98 Ibid. "Advantages to Government of Canada of Ontario's proposal of Aug. 21, 1951."

99 AO, RG 6-115, box 1, file 13, Rental Payments Data. Abbott to Frost, 10 Jan. 1952.

100 AO, RG 3-24, box 4, file D-PC, 7–9 May 1952. Frost to Walters, 28 Jan. 1952.

101 Ibid. Walters to Frost, 30 Jan. 1952.

102 AO, RG 6-115, container 2, file Mtg, Ottawa, 23 May 1952. "Discussions held by Ontario in the office of Dr. W.C. Clark, Dep. Minister of Finance, Ottawa, Thursday, May 22, 1952."

103 Ibid., file Corr. 1952 re: Tax Rental Agreement. K.W. Taylor to Chester Walters, 7 Aug. 1952.

104 AO, RG 6-115, container 2, file 13, Corr. 1952, re: Tax Rental Agreements (TRA) 1952, 1953. Frost to St. Laurent, 18 Aug. 1952.

105 AO, RG 3-24, box 4, file D-PC, May 7–9, 1952. Frost to Macdonald, 17 Sept. 1952.

106 Ibbitson, *Loyal No More*, 86.

4 "Ontario's Earnest Desire for National Unity"

1 Graham, *Old Man Ontario*, 196; see also, Ibbitson, *Loyal No More*.

2 AO, RG 3-24, box 4, file D-P, Economic Cttee, 1952, 1953. Frost to St. Laurent, draft, 16 Feb. 1953.

3 AO, RG 6-115, UC 5-6, box 6, file 13, 1955 Economic Cttee. Frost to St. Laurent, 29 April 1953.

· 4 Ibid.

5 LAC, St. Laurent Papers, vol. 97, file D-PR, 1952–53, Personal and Confidential. St. Laurent to Frost, 15 May 1953.

6 See AO, RG 3-24, box 7, file D-P, Economics Cttee, 1953. Gathercole to Frost, 18 Nov. 1953; and AO, RG 6-15, vol. 27, file Addresses delivered by Hon. Leslie M. Frost. "Address of Hon. Leslie M. Frost, QC, at the Fiftieth Anniversary Mtg of the Union of Manitoba Municipalities at Winnipeg, Nov. 25. 1953." In this latter address, Frost said "Ontario would welcome the re-establishment of the Economics Committee … [which] would help to keep under review ever-changing problems which are not going to be any less in the days of development which lie ahead."

7 AO, RG 6-41, box 15, file Tax Rental Payments. Gathercole to Frost, 5 Jan. 1954.

8 AO, F 4345, Leslie Frost Papers, new series, container 2, file 69, Donald O'Hearn to Frost, 7 July 1954, and container 1, file 34, Summary of points raised in conversation between George Gathercole and Mr. Graham Towers, Governor of the Bank of Canada, and with other Bank of Canada officials, Wed. 18 Aug. 1954, in Ottawa.

9 See LAC, St. Laurent Papers, vol 177, file D-PR (duplicate). St. Laurent to Egan Chambers, 28 Sept. 1954.

10 AO, RG 6-115, UC 3-4, box 4, file Preliminary Mtg, 15 Oct. 1954. "Memo re: D-PR," 5 Oct. 1954.

11 Ibid. Duplessis to St. Laurent, 11 Oct. 1954. Thomson, *St. Laurent*, 383–4.

12 AO, RG 3-23, box 37, file D-P, Ottawa Summary, 15 Oct. 1954. "Summary of Discussions … at Ottawa, Friday, Oct. 15, 1954."

13 Ibid.

14 Ibid.

15 AO, RG 6-115, UC 3-4, box 4, file 1955 Conference, Preliminary Mtg, 15 Oct. 1954. St. Laurent to Frost, 14 Jan. 1955.

16 See Burns, *Acceptable Mean*, 108–12, and Perry, *National Finances, 1955–56*, 18–19.

17 This was a betrayal of a promise made to the Liberal Opposition in Quebec, "who had been privately assured by the federal finance minister that the 5 percent credit was not negotiable." Stevenson, *Unfulfilled Union*, 134.

18 AO, RG 6-115, file 1955 Conference. St. Laurent to Frost, 14 Jan. 1955.

19 SA, Douglas Papers, R 33.4, file IX.12e, Ontario and Quebec. Al Johnson to Douglas (quoting from St. Laurent letter of 14 Jan. 1955), 26 Jan. 1955. In contrast, Douglas thought that the move "leads back to the old dog-eat-dog days of provincial rivalry and federal impotency. Ottawa has hoisted the white flag of surrender over the forts of full employment and a high level of national prosperity." [Ibid., Douglas, "Mr. St. Laurent Turns Back the Clock," on *Provincial Affairs Series*, 1 Feb. 1955.]

20 AO, RG 6-115, UC 3-4, box 4, file 1955 Conference, Preliminary Mtg, 15 Oct. 1954. "Observations on the Federal Government's Increase from 5 to 10 per cent of the personal income tax deduction for provincial income tax purposes," 21 Jan. 1955.

21 Ibid.

22 LAC, RG 19, vol. 3879, file 5515-04(55/2)-1. Cabinet Cttee on the F-PC, 1955, 23 June 1955.

23 Ibid.

24 Ibid.

25 Ibid.

26 AO, RG 3-24, box 7, file D-P, Philip Clark. Clark to Frost, 15 June. AO, RG 6-115, UC3-4, box 4, file 1955 Conf. Preparatory Cttee. 3rd Mtg. of the Pre-paratory Cttee for the F-PC, 1955, 4 July 1955.

27 Ibid.

28 LAC, RG 19, vol. 3879, file 5515-04(55/2)-1. Cabinet Cttee on the F-PC, 1955, 18 July 1955.

29 AO, RG 6-115, UC 3-4, box 4, file 1955 Conf. Preparatory Cttee. 4th Mtg. of the Preparatory Cttee for the F-PC, 1955, 11 Sept. 1955.

30 AO, RG 3-24, box 7, file D-PC, Sept.–Oct. 1955. Gathercole to Frost, Sunday night [11 Sept. 1955].

31 Blair Fraser, "A New Blueprint for Confederation," *Maclean's*, 26 Nov. 1955.

32 AO, RG 6-115, UC 3-4, box 4, file Preliminary Mtg, 15 Oct. 1955. "Some Unsettled FP Fiscal Relations Questions," 27 Oct. 1955.

33 SA, R-37, C.M. Fines Papers, file IV.6a, Tax Rental Agreements (hereafter TRA), 1946–60. T.C. Douglas to St. Laurent, 1 Nov. 1955.

34 LAC, Drew Papers, vol. 239, file 306.1. Roblin to Drew, 21 Nov. 1955.

35 Fraser, "New Blueprint for Confederation."

36 LAC, RG 19, vol. 3879, file 5515-04(55/2)-1/vol. 2. Burns to Harris, 10 Nov. 1955.

37 AO, RG 3-24, box 8, file D-PC, 1955, 1956. St. Laurent to Frost, 6 Jan. 1956.

38 Ibid. Frost to St. Laurent, 22 Feb. 1956.

39 AO, RG 3-23, vol. 38, file D-PC (Statement LMF). "Statement by the Hon. Leslie M. Frost ... on March 9th, 1956."

40 Ibid.

41 AO, RG 3-24, box 8, file D-PC, July 11, 1956. "Memo on F-PR ... Aug. 13, 1956." Perry, *Fiscal History of Canada*, 537; Perry, *Background of Current Fiscal Problems*, 59.

42 LAC, Martin Papers, vol. 32, file 60-2. R.B. Bryce to Martin, 20 Dec. 1954.

43 Struthers, *Limits of Affluence*, 172. House of Commons, *Debates*, 13 Jan. 1955, 140–4.

44 LAC, RG 19, vol. 3879, file 5515-04(55/1)-1. Minutes of the Cabinet Cttee on F-PC, 1955, 5 April 1955. AO, RG 4-2, file 77.9. R.E.G. Davis, Executive Director of the Canadian Welfare Council, to Dana Porter, 24 Jan. 1954. Struthers, *Limits of Affluence*, 174.

45 LAC, Martin Papers, vol 4, file 15. "F-PC, 1955, Preliminary Mtg, April 27th, 1955, Afternoon Session."

46 Ibid.

47 AO, RG 6-115, UC 3-4, box 4, file 1955 Conference, Saskatchewan. Gathercole to Al Johnson, 13 May 1955.

48 AO, RG 4-2, file 71.9. "Report of George Gathercole on the Second Mtg of the Preparatory Cttee of the F-PC, May 26, 27 and 30, 1955," 6 June 1955.

49 AO, RG 3-24, vol. 13, file Elections (Provincial, 1955), Manifesto, 12 May 1955. "A Report to the People: Address to the Electors by ... Frost ..." 12 May 1955.

50 AO, RG 4-2, "Report of George Gathercole on the Second Mtg," 6 June 1955.

51 AO, RG 3-24, vol. 7, file D-PC, Sept.–Oct. 1955. "Statement of the Hon. Leslie M. Frost ... June 20, 1955."

52 LAC, Martin Papers, vol. 4, file 15. F-P Mtg on Unemployment Assistance, Morning Session, 20 June 1955.

53 Ibid., Morning and Afternoon Sessions, 21 June 1955.

54 Ibid., Afternoon Session, 20 June 1955.

55 AO, RG 3-23, box 37, file D-PC Re: Unemployment Assistance, 20–21 June 1955. St. Laurent to Frost, 22 June 1955.

56 Ibid., file D-PC, Oct.–Nov. 1955. "Unemployment Relief Assistance," no author, n.d. This document also indicates that Ontario officials were concerned about the implications of unemployment assistance for the pro-

vincially funded mothers' allowance program, in which changes were also being considered. See Little, *"No Car, No Radio, No Liquor Permit,"* 116–25.

57 LAC, RG 29, Department of National Health and Welfare (hereafter DoNHW), vol. 1372, file 1-1. Davidson to Martin, "Health Insurance and Ontario," 5 Aug. 1955.

58 House of Commons, *Debates*, 15 Jan. 1954, 1143-4. LAC, RG 29, vol. 1372, file 1-5. Willard to Cameron, 25 April 1955.

59 See LAC, RG 19, vol. 3879, file 5515-04(55/1)-1. Minutes of the Cabinet Cttee on F-PC, 1955, 5 April 1955.

60 Government of Canada, *Federal-Provincial Conference, 1955: Preliminary Meeting*, 18.

61 LAC, Martin Papers, vol. 4, file 15. "F-PC, 1955, Preliminary Mtg, April 27th, 1955, Morning Session." Bryden, *Planners and Politicians*, 6–8.

62 Taylor, *Health Insurance and Canadian Public Policy*, 207–10.

63 AO, RG 3-24, box 7, file D-P, Gathercole, July–Aug. 1955. "Third Mtg of the Preparatory Cttee for the F-PC, 1955," 4 July 1955.

64 LAC, RG 19, vol. 3879, file 5515-04(55/1)-1. Maurice Lamontagne report, "Cabinet Cttee on the F-PC, 1955," 18 July 1955.

65 Taylor, *Health Insurance*, 127–9.

66 LAC, RG 29, vol. 1372, file 1-1. Davidson to Martin, "Health Insurance and Ontario," 5 Aug. 1955.

67 Ibid., vol. 1374, file Health Insurance Cttee Mtg, 1955. "Informal discussion concerning health care," 25 Aug. 1955.

68 AO, RG 3-24, box 7, file D-PC, Sept.–Oct. 1955. St. Laurent to Frost, 2 Sept. 1955.

69 LAC, RG 29, vol. 1372, file D-PC, 1955. G.D.W. Cameron to Martin, 16 Sept. 1955.

70 QUA, Dexter Papers, vol. 19, file Health Program, no. 183. Dexter draft, 16 Sept. 1955.

71 LAC, RG 29, vol. 1372, file 1-1. Davidson to senior NHW staff, 20 Sept. 1955.

72 AO, RG 3-24, box 8, file D-PC I, Oct. 1955. Frost to St. Laurent, draft, 27 Sept. 1955. St. Laurent's reply indicates that he received Corr. from Frost that was at the very least very similar to the draft letter. Ibid., St. Laurent to Frost, 29 Sept. 1955.

73 LAC, Martin Papers, vol. 6, file 40-5. Davidson to Martin, n.d.

74 Taylor, *Health Insurance*, 131.

75 See LAC, RG 29, vol. 1372: file 2-5, Health Insurance, Ontario, C.A. Roberts to F.W. Jackson, 23 Feb. 1956; file 1-7, Health Insurance, Current Discussion, J.W. Willard to G.D.W. Cameron, 12 April 1956; file 2-5, Health Insur-

ance, Ontario, "Statement to the Health Cttee of the Ontario legislature by the Canadian Life Insurance Officers Association," 22 March 1956.

76 LAC, Drew Papers, vol. 239, file 306.1. Robbins to Drew, 29 Feb. 1956.

77 Thomson, "Political Ideas of Louis St. Laurent," 153.

78 Camp, *Gentlemen, Politicians and Players*, 203; see, also, Bothwell and Kilbourn, *C.D. Howe*, 299–316; Fleming, *So Very Near*, 299–312.

79 Camp, *Gentlemen, Politicians and Players*, 201.

80 Stursberg, *Diefenbaker: Leadership Gained*, 5–7.

81 Goodman, *Life of the Party*, 74.

82 Hugh Latimer, "Political Reminiscences," quoted in Graham, *Old Man Ontario*, 330.

83 AO, Westcott Papers, F 2094-2-0-10, file Memos from Macauley. "Detailed Chronology of LMF and Politics, 1940–1964."

84 Diefenbaker, *One Canada*, vol. 1, 280–2.

85 Perry, *Fiscal History of Canada*, 537; Graham, *Old Man Ontario*, 322. AO, RG 47-27-1-2, Ontario Historical Studies Series Political Interviews. Interview with James Allen, 15 Aug. 1972, 8–9.

86 LAC, Michener Papers, vol. 88, file Diefenbaker, John, Corr. Diefenbaker to Michener, 28 Feb. 1957 [no. 2].

87 LAC, MG 26 M, John G. Diefenbaker Papers, reel M-5555, vol. 18, file 364. "Notes on Remarks by the Hon. Leslie M. Frost, QC, at Massey Hall," 25 April 1957. *Globe and Mail*, 26 April 1957.

88 LAC, PCP Papers, vol. 341, file Frost, 1954–57. Allister Grossart to Frost, 6 May 1957.

89 QUA, Dexter Papers, box 16, file 122. Tax Agreements no. 1. 11 May 1957.

90 Newman, *Renegade in Power*, 87.

91 See Smith, *Rogue Tory*, 203–4; Dyck, "Links between Federal and Provincial Parties," 148.

92 AO, RG 3-23, vol. 38, file D-PC, Nov. 1957. Diefenbaker to Frost, 16 Sept. 1957, and Diefenbaker to Frost, 31 Oct. 1957.

93 *Globe and Mail*, 25 Nov. 1957.

94 Graham, *Old Man Ontario*, 335-6.

95 *Globe and Mail*, 26 Nov. 1957.

96 AO, RG 6-115, UC 11-12, box 11, file F-P Corr., 1958. Douglas Campbell, premier of Manitoba, to Diefenbaker, 18 Dec. 1957.

97 Ibid., "Note on Hon. Douglas Campbell's letter of Dec. 18, 1957, to Rt. Hon. J.G. Diefenbaker," n.d.

98 Burns, *Acceptable Mean*, 169; Interview, Dalton Camp, 19 Feb. 1997.

99 Graham, *Old Man Ontario*, 336.

100 AO, RG 3-24, box 9, file D-PR, 1958. Frost to Gathercole, 16 Jan. 1958.

101 Quoted in Graham, *Old Man Ontario*, 337.

102 SA, Fines Papers, file IV.6a, TRA, 1946–60. Diefenbaker to Douglas, 24 Jan. 1958.

103 Quoted in English, *Worldly Years*, 199. On the leadership convention preparation, see Stursberg, *Pearson and the Dream of Unity*, 47–8; Martin, *A Very Public Life*, vol. 2, 313; Courtney, *Do Conventions Matter?*, 16.

104 Diefenbaker, *One Canada: The Years of Achievement*, 82; Granatstein, *Canada, 1957–1967*, 34–5.

105 LAC, MG 32 C65, Allister Grosart Papers, vol. 8, file 14. Dalton Camp to Grosart, 14 April 1958.

106 Graham, *Old Man Ontario*, 337.

107 QUA, Tom Kent Papers, box 1, file Corr., April–Dec. 1958. Kent to Col. Ted Leslie, 12 April 1958.

108 QUA, Dexter Papers, box 16 file 122. "D-P 3," 10 April 1958.

109 Smith, *Rogue Tory*, 285.

110 SA, Fines Papers, file IV.6a, TRA, 1946–60. Douglas to Diefenbaker, 30 May 1958, and Fleming to Douglas, 17 June 1958.

111 Ibid., file IV.6b. Douglas to Frost, 10 Dec. 1958.

112 AO, RG 6-14, vol. 94, file TRA: Sundry. Fleming to James Allan, 4 Feb. 1959.

113 AO, RG 3-23, box 38, file G, D-PR Re: Tax-Sharing Arrangements, 1958–59. Frost to Diefenbaker, 17 Feb. 1959.

114 LAC, Diefenbaker Papers, reel M-7936, vol. 328, file 364, Provincial Governments, Ontario 1957–62. "A Report to the People from … Frost," n.d. (ca. 4 May 1959).

115 Graham, *Old Man Ontario*, 351–2.

116 AO, RG 3-23, box 38 file G, D-PR Re: Tax-Sharing Arrangements, 1958–59. Gathercole, "Agenda for Hon. Leslie M. Frost Concerning discussions in Ottawa, Aug., 1959," 18 Aug. 1959.

117 Smith, *Rogue Tory*, 393–5.

118 AO, RG 6-115, UC 13-14, box 13, file 1959 F-PC. "Notes on the Mtg of the D-P Cttee of Ministers of Finance and Provincial Treasurers … Oct. 15–16 1959."

119 Harold Greer, "Sales Tax Alternative," *Globe and Mail*, 26 July 1960, 1.

120 LAC, RG 19, vol. 3879, file 5515-03 (vol. 2). "Notes on In Camera Proceedings of F-PC of July 25–27 1960," 26 July 1960.

121 *Globe and Mail*, 27 July 1960, 1.

122 LAC, Fleming Papers, vol. 136, file 6. "D-PC on Constitutional Amendment, Oct. 6–7 1960," 2-9.

Notes to pages 101–8 257

123 LAC, MG 32 B11, E. Davie Fulton Papers, vol. 68, file 10. Fulton to Diefen-
baker, 31 Jan. 1961. AO, RG 3-26, Office of the Premier: Premier John P.
Robarts General Corr., box 18, file BNA Act, AG, Nov. 1961–Dec. 1965.
Roberts to Fulton, 15 Feb. 1961.

124 AO, RG 3-24, box 9, file D-PC, 26–28 Oct. 1960. "Summary of Suggestions
made by the PM ...," no author, no date.

125 AO, RG 6-115, box 16, file F-PC, 11th Continuing Cttee, Sept. 1960.
Gathercole to Frost, 22 Sept. 1960.

126 QUA, Richard Malone Papers, box 2, file Dexter, Grant, 1961–62. Dexter
memo, "Talk with Ken Taylor," 24 Jan. 1961.

127 Ibid., Dexter memo, "Balance of evening with Ken Taylor," 25 Jan. 1961.

128 AO, RG 6-115, box 17, file FP-FM 61. Diefenbaker to Frost, 16 June 1961.
LAC, MG 32 B1, Richard Bell Papers, vol. 38, file 1960–61. A.S. Abell to the
Minister, 18 May 1961.

129 LAC, MG 32 B29, Waldo Monteith Papers, vol. 2, file DoNHW, Social Security, Report of Inter-Departmental Cttee, Aug. 1961.

130 AO, George Gathercole Papers, Acc. 12401, MU 5330, file Cttee Documents, 1960–63. "A Summary Report of the Ontario Cttee on Portable
Pensions, Feb. 1961."

131 AO, RG 3-24, box 9, file D-P, Premiers Conference, Quebec, 1–2 Dec. 1960.
Press release, 2 Dec. 1960.

132 Ibid. Duff Roblin to Frost, 6 Dec. 1960.

133 Ibid. Press release, 2 Dec. 1960.

5 "A Lasting Effect on Confederation Itself"

1 *Report of the Proceedings of the Fifteenth Annual Tax Conference*, Montreal, Nov.
1961. George Gathercole, 315.

2 Graham, *Old Man Ontario*, 401.

3 AO, Latimer Papers. Minutes of the Ontario PC Leadership Convention,
address by Diefenbaker, 24 Oct. 1961.

4 QUA, Malone Papers, box 2, file Dexter, Grant 1961–62. Dexter memo,
"Balance of evening with Ken Taylor," 25 Jan. 1961.

5 John Miller, "Ballyhoo Loud, Voters Uncertain," *Globe and Mail*, 25 Oct.
1961, 1.

6 Oliver, *Unlikely Tory*, 118–19.

7 McDougall, *Robarts*, 70–1.

8 Paikin, *Public Triumph, Private Tragedy*, 24, 34.

9 Newman, *Renegade in Power*, 175–91.

10 Granatstein, *Canada, 1957–1967*, 116–33.

11 See, e.g., AO, Frost Papers, box 1, file Diefenbaker, 1962. Various letters.

12 LAC, Diefenbaker Papers, reel M-7935, file 360, Provincial Govts., Gen., 1959–62. Memo to file, Derek Bedson, 21 Nov. 1961.

13 LAC, MG 31 E59, R.B. Bryce Papers, vol. 8, file 19. "Social Security – Views Expressed by Individual Ministers at Cabinet Mtgs Oct. 10th, 12th and 26th, 1961." 27 Oct. 1961.

14 Ibid.

15 AO, RG 3-26, box 18, file BNA Act, AG, Nov. 61–Dec. 65. Diefenbaker to Robarts, 17 Jan. 1962.

16 LAC, Fleming Papers, vol. 84, file 12. H.D. Clark to Fleming, 31 Jan. 1962.

17 LAC, Gordon Papers, vol. 6, file Constitutional Amendment 1964–68. "An Act to provide for the amendment in Canada of the Constitution of Canada," draft, 6 Nov. 1961.

18 AO, RG 3-26, box 18, file BNA Act, AG, Nov. 61–Dec. 65. Diefenbaker to Robarts, 17 Jan. 1962.

19 LAC, Fleming Papers, vol. 84, file 12. Clark to Fleming, 31 Jan. 1962.

20 House of Commons, *Debates*, 22 Jan. 1962.

21 AO, RG 3-26, box 18, file BNA Act, AG, Nov. 61–Dec. 65. Gathercole to Robarts, 1 Feb. 1962.

22 Ibid.

23 Bryden, *Old Age Pensions*, 165.

24 AO, RG 3-102, Office of the Premier. Press release, 9 Feb. 1962.

25 See Bryden, *Planners and Politicians*.

26 QUA, Kent Papers, box 2, file Corr.. Robarts to Pearson, 6 Feb. 1962.

27 LAC, RG 2, Privy Council Office, Series A-5-a, vol. 6192, 6 Feb. 1962.

28 LAC, MG 32 B9, Gordon Churchill Papers, vol. 84, file 12. Robert Clark to Donald Fleming, 2 March 1962.

29 AO, RG 3-26, vol. 403, file Pensions, Portable, March–May 1962. Clark to Robarts, 26 April 1962.

30 AO, RG 3-26, box 155, file Royal Commission on Health, Nov. 61–Dec. 65. McCutcheon to Robarts, 19 April 1962.

31 Saywell, "Parliament and Politics," in Saywell, ed., *Canadian Annual Review for 1962*, 13–14.

32 Newman, *Renegade in Power*, 436–9.

33 TUA, Frost Papers, box 12, file Diefenbaker, 1962 Election. Frost to Diefenbaker, 12 July 1962.

34 Ibid. Frost to Diefenbaker, 18 July 1962.

35 Newman, *Renegade in Power*, 439.

36 AO, RG 10-6, box 31, file 10-6-0-351. Draft statement of the Prime Minister of Ontario to the Royal Commission on Health Services, 15 Aug. 1962.

37 LAC, Churchill Papers, vol. 136, file D-PC, Constitutional. Memo for Cabinet, 30 July 1962.
38 Ibid., vol. 2, file DoNHW, Social Security, Jan.–Aug. 1962. Joe Willard to Diefenbaker, 30 July 1962.
39 AO, RG 3-26, box 287, file Premiers' Conference, Victoria, B.C., 1962, Portable Pensions. "Notes on Portable Pensions for the Use of the Hon. John Roberts ... Aug. 6th and 7th, 1962."
40 AO, RG 3-42, Office of the Premier: Premier John P. Robarts – Conference Files, box 13, file Provincial Premiers Conference, Aug. 1962, 127–139.
41 AO, Gathercole Papers, Acc. 12401, file Portable Pension Submissions. "Main Points Made in Submissions to Cttee at Sept. Hearings," 1962.
42 AO, RG 3-26, vol. 403, file Pensions, Portable, March–May 62. Monteith to Robarts, 4 Jan. 1963.
43 AO, RG 3-102, box 1, file Press Releases. Ontario Govt. Press Release, 19 March 1963.
44 Saywell, "Parliament and Politics," in *Canadian Annual Review for 1963*, 7–9.
45 Private Collection, *Canadian Annual Review* (hereafter CAR) Papers, clippings file. "Television Address by the Rt. Hon. John G. Diefenbaker ... March 22nd 1963."
46 AO, John Robarts Papers, Series F-15, MU 8004, box 8, file Ontario PCP, Election. George Hogan to Robarts, 11 April 1963.
47 AO, RG 3-26, box 404, file Portable Pensions, Treasury, 1963. "Statement by the Hon. John Robarts ... on the change of govt. at Ottawa, April 22nd, 1963."
48 English, *Worldly Years*, 277–8; Smith, *Gentle Patriot*, 155–79.
49 Bryden, *Planners and Politicians*, 91.
50 AO, Gathercole Papers, file Portable Pensions, Corr., 1963. Gathercole to Robarts, 8 May 1963; Gathercole to John Connolly, 1 May 1963.
51 AO, RG 3-26, box 404, file Portable Pensions, Treasury 1963. Pearson to Robarts, 12 July 1963.
52 Ibid. Robarts to Pearson, 18 July 1963.
53 QUA, Kent Papers, box 2, file Corr.. Kent to cabinet, 6 June 1963.
54 LAC, RG 2, Series A-5-a, vol. 6253. Cabinet minutes, 11 July 1963.
55 AO, RG 3-26, box 404, file Portable Pensions, Treasury 1963. Portable Pension Cttee comments, "Re: Compulsory Contributory social Security (Retirement Maintenance) Insurance Plans," 24 July 1963.
56 AO, RG 6-44, box UF 33, file F-PC, July 1963. Notes Taken at F-PC, 26 July 1963.
57 Ibid.
58 Bryden, *Planners and Politicians*, 94–7.

59 AO, RG 3-26, box 287, file Premiers' Conference, Aug. 1963. "Portable Pension Legislation and Inter-Provincial Cooperation," 29 July 1963.
60 Ibid.
61 QUA, Kent Papers, vol. 7, file F-PC on Pensions, 12–25 Nov. 1962. Pension strategy, 4 Sept. 1963. McDougall, *Robarts*, 106.
62 AO, RG 3-102, box 1, file Press Release, 9 Sept. 1963. "Statement by the Hon. John Robarts … at the F-PC on Pension Plans, Ottawa, Sept. 9th–10th, 1963."
63 Kent Papers, box 3, file Oct. 1963. Pearson to Robarts, 7 Oct. 1963.
64 AO, Robarts Papers, Series F-15-4-3, MU 8005, box 9, file Pearson, Lester B. 1963–67. Pearson to Robarts, 4 Oct. 1963.
65 Ibid. Robarts to Pearson, 9 Oct. 1963.
66 QUA, Kent Papers, vol. 7, file F-PC on Pensions, 12–25 Nov. 1963. DM Welfare to LaMarsh, 13 Nov. 1963.
67 AO, RG 3-26, box 488, file Fed. Govt., F-PC, 26–29 Nov. 1963. Gathercole to Robarts, 14 Nov. 1963.
68 Ibid., Notes on F-P Plenary Conference, 1.
69 Ibid., 18.
70 Ibid. Appendix B, 50. Courchene, *Equalization Payments*, 44.
71 AO, RG 3-26, box 488, file Fed. Govt., F-PC, State of the Economy, Nov. 1963. Robarts handwritten notes, n.d.
72 Bryden, *Planners and Politicians*, 105–6.
73 AO, RG 3-26, box 478, file Fed. Govt., Canada Pension Plan (hereafter CPP), 1963. Robarts's handwritten notes, n.d.
74 Ibid., box 490, file Pension Commentaries from the Pension Commission of Ontario. Memo from L.E. Coward, Nov. 1963.
75 Ibid., box 478, file Fed. Govt., CPP, 1964, no. 1. Memo from the PM of Canada to Provincial Premiers, confidential until 20 Jan. 1964.
76 Ibid. L.E. Coward, Comments on the Memo from the PM…, 15 Jan. 1964.
77 LAC, Pearson Papers, vol. 221, file 632.5 pt. 2. Robarts to Pearson, 13 Feb. 1964.
78 AO, RG 3-26, box 480, file CPP, L.B. Pearson, Fed. Govt., Nov. 61–Dec. 65. Pearson to Robarts, 25 Feb. 1964.
79 Ibid., box 478, file Fed. Govt., CPP 1964, no. 2. Coward to Robarts, 4 March 1964.
80 Ibid.
81 TUA, Frost Papers, box 62, file 15, Oakley Dalgleish. Confidential memo prepared by *Globe and Mail* representatives at off-the-record seminar on French Canada, May 1963.

82 AO, Robarts Papers, Series F 15-4-3, MU 8001, box 5, file OPC Party, April–June 1963. Remarks by JPR at Quebec Govt. Dinner, 15 June 1963. According to his adviser Hugh Segal, Premier Bill Davis "had always unfairly laboured in John Robarts' shadow" when it came to his relations with Quebec. "Robarts had gone to Quebec City, held one press gallery dinner, and become the great hero and saviour of Confederation despite not doing all that much." Segal, *No Surrender*, 96.

83 *Globe and Mail*, 15 June 1963.

84 AO, RG 3-26, box 478, file Fed. Govt., CPP, 1964, no. 2. Hogan to Robarts, 9 March 1964.

85 Ibid., file Fed. Govt., CPP, General 1964–65. Gathercole to Robarts, 10 March 1964.

86 Ibid., box 489, file F-PC, 31 March–2 April 1964; Hon. J.P. Robarts, Fed. Govt. W.B. Common and A.R. Dick to Robarts, 26 March 1964.

87 Private Collection, CAR Papers, file F-PC, 1964. "Statement by the Hon. John Robarts ... March 31 1964."

88 LAC, RG 29, vol. 2114, file 23-3-6, draft minutes, "CPP, F-PC, Quebec, April 1, 1964," 3–4.

89 LAC, MG 31 D78, Peter Stursberg Papers, vol. 33, file Judy LaMarsh, 1976, interview.

90 LAC, RG 29, vol. 2114, file 23-3-6. Draft minutes, "CPP, F-PC, Quebec, April 1, 1964," 3–4.

91 Ibid, 4.

92 LAC, Stursberg Papers, vol. 33, file Tom Kent, 1977, interview.

93 Bryden, *Planners and Politicians*, 116–20. Simeon, *Federal-Provincial Diplomacy*, 56–60. Morin, *Quebec vs. Ottawa*, 8–10.

94 LAC, Pearson Papers, vol. 221, file 632.5 pt. 2. "Statement by the Hon J. Robarts ... Given before the Orders of the Day in the Ontario Legislature on Wednesday, April 15, 1964."

95 LAC, Gordon Papers, vol. 16, file Pearson, Rt. Hon. L.B., Corr. and memos. Gordon to Pearson, 15 April 1964.

96 TUA, Frost Papers, box 83, file 8. Frost to Robarts, 18 April 1964. Gordon Papers, vol. 5, file CPP. Frost to Gordon, 18 April 1964.

97 Ibid. Gordon to Frost, 21 April 1964.

98 AO, RG 3-26, box 393, file F-P Tax-Sharing Agreement, 1961–65. Pearson to Robarts, 15 Aug. 1964.

99 AO, RG 10-06, box 12, file 10-6-0-130. Treasury Department, Research and Statistics Branch. "Interim Arrangements for Contracting-Out of Various Conditional Grants and Shared-Cost Programs," Sept. 1964, 23.

100 AO, Robarts Papers, MU 7998, box 2, file Hogan, George. Hogan to Robarts, 27 Aug. 1964.

101 McDougall, *Robarts*, 133. Hunt, "The Federal-Provincial Conference of First Ministers, 1960–1976," Hunt's interview with Robarts, 25 Sept. 1978.

102 AO, RG 75-21-0-20, Cabinet Office: Cabinet Agenda files, box 3. H.I. Macdonald, "The Role of Ontario in the Formation of National Policy," 8 March 1974.

103 AO, RG 3-26, box 490, file F-PC, Charlottetown, 1 Sept. 1964. Pearson to Robarts 19 Aug. 1964.

104 Ibid.

105 LAC, Gordon Papers, vol. 6, file Constitutional Amendment, 1964–68. "Constitutional Amendment in Canada," Cabinet document no. 385-64, 25 Aug. 1964.

106 Ibid.

107 AO, RG 3-26, box 490, file F-PC, Sept. 1964, Mr. Robarts's file. W.B. Common, Dep. AG, to Robarts, 17 Aug. 1964.

108 LAC, Gordon Papers. "Constitutional Amendment in Canada," Cabinet document no. 385-64, 25 Aug. 1964.

109 "PM Stresses Need for National Unity," *Globe and Mail*, 2 Sept. 1964.

110 *Chronicle-Herald*, 3 Sept. 1964. *Globe and Mail*, 3 Sept. 1964.

111 LAC, Gordon Papers, vol. 6, file Constitutional Amendment, 1964–68. Guy Favreau to Cabinet Cttee on F-PR, 14 Sept. 1964.

112 "Charlottetown Folly," *Globe and Mail*, 5 Sept. 1964. AO, RG 3-26, box 490, file F-PC, Sept. 1964, Mr. Robarts's file. W.B. Common to Robarts, 17 Aug. 1964.

113 AO, RG 3-26, box 484, file Constitution of Canada, Amendment of, General. Nov. 61–Dec. 64. Wishart to C.R. Magone, 3 Sept. 1964.

114 LAC, Gordon Papers, vol. 6, file Constitutional Amendment, 1964–68. Cabinet document no. 434/64, 30 Sept. 1964.

115 Ibid., Bryce to Walter Gordon, 25 Sept. 1964.

116 See AO, RG 3-26, box 478, file Fed. Govt., CPP, 1964, no. 1. L.E. Coward, memo re: Telephone call from Tom Kent, 29 Sept. 1964. TUA, Frost Papers, box 83, file 8. Frost to Robarts, 1 Oct. 1964. In this, Frost assures Robarts that "it is not a case of Ontario following along reluctantly on Fed. proposals." AO, RG 3-26, box 480, file CPP, Pearson, LB, Fed. Govt., Nov. 61–Dec. 65. Robarts to Pearson, 2 Oct. 1964.

117 AO, RG 3-26, box 484, file Constitution of Canada, Amendment, General, Nov. 61–Dec. 64. Wishart to Robarts, 8 Oct. 1964.

118 LAC, Gordon Papers, vol. 6, file Constitutional Amendment, 1964–68. Record of Cabinet Decision, 8 Oct. 1964.

119 "Provinces Have Won 'Sacred Guarantees,'" *Toronto Daily Star*, 15 Oct. 1964.

120 LAC, Pearson Papers, vol. 58, file 301, Govt., Constitution, Personal and Confidential. J.J. Connolley to Pearson, 15 Oct. 1964.

121 Simeon, *Federal-Provincial Diplomacy*, 68.

122 AO, RG 3-26, vol. 393, file F-P Tax-Sharing Agreements, Nov. 61–Dec. 65. Minutes of mtg on Tax Structure Cttee and F-PC, 9 Oct. 1964.

123 LAC, Pearson Papers, vol. 221, file 632.5 pt. 3. Pearson to Robarts, 18 Nov. 1964.

124 Private Collection, CAR Papers, clipping files, "Further Ottawa-Quebec Private Deals Won't Be Recognized by Ontario," *Chronicle-Herald*, 23 Oct. 1964. See also "Leading Canada toward the Abyss," *Province*, 24 Oct. 1964.

6 "Profound Changes in the Character of Canadian Federalism"

1 Simeon, *Federal-Provincial Diplomacy*, 51.

2 AO, RG 75-21-0-20, box 3. H. Ian Macdonald, "Role of Ontario in National Policy Formation," Carleton University, 8 March 1974.

3 McLarty, "Organizing for a Federal-Provincial Fiscal Policy," 414.

4 Simeon, *Federal-Provincial Diplomacy*, 54.

5 Kent, *Public Purpose*, 276.

6 AO, RG 3-26, box 490, file F-PC, Ottawa, 13–16 Oct. 1964. Economics Branch, Dept. of Economics and Development, "Notes for the F-P Tax Structure Cttee," 29 July 1964.

7 Russell, *Constitutional Odyssey*, 75–6.

8 Private Collection, Donald Stevenson Papers. "Points for use in remarks to seminar of Queen's Institute of Intergovernmental Affairs," 9 April 1984.

9 LAC, RG 19, vol. 4769, file 5710-06/65. Notes on a Discussion of the Intergovernmental Aspects of Implementing Fiscal Policy in Canada, 27–28 Aug. 1965.

10 AO, RG 3-48, box 1, file Tax Cttees. Minutes of mtg of cttee on F-P fiscal relations and tax structure, 13 Oct. 1965.

11 Ibid. Minutes of mtg re: Tax Structure Cttee, 6 Dec. 1965.

12 AO, RG 27-39, Management Board of Cabinet: Office of the Secretary, F-P Matters Files, box 8, file Feb. and before 1966, Statement by Ontario Treasurer. Submission by the Treasurer of Ontario to the 2nd F-PC of Finance and Treasury Ministers on Economic Problems, 9 Dec. 1965, 1.

13 Ibid., 1–2.

14 Ibid., 2. On the Rowell-Sirois Report, see Ferguson and Wardhaugh, "'Impossible Conditions of Inequality,'" 551–84.

15 AO, RG 27-39, Submission by the Treasurer of Ontario to the 2nd F-PC, 9 Dec. 1965, 3, 4.
16 Ibid., 5.
17 Ibid., 5–6.
18 Ibid., 6.
19 AO, RG 3-26, box 394, file F-P Tax-Sharing, Tax Structure Cttee, Dec. 65, Treasury. Macdonald to Robarts, re: Mtg of Ministers of Finance and Tax Structure Cttee, 20 Dec. 1965.
20 Ibid.
21 Taylor, *Health Insurance and Canadian Public Policy*, 340–1.
22 AO, RG 3, Series A-13-1, box 135, file Medical Insurance Cttee no. 1. R.A. Farrell to J.K. Reynolds, 4 Jan. 1965.
23 Quoted in MacDonald, *Happy Warrior*, 209.
24 AO, RG 3, Series A-13-1 box 135, file Medical Insurance Cttee 1. Report of the Special Caucus SubCttee Appointed to Review the Medical Health Insurance Act, 13 April 1965.
25 AO, Robarts Papers, MU 8007, box 11, file Rohmer, Richard, 1962–71. Handwritten memo, Rohmer to Robarts, April 1965.
26 Vaughan, *Aggressive in Pursuit*, 130.
27 AO, RG 3-26, box 491, file F-PC, 19–22 July 1965. Pearson to Robarts, 9 April 1965. LAC, RG 19, vol. 4720, file 5526-04(65/1)-1 pt. 1. Draft (by A.W. Johnson), Pearson to premiers, 12 May 1965.
28 Private Collection, Walter Gordon Papers. Bryce to Gordon, "The Horrors Ahead," 25 June 1965.
29 Kent, *Public Purpose*, 366.
30 LAC, RG 19, vol. 4854, file 5508-02 pt. 1. Johnson to R.B. Bryce, 16 July 1965.
31 LAC, RG 2, Series A-5-a vol. 6271. Cabinet conclusions, 19 July 1965. On the original four principles that the federal Liberals adopted, to which were subsequently added "compulsory" participation, see Taylor, *Health Insurance*, 363–5. Bryden, *Planners and Politicians*, 141–3.
32 Private Collection, CAR Papers, file July conference briefs, etc. 1965. F-PC, opening statement by the PM of Canada, 19 July 1965, 25.
33 Kent, *Public Purpose*, 369.
34 AO, Gathercole Papers, MU 5311, file Corr., 1965–71. Ontario Advisory Cttee on Confederation: terms of reference, 5 Jan. 1965.
35 Ibid.
36 Ibid. Robarts to Gathercole, 5 Jan. 1965.
37 The original committee members were Alexander Brady (Political Science, University of Toronto); John Conway (Humanities, York University); Donald

Creighton (History, University of Toronto); Richard Dillon (Engineering, University of Western Ontario); Eugene Forsey (Canadian Labour Congress and Carleton University); Paul Fox (Political Science, University of Toronto); George Gathercole (Vice-Chair, Ontario Hydro); Bora Laskin (Law, University of Toronto); W.R. Lederman (Law, Queen's University); C.R. Magone (Lawyer); Lucien Matté (President, University of Sudbury); John Meisel (Political Studies, Queen's University); R.C. McIvor (Economics, McMaster University); Edward McWhinney (Law, University of Toronto); Harvey Perry (Canadian Tax Foundation); Roger Seguin (lawyer); T.H.B. Symons (President, Trent University). [See AO, Gathercole Papers, MU 5311, file correspondence, 1965–71. Ontario Advisory Cttee on Confederation: terms of reference, 5 Jan. 1965.]

38 Interview, H. Ian Macdonald, 25 Jan. 2007.
39 AO, Gathercole Papers, MU 5325, Verbatim report of the proceedings of the Ontario Advisory Cttee on Confederation mtg, 19 March 1965, 6.
40 Ibid.
41 Russell, *Constitutional Odyssey*, 73–4; Thomson, *Jean Lesage*, 230.
42 LAC, Pearson Papers, vol. 58, file 301, Govt., Constitution, Corr. with Provincial Premiers. Lesage to Pearson, 31 March 1965.
43 Ibid.
44 Ibid. Pearson to Guy Favreau, 6 April 1965.
45 Ibid. Robertson to Pearson, 6 April 1965.
46 Ibid. Pearson to Robertson, 17 April 1965.
47 AO, Gathercole Papers, MU 5325, Verbatim report of the Ontario Advisory Cttee on Confederation mtg, 30 April 1965.
48 AO, RG 3-26, box 491, file F-PC, 18–22 July 1965. Macdonald to Robarts, 26 April 1965.
49 AO, Gathercole Papers, MU 5325, Verbatim report of proceedings of the Ontario Advisory Cttee on Confederation mtg, 17 Sept. 1965, 9–10.
50 Ibid.
51 Interview, Gary Posen, 27 Jan. 2007.
52 AO, Gathercole Papers, MU 5311, Forsey to Macdonald, 21 April 1966.
53 Struthers, *Limits of Affluence*, 211–16.
54 Quoted in ibid., 217.
55 Scott Young, "The War on Poverty," *Globe and Mail*, 29 Oct. 1965, 7. See also Splane, "Social Policy-Making in the Government of Canada," 227–30.
56 AO, RG 3-26, vol. 491, file F-PC, 19–22 July 1965, Gen., Fed. Govt. LaMarsh to Louis Cecile, 21 April 1965. See also Little, *"No Car, No Radio, No Liquor Permit,"* 141–2.
57 AO, RG 3-26, LaMarsh to Cecile, 21 April 1965.

58 Ibid. Band to Robarts, 14 May 1965.

59 Ibid. Macdonald to Robarts, 3 May 1965.

60 AO, RG 3-48, box 1, file Mtgs re: medicare. Mtg re: Federal Medicare Proposals, 29 July 1965.

61 AO, RG 3-48, box 1, file Mtgs re: Medicare. Mtg re: Federal Medical Services Plan, 11 Aug. 1965.

62 LAC, Pearson Papers, vol. 176, file 360.62, Provincial Governments, Interprovincial Conferences, Ministers of Health. Robarts to Pearson, 20 Aug. 1965.

63 AO, RG 3-26, box 133, file Medical Insurance, Health, Jan. 1964–Dec. 1965. Coward to Robarts, 20 Aug. 1965.

64 AO, RG 3-48, box 1, file Mtgs re: Medicare. Mtg re: Medical Services Insurance Plan, 26 Aug. 1965

65 LAC, Pearson Papers, vol. 176, file 360.62. Pearson to Robarts, 16 Sept. 1965.

66 In conversations between Tom Kent of the PMO and Colin Brown and Carman Naylor representing the Ontario insurance industry, the latter two reported that "Kent did not rule out the possibility of existing carriers participating in the Medicare plan." In fact, despite having a reputation for being "rather socialistic in his ideas," Kent seemed to the insurance men to be quite amenable to their position. "In general," they reported, "he endeavored to give us the impression that the Federal Government is taking a very relaxed and flexible position on Medicare, and giving the provinces considerable freedom to work out the details of their plan." There was considerable suspicion of this view among those more familiar with Kent: Matthew Dymond commented that "it is very interesting to read of the impressions gained of Mr. Kent's flexibility, particularly when one has knowledge and experience of the inflexibility of his view." [AO, RG 3-26, box 138, file Medical Services, Insurance Council, Nov. 1961–Dec. 1965. Report of Mtg of Colin Brown and C.A. Naylor with Mr. Tom Kent in Ottawa on 13 Oct. 1965; Dymond to J.K. Reynolds, 27 Oct. 1965.]

67 AO, RG 3-48, box 1, file Mtgs re: Medicare. Mtg re: Medicare, Conference of F-P Ministers of Health, 14 Sept. 1965.

68 AO, RG 3-26, box 133, file Medical Insurance, Health, Jan. 1964–Dec. 1965. Macdonald to Robarts, 5 Oct. 1965.

69 Ibid. Gordon, memo to self, 5 Dec. 1965.

70 LAC, Gordon Papers, file Cabinet Resignation. A.F. Gordon to Stephen Clarkson, 2 Dec. 1965. On the shifting Liberal power structure, see Bryden, *Planners and Politicians*, 145–63.

71 AO, RG 3-26, box 133, file Medical Insurance, Health, Jan. 1964–Dec 1965. Coward to Robarts, 20 Aug. 1965.

72 AO, Gathercole Papers, MU 5311, file Notices and Agendas, 1965–66. "Report from the Sub Cttee on Cultural Matters," 21 Jan. 1966.

73 LAC, Gordon Papers, vol. 6, file Constitutional Amendment, 1964–68. Pearson to Lesage, 26 Jan. 1966.

74 Ibid.

75 AO, RG 9-79, Subject files of the Executive Assistant to Chief Economist H.I. Macdonald, box 7, file Stevenson. "Summary notes taken on the report of the economic and fiscal subcommittee," 21 Jan. 1966.

76 Ibid.

77 AO, Gathercole Papers, MU 2326. Minutes of mtg of the Ontario Advisory Cttee on Confederation, 18 Feb. 1966.

78 AO, RG 9-79, box 7, file, Sub-Cttee on Finance and Economics. "Proposed Resolution on Postponement of Renewal of Financial Arrangements," n.d. (ca. spring 1966). AO, RG 3-48, box 1 B397411, file Tax Cttees. Mtg of Cttee on F-PR and on Tax Structure, 16 Mar. 1966.

79 AO, RG 3-26, vol. 393, file F-P Tax-Sharing Agreements, Jan.–Dec. 1966. Macdonald to Robarts, 21 March 1966.

80 Ibid. Notes from a mtg, 22 April 1966.

81 Ibid.

82 Ibid., Treasury, Jan.–Dec. 1966. Macdonald to Robarts, 22 July 1966.

83 AO, Robarts Papers, MU 8007, box 11, file Rathbun, W. A., 1966–67. Bill Rathbun, "Politics – Three Levels Commentary," 12 June 1966.

84 Ibid.

85 LAC, Bryce Papers, vol. 9, file Notes made of conversations with minister of finance and R.B. Bryce, n.d. and 1963–70. A.W. Johnson to R.B. Bryce, 21 June 1966.

86 AO, RG 3-26, box 393, file F-P Tax-Sharing Agreements, Treasury, Jan.–Dec. 1966. Macdonald to Robarts, 6 July 1966.

87 Ibid. Macdonald to Robarts, 8 July 1966.

88 Ibid. F-P Tax Negotiations, Ontario Position, n.d. (ca. 25 July 1966).

89 Ibid. Macdonald to Robarts, 14 July 1966.

90 AO, RG 3-26, box 493, file F-PC on Taxation, Ottawa, 24–28 Oct. 1966. "Summaries and Implications of the Provincial and Federal Statements… 14–15 Sept. 1966."

91 Ibid.

92 AO, RG 3-48, box 1 B 397411, file Tax Cttees. Mtg re: Tax Structure Cttee Mtg, 23 Sept. 1966.

93 Ibid.

94 Ibid.

95 Ibid.

96 Quoted in Simeon, *Federal-Provincial Diplomacy*, 84–5.

97 LAC, RG 19, vol. 4720, file 5515-04(66/1)-1 pt. 1. Ed Gallant to A.W. Johnson, 8 Nov. 1966.
98 AO, RG 3-26, vol. 466, file Ontario Advisory Cttee on Confederation, Jan.–June 1967. Macdonald to Robarts, 13 May 1966.
99 AO, Gathercole Papers, MU 5313, Series B, file Source Papers 1966. Charles Beer's notes on NDP Conference: Ontario's Role in Confederation, 24 Sept. 1966.
100 Simeon, *Federal-Provincial Diplomacy*, 84.

7 "See if We Can't Amend the Marriage Contract"

1 Coates, *Night of the Knives*.
2 LAC, Richard Bell Papers, vol. 109, file Camp, Dalton K. Camp to Bell, 28 April 1967.
3 Stevens, *Player*, 160–88; Stevens, *Stanfield*, 161–9; Smith, *Rogue Tory*, 543–8.
4 AO, Robarts Papers, MU 7997, box 1, file Diefenbaker, John, 1965 and 1967. Robarts to Diefenbaker, 11 May 1967.
5 LAC, Gordon Papers, vol. 15, file 8. MacEachen to members of the Ontario caucus, 22 March 1967. AO, RG 6-14, UB 144-45, file F-PC of Welfare Ministers. Andrew Murray, "Conference on Ministers of Welfare," 29 Jan. 1968.
6 AO, RG 3-26, box 134, file Medical Insurance, Health Jan.–Dec. 66. Dymond to MacEachen, 27 April 1967.
7 Ibid. MacEachen to Dymond, 11 May 1967.
8 TUA, Frost Papers, box 76, file 8, Political Correspondence 1967. Frost to Stanfield, 1 Dec. 1967.
9 See Bryden, "Other Battle," 75–92.
10 AO, RG 27-39, box 1, file Royal Commission on Taxation. Macdonald to Robarts, 1 March 1967.
11 AO, RG 3-26, box 395, file F-P Tax-Sharing Agreements, Jan.–Dec. 1967. Research and Statistics Branch, Treasury Dept., "Some Impressions of the Discussion re: The Carter Report … on June 13 and 14, 1967," 2.
12 AO, RG 6-14, vol. 82, file Cabinet Cttee, 1967. Macdonald to C.S. MacNaughton, 23 May 1967.
13 AO, RG 3-26, "Some Impressions of the Discussion re: The Carter Report," 9.
14 Ibid. Macdonald to Robarts, 23 June 1967.
15 LAC, Gordon Papers, vol. 16, file Pearson, Cabinet document 761/67. "Summary of views expressed by provincial ministers of finance," 20 Nov. 1967.
16 AO, Gathercole Papers, MU 5311, file Corr., 1965–71. Pearson to Robarts, 26 Jan. 1967.

17 CAR Papers, Robarts to Pearson, 1 Feb. 1967.

18 Ontario Legislative Assembly, *Debates*, 25 Jan. 1967.

19 AO, RG 9-79, box 2, file Confederation of Tomorrow Conference (hereafter CoTC). Johnson to Robarts, 16 March 1967.

20 AO, RG 3-26, box 517, file Provinces, Quebec, 1966–67. Macdonald to Robarts, 20 March 1967.

21 See, e.g., AO, RG 9-79, box 2, file CoTC. Mtg of the 1st plenary session of the planning cttee, 25 Aug. 1967; Progress report of the agenda sub-cttee, 5 Sept. 1967; Minutes of the 2nd plenary mtg, 5 Sept. 1967; 2nd progress report of the agenda sub-cttee, 11 Sept. 1967; Minutes of the 3rd plenary mtg, 11 Sept. 1967; Minutes of the 4th plenary mtg, 26 Sept. 1967.

22 AO, RG 3-26, box 444, file CoTC, Background Papers, 1967. Notes on a mtg held in Winnipeg, 10 Oct. 1967.

23 Ibid. Greathed, "Notes on a mtg with officials in Regina," 17 Oct. 1967.

24 AO, RG 9-79, box 2, file CoTC. Minutes of the 7th plenary mtg of the planning cttee, 24 Oct. 1967.

25 Ibid. Greathed, "Notes on a mtg with E.C. Manning of Alberta," 17 Oct. 1967.

26 Ibid.

27 AO, RG 3-26, box 444, file CoTC, Ontario Govt., Sept.–Oct. 1967. Posen to Stevenson, 16 Oct. 1967.

28 Ibid. Clarkson to file, "CoTC," 16 Oct. 1967.

29 Ibid.

30 Ibid. "Notes on a mtg held with officials in Halifax," 31 Oct. 1967.

31 AO, RG 9-79, box 2, file CoTC. "CoTC – Team Visit to Quebec," 26 Oct. 1967.

32 Ibid. Greathed to Stevenson, 31 Oct. 1967.

33 AO, RG 3-26, box 444, file CoTC, Ontario Govt., Nov.–Dec. 1967. Mtg of Confederation Cttee, 10 Nov. 1967.

34 AO, RG 9-79, box 2, file CoTC. Minutes of the 10th plenary mtg of the planning cttee, 9 Nov. 1967.

35 LAC, Gordon Papers, vol. 16, file 13. Gordon to Pearson, 22 Sept. 1967. On the matter of Gordon's deteriorating relationship with the PM, see Azzi, "Pearson, the Liberal Party and Economic Nationalism," 110–16. Smith, *Gentle Patriot*, 360–4.

36 Interview, H. Ian Macdonald. 18 Dec. 1996.

37 Private Collection, CAR Papers, Press Releases, "Opening Statement by the Hon. Daniel Johnson, Prime Minister of Quebec, to the CoTC," 27 Nov. 1967.

38 Gordon Pape, "Confederation Conference: Premiers Badly Divided," *Gazette*

(Montreal), 28 Nov. 1967. Of the four original provinces, Ontario was the least firm in its commitment to major constitutional change, a position in keeping with that advanced by the Ontario Advisory Cttee on Confederation. See Robarts's opening statement [Govt. of Ontario, *Preliminary Statement*, CoTC, Toronto, 27–30 Nov. 1967]. New Brunswick Premier Louis Robichaud, on the other hand, was "the most emotional voice heard in pleading with the rest of Canada to take action before it's too late to stem the separatist tide in Quebec." [*Gazette*, 1 Dec. 1967.]

39 Private Collection, CAR Papers, Notes on the minutes of the CoTC, 29 Nov. 1967. Gordon Pape, "Johnson Relaxes Hard Line Policy," *Gazette*, 30 Nov. 1967.

40 AO, RG 3-26, box 444, file CoTC, Ontario Govt., Nov.–Dec. 1967. Stevenson, "Follow-up on the Constitutional Questions Raised," 4 Dec. 1967.

41 AO, Robarts Papers, Series MU 7998, box 2, file Goldenberg, Carl, 1967–69. Goldenberg to Robarts, 4 Dec. 1967.

42 LAC, RG 19, vol. 4720, file 5517-04(68/1)-1. A.W. Johnson, "Summary of a talk on the CoTC," 4 Dec. 1967.

43 Ibid.

44 Ibid.

45 AO, RG 6-14, box 113, file Constitutional: F-PC, Feb. 1968. Gary Posen to Ed Greathed, 13 Dec. 1967.

46 Ibid.

47 Ibid. Posen and Metcalfe, "How Ontario might approach the F-PC called for the beginning of Feb.," n.d. (ca. mid-Dec. 1967).

48 Ontario Legislative Assembly, *Debates*, 27 Feb. 1968, 263.

49 AO, RG 3-26, vol. 466, file Ontario Advisory Cttee on Confederation, July–Dec. 1967. Macdonald to Robarts, 19 Dec. 1967.

50 LAC, RG 19, 4720, file 5517-04(68-1)-1. Cabinet document 10-68, 9 Jan. 1968.

51 Ibid.

52 AO, RG 6-14, vol. 113, file Constitutional: F-PC, Feb. 1968. Greathed to Stevenson, 11 Jan. 1968. LAC, RG 19, vol. 4720, file 5517-04(68/1)-1. A.W. Johnson to R.G. Robertson et. al., 4 Jan. 1968.

53 AO, RG 6-14, vol. 113, file Constitutional: F-PC, Feb. 1968. Macdonald to Robarts, 31 Jan. 1968.

54 Ibid. "Major points of the opening statement by the Hon. John Robarts ... Feb. 5th 1968."

55 Ibid.

56 Jack Cahill, "Robarts hailed for 'saving' nation," *Toronto Daily Star*, 8 Feb. 1968, 12.

57 See "Johnson opposes forcing provinces to turn bilingual," *Toronto Daily Star*,
    8 Feb. 1968, 12. (This is also the heart of Kenneth McRoberts's argument
    in *Misconceiving Canada*: that Trudeau's brand of bilingualism was not at all
    what Quebec was seeking in the 1960s, and gave rise to increasing separatist
    sentiment in the following decades.) Anthony Westell, "Manning Warns of a
    Munich," *Globe and Mail*, 6 Feb. 1968, 1.
58 AO, RG 6-14, box 116, file Constitutional Conference, Continuing Cttee,
    1968. Posen, "Report of the Mtg of the Continuing Cttee ... July 25–26 1968."
59 Ibid., box 110, file Propositions, Constitutional Cttee of Officials. Greathed
    to Reynolds, 18 July 1968.
60 Ibid., box 116. Posen, "Report of the Mtg ... July 25–26 1968."
61 Peter C. Newman, "The Impact of Television," *Montreal Star*, 7 Feb. 1968.
62 AO, Robarts Papers, MU 7998, box 2, file Johnson, Daniel. Robarts to Mde.
    Johnson, 5 March 1969.
63 AO, RG 3-42, AO, RG 3-42, box 3, file Material for visit to Montreal and
    Ottawa. "Report on the Continuing Cttee of Officials of the Constitutional
    Conference," 24 Oct: 1968.
64 AO, Robarts Papers, MU 7998, box 2, file Frost, Leslie. J.K. Reynolds to
    Robarts, 26 Nov. 1968.
65 LAC, RG 19, vol. 4721, file 5517-04(69/1)-1 pt. 1. A.W. Johnson to Turner,
    31 Jan. 1969.
66 Ibid.
67 Ibid.
68 Ibid.
69 Ibid.
70 Ibid.
71 AO, RG 3-42, box 2, file The Hon. J.P. Robarts. Memo re: Govt. of Ontario
    Organization for Constitutional Review, 16 May 1969.
72 AO, RG 6-14, UB 126-127. Greathed to Stevenson, 10 July 1969.
73 AO, RG 3-26, box 395, file Finance and Economics, Jan.–June 1969. Rath-
    bun to Robarts, 8 Apr. 1969.
74 AO, RG 3-42, box 2, file F-PC, Constitution, June 1969, Fed. Govt.. "The
    Ontario Position on the Spending Power," 6 June 1969. CAR Papers, Govt.
    of Ontario, "Intergovernmental Finance and Ontario's White Paper on
    Provincial-Municipal Taxation Reform," 6 June 1969. AO, RG 6-14, UB
    126-127, Constitutional Conference Papers, "Progress Report of the Cttee of
    Ministers on the Judiciary," 30 May 1969, and "Progress Report of the Cttee
    of Ministers on Fundamental Rights," 30 May 1969.
75 AO, RG 3-42, box 2, file The Hon. John Robarts, PM. Stevenson's handwrit-
    ten notes on "PM's Conf ., 11 June 1969."

76 Trudeau, "Quebec and the Constitutional Problem," 3–51. McRoberts, *Misconceiving Canada*, 60–9; English, *Just Watch Me*, 8–9.

77 AO, RG 6-14, UB 130-131. "Draft letter to the Hon. P.E. Trudeau from the Hon. J.P. Robarts," 3 Nov. 1969.

78 AO, RG 3-26, box 514, file Trudeau, Hon Pierre E., Jan.–Dec. 1969, Fed. Govt. Macdonald to C.S. MacNaughton, 3 Sept. 1969.

79 AO, RG 3-42, box 1. Dept. of Treasury and Economics, "Background material for the mtg of F-P Prime Ministers and Premiers, 16–17 Feb. 1970."

80 House of Commons, *Debates*, 15 Oct. 1970, 148.

81 AO, RG 3-42, box 1, file F-P Constitutional, 14–16 Sept. 1970. Posen, "The Process of Constitutional Review," n.d. (ca. Aug. 1970).

82 AO, Gathercole Papers, MU 5319, file Source Papers, Conferences, F-PC, Sept. 1970. Notes for the use of the Hon. John Robarts on the constitutional review process, 14–15 Sept. 1970.

83 AO, RG 3-105, Office of the Premier: Premier William G. Davis Cttee Files, box 3, 1970, file CCO, Constitutional Conference, Nov.–Dec. 1970. Greathed to Stevenson, 19 Nov. 1970.

84 Ibid. Stevenson to Macdonald, 20 Nov. 1970.

85 Ibid. Greathed to Stevenson, 19 Nov. 1970.

86 AO, RG 3-42, box 2, file Robarts. Notes in Robarts's handwriting, n.d. (ca. 1971).

87 For an introduction to the FLQ crisis, see Fournier, *FLQ: The Anatomy of an Underground Movement*, and Tetley, *October Crisis, 1970.*

88 Oliver, "Ontario," in Saywell, ed., *Canadian Annual Review of Politics and Public Affairs, 1971*, 99–103.

89 AO, RG 3-26, box 276, file Gen., Canadian Unity, Jan.–Dec. 1970. Robarts to Mrs. Dempster, 21 April 1970. AO, RG 3-59, box 1, 1971, file F-PC, Constitution, Victoria. Translation, "W. Davis Draws away from the role of mediator adopted by Mr. Robarts," article from *Le Droit*, 8 May 1971.

90 AO, RG 50-33, Treasury Department: Fiscal Policy Planning Branch, vol. 28, file F-P Mtgs. Stevenson to Macdonald, 6 Jan. 1971.

91 AO, RG 3-26, vol. 485, file Fed. Govt., Constitution Corr., Jan.–Feb. 1970. Michael Hunter (EA to Turner) to Reynolds, 22 Jan. 1971. AO, RG 3-59, box 1, 1971, file F-PC, Constitution, Victoria. "Rough Notes of a mtg in Toronto on April 13 of Ontario ministers with the Hon. John Turner." n.d.; box 2. Macdonald to Robarts, 5 Feb. 1971.

92 Ibid.

93 Ibid.

94 Ibid. Turner to Robarts, 29 Jan. 1971.

95 AO, RG 3-49, Office of the Premier: Premier William G. Davis Central

Registry Files, box 9, file FP 7-1, F-P Affairs Secretariat, 1971, Organization. Macdonald to McKeough, 17 March 1971 (courtesy of Peter Oliver
estate).

96 Ibid. Macdonald to McKeough, 1 April 1971 (courtesy of Peter Oliver
estate).

97 AO, RG 3-59, box 2, 1971, file F-PC, Constitution, Victoria. "Rough notes
of a Mtg ... with Turner," 13 April 1971; box 1, file Background material ...
Victoria. "Mtg in Toronto on April 13 ... with Turner," April 1971.

98 AO, RG 3-59, box 8, file FP 4 Constitution 1971 (March to May). Macdonald to Reynolds, 22 April 1971.

99 Ibid., box 2, 1971, file Background Material ... Victoria. F-P Affairs Secretariat, "The Constitutional Review," May 1971.

100 Ibid., box 1, 1971, file F-PC, Constitution, Victoria. Turner to Davis, 18 May
1971.

101 *Montreal Star*, 7 April 1971, editorial, quoted in AO, RG 3-49, box 8, file FP
4, Constitution 1971. Greathed to Stevenson, 19 May 1971.

102 Ibid.

103 AO, RG 3-59, box 1, file Summaries and Proceedings, F-PC, Victoria, 1971.
F-P Affairs Secretariat, "A Peek at Victoria," 3 June 1971.

104 Ibid.

105 Dominique Clift, "Confederation '71: Quebec," in *Montreal Star*, 12 June
1971.

106 Saywell, "Parliament and Politics," in *CAR, 1971*, 50.

107 Blake, "Intergovernmental Relations," 216.

108 Ibid., 218–22.

109 Saywell, "Parliament and Politics," *CAR, 1971*, 48–9.

110 Ibid., 52.

111 Blake, "Intergovernmental Relations," 222.

112 Private Collection, CAR Papers, "Notes for a Statement on Social Policy by
the Prime Minister of Ontario," n.d.

113 Saywell, "Parliament and Politics," *CAR, 1971*, 60.

114 RG 3-49, box 8, file FP 4-4, Quebec 1971 Constitution. W.A. Rathbun to
J.K. Reynolds, 24 June 1971.

115 Saywell, "Parliament and Politics," *CAR, 1971*, 42.

8 "Disentanglement" and Mega-intergovernmental Politics in Ontario

1 There has been relatively little scholarly attention paid to the Victoria
debacle in Canadian constitutional history. See, Russell, *Constitutional
Odyssey*, 77–91; Hurley, *Amending Canada's Constitution*, 35–41. Excellent

contemporary accounts can be found in Simeon, *Federal-Provincial Diplomacy,* 88–123, and Saywell, "Parliament and Politics," in Saywell, ed., *Canadian Annual Review of Politics and Public Affairs, 1971.*

2 AO, RG 6-32-2, container 39, file F-P Continuing Cttee on Fiscal and Economic Matters, 14–15 June 1972. Statement by the Hon. W. Darcy McKeough, 31 Jan. 1972, 2.

3 Ibid.

4 Ibid.

5 AO, RG 6-77, DoF: F-P Fiscal Program Files, TB 2026, file Cost-Sharing Welfare. Duncan [Allen] to T.M. Russell, 11 Jan. 1972.

6 AO, RG 50-33, box 26, file F-P Series, Minister's mtg with Mr. Turner, 11–12 March 1972. "Notes for Mr. McKeough's mtg with Mr. Turner," n.d.

7 Ibid. Mtg of Mr. Turner and Mr. McKeough, 11 July 1972. Stevenson handwritten notes, 11 July 1972.

8 Ibid. "Analysis of Federal Proposal for Sharing Health Costs," n.d.

9 Ibid. McKeough to Turner, 19 April 1972.

10 Ibid. McKeough memo to file, 14 March 1972.

11 Ibid. Stevenson to McKeough, 9 March 1972.

12 Ibid. Stevenson memo to file, 14 March 1972.

13 AO, RG 3-49, T 77-740, box 21, file P & A/ EN 6-3-1, Gas Pricing, Environment 1972. McKeough to Don Getty, Alberta Minister of Federal and Intergovernmental Affairs, 11 Feb. 1972 (courtesy of Peter Oliver estate).

14 *Globe and Mail,* 17 Nov. 1972, B1.

15 AO, RG 3-49, T 77-740, box 21, file P and A/EN 6-3-1. McKeough to Leo Bernier, Minister of Natural Resources, 17 Nov. 1972 (courtesy of Peter Oliver estate).

16 Oliver, "Ontario," in Saywell, ed., *Canadian Annual Review of Politics and Public Affairs, 1972,* 153.

17 AO, RG 3-49, T 77-740, box 21, file P and A/EN 6-3-1. McKeough to Davis, 15 Dec. 1972 (courtesy of Peter Oliver estate).

18 Ibid., box 10, file EX 3 Policy and Priorities BD 1972 (courtesy Peter Oliver estate). Mtg of the Cttee of Advisors, Report, 16 Oct. 1972.

19 Ibid., T 77-740, box 21. McKeough to Davis, 15 Dec. 1972.

20 Ibid.

21 In his editorial in *Le Devoir* (7 July 1972), Claude Ryan addressed the evolution of the Ontario-Quebec axis through the Robarts and early Davis years. He maintained that however friendly Robarts had been to various Quebec premiers, "due to its wealth, its geographical position, its large population and its economic interests, Ontario is prevented from behaving 'as a province' and is held to identify itself with the national objectives of Canada as a whole. Quebec, because of its social and cultural characteristics, very natu-

rally adopts a distinctive attitude, often even a dissident one, in its relations with the central authority. Such is not the case with Ontario: even when its immediate interests and its convictions suggest the opposite, Ontario feels obligated to support the central authority on questions of major impor-tance." On the difference between Robarts's and Davis's relationship with Quebec, see also Segal, *No Surrender*, 96.

22 AO, RG 50-33, box 26, file F-P, Ontario-Quebec, mtg on Tax Sharing. Brief Notes on Ontario-Quebec Common Interests re: Fiscal Relationship, 9 Nov. 1972.

23 Ibid. "The Constitutional Review," Nov. 1972.

24 Ibid. Stevenson to Russell, 17 Nov. 1972; Ploeger to Russell, 21 Nov. 1972; "Mtg with Officials of the Quebec Govt. on Tax Sharing with the Fed. Govt," 7 Dec. 1972.

25 TUA, Frost Papers, box 83, file 2. Frost to Stanfield, 5 Feb. 1973.

26 Oliver, "Ontario," in *CAR, 1973*, 113–14. AO, RG 75-14, Cabinet Office: Minutes, vol. 4, file Minutes 30/73, 16 May 1973.

27 CAR Papers, Opening Statement by The Hon. William G. Davis, 22 Jan. 1974.

28 Saywell, "Parliament and Politics," in Saywell, ed. *Canadian Annual Review, 1974*, 96.

29 See ibid. 98–107, for a review of the correspondence between the two levels of government.

30 AO, Westcott Papers, F-2094-4-1-196, Prime Ministers Conference. Greathed to Westcott, notes on mtg re: premiers' conference, 13 March 1974.

31 AO, RG 6-77, Acc. 32779, TB 2038, file Loose Material. Stevenson to Rendell Dick, 30 Aug. 1974.

32 Ibid.

33 Ibid. Rendell Dick to Richard Dillon, 18 Nov. 1974.

34 AO, Westcott Papers, F-2094-4-1, file Conference of First Ministers, 1974. 15th Annual Premiers Conference, 12–13 Sept. 1974: Ontario Briefing Material, 19.

35 AO, RG 58-9, Ministry of Intergovernmental Affairs, F-P Relations Branch, box 12, file FD 16, IGA. Office of IGA, "Report on Intergovernmental Rela-tions, 1974," Dec. 1974, 1.

36 Ibid., 8–9.

37 Ibid., 10.

38 Ibid., 13.

39 AO, RG 6-77, Acc. 32779, TB 2043, file Loose Material. Stevenson notes on mtg between McKeough and MacDonald, 8 Oct. 1975; Posen to Greathed, 30 Jan. 1975.

40 AO, RG 3-49, T 80-293, box 21, file P & A/ EG 7-2-1, Pricing Oil, June–April

1975, Liquid fuels (courtesy of Peter Oliver estate). B. Rynard to Davis, 10 April 1975.

41 Ibid. Davis to Rynard, 21 April 1975.

42 Ibid. Nixon Notes for Address to Kiwanis Club of Ottawa, 27 June 1975.

43 AO, RG 6-77 Acc. 32779, TB 2038, file Loose Material. Telex, Davis to Trudeau, 19 June 1975.

44 Private Collection, Stevenson Papers. Stevenson, "F-PR and Trends in Canadian Federalism," York University presentation, Oct. 1975.

45 CAR papers, Opening Statement of the Hon. William G. Davis to the F-PC of First Ministers, 23–25 May 1973.

46 AO, RG 58-9-1, box 12, file FD-1c. Office of IGA, "Considerations toward an Intergovernmental Strategy for Ontario," June 1973.

47 AO, RG 3-49, box 36, file P & A/ TE 7, IGA 1973 (courtesy of Peter Oliver estate). T. Campbell (Sec. to Cabinet) to C.E. Brannan, 12 Feb. 1973.

48 AO, RG 58-9-1, "Considerations toward an Intergovernmental Strategy for Ontario," June 1973.

49 Ibid.

50 Ibid.

51 AO, RG 58-9-1, box 12, file FD-3, Intergovernmental Matters. David H. to Andy, 26 June 1973.

52 AO, RG 6-77 Acc. 30094, TB 67, file Fiscal Management Negotiations, 1975–76. Stevenson to Dick, 23 Feb. 1976.

53 AO, RG 3-59, T 79-911, box 10, file Conferences, 1976, Gen. Stevenson, Note for file, 12 Jan. 1976.

54 Ibid. Posen to Greathed, 15 Jan. 1976.

55 Ibid. Stevenson, Note for file, 12 Jan. 1976.

56 House of Commons, *Debates*, 2 Oct. 1974.

57 AO, RG 50-5-1, Treasury, Economics and Intergovernmental Affairs, Minister's and Deputy Minister's Corr. Files, 1976–78, box 27, file 705-2, Constitutional Conferences, Gen. F-P and Interprovincial Affairs Secretariat, "Proposal for the Patriation of the Canadian Constitution and the Adoption of an Amending Formula," 17 Feb. 1976.

58 Ibid. Robertson remembers that it was New Brunswick's Richard Hatfield who was the only premier "with any discernible understanding of and sympathy for the dissatisfactions of Quebec," although he acknowledged that Davis might "have shared Hatfield's understanding to some extent." See Robertson, *Memoirs*, 286.

59 Ibid.

60 AO, RG 50-5-1, box 27, file 705-2. Greathed to Dick, 20 Feb. 1976.

61 AO, RG 3-49, T 80-1156, box 29, file FP 4-1, Constitution, Amendment to

the Constitution of Canada 1976 (courtesy of Peter Oliver estate). Trudeau to Davis, 31 March 1976.

62 AO, RG 50-5-1, "Proposal for the Patriation of the Canadian Constitution and the Adoption of an Amending Formula," 17 Feb. 1976.

63 Ibid.

64 AO, RG 3-49, T 80-1156, box 29, file FP 4-1. "Options for an Ontario Position on the Patriation of the Canadian Constitution," 10 March 1976.

65 AO, RG 50-5-1, box 28, file First Ministers Conference (Trudeau). Draft, Davis to Trudeau, 5 April 1976, and Stevenson to Dick, 12 April 1976.

66 Ibid. Statement by the Hon. Darcy McKeough in Ontario Legislature, 9 April 1976.

67 Ibid., box 27, file 705-2, Constitutional Conferences, Gen. Stevenson to McKeough, 29 April 1976.

68 AO, RG 58-9-1, box 10, file Health Financing. Michele Fordyce to Gary Posen, 13 April 1976.

69 AO, RG 50-5-1, box 27, file 705-2. Posen draft memo for McKeough to Davis, 14 May 1976.

70 Ibid. Posen to Greathed, 14 May 1976.

71 AO, RG 6-77, Acc. 32779, TB 2037, file Background Material for mtg. "Statement Tabled by the Prime Minister," 7 June 1976.

72 Private Collection, CAR Papers, F-PC of First Ministers, Statement by the Hon. William G. Davis, 14 June 1976.

73 AO, RG 50-5-1, container 12, file Fed. Govt., Gen. McKeough, memo to file, 27 July 1976.

74 Ibid., container 27, file 705-2, Constitutional Conferences. Gen. Davis's report to Cabinet on discussions at the 17th Annual Premiers' Conference, 25 Aug. 1976.

75 Ibid.

76 Private Collection, CAR Papers, 17th Annual Premiers Conference, Communiqué, F-P Financial Negotiations, Aug. 1976.

77 AO, RG 50-5-1, container 27, file 705-2. Ministry of the Attorney General, "The Premiers' Conference Revisited," 15 Sept. 1976.

78 Ibid. (original emphasis).

79 Ibid.

80 Ibid., container 27, file 705-2. Dick to E.E. Stewart, 28 Sept. 1976.

81 LAC, RG 33/118, Pepin-Roberts Task Force on Canadian Unity, vol. 9, file Alberta. Lougheed to Trudeau, 14 Oct. 1976.

82 Ibid.

83 A0, RG 50-5-1, container 27, file 705-2. Trudeau to Lougheed, 19 Oct. 1976. (In original "quote" and "unquote," "begin underline" and "end underline.")

84 AO, RG 3-49, T 80-1156, box 30, file FP 11-1, Air Transportation 1976. Mc-Keough to Davis, 12 July 1976 (courtesy of Peter Oliver estate).

85 Poliquin, *René Lévesque*, 135–6.

86 AO, RG 3-49, T 80-1156, box 30, file FP 9-8, Provinces Quebec 1976. Stevenson to Dick, 9 Nov. 1976 (courtesy of Peter Oliver estate).

87 AO, RG 50-5-1, container 27, file 705-2. Greathed to McKeough, "The cornflake theory of Confederation," 2 Dec. 1976.

88 AO, RG 3-49, T-80-1156, box 30, file FP 9-8, Provinces Quebec 1976. Stevenson to McKeough, 3 Dec. 1976.

89 Ontario bureaucrat Donald Stevenson spoke to the Assistant Deputy Minister of Finance in Quebec – Michel Audet – following the mtg, and learned that Lévesque's "violent reaction to the conference results". was probably due to the premier's "political sense that it would give him a good platform to call the conference a failure." Stevenson thought instead that "it was not too useful a thing for future inter-provincial collaboration because a number of people were beginning to wonder if Lévesque would have called it a failure even if all of Quebec's demands had been agreed to." [AO, RG 50-5-1, container 28, file First Ministers Conference (Trudeau). Stevenson to Dick, 16 Dec. 1976.]

90 Ibid., container 62, file Advisory Cttee/Cabinet Cttee on Confederation. Stevenson to René Brunelle, 13 April 1977.

91 AO, RG 3-49, T 80-1156, box 30, file FP 9-8, Provinces Quebec 1976. Ian Macdonald, "A Proposal for an Advisory Cttee on Ontario's Role in Confederation," 23 Nov. 1976 (courtesy of Peter Oliver estate).

92 The new mtg was to be called "Destiny Canada Destinée" and was scheduled for June 1977. See AO, RG 50-5-1, container 62, file Advisory Cttee/Cabinet Cttee on Confederation #1. Cabinet Cttee Rep, 20 April 1977.

93 AO, MG 32 C55, vol. 2, file 12. Ramsay Cook to Eugene Forsey, 18 Jan. 1977; Forsey to Arthur Lower, 21 Jan. 1977; Forsey to Cook, 24 Jan. 1977. In Cook's memoir of his relationship with Trudeau, he makes no mention of the group of advisers, suggesting that it never really got off the ground. See Cook, *Teeth of Time*, 130–2.

94 AO, F 15-5, MU 8050, file Task Force on Canadian Unity. Summary of understanding between Pepin and Robarts, 15 June 1977.

95 AO, RG 50-5-1, container 62, file Advisory Cttee/Cabinet Cttee on Confederation #1. Greathed to Dick, drafts and copies of intergovernmental correspondence, 7 April 1977.

96 Ibid.

97 Ibid.

98 Ibid., container 14, file 311-2 F-P Affairs Secretariat, Gen. Posen and Greathed to Stevenson, 20 Oct. 1976.

 99 Ibid

100 Clarkson and McCall, *Trudeau and Our Times*, vol. 1, 136–9, 270–1.

101 AO, RG 50-5-1, container 62, file Advisory Cttee/Cabinet Cttee on Confederation #2. Stevenson memo to file, 22 July 1976. Rendell Dick "had to
smile" when he read Stevenson's report of Ian Macdonald's views on asym-
metry: "It takes me back to my memo of several months ago when I made
the same observation and received some very pointed comments on my
copy!" [Ibid., Dick to Stevenson, 25 July 1977.]

102 AO, RG 3-49, T 82-1018, box 17, file FP 9-8, Provinces Quebec 1977.
"Ontario-Quebec Officials mtg ... Impressions," 15 Aug. 1977 (courtesy
Peter Oliver estate).

103 Ibid. "Statement by the Hon. Roy McMurtry," n.d. (ca. Sept. 1977), and
Greathed to Dick, "Constitutionality of Quebec's language legislation," 13
Sept. 1977.

104 AO, RG 50-5-1 (2562), container 62, 1977, file 570 – Advisory Cttee/Cabi-
net Cttee on Confederation. Greathed to Dick, 8 Sept. 1977.

105 AO, RG 3-49, T 82-1018, box 12, file CV 1-5, Priorities and Future Directions of the Govt., Responses 1977. McKeough to Davis, 12 Sept. 1977
(courtesy Peter Oliver estate).

106 AO, RG 50-5-1 (2562), container 62, 1977, file 570 – Advisory Committee/
Cabinet Committee on Confederation. Stevenson memo to file, Oct. 1977.
The idea of a third option, of course, plays on the Trudeau government's
own earlier third option in Canadian foreign policy, which envisioned a
decentering of Canada's reliance on U.S. trade and a repositioning within
the European and Asian markets. Like Ontario's intergovernmental option, the foreign policy version also came to naught.

107 Ibid., Cabinet Cttee Report, 2 Nov. 1977.

108 RG 58-9-1, box 4. Stevenson memo to file, 13 March 1978. AO, RG 3-59,
box 2, file Conferences 1975, Min. on Constitution CF Fed./Prov., C8, 30
Oct.–1 Nov. 1978. Greathed to McKeough, 5 June 1978; Greathed to McK-
eough, 12 June 1978.

109 Trudeau, *Memoirs*, 248.

110 Canada, *A Time for Action*, 25.

111 AO, RG 6-77 Acc. 30720, file Constitutional Matters. Premier's Advisory Cttee on the Economic Future, Notes from the mtg of 12 June 1978. Private
Collection, CAR Papers, unorganized material. "The Kingston Statement:
A mtg of four provincial premiers with the leader of the Progressive Conservative Party of Canada," 16 Sept. 1977. Trudeau, *Memoirs*, 248.

112 AO, RG 3-59, T 82-642, box 2, file Conferences 1975, Min. on Constitution
CF Fed./Prov., C8, 30 Oct.–1 Nov. 1978. 1st mtg of the Provincial Ministers
Responsible for the Constitution, Saskatoon, 7 July 1978.

113 Ibid., file Conferences, Saskatoon, Constitution, 7 July 1978, CF Interprovincial mtg 1978. Office of Intergovernmental Affairs, "Ontario Preparations for Intergovernmental Discussions on the Constitution," 11 July 1978.
114 Private Collection, CAR Papers, unorganized material. Remarks by the Hon. William G. Davis, Premier of Ontario, on the Economy. 1978 Premiers Conference, 9–10 Aug. 1978.
115 AO, RG 6-77, Acc. 30094, file FP Cost-Sharing/Social Services Review 1976. Davis to Trudeau, 9 Feb. 1978.
116 Ibid., file Fiscal Arrangements, 1979–80. Davis to Trudeau, 12 Sept. 1978.

9 "The Hot Gospel of Confederation"

1 See, e.g., Graham, *Last Act*, in which Trudeau and the Gang of Eight are the key players.
2 AO, RG 6-77, Acc. 30094, file Fiscal Arrangements, 1979, 1980. Trudeau to Davis, 2 Oct. 1978.
3 AO, RG 3-49, box 15, file 4-1-1, PM, Premiers and Ministers 1978. Miller to Davis, 27 Oct. 1978. Miller had been named both treasurer and minister of intergovernmental affairs following a cabinet shuffle in the summer of 1978.
4 AO, RG 6-77, Acc. 32779, file Loose Material. Gough to Jill Logan, Senior Adviser Intergovernmental Finance, 27 Oct. 1978.
5 Davey, *Rainmaker*, 234–5; English, *Just Watch Me*, 380–1.
6 Government of Alberta, *Harmony in Diversity: A New Federalism for Canada*, 1978, "Lougheed Expects to Raise Ottawa Hackles with 'Confrontation' Paper on Constitution," *Globe and Mail*, 20 Oct. 1978. The document outlined the now familiar elements of Alberta's vision of the division of powers, including plans for provincial control of natural resources and changes to the Supreme Court.
7 Romanow, Whyte, and Leeson, *Canada ... Notwithstanding*, 22.
8 Trudeau, *Memoirs*, 249–50.
9 LAC, MG 32 C55, Carl Goldenberg Papers, vol. 2, file Constitutional Conference Federal (1979), Draft proposals. "List of 'Best Effort' Draft Proposals," 5–6 Feb. 1979.
10 AO, RG 6-77, Acc. 30094, file F-P Constitutional Discussions. B. Jones to Don Stevenson, 10 Jan. 1979.
11 Private Collection, Stevenson Papers. "Notes for Use on Thursday, October 19th, 1978 at a Seminar with the Niagara Institute." AO, RG 6-77, Jones to Stevenson, 10 Jan. 1979.

12 Task Force on Canadian Unity, *A Future Together: Observations and Recom-mendations*; Peter Miller, "Task Force Naïve to Entrust Language Rights to Provinces, PM Says," *Globe and Mail*, 27 Jan. 1979, 13. AO, RG 3-105, box 14, file Task Force on Canadian Unity. Stevenson memo to file, 30 Jan. 1979.

13 William Johnson, "A Diagnosis with a Ring of Truth," *Globe and Mail*, 26 Jan. 1979, 8.

14 AO, RG 58-9-1, FD-1, box 1, TL 83-1499. Paul Brown to Gary Posen, 22 Feb. 1979. See also Romanow et al., *Canada*, 23–54.

15 Trudeau insisted on campaigning on the constitution, which his chief or-ganizer Keith Davey knew wouldn't help the party at the polls. [English, *Just Watch Me*, 384–5; Davey, *The Rainmaker*, 238–9]. See also Byers, ed., *Canadian Annual Review of Politics and Public Affairs, 1979*, 24–5. Trudeau's approach to the constitution was also in the process of being formally rejected: in *Reference Re: Legislative Authority to Alter or Replace the Senate* [[1980] 1 S.C.R. 54], the Supreme Court ruled that Bill C-60 went beyond the federal govern-ment's capacity to unilaterally alter the constitution. On the Conservative campaign and victory, see Courtney, "Campaign Strategy and Electoral Vic-tory," 121–51.

16 AO, RG 58-9-1, FD-1, box 1, TL 85-830, file Ontario. Clark to Davis, 26 July 1979.

17 Ibid., file Economic Issues no. 5. Office of Intergovernmental Affairs, "Oil Pricing and Security: A Comprehensive Policy Framework for Canada," 7 Aug. 1979. NSARM, RG 55, Department of Development, vol. 8, file Inter-governmental Affairs. Peckford to Clark, 23 Aug. 1979.

18 AO, RG 58-9-1, "Oil Pricing and Security," 7 Aug. 1979.

19 AO, RG 3-49, box 53, file P&A/IA 5, F-P IGA. David Redgrave and Ed Greathed to Rendell Dick and Don Stevenson, 27 Aug. 1979.

20 AO, RG 6-77, Acc 30094, file Hall Commission. Joyce Feinberg to Carolyn Sherk, 23 Oct. 1979. Vaughan, *Aggressive in Pursuit*, 250–2.

21 English, *Just Watch Me*, 428.

22 See Clarkson, *Big Red Machine*, 87.

23 See English, *Just Watch Me*, 428–38; Simpson, *Discipline of Power*, 3–47.

24 Clarkson, *Big Red Machine*, 98–100; Irvine, "Epilogue: The 1980 Election," 355–78.

25 AO, RG 58-9-1, FD-1, TL 85-830, file Ministry Business "C." Stevenson to Greathed, "Post-election Thoughts," 19 Feb. 1980.

26 Ibid., Ministry of Intergovernmental Affairs, "Federal Election Results: Inter-governmental Implications," 20 Feb. 1980.

27 AO, RG 3-49, box 16, file F-P Gen. Davis to Trudeau, 7 March 1980.

28 Ibid., box 17, file Constitutional Matters, Gen. Stevenson to Wells, 23 Jan.

1980; AO, RG 6-32-2, box 1069, file 1980 Ontario Policy Perspectives. Ministry of Intergovernmental Affairs, "Analysis of the Report of the Constitutional Cttee of the Quebec Liberal Party," 12 Feb. 1980. AO, RG 58-9-1, box 3, TL 83-1499, file Federal-Ontario Issues. "Items for Discussion with M. Kirby," 2 April 1980.

29 Ibid., "Notes on conversation with Mike Kirby," 2 April; FD-1, TL 85-830, file Ministry Business "C." Stevenson to Greathed, "Post-election Thoughts," 19 Feb. 1980.

30 See Pinard, "The Dramatic Re-emergence of the Quebec Independence Movement," 478–85, and McRoberts, *Misconceiving Canada*, 155–8. On the PQ campaign, see Poliquin, *René Lévesque*, 158–60; Fraser, *René Lévesque*, 215–40.

31 Quoted in McRoberts, *Misconceiving Canada*, 158. See also, English, *Just Watch Me*, 451–6.

32 AO, RG 3-49, box 17, FP 4, file Constitutional Matters, Gen. Ministry of Intergovernmental Affairs, "Report to Cabinet on the Discussions to Date of the Continuing Cttee of Ministers on the Constitution," 30 July 1980.

33 AO, RG 6-32-2, box 1061, file Policy Perspectives, Aug. 1980. "IGA: Priorities for the Early Eighties," n.d.

34 Ibid.

35 AO, 3-49, box 17, file FP 4-2-1, Constitutional Matters, Confederation 1980. Greathed to Segal. 13 Aug. 1980.

36 Ibid.

37 AO, RG 3-105, TL 83-1495, box 10, file Cttees 1980, Advisory Cttee on Confederation. Summary Record of Proceedings, F-PC of First Ministers on the Constitution, 8–13 Sept. 1980, 51–2.

38 Russell, *Constitutional Odyssey*, 110. AO, RG 3-105, Summary Record of Proceedings, F-PC of First Ministers on the Constitution, 8–13 Sept. 1980, 56–8. At some point during a formal dinner, Trudeau stormed out before dessert had been served or the governor general had departed, underlining the frayed tempers at the conference. Russell places this on the evening prior to the closing remarks; Saskatchewan Premier Allan Blakeney is probably more accurate as dating it at the beginning of the conference – 7 September, his birthday. The dessert that the prime minister missed out on was Blakeney's birthday cake. [Blakeney, *An Honourable Calling*, 174.]

39 AO, RG 3-49, box 17, file FP 4-1-1, Amendment to Constitution. Davis to "Fellow Conservatives," 16 Sept. 1980.

40 Ibid.

41 Ibid.

42 See Bryden, "Constitutional Dialogue," 44–5; Robertson, *Memoirs*, 323–4.

43 The Constitution Act that Trudeau proposed to introduce in Parliament included an amending formula, a referendum to break any intergovernmental impasse, a Charter of Rights and Freedoms, and a commitment to equalization. Davis proposed restrictions to the federal use of referenda, although he also admitted that "Ontario can live with the existing package." AO, RG 3-49, box 17, file FP 4-1-1, file Amendment to the Constitution. Davis to Trudeau, 27 Oct. 1980.

44 AO, RG 3-59, box 5, 1981, file F-PC 1981. "Notes for a Possible Discussion between Premier Davis and Prime Minister Trudeau," n.d.

45 AO, RG 6-77, Acc. 29115, TB 135, file FAA, Notes, Mtgs, etc. Rendall Dick to Frank Miller, 6 Feb. 1981. AO, RG 58-9-1, FD-1, box 1, TL 85-830, file Ministry Business 'C.' Deputy Ministers' Council, "Some Intergovernmental Perspectives, 27 March 1981.

46 AO, RG 6-77, Acc. 32780, TB 83, file Equalization 1981. "Note on Ontario's Position with Respect to Equalization," n.d.

47 AO, RG 58-9-1, "Some Intergovernmental Perspectives," 27 March 1981. On the NEP, see Scarfe, "Federal Budget and Energy Program," 1–14.

48 AO, RG 58-9-1, "Some Intergovernmental Perspectives," 27 March 1981.

49 Russell, *Constitutional Odyssey*, 111–13; Romanow et al., *Canada*, 112–14; Kome, *Taking of Twenty-Eight*; Hosek, "Women and the Constitutional Process," 286–91; Sanders, "The Indian Lobby," 310–14; Behiels, "Aboriginal Nationalism in the Ascendancy," 266–72.

50 English, *Just Watch Me*, 496.

51 Romanow et al., *Canada*, 158–68. Each of the provincial courts were asked a slightly different question, based on the historic evolution of the province and the particular objections each provincial government had with the Trudeau approach. Newfoundland's was based on its entry into Confederation in 1949; Manitoba had already done the most preparation for the court challenge and was the most eager to move forward on this front; Quebec needed to be seen as doing everything it could to stop the federal initiative. Determining which provinces would mount court challenges was a joint decision undertaken by all the dissident premiers.

52 AO, RG 3-49, box 83, file FP-4-1-1, PM – Amendment to the Constitution of Canada, vol. 1, Jan.–April. Stevenson to Wells, re: Conversation with Mike Kirby, 9 April 1981.

53 Ibid. Davis to William Bennett, premier of BC, 9 April 1981.

54 Segal, *No Surrender*, 98.

55 AO, RG 3-49, box 83, file FP-4-1-1, Stevenson to Stewart, 13 April 1981.

56 Ibid. Davis to Bennett, 9 April 1981. New Brunswick was the other province that supported the federal initiative.

57 Ibid. Stevenson to Stewart, 13 April 1981.

58 Girard, *Bora Laskin*, 506.

59 AO, RG 3-49, box 83, file FP-4-1-1. Segal, London and Patriation Situational Review, 16 April 1981.

60 Quoted in McMurtry, "Search for a Constitutional Accord," 47.

61 See Girard, *Bora Laskin*, 507–8; Sharpe and Roach, *Brian Dickson*, 269.

62 McMurtry, "Search for a Constitutional Accord," 50.

63 AO, RG 3-49, box 99, file P&A/ 1A 5, 1981, IGA. "Notes on Meeting with F-P Relations Office, June 22, 1981."

64 AO, RG 3-59, TL 83-1495, box 5, file Conferences CF, F-PC 1981. Trudeau to Davis, 30 June 1981.

65 Nurgitz and Segal, *No Small Measure*, 110; see also Robertson, *Memoirs*, 322–7.

66 Private Collection, Stevenson Papers, "Chronology of Steps Leading to Constitutional Agreement on November 5th, 1981."

67 Roy Romanow disagrees that Ontario was in any way able to act as a conciliator at this stage. See his "'Reworking the Miracle,'" 80.

68 McMurtry, "Search for a Constitutional Accord," 52. Laskin and Estey both stayed away from the debate itself, although the former was keen to sit in the audience. Estey had to convince him of the inappropriateness of receiving extrajudicial input into a decision on which the Court had yet to rule. Girard, *Bora Laskin*, 509.

69 Even after joining the Gang of Eight, the last province to do so, "Saskatchewan would continue its efforts to modify the federal resolution and thereby broaden its support among Canadians" according to Romanow. "'Reworking the Miracle,'" 81.

70 Martin, *Chrétien*, vol. 1, 293–5.

71 McMurtry, "Search for Constitutional Accord," 53.

72 Private Collection, Stevenson Papers, "Chronology of Steps."

73 Much has been written about the Supreme Court's decision. Peter Russell has offered numerous clear-headed explanations of the decision, including the original commentary he made as the decision was being read over the airwaves. His most useful published accounts can be found in *Leading Constitutional Decisions*, 501–6, and "Bold Statecraft, Questionable Jurisprudence," 210–38. Much has also recently been written trying to uncover the authorship behind the rare, unauthored majority and dissenting decisions in the case. See, Sharpe and Roach, *Brian Dickson*, 269–74, and Girard, *Bora Laskin*, 508–15.

74 Private Collection, Stevenson Papers, "Chronology of Steps."

75 Ibid. The events that occurred between 28 September 1981 and the making

of the final deal on 5 November have been guardedly recounted by some of the participants. For their own recollections of the events, see Segal, *No Surrender*, 102–8; Romanow, "'Reworking the Miracle,'" 82–8; Romanow et al., *Canada*, 188–215; McMurtry, "Search for a Constitutional Accord," 54–68.

76 Private Collection, Stevenson Papers, "Chronology of Steps."

77 AO, RG 3-59, TL 83-1495, box 5, file Conferences 1981 on Constitution CF Fed./Prov. Cf, Nov. 1981. First Ministers. Trudeau to Bennett, telex, 23 Oct. 1981, and Bennett to Trudeau, telex, 23 Oct. 1981.

78 Ibid. Bennett to Trudeau, telex, 23 Oct. 1981. Private Collection, Stevenson Papers, "Chronology of Steps."

79 Romanow et al., *Canada*, 188–215.

80 Private Collection, Stevenson Papers, "Chronology of Steps." The key people included in the discussions were Norman Specter and Jim Matkin of B.C., Don Dennison of N.B., and Howard Leeson of Saskatchewan.

81 Roy McMurtry remembers things slightly differently, claiming that "Alberta would be the key to any breakthrough." ["Search for a Constitutional Accord," 61–3.] While it was certainly true that little could be done without the agreement of at least one of the provinces most staunchly opposed to the Trudeau approach – Alberta or Quebec – in the days leading up to the meeting it seems clear that it was British Columbia's people who were most important to Ontario's efforts to bridge the gap between the two sides.

82 Private Collection, Stevenson Papers, "Chronology of Steps."

83 Lougheed to Lévesque, 8 March 1982, reprinted in *Constitutional Patriation: The Lougheed-Lévesque Correspondence*, 22.

84 This is one of the key issues upon which the understanding of what happened over the next few days rests. From Alberta's perspective, what the group had agreed to was an alliance "*only* so long as Mr. Trudeau continued with his *process* of unilateral action. If he abandoned his unilateral process and was prepared to modify the resolution and undertake serious negotiations, then every one of the eight premiers was freed from any commitment arising out of the Accord of April 16, 1981, leaving each of us free to modify or alter his government's position on the amending formula or any other constitutional matter." As would become clear, Quebec politicians and advisers disagreed with this interpretation of the commitments made to the other provinces. Lougheed to Lévesque, 8 March 1982, 22.

85 Private Collection, Stevenson Papers, "Chronology of Steps."

86 Lougheed to Lévesque, 8 March 1982, 22.

87 McMurtry, "Search for a Constitutional Accord," 63–4.

88 Ibid. The limitation on the Charter was the much-criticized "notwithstanding clause" which gave governments the opportunity to pass legislation that
contravened the Charter by invoking it.

89 Clarkson and McCall's account of the events leading to the agreement on
5 November was pieced together from hundreds of interviews with participants and is probably the most thorough description of the circumstances
that we will ever have. At the heart of their story, however, lies Trudeau,
which necessarily skews the way the story is told. *Trudeau and Our Times*,
vol. 1, 357–86.

90 Davis's biographer notes, for example, the absence of more than one reference to Davis in McMurtry's long account of the process of securing a deal
published in the *Queen's Law Review.*

91 AO, RG 6-77, Acc. 32780, file Equalization 1981. Briefing Notes, Federal
Equalization Proposal, ca. 12 Nov. 1981.

92 Ibid., Acc. 29115, file EPF: Briefing, Notes, Etc. Briefing Notes, Established
Programs Financing, ca. 12 Nov. 1982.

93 AO, RG 6-32-2, container 1038, file 560: Economic Advisory Group (Premier's). Minutes, Premier's Advisory Cttee on the Economic Future, 7 Dec.
1981.

94 AO, RG 6-77, Briefing Notes, Federal Equalization Proposal, ca. 12 Nov.
1981.

95 AO, RG 58-1-1, container 1, file Dep. Minister, 1981–82. "Points for draft
letter to all deputies," 13 Jan. 1982.

96 Ibid. Stevenson memo to file, 14 Jan. 1982.

97 AO, RG 3-47, box 121, file F-P and/or Provincial Matters, Provinces, FP 9-8,
Quebec 1982. Stevenson to all deputies, 5 Jan. 1982.

98 AO, RG 6-77, Acc. 30094. File Court challenge on EPF. Brock Smith to
Graham Stoodley, 8 Feb. 1982, and Acc. 29115, F-PC of First Ministers on
the Economy, unrevised text, 4 Feb. 1982.

99 Ibid., Acc. 32780, file Internal memoranda, 1982. Ron McGinley to Brock
Smith, 26 March 1982.

100 AO, RG 6-32-2, container 1064, binder: F-P Finance Ministers' Meeting,
5 July 1983. Davis to Trudeau, 29 April 1983 (mailed 3 May 1983).

101 Davis, Toronto Empire Club address, 5 March 1981.

Epilogue

1 AO, David Peterson Papers, F 2093-11-3-68, box 53 HA, Mtgs with PM Mul-
roney 1985. Ministry of Intergovernmental Affairs, "Halifax First Ministers'
Conference," 7 Aug. 1985. F 2093-11-3-70, Premiers' Conference, Quebec,
Issues 1985. Posen to Peterson, 1 Aug. 1985.

2 Ibid.

3 AO, F 2122-3-0-070, Hershell Ezrin Papers, Private mtg of the Premier and PM. Posen to Peterson, 7 Aug. 1985.

4 Ibid.

5 AO, Peterson Papers, F 2093-1-3-68. Posen to Peterson, 9 Aug. 1985.

6 AO, F-2093-39-0-49. Ministry files, Ministry of Intergovernmental Affairs, June–Dec. 1989. Speaking Notes for Dan Gagnier, n.d.

7 By this I mean the province whose citizens most frequently identify with the nation more than the province or, alternatively, where the sense of provincial identity is weakest. Morton, "*Sic Permanent.*"

Bibliography

Primary Sources

Archives of Ontario (AO)

GOVERNMENT RECORDS

Cabinet Office: Cabinet Agenda Files (RG 75-12)

Cabinet Office: L.R. MacDonald, Secretary to Cabinet (RG 75-42)

Cabinet Office: Minutes (RG 75-14)

Department of Finance: Correspondence and Subject Files of the Minister and Deputy Minister (RG 6-32).

Department of Finance: Deputy Minister's General Correspondence, 1924–1971 (RG 6-14)

Department of Finance: Dominion-Provincial Conferences, 1935–1955 (RG 6-41)

Department of Finance: Inter-Ministerial and Intergovernmental Correspondence, 1924–1958 (RG 6-15)

Department of Finance: Federal-Provincial Fiscal Program Files (RG 6-77)

Department of Finance: Federal-Provincial Relations Correspondence Files, 1950–1962 (RG 6-115)

Department of Finance: Policy Division Subject Files (RG 6-44)

Department of Finance: Reports on Federal-Provincial Tax Agreements, 1941–1961 (RG 6-116)

Department of Health: Dominion Council of Health Files (RG 10-5)

Department of Health: Correspondence of the Deputy Minister of Health (RG 10-6)

Management Board of Cabinet: Office of the Secretary, Federal-Provincial Matters Files (RG 27-39)

Ministry of Intergovernmental Affairs, Federal-Provincial Relations Branch
    Records (RG 58-9-1)
Office of the Attorney General: Attorney-General's Correspondence Files,
    1926–1964 (RG 4-2)
Office of the Premier: George Drew Election Material (RG 3-21)
Office of the Premier: George Drew, Letterbooks (RG 3-18)
Office of the Premier: Frost General Correspondence (RG 3-23)
Office of the Premier: Frost Premier's Correspondence (RG 3-24)
Office of the Premier: Premier John P. Robarts – Conference Files (RG
    3-42)
Office of the Premier: Premier John P. Robarts General Correspondence
    (RG 3-26)
Office of the Premier: Premier John P. Robarts Press Releases (RG 3-102)
Office of the Premier: Premier William G. Davis Central Registry Files (RG
    3-49)
Office of the Premier: Premier William G. Davis Committee Files (RG 3-105)
Ontario Historical Studies Series Political Interviews (RG 47-27-1)
Subject files of the Executive Assistant to Chief Economist H.I. Macdonald
    (RG 9-79)
Treasury Department: Fiscal Policy Planning Branch (RG 50-33)
Treasury, Economics and Intergovernmental Affairs Papers: Minister's and
    Deputy Minister's Correspondence Files, 1976–1978 (RG 50-5-1)

MANUSCRIPT RECORDS
Ezrin, Hershell (F 2122)
Frost, Leslie (F 4345)
Gathercole, George (MU 5330)
Latimer, Hugh (MU 4543)
Peterson, David (F 2093)
Robarts, John (F 15)
Westcott, Clare (F 2094)

Library and Archives of Canada (LAC)

GOVERNMENT RECORDS
Department of Finance (RG 19)
Department of National Health and Welfare (RG 29)
Pepin-Robarts Task Force on Canadian Unity (RG 33/118)
Privy Council Office (RG 2)
Royal Commissions – Hall (RG 33/78)

MANUSCRIPT RECORDS

Bell, Richard (MG 32 B1)
Bracken, John (MG 27 III C16)
Bryce, R.B. (MG 31 E59)
Canadian Council on Social Development (MG 28 I10)
Churchill, Gordon (MG 32 B9)
Claxton, Brooke (MG 32 B5)
Cooperative Commonwealth Federation/New Democratic Party (MG 28 IV 1)
Diefenbaker, John G. (MG 26 M)
Drew, George (MG 32 C3)
Fleming, Donald (MG 32 B39)
Fulton, E. Davie (MG 32 B11)
Goldenberg, Carl (MG 32 C55)
Gordon, Walter (MG 32 B44)
Graydon, Gordon (MG 27 III C15)
Grosart, Allister (MG 32 C65)
King, William Lyon Mackenzie (MG 26 J)
Martin, Paul Sr. (MG 32 B12)
Michener, Roland (MG 32 A4)
Monteith, Jay Waldo (MG 32 B29)
Pearson, L.B. (MG 26 N)
Pickersgill, J.W. (MG 32 B34)
Progressive Conservative Party (MG 28 IV 2)
Robertson, R. Gordon (MG 31 E87)
St. Laurent, Louis (MG 26 L)
Stursberg, Peter (MG 31 D78)
Whitton, Charlotte (MG 30 E256)

Nova Scotia Archives and Record Management (NSARM)

Department of Development (RG 55)
Macdonald, Angus L. (MG 2)

Private Collections

Clipping Files (P.E. Bryden)
Canadian Annual Review Papers (P.E. Bryden)
Drew, George (John T. Saywell)
Gordon, Walter (J.L. Granatstein)
Stevenson, Donald (Donald Stevenson)

Public Archives of New Brunswick (PANB)

McNair, John (RS 414)

Public Archives and Record Office – Prince Edward Island (PARO-PEI)

Federal-Provincial Affairs Papers: Conference Files (RG 21-1)
Premiers Papers: Walter Jones (RG 25)

Queen's University Archives (QUA)

Dexter, Grant
Kent, Tom
Malone, Richard

Saskatchewan Archives (SA)

T.C. Douglas Papers (R-33)
C.M. Fines Papers (R-37)

Trent University Archives (TUA)

Frost, Leslie (77-024)
Progressive Conservative Association of Ontario

Interviews

Bryce, R.B.
Dick, Rendell
Cameron, David
Camp, Dalton
Carman, Robert
Goodman, Eddie
Kent, Tom
Macdonald, H. Ian
McKeough, Darcy
McMurtry, Roy
Peterson, David
Posen, Gary
Rae, Bob

Reisman, Simon
Robertson, Gordon
Segal, Hugh
Stevenson, Donald
Stewart, E. E.
Wells, Thomas

Magazines and Newspapers

Canadian Forum
Globe and Mail
Montreal Star
Ottawa Journal
Saturday Night
Toronto Star
Toronto Telegram
Winnipeg Free Press

Government Publications

Government of Alberta. *Harmony in Diversity: A New Federalism in Canada.* Edmonton: Author. 1978.

Government of Canada. *Proceedings of the Constitutional Conference of Federal and Provincial Governments,* Quebec, 25–28 Sept. 1950.

Government of Canada. *Proceedings of the Conference of Federal and Provincial Governments,* Ottawa, 4–7 Dec. 1950.

Government of Canada. *Federal-Provincial Conference, 1955: Preliminary Meeting,* Ottawa, 26 April 1955.

Government of Canada. *Proceedings of the Federal-Provincial Conference, 1955,* Ottawa, 3 Oct. 1955.

Government of Canada. *Proceedings of the Dominion-Provincial Conference, 1957,* Ottawa, 25–26 Nov. 1957.

Government of Canada. *A Time for Action: Toward the Renewal of the Canadian Federation,* Ottawa, 1978.

Government of Canada. House of Commons. *Debates,* 1943–1990.

Legislative Assembly of Ontario. *Debates,* 1945–1990.

Legislative Assembly of Ontario. George Alexander Drew biography. http://www.ontla.on.ca/web/members/members_all_detail.do?locale=en&ID=453.

Task Force on Canadian Unity, *A Future Together: Observations and Recommendations.* Ottawa, 1979.

Secondary Sources

Armstrong, Christopher. "The Mowat Heritage in Federal-Provincial Relations." In *Oliver Mowat's Ontario*, ed. Donald Swainson, 93–119. Toronto: Macmillan, 1972.

Armstrong, Christopher. *The Politics of Federalism: Ontario's Relations with the Federal Government, 1867–1942*. Toronto: University of Toronto Press, 1981.

Bakvis, Herman, Gerald Baier, and Douglas Brown. *Contested Federalism: Certainty and Ambiguity in the Canadian Federation*. Toronto: Oxford University Press, 2009.

Barnett, Enid. *The Keynesian Arithmetic in War-Time Canada: Development of the National Accounts, 1939–1945*. Kingston: Harbinger House Press, 1998.

Barnett, Enid. *The War Budget of September 1939: Keynes Comes to Canada*. Kingston: Harbinger House Press, 2000.

Barnett, Enid. *Keynes's How to Pay for the War in Canada: The Story of Compulsory Savings 1939–1944*. Kingston: Harbinger House Press, 2001.

Behiels, Michael D. "Aboriginal Nationalism in the Ascendancy: The Assembly of First Nations' First Campaign for the Inherent Right to Self-Government, 1968–1987." In *Canadas of the Mind: The Making and Unmaking of Canadian Nationalisms in the Twentieth Century*, ed. Norman Hillmer and Adam Chapnick, 260–86. Montreal and Kingston: McGill-Queen's University Press, 2007.

Behiels, Michael D., ed. *The Meech Lake Primer: Conflicting Views of the 1987 Constitutional Accord*. Ottawa: University of Ottawa Press, 1989.

Béland, Daniel, and André Lecours. *Nationalism and Social Policy: The Politics of Territorial Solidarity*. New York: Oxford University Press, 2008.

Bercuson, David. *True Patriot: The Life of Brooke Claxton, 1898–1960*. Toronto: University of Toronto Press, 1993.

Bickerton, James P. *Nova Scotia, Ottawa and the Politics of Regional Development*. Toronto: University of Toronto Press, 1990.

Black, Conrad. *Duplessis*. Toronto: McClelland and Stewart, 1977.

Blake, Raymond B. "Intergovernmental Relation Trumps Social Policy Change: Trudeau, Constitutionalism and Family Allowances." *Journal of the Canadian Historical Association* 18, no. 1 (2007): 207–39.

Blake, Raymond B. *From Rights to Needs: A History of Family Allowances in Canada, 1929–92*. Vancouver: UBC Press, 2009.

Blakeney, Allan. *An Honourable Calling: Political Memoirs*. Toronto: University of Toronto Press, 2008.

Bothwell, Robert, and William Kilbourn. *C.D. Howe: A Biography*. Toronto: McClelland and Steward, 1979.

Boychuk, Gerard W. *National Health Insurance in the United States and Canada: Race, Territory and the Roots of Difference*. Washington, DC: Georgetown University Press, 2008.

Brownsey, Keith. "Opposition Blues: Leadership, Policy, and Organization in the Ontario Conservative Party, 1934–43." *Ontario History* 88, no. 4 (1996): 273–96.

Bryden, Kenneth. *Old Age Pensions and Policy-Making in Canada*. Montreal and Kingston: McGill-Queen's University Press, 1974.

Bryden, P.E. *Planners and Politicians: Liberal Politics and Social Policy, 1957–1968*. Montreal and Kingston: McGill-Queen's University Press, 1997.

Bryden, P.E. "Money and Politics: Relations between Ontario and Ottawa in the Diefenbaker Years." In *The Diefenbaker Legacy: Canadian Politics, Law and Society Since 1957*, ed. D.C. Storey and R. Bruce Shepard, 123–36. Regina: Canadian Plains Research Centre, 1998.

Bryden, P.E. "Beyond the Green Book: The Ontario Approach to Intergovernmental Relations, 1945–1955." In *Cultures of Citizenship in Post-war Canada*, ed. Nancy Christie and Michael Gauvreau, 133–62. Montreal and Kingston: McGill-Queen's University Press, 2003.

Bryden, P.E. "Ontario's Agenda in Post-Imperial Constitutional Negotiations, 1949–1968." In *Canada at the End of Empire*, ed. Philip Buckner, 216–31. Vancouver: UBC Press, 2005.

Bryden, P.E. "The Constitutional Dialogue between Federal and Provincial Governments: Ontario Opens the Conversation." *Supreme Court Law Review*, 2nd series 36 (2007): 31–50.

Bryden, P.E. "The Other Battle: The Achievement of National Medicare." *Canadian Bulletin of Medical History* 26, no. 2 (2009): 75–92.

Burns, R.M. *The Acceptable Mean: The Tax-Rental Agreements, 1941–1962*. Toronto: Canadian Tax Foundation, 1980.

Byers, R.B., ed. *Canadian Annual Review of Politics and Public Affairs, 1979*. Toronto: University of Toronto Press, 1981.

Cairns, Alan C. "The Judicial Committee and Its Critics." *Canadian Journal of Political Science* 4, no. 3 (1971): 301–45. http://dx.doi.org/10.1017/S0008423900026809.

Cameron, David, and Richard Simeon. "Ontario in Confederation: The Not-So-Friendly Giant." In *Government and Politics of Ontario*, 5th ed., ed. Graham White, 158–85. Toronto: University of Toronto Press, 1997.

Camp, Dalton. *Gentlemen, Players and Politicians*. Toronto: McClelland and Steward, 1970.

Christie, Nancy. *Engendering the State: Family, Work and Welfare in Canada*. Toronto: University of Toronto Press, 2000.

Clarkson, Stephen. *The Big Red Machine: How the Liberal Party Dominates Canadian Politics.* Vancouver: UBC Press, 2005.

Clarkson, Stephen, and Christina McCall. *Trudeau and Our Times,* vol. 1, *The Magnificent Obsession.* Toronto: McClelland and Stewart, 1990.

Coates, Robert C. *The Night of the Knives.* Fredericton: Brunswick Press, 1969.

Cohen, Andrew. *A Deal Undone: The Making and Breaking of the Meech Lake Accord.* Vancouver: Douglas and McIntyre, 1990.

Connors, Richard, and John M. Law, eds. *Forging Alberta's Constitutional Framework.* Edmonton: University of Alberta Press, 2005.

Constitutional Patriation: The Lougheed-Lévesque Correspondence. Kingston: Institute of Intergovernmental Relations, 1999.

Cook, Ramsay. *The Teeth of Time: Remembering Pierre Elliott Trudeau.* Toronto: University of Toronto Press, 2006.

Courchene, Thomas J. *Equalization Payments: Past, Present and Future.* Toronto: Ontario Economic Council, 1984.

Courtney, John C. "Campaign Strategy and Electoral Victory: The Progressive Conservatives and the 1979 Election." In *Canada at the Polls, 1979 and 1980: A Study of the General Elections,* ed. Howard R. Penniman, 121–51. Washington: American Enterprise Institute for Public Policy Research, 1981.

Courtney, John C. *Do Conventions Matter? Choosing National Party Leaders in Canada.* Montreal and Kingston: McGill-Queen's University Press, 1995.

Davey, Senator Keith. *The Rainmaker: A Passion for Politics.* Toronto: Stoddart, 1986.

Diefenbaker, John G. *One Canada: The Crusading Years, 1895–1956.* Toronto: Macmillan, 1975.

Diefenbaker, John G. *One Canada: The Years of Achievement, 1957–1962.* Toronto: Macmillan, 1976.

Dion, Stéphane. "My Praxis of Federalism." In *Straight Talk: Speeches and Writings on Canadian Unity,* 114–27. Montreal and Kingston: McGill-Queen's University Press, 1999.

Dion, Stéphane. "Ontario and Canada: Loyal Forever," Distinguished Speaker Series, Faculty of Law, University of Western Ontario, 2001. http://www.pco-bcp.gc.ca/aia/index.asp?lang=eng&Page=archive&Sub=speeches-discours&Doc=20010921-eng.htm

Dyck, Rand. "Links between Federal and Provincial Parties and the Party System." In Herman Bakvis, ed., *Representation, Integration and Political Parties,* vol. 14 of the research studies, Royal Commission on Electoral Reform and Party Financing, 129–77. Toronto: Dundurn Press, 1991.

English, John. *The Worldly Years: The Life of Lester B. Pearson,* vol. 2, *1949–1972.* Toronto: Knopf, 1992.

English, John. *Just Watch Me: The Life of Pierre Elliott Trudeau, 1968–2000.* Toronto: Knopf Canada, 2009.

Evans, A. Margaret. *Sir Oliver Mowat.* Toronto: University of Toronto Press, 1992.

Ferguson, Barry, and Robert Wardhaugh. "'Impossible Conditions of Inequality': John W. Dafoe, the Rowell-Sirois Royal Commission and the Interpretation of Canadian Federalism." *Canadian Historical Review* 84, no. 4 (2003): 551–84. http://dx.doi.org/10.3138/CHR.84.4.551.

Finkel, Alvin. "Paradise Postponed: A Re-examination of the Green Book Proposals of 1945." *Journal of the Canadian Historical Association,* new series, vol. 4 (1993): 120–42.

Finkel, Alvin. "Welfare for Whom? Class, Gender, and Race in Social Policy." *Labour/Le Travail,* vol. 49 (Spring 2002): 247–61.

Fleming, Donald M. *So Very Near: The Political Memoirs of the Honourable Donald M. Fleming,* vol. 1, *The Rising Years.* Toronto: McClelland and Stewart, 1985.

Fournier, Louis. *FLQ: The Anatomy of an Underground Movement,* trans. Edward Baxter. Toronto: NC Press, 1984.

Fraser, Graham. *René Lévesque and the Parti Québécois in Power.* Montreal and Kingston: McGill-Queen's University Press, 1984.

Gibbons, Roger. "Alberta and the National Community." In *Government and Politics in Alberta,* ed. Allan Tupper and Roger Gibbons, 67–84. Edmonton: University of Alberta Press, 1992.

Gibbons, Roger, ed. *Meech Lake and Canada: Perspectives from the West.* Edmonton: Academic Print and Publishing, 1988.

Girard, Philip. *Bora Laskin: Bringing Law to Life.* Toronto: University of Toronto Press for the Osgoode Society for Canadian Legal History, 2005.

Goodman, Eddie. *Life of the Party.* Toronto: Key Porter, 1988.

Gotlieb, Marc J. "George Drew and the Dominion-Provincial Conference on Reconstruction, 1945–46." *Canadian Historical Review* 66, no. 1 (1985): 27–47. http://dx.doi.org/10.3138/CHR-066-01-02.

Graham, Roger. *Old Man Ontario: Leslie M. Frost.* Toronto: University of Toronto Press, 1990.

Graham, Ron. *The Last Act: Pierre Trudeau, the Gang of Eight, and the Fight for Canada.* Toronto: Penguin, 2011.

Granatstein, J.L. *The Politics of Survival: The Conservative Party of Canada, 1939–1945.* Toronto: University of Toronto Press, 1967.

Granatstein, J.L. *Canada, 1957–1967: The Years of Uncertainty and Innovation.* Toronto: McClelland and Stewart, 1986.

Granatstein, J.L. *Canada's War: The Politics of the Mackenzie King Government, 1939–1945.* Toronto: University of Toronto Press, 1990 (Oxford University Press, 1975).

Haddow, Rodney. "Ontario Politics: Plus ça change?" In *Canadian Politics.* 2nd ed., ed. James Bickerton and Alain-C. Gagnon, 469–90. Peterborough: Broadview Press, 1994.

Henderson, T. Stephen. *Angus L. Macdonald: A Provincial Liberal.* Toronto: University of Toronto Press, 2007.

Hodgins, Bruce W., and Robert C. Edwards. "Federalism and the Politics of Ontario, 1867–80." In *Federalism in Canada and Australia: The Early Years,* ed. Bruce W. Hodgins, Don Wright, and W.H. Heich, 61–96. Waterloo: Wilfrid Laurier University Press, 1978.

Hosek, Chaviva. "Women and the Constitutional Process." In *And No One Cheered: Federalism, Democracy and the Constitution Act,* ed. Keith Banting and Richard Simeon, 280–300. Toronto: Methuen, 1983.

Hoy, Claire. *Bill Davis: A Biography.* Toronto: Methuen, 1985.

Hurley, James Ross. *Amending Canada's Constitution: History, Processes, Problems and Prospects.* Ottawa: Minister of Supply and Services, 1996.

Ibbitson, John. *Loyal No More: Ontario's Struggle for a Separate Destiny.* Toronto: HarperCollins, 2001.

Irvine, William P. "Epilogue: The 1980 Election." In *Canada at the Polls, 1979 and 1980: A Study of the General Elections,* ed. Howard R. Penniman, 337–98 Washington, DC: American Enterprise Institute for Public Policy Research, 1981.

Kendle, John. *John Bracken: A Political Biography.* Toronto: University of Toronto Press, 1979.

Kome, Penney. *The Taking of Twenty-Eight: Women Challenge the Constitution.* Toronto: Women's Press, 1983.

Little, Margaret Jane Hillyard. *"No Car, No Radio, No Liquor Permit": The Moral Regulation of Single Mothers in Ontario, 1920–1997.* Toronto: Oxford University Press, 1998.

Lower, A.R.M. "Does Ontario Exist?" *Ontario History* 60, no. 2 (1968): 65–9.

MacDonald, Donald C. *The Happy Warrior: Political Memoirs.* Toronto: Dundurn Press, 1998.

Macdonald, H. Ian. "A View from the Chair." In *Ontario Advisory Committee on Confederation: Background Papers and Reports.* Toronto: Queen's Printer of Ontario, 1967.

Manthorpe, Jonathan. *The Power and the Tories: Ontario Politics – 1943 to the present.* Toronto: Macmillan, 1974.

Marshall, Dominique. *The Social Origins of the Welfare State: Quebec Families, Compulsory Education, and Family Allowances,* trans. Nicola Doone Danby. Waterloo: Wilfrid Laurier University Press, 2006.

Martin, Lawrence. *Chrétien,* vol. 1, *The Will to Win.* Toronto: Lester Publishing, 1995.

Martin, Paul. *A Very Public Life*, vol. 2, *So Many Worlds*. Toronto: Deneau, 1985.

McCormick, Peter. "Provincial Political Party Systems, 1945–1986." In *Canadian Parties in Transition: Discourse, Organization, Representation*, ed. Alain G. Gagnon and A. Brian Tanguay, 152–85. Toronto: Nelson, 1989.

McDougall, A.K. *John P. Robarts: His Life and Government*. Toronto: University of Toronto Press, 1986.

McLarty, R.A. "Organizing for a Federal-Provincial Fiscal Policy." *Canadian Tax Journal* 15 (1967): 412–20.

McMurtry, R Roy. "The Search for a Constitutional Accord – A Personal Memoir." *Queen's Law Journal* 8 (1982–1983): 28–73.

McRoberts, Kenneth. *Misconceiving Canada: The Struggle for National Unity*. Toronto: Oxford University Press, 1997.

Meekison, J. Peter. "The Annual Premier's Conference Forging a Common Front." In *Canada: The State of the Federation 2002 – Reconsidering the Institutions of Canadian Federalism*, ed. J. Peter Meekison, Hamish Telford, and Harvey Lazar, 141–82. Kingston: McGill-Queen's University Press for the Institute of Intergovernmental Relations and School of Policy Studies, Queen's University, 2004.

Mendelsohn, Matthew, and J. Scott Matthews. "The New Ontario: The Shifting Attitude of Ontarians toward the Federation," *Mowat Note*, 1. Toronto: Mowat Centre for Policy Innovation, Feb. 2010.

Monahan, Patrick J. *Meech Lake: The Inside Story*. Toronto: University of Toronto Press, 1991.

Morin, Claude. *Quebec versus Ottawa: The Struggle for Self-Government, 1960–77*. Toronto: University of Toronto Press, 1976.

Morton, Desmond. "*Sic Permanent*: Ontario People and Their Politics." In *Government and Politics of Ontario*. 5th ed., ed. Graham White, 3–18. Toronto: University of Toronto Press, 1997.

Nelles, Viv. "Red Tied: Fin de Siecle Politics in Ontario." In *Canadian Politics*, 3rd ed., ed. Michael Whittington and Glen Williams, 76–97. Scarborough: Nelson Canada, 1990.

Newman, Peter. *Renegade in Power: The Diefenbaker Years*. Toronto: McClelland and Stewart, 1963.

Noel, Sid. "The Ontario Political Culture: An Interpretation." In *Government and Politics of Ontario*, 5th ed., ed. Graham White, 49–68. Toronto: University of Toronto Press, 1997.

Nurgitz, Nathan, and Hugh Segal. *No Small Measure: The Progressive Conservatives and the Constitution*. Ottawa: Deneau, 1983.

Oliver, Peter. "Ontario." In *Canadian Annual Review of Politics and Public Affairs, 1971*, ed. John Saywell, 99–129. Toronto: University of Toronto Press, 1972.

Oliver, Peter. "Ontario." In *Canadian Annual Review of Politics and Public Affairs, 1972*, ed. John Saywell, 129–55. Toronto: University of Toronto Press, 1973.

Oliver, Peter. "Ontario." In *Canadian Annual Review of Politics and Public Affairs, 1973*, ed. John Saywell, 102–26. Toronto: University of Toronto Press, 1974.

Oliver, Peter. *Unlikely Tory: The Life and Politics of Allan Grossman*. Toronto: Lester and Orpen Dennys, 1985.

Owram, Doug. *The Government Generation: Canadian Intellectuals and the State, 1900–1945*. Toronto: University of Toronto Press, 1986.

Paikin, Steve. *Public Triumph, Private Tragedy: The Double Life of John P. Robarts*. Toronto: Viking Canada, 2005.

Perry, J. Harvey. *Background of Current Fiscal Problems*. Toronto: Canadian Tax Foundation, 1982.

Perry, J. Harvey. *A Fiscal History of Canada – The Postwar Years*. Toronto: Canadian Tax Foundation, 1989.

Perry, J. Harvey. *The National Finances, 1955–56*. Toronto: Canadian Tax Foundation, n.d.

Petter, Andrew. "Federalism and the Myth of the Federal Spending Power." *Canadian Bar Review* 68 (Sept. 1989): 448–79.

Pickersgill, J.W. *My Years with Louis St. Laurent: A Political Memoir*. Toronto: University of Toronto Press, 1975.

Pickersgill, J.W., and D.F. Forster. *The Mackenzie King Record*, vol. 2, *1944–1945*. Toronto: University of Toronto Press, 1968.

Pickersgill, J.W., and D.F. Forster. *The Mackenzie King Record*, vol. 3, *1945–1946*. Toronto: University of Toronto Press, 1970.

Pinard, Maurice. "The Dramatic Re-emergence of the Quebec Independence Movement." *Journal of International Affairs* 45, no. 2 (1992): 471–97.

Poliquin, Daniel. *René Lévesque*. Toronto: Penguin Canada, 2009.

"Public Opinion Polls." *Public Opinion Quarterly* 8, no. 3 (1944): 435–57. http://dx.doi.org/10.1086/265702.

Rea, J.E. *T.A. Crerar: A Political Life*. Montreal and Kingston: McGill-Queen's University Press, 1997.

Report of the Proceedings of the Fifteenth Annual Tax Conference. Montreal: Canadian Tax Foundation Nov. 1961.

Richmond, D.R. *The Economic Transformation of Ontario: 1945–1973*. Toronto: Ontario Economic Council, 1974.

Robertson, Gordon. *Memoirs of a Very Civil Servant: Mackenzie King to Pierre Trudeau*. Toronto: University of Toronto Press, 2000.

Romanow, Roy. "'Reworking the Miracle': The Constitutional Accord 1981." *Queen's Law Journal* 8 (1982–1983): 74–98.

Romanow, Roy, John Whyte, and Howard Leeson. *Canada ... Notwithstanding: The Making of the Constitution, 1976–1982*. Toronto: Carswell/Methuen, 1984.

Russell, Peter H. "Bold Statescraft, Questionable Jurisprudence." In *And No One Cheered: Federalism, Democracy and the Constitution Act*, ed. Keith Banting and Richard Simeon, 210–38. Toronto: Metheun, 1983.

Russell, Peter H. *Leading Constitutional Decisions*. 3rd ed. Ottawa: Carleton University Press, 1984.

Russell, Peter H. *Constitutional Odyssey: Can Canadians Become a Sovereign People?* 2nd ed. Toronto: University of Toronto Press, 1993.

Sanders, Douglas. "The Indian Lobby." In *And No One Cheered: Federalism, Democracy and the Constitution Act*, ed. Keith Banting and Richard Simeon, 301–32. Toronto: Methuen, 1983.

Saywell, John T. *"Just call me Mitch": The Life of Mitchell F. Hepburn*. Toronto: University of Toronto Press, 1991.

Saywell, John T. *The Lawmakers: Judicial Power and the Shaping of Canadian Federalism*. Toronto: University of Toronto Press, 2002.

Saywell, John, ed. *Canadian Annual Review for 1962*. Toronto: University of Toronto Press, 1963.

Saywell, John, ed. *Canadian Annual Review for 1963*. Toronto: University of Toronto Press, 1964.

Saywell, John, ed. *Canadian Annual Review of Politics and Public Affairs, 1971*. Toronto: University of Toronto Press, 1972.

Saywell, John, ed. *Canadian Annual Review of Politics and Public Affairs, 1974*. Toronto: University of Toronto Press, 1975.

Scarfe, Brian L. "The Federal Budget and Energy Program, October 28th, 1980: A Review." *Canadian Public Policy* 7, no. 1 (1981): 1–14. http://dx.doi.org/10.2307/3549850.

Segal, Hugh. *No Surrender: Reflections of a Happy Warrior in the Tory Crusade*. Toronto: Harper Collins, 1996.

Sharpe, Robert J., and Kent Roach. *Brian Dickson: A Judge's Journey*. Toronto: University of Toronto Press for the Osgoode Society for Legal History, 2003.

Simeon, Richard. *Federal-Provincial Diplomacy: The Making of Recent Policy in Canada*. Toronto: University of Toronto Press, 1972.

Simeon, Richard, and Ian Robinson. *State, Society and the Development of Canadian Federalism*. Royal Commission on the Economic Union and Development Prospects for Canada, vol. 71. Toronto: University of Toronto Press, 1990.

Slater, David. *War, Finance and Reconstruction: The Role of Canada's Department of Finance, 1939–1946*. Ottawa, 1995.

Smith, Denis. *Gentle Patriot: A Political Biography of Walter Gordon*. Edmonton: Hurtig, 1973.

Smith, Denis. *Rogue Tory: The Life and Legend of John G. Diefenbaker*. Toronto: Macfarlane Walter Ross, 1995.

Splane, Richard. "Social Policy-Making in the Government of Canada." In *Canadian Social Policy*, rev. ed., ed. Shankar A. Yelaja, 224–65. Waterloo: Wilfrid Laurier University Press, 1987.

Stevens, Geoffrey. *Stanfield*. Toronto: McClelland and Stewart, 1973.

Stevens, Geoffrey. *The Player: The Life and Times of Dalton Camp*. Toronto: Key Porter, 2003.

Stevens, Paul, and John Saywell. "Parliament and Politics." In *Canadian Annual Review of Politics and Public Affairs, 1971*, ed. John Saywell, 3–98. Toronto: University of Toronto Press, 1972.

Stevenson, Don. "Ontario and Confederation: A Reassessment." In *Canada: The State of the Federation 1989*, ed. Ronald L. Watts and Douglas Brown, 53–74. Kingston: Institute of Intergovernmental Relations, 1989.

Stevenson, Garth. *Unfulfilled Union: Canadian Federalism and National Unity*. 3rd ed. Toronto: Gage, 1989.

Stevenson, Garth. *Ex Uno Plures: Federal-Provincial Relations in Canada, 1867–1896*. Kingston and Montreal: McGill-Queen's University Press, 1993.

Struthers, James. "A Profession in Crisis: Charlotte Whitton and Canadian Social Work in the 1930s." *Canadian Historical Review* 62, no. 2 (1981): 169–85. http://dx.doi.org/10.3138/CHR-062-02-02.

Struthers, James. "Shadows from the Thirties: The Federal Government and Unemployment Assistance, 1941–1956." In *The Canadian Welfare State*, ed. Jacqueline S. Ismael, 3–32. Edmonton: University of Alberta Press, 1987.

Struthers, James. *The Limits of Affluence: Welfare in Ontario, 1920–1970*. Toronto: University of Toronto Press, 1994.

Stursberg, Peter. *Diefenbaker: Leadership Gained, 1956–1962*. Toronto: University of Toronto Press, 1975.

Stursberg, Peter. *Lester Pearson and the Dream of Unity*. Toronto: Doubleday, 1978.

Stursberg, Peter. *The Last Viceroy: Roland Michener*. Toronto: McGraw-Hill Ryerson, 1989.

Taylor, Malcolm G. *Health Insurance and Canadian Public Policy: The Seven Decisions that Created the Canadian Health Insurance System and Their Outcomes*. 2nd ed. Kingston and Montreal: McGill-Queen's University Press, 1987.

Tetley, William. *The October Crisis, 1970: An Insider's View*. Montreal and Kingston: McGill-Queen's University Press, 2007.

Thomson, Dale C. *Louis St. Laurent: Canadian*. Toronto: Macmillan, 1967.

Thomson, Dale C. "The Political Ideas of Louis St. Laurent." In *The Political Ideas of the Prime Ministers*, ed. Marcel Hamelin, 139–53. Ottawa: Les éditions de l'Université d'Ottawa, 1969.

Thomson, Dale C. *Jean Lesage and the Quiet Revolution*. Toronto: Macmillan, 1984.

Trudeau, Pierre Elliott. "Quebec and the Constitutional Problem." In *Federalism and the French Canadians*. Toronto: Macmillan, 1968.

Trudeau, Pierre Elliott. *Memoirs*. Toronto: McClelland and Stewart, 1993.

Vaughan, Frederick. *Aggressive in Pursuit: The Life of Justice Emmett Hall*. Toronto: University of Toronto Press for the Osgoode Society for Legal History, 2004.

Vipond, Robert C. *Liberty and Community: Canadian Federalism and the Failure of the Constitution*. Albany: State University of New York Press, 1991.

White, Randall. *Ontario, 1610–1985: A Political and Economic History*. Toronto: Dundurn Press, 1985.

Williams, David R. *Duff: A Life in the Law*. Vancouver: UBC Press, 1984.

Wiseman, Nelson. "Change in Ontario Politics." In *Government and Politics of Ontario*, 5th ed., ed. Graham White, 418–41. Toronto: University of Toronto Press, 1997.

Wiseman, Nelson. *In Search of Canadian Political Culture*. Vancouver: UBC Press, 2007.

Young, R.A. " 'And the People Will Sink into Despair': Reconstruction in New Brunswick, 1942–1952." *Canadian Historical Review* 69, no. 2 (1988): 127–66. http://dx.doi.org/10.3138/CHR-069-02-01.

UNPUBLISHED MANUSCRIPTS AND THESES

Brownsey, Keith. "Tory Life: The Life Cycle of the Progressive Conservative Party of Ontario, 1935–1985." Doctoral dissertation, Queen's University, 1994.

Hunt, Wayne Austin. "The Federal-Provincial Conference of First Ministers, 1960–1976." Doctoral dissertation, University of Toronto, 1982.

Index